E-BUSINESS
ST@RT-UP

THE SUNDAY TIMES

E-BUSINESS ST@RT-UP

THE COMPLETE GUIDE TO LAUNCHING YOUR INTERNET AND DIGITAL ENTERPRISE

PHILIP TRELEAVEN

KOGAN
PAGE

First published in 2000

Kogan Page Limited
120 Pentonville Road
London N1 9JN

© Philip Treleaven, 2000

The views expressed in this book are those of the author and are not necessarily the same as those of Times Newspapers Ltd.

British Library Cataloguing in Publication Data

A CIP record for this book is available from the British Library.

ISBN 0 7494 3145 8

Typeset by Saxon Graphics Ltd
Printed and bound in Great Britain by Clays Ltd, St Ives plc

About the author

Philip Treleaven is professor of computing at University College London (UCL). His mission is to introduce America's entrepreneurial culture into British universities. He has launched the popular 30-lecture foundation course *Digital Business*, and encouraged students to set up the *Students' Business Club* and website (www.students.co.uk) to help them launch their own companies. He is a director of three companies and is also involved in London's venture capital community.

Philip is a European authority on electronic commerce and on so-called 'intelligent systems' (eg neural networks, genetic algorithms). He has pioneered the use of 'intelligent' computing techniques for data mining and forecasting in banking, insurance and the retail trade. He has consulted for many of the leading American, Japanese and European high-tech companies including Fujitsu, Mitsubishi, NCR, Philips, Siemens and Thomson, major banks such as Barclays and TSB, and many leading retailers including John Sainsbury.

Recently, Philip led a UK Department of Trade & Industry delegation to the United States, Israel and East Asia to look at organizations and seed funding for helping high-tech start-ups.

Philip Treleaven has published over 150 papers, has lectured in over 30 countries, and has been an invited speaker at a number of international conferences.

Contents

Foreword

Small firms play an important part in the modern economy, and none more so than those with an entrepreneurial flair and an ambition for growth. As well as generating wealth and employment, they bring substantial value to the UK through their agility and capacity for innovation – developing new products and services, opening new markets and challenging existing competitive situations.

Yet the challenges of starting and growing a small entrepreneurial firm are tremendous, especially when high-tech products or processes are involved. As well as juggling the intricacies of setting up a company – from preparing a business plan to finding office space to recruiting staff – the high-tech entrepreneur will often face the additional hurdles of raising substantial amounts of equity capital, undertaking a global market analysis and establishing a presence on the Internet. None of these are simple issues, yet many entrepreneurs find that they will often have to be dealt with 'on the wing'. Therefore, it is vital that there are sources of advice and help to which they can turn during the early years of vulnerability.

There can be few areas more important in determining the future competitiveness of UK companies than electronic commerce. Information technology offers businesses the opportunity to access wider markets and to deliver completely new products and services. It allows them to work with a wide range of people irrespective of location, to streamline and automate their business processes – from dealing with customers and suppliers to completing transactions online – and most importantly, it allows them to improve the quality of service enjoyed by their customers. UK businesses cannot afford to ignore e-commerce, and I hope that they find the advice contained within this book helpful in formulating the IT strategies they need to remain competitive in the new digital economy.

The Government is committed to improving the quality of help that small entrepreneurial firms deserve, and the successful exploitation of technological creativity for which the UK can be justly proud. This book is very much in the same spirit of providing practical advice, and I would like to send my personal best wishes for a prosperous and successful future to those high-tech entrepreneurs who read it.

Patricia Hewitt, MP
Minister for Small Business and E-Commerce
Department of Trade and Industry
February 2000

Preface

This book is dedicated to *young high-tech entrepreneurs* – especially students – to help you become the next Richard Branson or Bill Gates. *High-tech* start-ups are different. They are built on the idea of working like crazy for two to three years and then going public or selling out for a vast amount of money.

In the United States, starting your own high-tech company is part of the American dream. Bill Gates of Microsoft, Michael Dell of Dell Computers, Marc Andreessen of Netscape, and Jerry Yang of Yahoo! are role models who have become enormously wealthy at a very early age. They have also helped revitalize America. They have produced global products and services like Windows and Yahoo! that have literally changed the world. And, more importantly, they have created jobs for millions of people.

Opportunities abound in the Internet revolution and the coming digital media revolution of interactive television. This is not just an American dream; young people in Europe and Asia are also starting high-tech companies. It is a global competition for new ideas, money and jobs.

Today, the 'job for life' and the 'student grant' are rapidly becoming history. So turning necessity into a virtue, more and more young people are starting high-tech companies and working their way through college. Rather than delivering newspapers or working in a bar, if you are going to work hard, it is nice to feel that with a bit of luck you might make your fortune. If the right balance is struck between working and studying, having your own company gives security, pays the bills and certainly gives you a valuable business education – at the 'university of life'.

Starting your own company is probably the most exciting thing you will ever do. Seeing the company grow, overcoming problems, creating jobs for people, making money, and retiring to the Caribbean. Well, let's not get too carried away just yet. But as Richard Branson has shown, the sooner you start, the more you can achieve. In fact, being an *entrepreneur* is probably the most socially useful thing you can do, because, as Silicon Valley has shown, new high-tech companies create large numbers of well-paid jobs for people.

This book will help you start your high-tech company by drawing together in a single source all the information you will need. There are a number of excellent books covering a specific area of small business, and these are brought together in the bibliography and suggested further reading at back.

The focus is on 'high-tech' start-ups, and especially those making maximum use of the Internet, because *electronic commerce* companies that interact with their customers over the Internet will be the major source of new businesses in the coming decade.

This guide has seven parts. Part 1 – *Making your fortune* – looks at role models, such as Richard Branson, Jerry Yang and Bill Gates, and how they started their companies. It then surveys briefly the exciting digital technologies that could inspire your business. It covers setting up your company, including getting an Internet presence, and how to make 'real' money by floating your company on a stock market.

Part 2 – *Launching your start-up* – covers all aspects of starting your company, from choosing a money-making idea, preparing a business plan, doing market research to see whether the idea is viable, registering your company, plus the essential but more mundane things of setting up your office, hiring staff and ordering the stationery.

Part 3 – *Business on the Internet* – looks at putting the Internet to work for you. It covers setting up your website, using the Internet to advertise your company, how to use the Internet to service your customers, and different types of electronic commerce businesses.

Part 4 – *Financial management for small business* – is the serious part, covering how to raise money to finance your venture, how to read a balance sheet and control the finances of your business, financial planning and forecasting, how to cost your products and services, and even an overview of taxation.

Part 5 – *Law for small businesses* – covers company law, contracts and intellectual property rights (IPR), which are especially important for high-tech start-ups. It is about protecting yourself and your assets. The contracts chapter focuses on software, the Internet and electronic commerce. IPR covers confidential information, copyright, trademarks and patents, with specific reference to 'high-tech'.

Part 6 – *Marketing for start-ups* – covers the essential topics of marketing, branding, public relations, advertising, sales, plus global marketing and exporting.

Part 7 – *Information sources and glossary* – lists sources of help and advice, covering the contact details of organizations in the United Kingdom and the Republic of Ireland, and a comprehensive glossary of business, technical, financial and legal terms.

Acknowledgements

In the USA, young entrepreneurs making their fortune through high-tech start-ups are 'part of the American dream'. From Boston to Bangalore, Tel Aviv to Taipei, there is a frenzy of high-tech start-ups with entrepreneurs dreaming of $1 billion fortunes. We need to make this 'our dream' if we are to be successful in the coming 'digital' decade.

Through this book and the companion 30-lecture *Digital Business* course (first started at University College London), we are seeking to change the entrepreneurial culture. (A lecturer pack for the *Digital Business* course is available for any university and college wishing to offer the course.)

In this endeavour, I would like to acknowledge the support of my friends and colleagues who have contributed greatly to this start-up guide. I would like to start by acknowledging Dr Suran Goonatilake (Founder, SearchSpace Ltd), a visionary entrepreneur, Dr Jeff Skinner (Director, UCL Ventures) and Charles Johnson (PriceWaterhouseCoopers) who gave extensive help and advice on the guide's contents.

Dr Andrew Scott (Director, UCL Management Studies Centre) reviewed and commented on Part 2, *Launching your start-up*.

My good friend, Dr Raghbir Sandhu (NVision), an expert on electronic commerce, made many contributions to Part 3, *Business on the Internet*.

Chris Wayman and Humphrey Nokes assisted me with Part 4, *Financial management for small business*. Humphrey Nokes is a leading UK investor in high-tech start-ups.

Stephen Walker (Partner, Bray Walker), Graham Farrington (Lagner Parry) and David Marsh (Partner, Needham Grant) gave me extensive help with Part 5, *Law for small businesses*. Stephen Walker specializes in high-tech start-up law, Graham Farrington is a well-known

Trademark Attorney, and David Marsh is one of Britain's leading intellectual property rights lawyers.

Andrew Wettern (Deputy Director, UCL Ventures) and Susannah Hart (Interbrand) reviewed and commented on Part 6, *Marketing for start-ups*. Andrew Wettern is responsible at UCL for commercialization of intellectual property in information technology. Susannah Hart, one of Europe's leading authorities on brand management, helped me with Chapter 31, *Branding*; branding being central to the success of every high-tech start-up.

Finally, I would like to thank Carol Webb, an aspiring entrepreneur, for reading the manuscript of the whole guide.

Screenshots, screen splashes, images and clip art

The author acknowledges and thanks the following companies and organizations for permission to reproduce screen shots, screen splashes, images and clip art:

IMSI (UK) Ltd; Nominet (www.nic.uk); Netnames (www.netnames.co.uk); HMSO Cabinet Office; Bank of Ireland (www.boi.ie); Infoseek (www.infoseek.com screenshots reprinted by permission. Infoseek Ultraseek and Ultraseek Server are trademarks of Infoseek Corporation which may be registered in certain jurisdictions. Other trademarks shown are marks of their respective owners. Copyright ©1994–1999 Infoseek Corporation; all rights reserved. GO Network is a trademark of Disney Enterprises Inc, 1998–1999, an Infoseek Corporation authorized licensee); Nasdaq (www.nasdaq.com screenshot of website copyright ©1999, Nasdaq Stock Market Inc. Reprinted with permission of the Nasdaq-Amex Market Group); Easdaq (www.easdaq.be); London Stock Exchange (www.stockex.co.uk); Neuer Markt (www.neuer-markt.de); Sage (Instant Accounting); WinZip (copyright ©1991–1998, Nico Mak Computing Inc. WinZip is a registered trademark of Nico Mak Computing Inc. WinZip is available from www.winzip.com. WinZip screen image reproduced with permission of Nico Mak Computing Inc); Yahoo! (www.yahoo.com); Regus (www.regus.com); BtInternet (www.btinternet.com); Dell Computer Corporation Ltd (www.euro.dell.com); Hensa (http://mic2.hensa.ac.uk – to be changed to www.mirror.ac.uk in the near future); Exploit (www.exploit.com); Link Exchange (www.linkexchange.com); CNN (www.cnn.com); Real (www.real.com, copyright ©1995–1999 RealNetworks Inc, 2601 Elliott, Suite 1000, Seattle, Washington 98121, USA; all rights reserved. Real Networks, Real Audio, Real Video, Real Media, Real Player, and other names and logos are trademarks or registered trademarks of RealNetworks Inc); Pointcast (www.pointcast.com); Gap (www.gap.com); Tesco (http://shop.tesco.co.uk); DHL (www.dhl.com); Microsoft MSN; Ebay (www.ebay.com); *Internet Magazine*; Symantec (WinFax, www.symantec.com); Business Links (www.businesslink.co.uk); Enterprise Ireland (www.enterprise-ireland.com); British Venture Capital Association (www.bvca.co.uk); Charles Schwab (www.schwab-world-wide.com); Irish Revenue Commissioners (www.revenue.ie); Hoover (courtesy of Hoover's Online, www.hoovers.com); E-Centre (www.e-centre.org.uk).

Disclaimer

The author has taken great care and effort to check all the information and advice in this guide for accuracy. However, given the comprehensive nature of these notes, mistakes are almost inevitable. I regret, therefore, that I cannot be held responsible for any loss that you may suffer as a result of any omissions or errors.

Part 1

Making *your* Fortune

---

1   High-tech Entrepreneurs

In the 1960s and 1970s, the cover of *TIME* magazine was a place reserved for rock stars. In the 1990s, another group of people dominated this *de facto* measure of popular cultural fame: Bill Gates, Steve Jobs, Marc Andreessen and Jerry Yang. Both rock and high-tech are creative industries, driven by one or two key individuals who believe they can succeed against all the odds.

High-tech start-ups are about *show business*. They are about going for it – taking your technical skills, identifying a market niche, promoting yourself and your company to the media, becoming the dominant market leader (*the Gorilla*), and rapidly realizing a £100 million company. It's about Microsoft, Virgin, Amazon.com, Yahoo!, Hotmail, Lastminute.com and Freeserve.

Nearly every high-tech start-up is built on the idea of working like crazy for two to three years and then going public or selling out for a vast amount of money. In 1994 two Stanford University students, Jerry Yang and David Filo, started to build a 'yellow pages' of their favourite websites and made it available over the Internet from their student room. Yahoo! rapidly became a sophisticated directory and search engine, and a *cult* site for Internet users. Today Yahoo! has a market capitalization of $30 billion and rising. Not bad for a few years' work!

Starting your own high-tech business is pure adrenaline. Winning the National Lottery or becoming a rock star is living in the poor house by comparison. To put things in perspective, Elvis Presley made $100 million during his lifetime – Bill Gates is worth $100 billion.

Entrepreneurs like Richard Branson, Bill Gates and Jerry Yang and their high-tech companies make great role models for thrusting start-ups.

In this chapter we look at:

☐ ten golden rules for helping you focus on making your fortune;
☐ high-tech entrepreneurs and companies that provide excellent role models;
☐ how other young entrepreneurs launched their businesses;
☐ what gives specific high-tech companies like Amazon.com their edge;
☐ the 'technology adoption life-cycle' – the business strategy followed by successful high-tech companies.

To start with, forget what they teach you in business school.

Ten golden rules for success

You might say this book is about *up-start* businesses, rather than *start-ups*. *Up-start entrepreneurs* need the right showbusiness mind set to succeed. Figure 1.1 lists the *ten golden rules* for you to bear in mind when launching your start-up:

☑	**Think big**	Aim for a £100 million international company in 3–5 years.
☑	**Branding**	Create an integrated image for your company; company name, Internet site, and product (eg Amazon.com).
☑	**The gorilla**	Identify a market niche where you can totally dominate the market; hence the analogy of the 800-pound gorilla (eg CNN).
☑	**Focus**	Focus on an entry-level product that is a 100% complete offering; real customers don't buy research (eg PeopleSoft).
☑	**Ruthless**	Capture the customer base; drive down the price, drive out the competition (eg Oracle).
☑	**Superstar**	Choose a product with glamour, then promote yourself and your business as a 'superstar' (eg Virgin).
☑	**Leverage**	Generate cash to grow your business. Start by contracting, then bespoke systems, next niche products, till you become the gorilla (eg Microsoft).
☑	**Early adopter**	Identify an 'early adopter' who will pay you to develop your first product.
☑	**Venture capital**	As soon as your idea is 'proved' use venture capital to accelerate growth to £10 million and then £100 million (eg Hotmail).
☑	**Realize your investment**	Think of a dream buyer for your £100 million company, then build the business for them, even if you subsequently decide to 'float' instead.

Figure 1.1 The Ten Golden Rules checklist

The people

If you want to see how it is done, study the experts. We will look at a few entrepreneur role models – Richard Branson (Virgin), Bill Gates (Microsoft), Herman Hauser (Acorn), Michael Dell (Dell), Jerry Yang (Yahoo!), Jeff Bezos (Amazon), and Kim Polese (Marimba). As you will see, most started their businesses in their teens or while they were still students. Often, their first business ventures failed. They started small, launched using their own money, and learnt about management as they grew.

Richard Branson

Richard Branson is undoubtedly Britain's best known entrepreneur and Virgin is one of the best known groups of companies. Branson showed little interest in education at school, but excelled in sports. He passed O-levels in English Language, English Literature, French, History, Ancient History and Scripture, but failed Elementary Mathematics three times. In fact, he professes not to be able to read a balance sheet even to this day; so much for education! What he *really* wanted to do was work.

Branson's first successful venture was Virgin Records, started in 1969 when he was nineteen. This mail-order record business – run from his parents' *pied-à-terre* in Albion Street, Paddington, London – offered discount records advertised in magazines like *Melody Maker*. However, this was not in fact his first venture. That honour goes to *Student*; a national student magazine which, although a literary success, failed to make money. Fortunately, Virgin Records, most staff of which were even younger than Richard Branson, was a roaring success.

Virgin Records mushroomed into the Virgin Music Group empire; to be followed by Virgin Radio and Virgin Atlantic Airways, etc. In contrast to many entrepreneurs who make money by buying tired companies and re-invigorating them, Branson's speciality is creating new companies from scratch. And he is not afraid of failure.

Today, Branson is reputedly worth over £1 billion. To summarize his great strengths, they are his enthusiasm, his capacity to motivate others, and his truly amazing ability to get free publicity for his new ventures. Richard Branson is not just a multimillionaire entrepreneur, he is a *daredevil* multimillionaire entrepreneur!

Bill Gates

In just sixteen years, William Gates III, and his partner Paul Allen, grew Microsoft from scratch to become the first software company to sell a billion dollars' worth of products in a single year. At 35, Gates was the youngest billionaire in the history of America.

Bill Gates is the archetypal *student* entrepreneur. His interest in computers and making money started at Lakeside School in Seattle, which fortuitously installed a teletype computer terminal that communicated via a telephone line with a Digital PDP-10 minicomputer in downtown Seattle. Gates 'got hooked', and he and Allen formed the Lakeside Programmers Group to make money from their somewhat unique programming skills. Much of this early income was generated in free computer time.

In 1973 Bill Gates enrolled at Harvard, and developed a reputation for working 36 hours on the trot, collapsing for 10 hours, grabbing a pizza, and then starting all over again. Gates' life changed in December 1974 when Allen spotted an article on the front cover of *Popular Electronics* about the Altair 8080 – the 'World's First Microcomputer Kit'. Both of them recognized the coming personal computer revolution. In eight weeks, working night and day, Gates and Allen produced a BASIC programming system for the 4K memory of the primitive Intel 8080 microprocessor that formed the heart of the Altair. Gates and Allen formed Microsoft in 1975, and Gates later dropped out of Harvard. One may be tempted to say 'and the rest is history', but with Microsoft who can tell? Today, Bill Gates is worth $100 billion dollars, making him the richest person on the planet.

Herman Hauser

Herman Hauser is the leading light of the Cambridge entrepreneurs and almost single-handedly jump-started 'Silicon Fen'. Hauser, an Austrian, went to Cambridge in 1973 as a physics PhD student. Since then he has started, or co-founded, 25 companies in the Cambridge area. Hauser is one of several Cambridge high-tech personalities who cut their teeth at Acorn, the British computer company. Acorn, with support from Apple, has spun off Advanced RISC Machines (ARM), a specialized chip manufacturer whose microprocessors are being adopted as an industry standard of consumer devices from cellular phones to video editing machines. ARM is Cambridge's first $1 billion high-tech company. Other Hauser businesses include ESI (Electronic Share Interchange), an online share brokerage, NetChannel, producing Internet set-top boxes, and Amadeus, the technology venture capital fund. Amadeus is one of the UK's few specialist 'tech' funds. Backed by Microsoft, Reuters, Deutsche Telekom and others, Hauser's Amadeus Capital Partners have raised $80 million.

Michael Dell

Michael Dell started his computer business from his dorm room at the University of Texas. Today, Dell is the world's leading direct marketer of personal computers and the richest man in Texas. Dell says his vision of a direct-sale computer company came to him when he was a first-year undergraduate studying biology at UT Austin. In his second year, with $1000 capital, he incorporated his business and dropped out. Dell then perfected the direct-order method of marketing his products through mail order, direct telephone sales and online, through the Internet. Dell achieves competitive advantage by taking an order, configuring it for the customer, and shipping it quickly by courier. The computer is assembled to the customer's exact specification, boxed and sent directly to a customer in under a week. This cuts inventory, overheads and prices.

Since 1995, Dell is probably the only Fortune 500 company that has increased both sales and earnings by 40 per cent in each consecutive year. For the future, Dell expects to increase sales by making major use of the Internet and also by expanding overseas. The company has built plants in Malaysia, Ireland and China. Today, Dell Computer is an $18 billion company, with its website taking $15 million per day in sales. Dell's stock has soared 37,000 per cent since 1990, with $10,000 invested in 1996 now worth over $100,000.

Jerry Yang

To quote *TIME* magazine, 'Four years ago, he was a graduate student living in a trailer. Today Jerry Yang is a billionaire who runs the most visited site on the Net.' Jerry Yang and David Filo started Yahoo! while doing their PhDs at Stanford University. Becoming increasingly bored with laborious research, they started to spend increasing amounts of time surfing the Internet and putting together a 'hotlist' of their favourite sites. Initially it was called 'Jerry's Guide to the World Wide Web', but this was changed to 'Yahoo!' reputedly standing for 'yet another hierarchical officious oracle!'

Before long, people from all over the world were using this database. Once the business potential of their 'hobby' was realized, they approached a venture capital firm and received one million dollars in funding in return for giving up 25 per cent of the company.

Then, with the help of the new investors, they recruited an excellent management team; Tim Koogle and Jeff Mallet. It was these experienced managers who really took the raw gem of an operation and turned it into the Yahoo! success story. High-tech entrepreneurs increasingly acknowledge this trend of hiring professional management talent to shape and grow a high-tech start-up at record speeds. And, as we will in fact see, venture capitalists value management talent far more than a brilliant idea.

Today, Yahoo! is the most visited site on the Internet (100 million 'hits' a day), and the company is worth $30 billion dollars at the time this book went to press.

Kim Polese

Many pundits predict that female entrepreneurs will dominate the next decade; what *Newsweek* branded *womenomics*. Kim Polese (pronounced Poh-Lay-Zay) is Chief Executive of Marimba (www.marimba.com) which makes software technology that corporations and publishers can use to broadcast information to computer users via the Web. She has a BS in biophysics from the University of California, Berkeley, and studied computer science at the University of Washington in Seattle.

Polese first made a name for herself at Sun Microsystems, where she was product manager for the much-celebrated Java programming language. In February 1996, she and three top Java engineers left Sun to create their own company, Marimba, with $4 million venture capital from Kleiner, Perkins, Caufield & Byers. Now, as chief executive of Internet start-up Marimba Inc., she lunches with Vice-President Al Gore and ranks as the only computer industry executive on *TIME* magazine's list of the 25 most influential people in America. Marimba's main product, Castanet, allows users to download a 'Castanet Tuner' that creates 'company channels' which automatically 'push' content to people rather than requiring them to 'pull' content from Web sites. Marimba floated in 1999 and has a market capitalization of $700 million, with Polese owning 10 per cent of the company.

Next, we will look at high-tech company role models, in many cases synonymous with their charismatic entrepreneur.

The companies

If you had to pick the world's hardest-charging high-tech companies, which would you pick? Probably IBM or Microsoft. However, as *Business Week* showed in its November 1998 article, 'The world's best-performing information technology companies, many of the top five, ranked by growth, return or profits, were mere start-ups just a few years ago (Table 1.1).

The amazing success of these companies centres on a relatively few high-tech business strategies:

❑ *The gorilla* – the strategy is to identify a market niche and try to totally dominate it (eg Amazon.com www.amazon.com and Cisco www.cisco.com).

❑ *Acquisition* – the strategy is to grow rapidly by acquiring complementary businesses (eg AOL's www.aol.com acquisition of Netscape and ICQ, or Eidos' www.eidos.com purchase of a string of games companies).

❑ *Portal* – the strategy is to become a major gateway or 'on-ramp' to the Internet (eg Yahoo www.yahoo.com).

❑ *Free service* – the strategy is to build valuation by registering subscribers for a free service (eg Hotmail www.hotmail.com and Dixon's FreeServe www.freeserve.net).

Table 1.1 Top five IT companies by size, growth, shareholder return and profits (source: *Business Week*, 2 November 1998)

Revenue (millions)		Growth (%)		Shareholder Return (%)		Profits (%)	
IBM	78,769	At Home	722	Mindspring	476	Vanguard	228
HP	46,624	Amazon.com	444	Yahoo!	417	Vodaphone	148
Lucent Tech.	29,042	Verio	384	Earthlink	340	Dell	74
BT	26,933	Excite	216	Amazon.com	329	HongKong Tel.	46
SBC Comm.	25,944	Doubleclick	197	America Online	196	Cable & Wireless	42

Amazon.com

Amazon.com and its founder, Jeff Bezos, virtually invented Internet retailing with its global online bookstore. Back in 1994, Jeff Bezos was a young, senior vice president of DE Shaw, the Wall Street hedge fund. With his background in computing he recognized the retail potential of the Internet. Bezos drew up a list of 20 products that could be sold online, including books, music, magazines, PC hardware and software, and shares. After narrowing the list to books and music, Bezos settled on books for two reasons. Firstly there are more to sell; there are 1.3 million books in print compared with 300,000 music titles. Secondly there are no '800-pound gorillas' in book publishing and distribution. The biggest US book chain Barnes & Noble (www.barnesandnoble.com) accounts for under 12 per cent of the industry's $25 billion annual sales, whereas six companies dominate the music industry.

Bezos then relocated to Seattle to start Amazon. He chose Seattle for its proximity both to high-tech talent and a major book distributor, Ingram's warehouse in Roseburg, Oregon. He rented a house and in true American style set four programmers to work in his garage building the Internet software.

Amazon, although a multimillion dollar business, employs only a few hundred people. It is a virtual company; no storefront and no inventory. When customers browse Amazon's database and request a book, orders are passed to a distributor or publisher, who deliver books to Amazon's warehouse for dispatch. Bezos attributes Amazon's success firstly to offering every book in print, and secondly to offering discounts on most books. Like most gorillas, the goal is for market share first and profits later.

Cisco

Cisco dominates the network router market. Routers are devices that allow different types of networks to work together, moving messages between networks and selecting the 'best route' for message distribution.

Cisco was founded in 1984 by the husband and wife team Leonard Bosack and Sandy Lerner, academics at Stanford University. Bosack ran the computers for the Computer Science Department, and Lerner ran those for the Business School. Bosack came up with a high-speed, inexpensive 'router' device to forward data from one department network to another, and also the necessary software allowing the data to be read by any computer on these networks.

Fortunately, Stanford refused Bosack and Lerner permission to produce routers for outside companies, so they mortgaged their house for seed capital, even borrowed on their credit cards, and launched Cisco.

In 1987, the legendary Silicon Venture capitalist Don Valentine of Sequoia Capital, who had financed Apple and Oracle, gave Cisco its only investment of venture capital. Interestingly, the first thing most venture capitalists do is look at the management experience of the people launching the start-up. Bosack and Lerner had next to none. However, Cisco did have revenue of $200,000 and the potential market was enormous. After the investment, Bosack and Lerner held 35 per cent of stock and Sequoia Capital 33 per cent. Cisco's first stock issue (IPO) was in February 1990 at a price of $18. Today, Cisco has a market capitalization of $100 billion dollars.

Hotmail

Hotmail was founded in 1995 by Sabeer Bhatia and Jack Smith, with the vision of offering free, globally accessible, Web-based e-mail to all users and personalized advertising for company promotions. Upon registration a user instantly gets an e-mail account ('user@hotmail.com') which operates independently of the customer's internet service provider, geographic location, or employer. Hotmail's great value was its database of 9 million subscribers world-wide. This was the reason why Microsoft acquired Hotmail in December 1997, paying a reputed $400 million.

The culture

Teenagers who want to be seriously rich and famous are no longer forming rock groups. Now, they are starting high-tech companies for fun, excitement, hype, instant fortunes and fame. Start-ups like Yahoo!, Hotmail, ICQ and Amazon.com are global icons for the young. And new 'silicon' Motowns – Cambridge, Tel Aviv, Taipei and Bangalore – are emerging quickly. The only difference between the two industries is that rock stars think in millions and tech stars think in billions!

High-tech is the new rock 'n' roll

High-tech is the mega-trend, but rock 'n' roll provides the industry blueprint. Table 1.2 shows this clearly.

Take a closer look at the mechanics of music industry success stories. You buy your first guitar and practise in your bedroom. You form a group and hire a manager, cut a record and go on tour. You then reach number one on the US *Billboard* charts. Enjoying the excesses of fame and fortune has always been every wide-eyed teenager's dreams.

Now, however, rock 'n' roll is *passé*. Today's teenagers look up to a new generation of superstars, but the process is remarkably similar. In fact, the parallels are incredible: buying your first PC, getting together with some friends, 'cutting' some software, starting a company, and getting a listing on NASDAQ, the tech-stock-market. These are today's dreams.

Tech stars are beginning to learn from their rock counterparts. Like rock stars, tech stars – the creative types – are not necessarily the best people to *manage* their business affairs. Rock stars have long recognized this and employ managers to negotiate contracts, juggle logistics, and co-ordinate the press. Now, there is a growing realization among tech stars that management has to be separated from the creative process. Tech stars create the initial idea and develop the technology. Then they hire professional managers to run the company, handle marketing and manage growth – just like the rock industry. Yahoo! is a classic example. But where and how does it all begin?

Table 1.2 Industry parallels

Mega-trends	Rock 'n' Roll (1960–1980)	High-tech (1990–)
Inspiration	rock band	start-up
Celebrity	rock star	tech star
Culture	sex, drugs and rock 'n' roll	risk-taking, cracking code
Cities	motown, Liverpool	Silicon Valley, Cambridge
Girl Power	female bands	female entrepreneurs
Rewards	millions	billions

The cities

Motown and Silicon Valley both have magical ingredients for creating 'entrepreneurs'; one for music, the other for high-tech.

Motown – Liverpool, Dublin, and Nashville – had an 'ecology' that made them work. They had good producers, good recording studios, the best entertainment lawyers, and the *clubs* to launch new acts. This was the infrastructure that took the raw product, a youngster with dreams and music talent, and fashioned it into the finished, glowing product: the music *superstar*.

Silicon Valley has a similar ecology.

The premier tech-city has remarkable parallels to the music cities. Its intricate ecology defines its product, its venture capital companies, its incubators (serving a similar role to music clubs), and a style of doing business. The universities in the region, principally Stanford, have provided Silicon Valley with the raw materials: the technology students. The value of Silicon Valley companies, $450 billion, is ten times the total value of Hollywood. In fact, there are two companies in the Valley, Intel and Cisco, each of them having a market capitalization that is more than twice the value of Hollywood (Intel $140 billion, Cisco $100 billion). Last year, on average, a Valley company went public every five days, creating 62 new millionaires – every day!

Now, other 'silicon valleys' are emerging: Cambridge, Tel Aviv, Prague, Bangalore, Taipei and Rio de Janeiro. All of them have the raw materials – excellent educational institutions producing technical talent. Some of the cities are beginning to have the financial networks and ingredients that make the Valley work. And recently, there are signs that Silicon Valley is becoming a victim of its own success, with spiralling salaries and office rents, massive traffic congestion and an acute shortage of the raw material they need. Just as manufacturing shifted from the West to the then emerging economies of Japan, South Korea and Singapore over the last three decades, one is now witnessing the beginning of a shift in computer software production from the United States to the rest of the world. The cities that win this race will define the face of the twenty-first century.

To understand how these tech stars build market share, you need to understand the *technology adoption life-cycle* – the Ten Commandments of high-tech!

(*Note*: Dr Suran Goonatilake is acknowledged for suggesting this section.)

The business strategy

If you only ever read one book on high-tech business strategy, then I highly recommend Geoffrey Moore's *Inside the Tornado*. Most successful marketing strategies for high-tech businesses are based on the so-called 'technology adoption life-cycle' that divides *markets* and *customers* into five groups (Figure 1.2). Moore, with laser clarity, zeros in on the marketing strategy to successfully unlock each customer group.

- ❑ *Innovators.* These are the *technology enthusiasts* who just love innovation and cannot wait to get their hands on your new product. Gaining the innovators' endorsement of your product is essential for its successful launch. But remember; innovators do not control the real purse strings.
- ❑ *Early adopters.* These are the *visionaries* who believe in gaining competitive advantage by adopting new products. They have money to spend. Early adopters are important for entrepreneurs for a number of reasons. Firstly they provide a sort of 'seed' funding without demanding shares. Secondly they love to boast in the media about their new toy, which gives you both free publicity and a valuable endorsement. Thirdly, however, they frequently demand that you customize your product for their needs, which can be a distraction for a start-up.
- ❑ *Early majority.* These are the *pragmatists* who adopt innovation

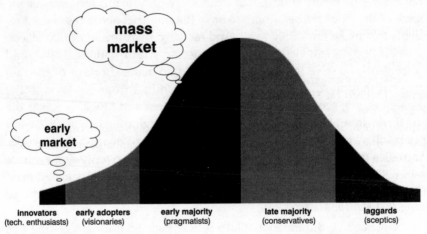

| innovators
(tech. enthusiasts) | early adopters
(visionaries) | early majority
(pragmatists) | late majority
(conservatives) | laggards
(sceptics) |

Figure 1.2 The technology adoption life cycle (adapted from Geoffrey Moore's 'Inside the Tornado')

when it has a proven track record of delivering productivity improvements. The early majority has most money. They also like to purchase from the market leader: firstly for product reliability, and secondly because it attracts additional supplier companies.

❑ *Late majority.* These are the *conservatives* who adopt innovation only because they are afraid of being left behind by the market. They represent a highly valuable market for simple, reliable and commoditized systems.

❑ *Laggards.* Finally we have the *sceptics*, who are the ever-present critics of high-tech products. Avoid them.

Your start-up goal is a business strategy that rapidly and successfully develops each market in turn:

1. *Enthusiasts* – seed new products with the technology enthusiasts so they educate the visionaries;
2. *Visionaries* – clinch sales to the visionaries, as a reference for the pragmatists;
3. *Pragmatists* – dominate the pragmatists' market, and become the market leader to attract the conservatives;
4. *Conservatives* – dominate the conservatives' market by commoditizing your product;
5. *Sceptics* – ignore them; they are a waste of time.

Sources of help

British Venture Capital Association (BVCA). Essex house, 12–13 Essex Street, London, WC2R 3AA, tel: 020 7240 3846, fax: 020 7240 3849, www.bvca.co.uk

Cringely, R (1996) *Accidental Empires – how the boys of Silicon Valley make their millions, battle foreign competition and still can't get a date*, Harper Business, London

Kaplan, D (1999) *The Silicon Boys – and their valley of dreams*, William Morrow & Co., New York

Kaplan, J (1996) *Startup – a Silicon Valley Adventure*, Penguin Books, London

Red Herring. The principal magazine of the venture capital community. 1550 Bryant Street, Suite 450, San Francisco, CA 94103, USA, *www.redherring.com*

Steiner, R (1998) *My First Break – how entrepreneurs get started*, The Sunday Times, London

Stone, R (1998) *The Microsoft Way*, Warner Books, London

2 High-tech Opportunities

Do you feel overwhelmed by the opportunities? We are currently experiencing a veritable explosion of new technologies and high-tech start-ups launching to exploit their potential. As the National Lottery adverts say, 'It could be you!'

In this chapter we look at:

- ❏ opportunities in the 'digital' TIME (telecommunications, information technology, media and entertainment) industries;
- ❏ the convergence of digital television, consumer electronics, computing and communications to a universal *digital* medium;
- ❏ the information superhighway, where every electronic device is Internet-enabled;
- ❏ the exciting digital technologies that are driving new business opportunities, like cyber life, mobile information services, electronic commerce, virtual reality, etc.

Most new businesses in the coming decade will be *digital businesses*. Either they will involve computing, digital media and Internet products and services; or they will make substantial use of the Internet and interactive digital television to deliver products and services directly into the office or home. In fact, the boundary between the so-called TIME industries is rapidly disappearing into an all-pervasive medium of *interactive digital media*.

Interactive digital media is exciting because of the potential for making money – and we are still looking for the new *digital* Tesco, BA and Barclays Bank.

The major advantage of digital business is cost. Advertisements, orders and product delivery are tied together for information-based products and services, and can be processed in seconds. And setting up a company is low-risk: a virtual store merely involves renting £500-worth of disk storage on a computer connected to the Internet. Communication with customers is by electronic mail, costing as little as £5 to send 1000 messages winging around the globe in a few seconds. In addition, customers type their orders directly into your computer, thereby reducing by 75 per cent the costs of processing orders, compared with telephone and paper-based ordering. As Amazon.com (www.amazon.com) shows, customers can be serviced anywhere in the world with advertising, personalized marketing, online ordering and sales support.

Before we look at the digital marketplace, digital multimedia will be reviewed briefly.

Digital multimedia

Digital multimedia is any combination of text, graphics, sound, animation and video delivered to you by computer or other electronic means. If you are looking for a good in-depth introduction to digital multimedia, then I highly recommend Fluckiger's *Understanding Networked Multimedia*.

Some definitions

The important 'digital' terms are:

- ❏ *analogue signal* – a physical value that varies continuously with time and/or space;
- ❏ *digital signal* – a time-dependent or space-dependent sequence of values coded in binary format and resulting from the transformation of an analogue signal;
- ❏ *digitization* – the process involved in transforming an analogue signal into a digital signal;
- ❏ *conversion* – analogue-to-digital (A/D) and digital-to-analogue (D/A) conversions are necessary because multimedia information is stored in digital format, but humans only react to physical sensory stimuli.

The conventional classification of media types is shown in Figure 2.1.

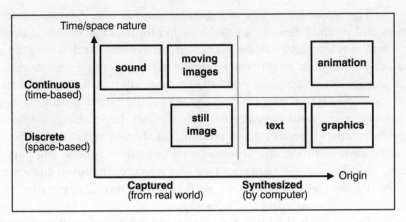

Figure 2.1 Multimedia classification

Convergence

Once a digital media product is created and stored in an electronic database, it will be available in the home, at work, at leisure or on the move uniformly over the telephone network, through cable and via satellite. It will also be accessible on-demand through a variety of devices: PC, TV, electronic kiosk, cellular phone, or personal digital assistant (PDA). More importantly, a customer will be able to access information on an individual basis, rather than after it has been broadcast to a group, and will be able to interact with the information. This convergence is captured in Figure 2.2. The principal digital media sectors are illustrated in Figure 2.3.

Next we look at the high-tech sectors and novel technologies that are inspiring new businesses.

Digital entertainment and consumer electronics

Digital entertainment, media and consumer electronics might be described as where *Hollywood meets Silicon Valley*, or *News Corporation confronts Microsoft*. Important converging sectors are:

- ❑ *digital television* – television supporting interactive entertainment, information, education and shopping;
- ❑ *digital multimedia* – full multimedia is any combination of text,

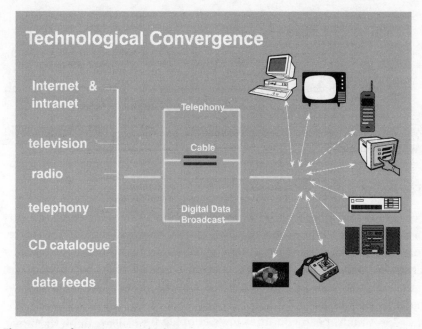

Figure 2.2 Information superhighway

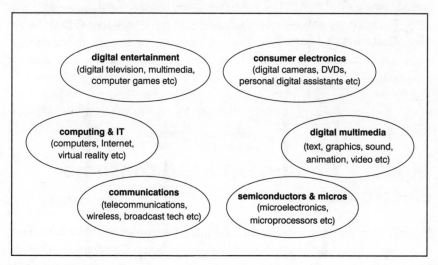

Figure 2.3 Digital media sectors

graphics, sound, animation and video delivered to you by television, computer or other electronic means;

☐ *consumer electronics* – digital cameras, digital video disks (DVD), personal digital assistants (PDA), and much more;

☐ *computer games* – not just the Tamagotchi or Lara Croft, but an increasing range of sophisticated and lifelike games.

We will focus here on (interactive) digital television – technology's Wild West.

Technologies

For the second time in history, Britain is pioneering television. The first occasion was in 1936 when the BBC started the first regular TV service intended for home viewing: a 405-line, all-electronic system developed by EMI. In 1998–99 the BBC and the commercial television companies launched the world's first terrestrial digital TV services intended for nationwide viewing.

All European countries have adopted a common digital TV standard called DVB (after the industry-led Digital Video Broadcasting group) based largely on the MPEG-2 video compression standard.

There are three basic configurations for interactive digital television, illustrated by Figure 2.4.

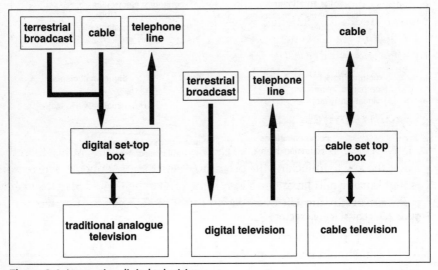

Figure 2.4 Interactive digital television

❏ *Analogue TV*. To view digital programmes on your analogue television you need a set-top box that receives the digital signal broadcast either terrestrially or via cable. Once received, the set-top box converts the signal to analogue for display on your traditional television. Interaction is supported by connecting the set-top box to a telephone line, just as with an internet service provider (ISP).

❏ *Digital TV*. A special digital television directly receives and displays the broadcast digital signal. Again, interaction is supported by connecting the television set with a built-in modem to the telephone line.

❏ *Cable TV*. A digital set-top box connects the cable to a digital television, as with current cable systems. However, interaction is via the cable.

Companies

This really is the clash of the titans: media conglomerates (eg News Corporation, AOL Time Warner), consumer electronic companies (eg Sony, Matsushita) and computing (eg Microsoft). All want to own the entertainment and media 'food chain', from production to distribution. Television, print, cinema, games, Internet, CD ROM etc; the whole shebang!

Of the titans, Rupert Murdoch's News Corporation is the global business model most media competitors scramble to emulate, spanning movie studios (Twentieth Century Fox), television networks (Fox TV, Sky TV, Star TV), a cable network, book publisher (HarperCollins) and newspapers (*New York Post, The Times, The Sun*).

So what are the business opportunities?

Opportunities

Many people in Europe believe that interactive television, rather than the PC, is the key to unlocking the promise of electronic commerce. The reason is that Europe and Japan are *TV societies*, unlike the United States which is a *PC society*. In the US over one-in-three homes has a PC, whereas in Europe numbers are far lower.

If you considered setting up an Internet company four years ago, today you should be thinking of interactive TV. Look at the opportunities here:

❏ *Home shopping.* Interactive TV shopping will obviously be enormous, based either on TV programmes where you can 'click' on the images to buy, or CD catalogues that go online when you purchase. Many large catalogue companies and retailers are planning to launch their own shopping channels.

❏ *Interactive games.* There will be interactive game shows where you can join in at home, just as we have seen multi-person games on the Internet.

❏ *Interactive dramas.* You will also be able to influence the plot of your favourite 'soap', such as choosing a happy, sad or even gory ending.

❏ *Infotainment.* The potential for providing interactive information and education is clearly enormous.

❏ *Interactive karaoke.* Karaoke is hugely popular (apart from with me), and interactive TV will allow you get fully customizable audio and video backings at home. You could even have your own TV show. All you need is a simple video camera connected to your digital TV.

If interactive TV really is the land of opportunity, what's left in computing?

Computing and information technology

In the summer of 1998/99 Microsoft became the most valuable company in the world with a market capitalization of over $460 billion. Yet the world of computing does not end at the personal computer, as shown by the surging value of Internet companies. Broadly, information technology (IT) comprises:

❏ *computers* – covering personal computers (eg Compaq, Dell) and workstations (Sun);

❏ *software* – covering Windows software (eg Microsoft), databases (eg Oracle), enterprise software (eg Sap, Sage), and bespoke software;

❏ *the Internet* – browsers (eg Microsoft, Netscape), service providers (eg AOL), and online shops (eg Amazon.com), etc.

A key driver in computing is the Internet and global access to multimedia information. Central to this uniform access is each device having a unique Internet (IP) address, just like every telephone and fax having its unique telephone number. However, there are other underlying computing technologies that are becoming increasingly ubiquitous.

Technologies

Important technologies are reshaping computing. They include the following:

Virtual reality. The potential of VR is all too clearly demonstrated by *Jurassic Park.* This ability to animate scenes and create virtual environments will soon appear on a PC near you. An obvious application for the home user is having your own on-screen mannequin or avatar, which can try on clothes and visit places for you.

Intelligent systems. Artificial intelligence (AI) techniques, such as neural networks and genetic algorithms, are being applied to business in areas including customer and product profiling, asset and sales forecasting, fraud detection, and retail optimization. These 'intelligent' systems provide powerful (static) decision support tools and (dynamic) personalization tools for Web systems.

Web casting. This allows users to register with online systems to receive information on selected topics automatically. The simplest mechanisms use e-mail to deliver information, while in the more sophisticated version a user downloads a screen saver that periodically fetches and displays information. Web casting is referred to as 'push-technology' as opposed to traditional web surfing, known as 'pull-technology'.

Companies

In computer hardware there are no real 800-pound gorillas, such as IBM used to be. Compaq is big in retail sales, Dell in direct telephone and Internet sales. Sun is big in workstations.

In software, Microsoft is the clear 'gorilla'; the company everybody looks to beat. So are there any opportunities left? The key trend is that virtually every consumer electronic product is being given 'computing' capabilities.

Opportunities

Computing products are increasingly embodying:

- ❏ *multimedia* – full integration of text, graphic art, sound, animation and video delivered to the consumer electronic device;
- ❏ *interfaces* – you can connect the device to any other consumer electronic device to exchange information;
- ❏ *mobility* – you can use it anywhere;
- ❏ *intelligence* – sophisticated computer programmes are being embedded in the devices to imbue them with human-like 'knowledge' and 'artificial intelligence' behaviour.

The epitome of these trends is the much-derided Tamagotchi hand-held game. This 'digital pet' has single-handedly created a whole new segment of the games industry and a family of similar products, such as 'Pocket Monster'. *Cyberlife* is the technical term for these gadgets. The latest phenomenon of *Cyberlife* is the so-called 'virtual idol'; Kyoko Date in Japan and Lara Croft in Britain. Ms Date even has fan clubs in Germany and France. Very strange people! The potential of 'cyberlife' for advertising and marketing appears enormous.

Tying all the above together is communications.

Communications

Communications encompass sectors involving the distribution of information from one location to another, spanning telephone, cable, broadcast satellites and wireless channels, where the boundaries are becoming distinctly blurred.

- ❏ *Telecommunications.* This principally covers the telephone companies (telcos), but also reaches over to the cellular operators.
- ❏ *Wireless communications.* The 'wireless world' covers WAP cellular phones, pagers, personal communications systems (PCS), private radio networks of the armed forces, the police and taxi industry, and the increasingly popular wireless data networks for connecting PCs and peripherals.
- ❏ *Networks.* This covers the equipment to interconnect computers, such as routers and hubs. Routers are the devices that interconnect different networks controlling the 'routing' of messages. Hubs are the focal points of networks ensuring that, if one computer breaks down, the networks will continue to function. Cisco (www.cisco.com) and Bay Networks dominate these areas.

❏ *Broadcast satellites.* These have traditionally provided broadcast television, but with the rise of the Internet they are now expanding to include digital data broadcasting.

Technologies

The following are some of the interesting communications technologies to watch are:

❏ *Cellular technology.* This is getting ever more sophisticated. Some of the latest phones have built-in Internet connections and Web browser technology.

❏ *Wireless Application Protocol (WAP).* This is a ubiquitous digital wireless telecommunication service that will allow uniform access to voice and data anywhere.

❏ *IP-enabled.* Internet protocol (IP) addresses, like telephone numbers, are being assigned to an increasing number of devices, allowing them to communicate intelligently with other devices on the Internet. The next generation of cellular phones will be 'IP-enabled'.

Companies

The world telecommunications market is estimated to be worth around $700 billion a year, and is growing rapidly as countries privatize their national telcos. This has led to a frenzy of mergers and acquisitions. For instance, WorldCom through its acquisition of MCI (for $30 billion), and the Internet companies UUNET plus CompuServe, leapt to become the second largest US phone company after AT&T, and the world's largest provider of Internet services.

In networking, the routers market is dominated by Cisco and 3COM, and the hub market by Bay Networks and Cabletron. This is one of the hottest areas of the stock market, with companies growing rapidly through acquisitions.

Opportunities

In communications, 'wireless' is considered by many as the primary growth area for the next decade. However, there are a number of other opportunity-areas for start-ups:

- ❑ *Internet telephony.* The market for so-called *voiceover IP* and *video-conferencing* over the Internet is set for major growth. Already a number of companies market software for audio and video telephony over the Internet, allowing users to conduct international telephone calls and teleconferencing at the cost of a local telephone call.
- ❑ *Mobile information services.* Cellular phone companies now have the technology to pinpoint the geographical location of a mobile phone user to within one metre. On the back of this ability to accurately locate a mobile phone, a mobile information services industry will be created.

Semiconductors and microprocessors

Have you ever wondered how *Silicon Valley* got its name? Why not *PC* or *Internet* valley? The reason is simple: silicon microchips are the steam engine of the era. Each microchip, or semiconductor, is an integrated circuit of millions of transistors built on a single crystal of silicon. A single-chip microprocessor contains all the arithmetic, logic plus control circuitry, and possibly also the memory, of a complete computer. The key terms here are:

- ❑ *microelectronics* – the building of integrated circuits on silicon and other semiconductor devices;
- ❑ *microchip* – any silicon chip containing an integrated circuit, whether a memory, special-purpose device, or general-purpose microprocessor;
- ❑ *microprocessors* – silicon chips containing the central processing unit (CPU) of a computer.

Today, the semiconductor industry is worth around $200 billion and is growing at a rate of 40 per cent a year. Although the cost of manufacturing a single microchip is negligible, it costs a staggering $1–$2 billion to build a typical fabrication plant.

Companies

The 800-pound gorilla of the semiconductor industry is Intel, which owns

75 per cent of the microprocessor market. Gordon Moore and Robert Noyce founded Intel in 1968, with capital of less than $5 million dollars and a famous one-page business plan. Well, they *had* done it before when they launched Fairchild.

Opportunities

Before asking your local bank manager for $1 billion to set up your own fabrication plant (or fab' line), you need to understand the two so-called *laws* that govern the semiconductor industry:

❑ *Moore's Law* – the number of transistors that can be placed on a single microchip doubles every 18 months;
❑ *Rock's Law* – the cost of the facilities and equipment to fabricate these semiconductors doubles every four years.

Obviously this escalating fabrication cost cannot go on rising indefinitely. An opportunity for some device physicist or electronics engineer perhaps?

Sources of help

Fluckiger, F (1995) *Understanding Networked Multimedia*, Prentice-Hall, London
Gates, B (1999) *Business @ the speed of thought*, Penguin Books, London
Gershenfeld, N (1999) *When things start to Think*, Henry Holt, New York
Kelly, K (1999) *New Rules for the New Economy*, Fourth Estate, London
Norman, D (1998) *Invisible Computers*, MIT Press, Cambridge, Mass
Shapiro, C and Varian, H (1999) *Information Rules*, Harvard Business School Press, Boston
Trapunski, E (1998) *The Secrets of Investing in Technology Stocks*, John Wiley & Sons, Toronto

3 Your High-tech Start-up

So, you have a brilliant idea and a strategy for turning it into money. Now you need to set up your company, get an Internet presence and open a bank account. But before doing any of these things, think of how you will convey your idea to potential customers. The better they understand your company's mission and recognize its brand name, the more likely they are to do business with you, and the more valuable your company.

This chapter gives you a complete overview of setting up your high-tech start-up – how to go about:

☐ creating your company's 'branding', starting with your company name and Internet address;
☐ registering your Internet domain name and getting a presence;
☐ registering your business as a limited company;
☐ finding the initial money to fund your start-up;
☐ opening a business bank account.

Remember, *up-start* start-ups are all about image and branding.

The importance of branding

Good branding suggests the mission of your company, the branded products and services it offers, your Internet name, possibly your company address. Even having consecutive telephone and fax numbers gives the impression of a 'well organized' company. In contrast, having a different company name and Internet name makes you look like a bunch of clowns! Microsoft illustrates good branding:

- ☐ company name *Microsoft* – the company selling software for microcomputers;
- ☐ product name – *MS Office* – the Microsoft word processing application package, etc;
- ☐ Internet domain name – *www.microsoft.com* – the Microsoft Web address;
- ☐ e-mail address *b.gates@microsoft.com* – the Microsoft electronic mail address.

As an example, consider the Students' Business Club website at UCL that helps students to find part-time professional work. When we set up the Club we wanted an easy-to-remember name that also conveyed the Club's mission to prospective employers:

Helping **students** find commercial work and start **companies** in the **UK**.

Fortunately, the Internet domain name was available. To build brand recognition amongst potential employers, the literature also refers to the organisation as *students.co.uk*.

The last action would be to register *students.co.uk* as a trademark (see Chapter 27). However, here we face an interesting problem. The UK trademark authorities will consider only the 'students' part of the Internet address when registering the trademark. Since 'students' is considered generic, then the mark is essentially non-registerable.

So before you start your high-tech company give some thought to its branding: *company* (name, logo, address), *products* (names, logos), *Internet* (domain name, website, electronic mail address), *telephone* (number, fax), and *business stationery* (letterheads, business cards, compliments slips, documents, brochures). Lastly, do not forget the business' *mission statement*.

Having chosen your desired company name and designed your branding, you next need to confirm whether your Internet name and company names are available. This can be done online.

Getting an Internet presence

Before you register your Internet name you need to decide whether it needs to be global (.com) or national (.co.uk). You might assume that a global name is always preferable, if available. However, if you are providing a purely national service, the global name may put off potential customers. For instance, the bookseller Amazon.com has both a global name (www.amazon.com) and a UK name (www.amazon.co.uk). The implication of this is that the UK site specializes in serving UK customers, and therefore offers you the books faster and cheaper.

Global Internet 'domain' names – those ending in .com and .net – are administered in the United States by an organization called *InterNIC* (www.internic.net). InterNIC provides an online search and registration facility.

All other countries, the United Kingdom (.uk), Germany (.de), Japan (.jp), Australia (.au) etc handle their own national registrations. UK Internet names – those ending in .co.uk and .org.uk – are handled by an organization called *Nominet UK* (www.nic.uk) (see Figure 3.1). Typically, to register a domain name in a country you either need to be doing business there already or intend to establish a business.

The simplest way to register a name is to use one of the commercial Internet name companies, who, for a fee, will handle all registration details. For instance, NetNames (www.netnames.co.uk) (see Figure 3.2) or NetBenefit (www.netbenefit.co.uk) in the UK, and Tabnet (www.tabnet.

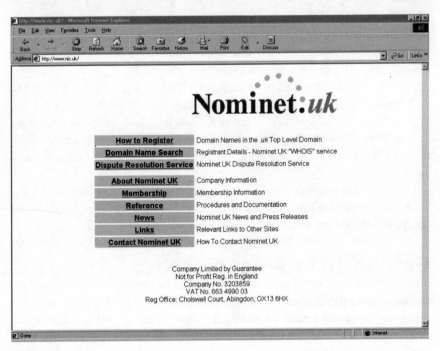

Figure 3.1

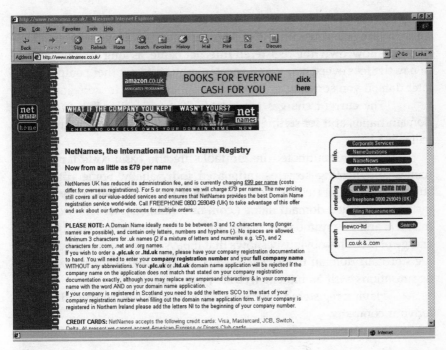

Figure 3.2

com) for the USA.

This is the usual process to register an Internet name:

1. Load the Web page of an Internet 'domain' name registration company.
2. Enter your chosen Internet name in the search box and 'click' the search button.
3. If the name is available, go to step 4; otherwise choose a new name and go to step 2.
4. Request the domain company to register your chosen Internet name by entering the name and domain in the form.

The company may want you to sign a paper form and fax/post the form back to them with a cheque. To speed up the registration process, telephone the company and ask them to fax you a registration form, complete the form, including your credit card number, and fax it back to them.

The registration company can also set up an Internet site for you.

This can be merely a 'dummy' site as part of your name registration, or they can provide you with a Web page for your company and e-mail facilities. You now 'own' the registered Internet name, as long as you continue to pay the fees every two years, and can move it to another computer at a later date, if you so wish.

The current charges (circa late 1999) for registering an Internet domain name, and for setting up a website and e-mail facility, are shown in Table 3.1.

The figures quoted in the table are the basic costs for domain names and hosting services purchased individually. Some companies, such as NetBenefit (tel 020 7336 6777), offer package deals. They will, for instance, supply a domain name (.com or .co.uk, etc), website hosting, e-mail IDs and any number of aliases, for a basic fee of £90, plus a monthly charge of £25. This obviously shows that it pays to shop around before you register your domain name. For a list of competitive domain registration organisations, visit Nominet's website (www.nic.uk).

Having registered your Internet presence, you next need to register your company.

Registering your company

When forming your company you have three basic options (Chapter 24 gives more details):

- ☐ *sole trader* – running a one-person business;
- ☐ *partnership* – working together with partners;
- ☐ *limited company* – forming a company with limited liability.

Table 3.1 Internet domain name registration costs

Organization	.com Cost	.co.uk Cost	Website	E-mail
InterNIC (via Network Solutions)	£45			
Nominet		£80		
NetNames	£144	£119		
NetBenefit	£150	£120	£50 + £240 pa	£50 pa

Most people choose to form a limited company because of the protection given to shareholders by the limited liability. Although the directors of a company have legal obligations, such as not knowingly incurring debts that they believe the company will be unable to pay, all you should lose, if things go wrong, are your investments in the company.

The common approach to forming a limited company is to have your solicitor buy an already registered 'off-the-shelf-company'. (A specialist registration service is provided, for example, by Companies Limited: www.limited-companies.co.uk.) You then change this off-the-shelf company's name to your preferred name. Your solicitor will make a search of registered company names, and if the name is available and acceptable will make the change by submitting the necessary form to the Companies Registration Office at Companies House (www.companies-house.gov.uk) (see Figure 3.3).

Alternatively you can also register your company name yourself at the UK Registrar of Companies or the Irish Republic Registry of Business Names. Addresses for these are in a section at the back of this book.

Companies House will supply the appropriate forms and there is

Figure 3.3

a customer department to help with queries. Its website provides an extensive list of online information. Companies House also publishes a CD ROM directory of all the companies currently registered in England, Wales and Scotland, along with companies that have been dissolved, converted or closed in the last 12 months. The CD ROM also comes with a sophisticated search tool that allows you to access companies by their company name or company number, town or postcode, etc. The directory is produced monthly; single copies of the CD ROM cost £30, and a year's subscription costs £300. They are available from any Companies House Information Centre, including Companies House in Cardiff (tel 02920 380 801).

Funding your start-up

Most people's idea of raising money to finance their start-up centres on *venture capital*. However, venture capitalists in general do not provide money for brand-new companies at the 'idea' stage. Because only about 10 per cent of venture-backed businesses are successes, VCs need a high rate of return (say 50 per cent a year) on their investments, and therefore want a high percentage (20–30 per cent of the shares) of your business.

So in reality, 70 per cent of start-ups are funded by the so-called Three Fs – founders, family and friends. With this *low-risk* route, you start small, fund your first product, focus your business on a market niche, generate some cash, and learn about management as you grow. To fund this start-up phase, US entrepreneurs even use their credit cards. Once your business is a proven success you can then approach a venture capitalist for funding to accelerate the growth of your business, and negotiate with them from a position of greater strength.

Opening a bank account

Your new company needs to have its own bank account – separate from your personal bank account – as soon as possible. There are a number of considerations:

- [ ] *Account name.* Your bank account needs a name; ideally the same name as your company.
- [ ] *Deposit.* You will be required to deposit a sum of money when setting up the account (this is known as 'capital introduced').

- ❏ *Signatures.* Sample signatures of all signatories for the account need to be provided.
- ❏ *Signatories.* You must decide how many of the designated signatures need to be provided when signing a cheque or other document – normally two.
- ❏ *Statements.* You will need to arrange for a bank statement each month, or even weekly.
- ❏ *Overdraft.* Do you need an overdraft facility? If so, what is the fee and how long will the arrangement last?
- ❏ *Paying-in book.* You need a paying-in book for money received.
- ❏ *Bank charges.* You will need to understand the bank's charges, even if they offer you free banking for a period.
- ❏ *Deposit account.* Consider opening a deposit account to earn interest on money not needed immediately.
- ❏ *Internet banking.* Lastly, make sure your bank provides an Internet banking service allowing you instant access to your account.

Most UK and Irish banks, for instance the Bank of Ireland (www.boi.ie), offer online banking to both personal and business customers. Online banking allows you to: 1) access account balances; 2) access all transaction records for the previous six weeks; 3) pay your bills online; 4) transfer money between accounts; 5) send e-mail messages to the bank's personnel; and 6) request a cheque book, bank card, overdraft, loan or additional accounts.

Banks currently offer two types of online banking:

- ❏ *Internet banking* allows you to access your bank accounts via the Web from any Internet-connected PC. Typically, you can do everything apart from paying bills (for security reasons).
- ❏ *PC banking* allows businesses full access to the bank's services, including paying bills. Typically this uses proprietary software that provides an additional level of security, and also interfaces with common accounting packages such as SAGE, Quicken and Money.

Costs for the online banking services are currently £10–15 for registration, and an annual fee of £10–15. However, owing to competition, banks are starting to provide these services free of additional charges. The competition for new business accounts is fierce, so it pays to shop around.

Sources of help

British Chamber of Commerce (BCC). 4 Westwood House, Westwood Business Park, Coventry CV4 8HS, tel: 02476 694492, fax: 02476 695844, email: enquiry@britishchambers.org.uk, *www.britishchambers.org.uk*

Clayton, P (1997) *Forming a Limited Company*, Kogan Page, London

Companies House. (England and Wales). Crown Way, Maindy, Cardiff, CF4 3UZ, tel: 02920 388 588, *www.companies-house.gov.uk*

Companies House. (Scotland). 37 Castle Terrace, Edinburgh, EH1 2EB, tel: 0131 535 5800, *www.companies-house.gov.uk*

Companies Registration Office. (Northern Ireland). Companies Registry, IBD House, 64 Chichester Street, Belfast BT1 4JX, tel: 01232 234 488, *www.companies-house.co.uk*

Hart, S and Murphy, J (1998) *Brands – The New Wealth Creators*, Macmillan Business, London

Institute of Directors (IoD). Institute of Directors. 116 Pall Mall, London SW1Y 5ED, tel: 020 7839 1233, fax: 020 7930 1949, *www.iod.co.uk*

Irish Republic Registry of Business Names. Parnell House, 14 Parnell Square, Dublin, tel: 011 804 5200

Irish Republic Small Firms Association (SFA). SFA Dublin Office, 84–86 Lower Baggot Street, Dublin 2, tel: 011 660 1011, fax: 011 611 2861, email: sfa@iol.ie, *www.ireland.iol.ie/sfa*

Seybold, P and Marshak, R (1998) *Customers.Com*, Century/Arrow, London

4 Making Real Money

High-tech start-ups, unlike traditional businesses, are all about pushing the value of your company to £100 million, and then realizing your investment in the shortest possible time.

This is the 'Silicon Valley culture' everyone is trying to emulate. It is about taking your technical skills, identifying a market niche, promoting yourself and your company to the media, becoming the dominant market leader (*the gorilla*), and making *real* money.

In this chapter we look at:

❑ how high-tech start-ups make real money – the $100 million home run;

❑ how start-ups use venture capital to accelerate growth;

❑ using share options and the initial public offering to motivate staff;

❑ the principal high-tech stock markets, NASDAQ, EASDAQ and AIM.

Yahoo! – the most visited site on the Internet with 100 million 'hits' a day – is in many ways the *classic* high-tech start-up. As we saw in Chapter 1, Yahoo! was launched in 1994 by two students who built a 'yellow pages' for the Internet. Once the business potential of their 'hobby company' was demonstrated, they approached a venture capital (VC) firm, Sequoia, and received $1 million dollars in funding in return for giving up 25 per cent of the company. The VC then helped them recruit the excellent management team, Tim Koogle and Jeff Mallet, who took the raw gem of an operation and turned it into a commercial success. Today, Yahoo! has a market capitalization of over $30 billion dollars, and Jerry Yang is worth $3 billion.

This is the classic high-tech start-up scenario:

❏ *Launch.* Use the *low-risk* start-up model to demonstrate your business idea. Start small, raise launch funding from friends and family, and develop your product.

❏ *Focus.* Focus on an entry-level product that is a 100 per cent complete offering.

❏ *Silicon Valley.* If you are an *up-start* start-up wanting to make a fortune fast, you need visibility, you need to dominate the US market, you need American VC money and the associated kudos, etc. Arguably the easiest place to do this is Silicon Valley. In addition, US VCs will insist that you are a US company and located nearby (eg in the Valley).

❏ *Share options.* Give everybody in the company, from the receptionist up, share options, to motivate them. Typically 10–25 per cent of the company is allocated for share options.

❏ *Venture capital.* As soon as your idea is proven, use venture capital to accelerate growth to a $100 million company.

❏ *Promotion.* Choose a product with glamour, then promote yourself and your business as a superstar. Remember the ultimate accolade is to get on the cover of *TIME* or *Newsweek*.

❏ *Initial public offering.* Aim for an *initial public share offering* (IPO) that will value your company at over $1 billion, or aim to sell the company to a *trade buyer* (typically a larger, established company) for $100–200 million.

This might sound like fantasy-land, but this is the classic US high-tech route to fame and fortune.

Digital 'show' business

Launching a high-tech start-up is about *show business*. Today, high-tech heroes like Bill Gates, Marc Andreessen and Jerry Yang are more likely to appear on the cover of *TIME* magazine than are film stars. The reason is that they are worth considerably more, and also have captured the sense of adventure in current times.

Our typical high-tech entrepreneur starts off contracting; building bespoke systems often for 'pocket money'. The breakthrough comes from the first major sale to a prestigious client. Our entrepreneur then sees the opportunity to turn the 'hobby' business into a highly profitable company dominating a market niche. As soon as the business demonstrates its financial potential, venture capital is introduced to accelerate growth. In parallel, professional managers are brought in to shape and focus the business.

Large valuations versus revenue

A classic difference between high-tech companies and conventional ones is that 'market capitalization' or valuation is often considered more important than profits. *Circa* 1998/99, Amazon.com (www.amazon.com) had a market capitalization of $22 billion and revenues of $610 million; Yahoo!'s (www.yahoo.com) corresponding figures were $31 billion and $203 million; and eBay's (www.ebay.com) were $15 billion and $47 million. Revenue growth drives valuation, indicating capture of market share, as opposed to quick profits.

Valuing your business

Many digital businesses seem to have *fantasy* values. So how do you and venture capitalists value your business? There are several ways:

❑ *Comparison with similar companies*. Calculate the value of your company by comparing it with similar companies, ideally quoted on a stock market. The key to this calculation is the price/earnings (P/E) ratio; the multiple of post-tax profits placed on a company to establish its market value. Ratios of 10:1 are normal, apart from high-tech stocks where they can be far higher. However, for loss-making companies this does not work.

❑ *Comparison of revenue*. Calculate the market capitalization to revenue ratio for an existing publicly quoted similar company, and apply this to your revenues.

❑ *Existing net assets*. This values a business on existing or projected net assets, such as buildings, and their realizable values; or even in electronic commerce the number of subscribers to an Internet service, and the potential revenue of advertising to them.

Having valued your business, the next big question is when to take venture capital.

Venture capital's role

There are two basic models for starting a business (see Chapter 18):

- ☐ *The venture-capital model.* You identify an opportunity in a large and growing market, hire a complete team of experienced and successful managers, raise millions of dollars of venture capital, and spend it to accelerate your business development.
- ☐ *The low-risk model.* You raise a small amount of money from friends, family and other entrepreneurs, develop your product, and slowly expand your business.

Most books (and most people's concept) of raising finance centre on the *venture-capital* model. However, as noted, reputable VCs in general do not provide money to brand-new companies at the 'idea' stage, owing to the high mortality rate of start-ups. Due to the fact that VCs need to aim for a high rate of return on investment (eg 50 per cent a year), they will therefore want a high percentage of your business (eg 20–30 per cent of the shares). Another prerequisite is that venture capitalists generally assume that young entrepreneurs and technologists cannot manage a business, especially in a situation of rapid growth. They will therefore want to bring in experienced, professional managers who will also need shares as an inducement.

The alternative is the low-risk model. You start small and focus your business on a market niche. To fund this start-up phase you raise a small amount of money from friends, family and other entrepreneurs; even on your credit card. You learn to control your finances, the basics of taxation and law, and hire people as your business grows. You deliver a better product or service to a few customers, rather than trying to capture a slice of the world market. In many ways this is *the* common sense approach, forcing you to address the most fundamental principles of building a profitable business.

In fact, the optimum approach is to use the low-risk model to start your company, and then, once your business is established, use venture capital to accelerate growth. You can raise investment capital as required, and because your increasingly successful company will receive successively higher valuations, venture capital will be less expensive. This ensures that you retain a much bigger share of your company.

Professional management

In return for investment, the VC or wealthy private investor will want a seat on your board and will take an active part in helping your company grow. This is an invaluable source of advice. Most high-tech entrepreneurs are confident of their own ability (bordering on arrogance), strong on technology and future trends, but usually weak on management. A good VC has an extensive network of contacts, and is well placed to help you recruit a strong management team, especially for managing ballistic growth. Although you may be reluctant to give up equity and be worried about losing control of your 'baby', both you and your VC are looking for success.

Share options

In Silicon Valley, 'stock options are the oil that lubricates high-tech start-ups'. Many receptionists in start-ups have become millionaires through their stock options.

Stock (or share) options allow employees to purchase shares in their company at a price fixed when the option was granted (the grant price) for a definite number of years in the future. For instance, a company in 1998 may have given an employee the right to buy 1000 shares at the current price of $10 per share vested over a four-year period. This means that after the first year (1999) the employee could buy 25 per cent of the options (250 shares) each year at the $10 price. A limit of 10 years is typically placed on the exercise. The rationale is that if a company goes public or is bought, then these shares will be worth a lot more (eg $100 per share, netting the employee $90,000 before tax).

In the UK, share option schemes fall into two broad categories, namely Inland Revenue approved schemes and unapproved schemes. Approved schemes have tax advantages while unapproved schemes are more flexible. The two Inland Revenue approved schemes are:

❑ *The share save scheme (SAYE)*. An employee takes out a certified Save As You Earn contractual savings scheme with a building society, bank, or Department of National Savings, and receives a tax-free bonus at the end of a designated period. The proceeds from the savings contract are then used by the employee to pay when exercising the share options.

❏ *The executive (or discretionary) scheme.* Various conditions must be met to qualify for tax relief. For instance, the employee is not allowed to have options over shares valued at more than £30,000 at the date of issue, and options can be exercised only after three years from being granted.

In the United States there are two main kinds of options:

❏ *Incentive stock options (ISO).* With an ISO, if certain rules are met, the employee does not have to pay tax on the 'spread' between the grant and exercise price until the shares are sold. Capital gains would then be due.

❏ *Nonqualified stock options (NSO).* With an NSO, the employee pays tax on the spread just as if it were wages, and the company can take a corresponding tax deduction.

Accelerating growth

So, when should you approach a VC? As discussed above, the best advice is to self-fund the start-up phase of your company and when you have a proven track record, approach a VC to fund expansion. This will put you in a strong negotiating position with the VC. Besides getting the best financial deal, also look to see what 'added-value' the VC can contribute. For example, an increasing number of corporations like Reuters and WPP are investing in start-ups close to their core business. These blue-chip companies bring an obvious endorsement and a large potential customer. Likewise, if you are planning to expand abroad – opening an office in Silicon Valley for instance – then look for a VC with offices in the Valley.

Realizing your investment

Recall that high-tech start-ups are about making your fortune, not about earning your living. So, when you start, think in terms of a £100 million company in 2–3 years. The principal 'exit' routes for realizing your investment are:

❏ *Trade sale.* Sell your business to another company.
❏ *Going public.* Obtain a share quote on one of the major stock exchanges.

Moving to Silicon Valley

As SAP (www.sap.com) and SAGE (www.sage.com) have clearly demonstrated, you can start a world-class, high-tech company in Europe. However, if your start-up has pretensions of being a global electronic commerce player, like Yahoo! or Amazon.com, then it is best to move your business to the United States, probably Silicon Valley, Boston or New York. The following is advice anyone in the Valley will give you:

❑ *Your Internet domain name.* This needs to end in 'dot com' (.com), or at the very least .net.
❑ *Venture capital.* You need the prestige of being backed by one of the legendary Silicon Valley 'tech' VCs: Sequoia (www.sequoiacap.com), Kleiner Perkins (www.kpcb.com), or Hummer Winblad (www.humwin.com).
❑ *Lawyers.* You need, likewise, the prestige of being represented by a leading Valley 'tech' law firm: Wilson Sonsini (www.wsgr.com), Venture Law (www.venturelaw.com), or McCutchen (www.mccutchen.com).
❑ *Bank account.* You should probably open an account at Silicon Valley Bank (www.svb.com).
❑ *Accountant.* Appoint one of the big five (Arthur Andersen, PWC...) accountancy firms to show you mean business.
❑ *Registration.* Your US VC will first of all demand that you register your company in the United States (ie Delaware). Secondly, the VC will want your head office based within a radius of 30 miles (ie in the Valley), so they can see you regularly.
❑ *Flotation.* Aim to float your company on NASDAQ, the pre-eminent 'tech' stock market.

The initial public offering

An initial public offering or IPO is the first public issuance of stock from a company that has not been traded before. You have a number of IPO options:

❑ *NASDAQ* – the North American Securities Dealers Automated Quotation system;
❑ *EASDAQ* – the European Association of Securities Dealers Automated Quotation system;

☐ *AIM* – the Alternative Investment Market; the junior stock market of the London Stock Exchange;

☐ *Neuer Markt* – the German stock market for small companies;

☐ *Internet IPO* – direct IPOs over the Internet (www.directipo.com).

Internal IPOs are set to become increasingly popular for small companies as vehicles for raising capital. Using the Internet has several advantages. Firstly, it avoids the expensive brokerage fees charged by underwriters. Secondly, it reaches a wider audience of potential investors. Finally, the Internet offers major reductions in time and cost for delivery of the materials offered.

Further details on NASDAQ, EASDAQ, AIM and Neuer Markt are given below.

Stock markets

The four principal Stock Markets for high-tech start-ups are the US's NASDAQ (and Euro NASDAQ), the European/Belgium EASDAQ, the UK's AIM (and TechMARK) and Germany's Neuer Markt. (A complete listing of all the European exchanges is given on the Federation of European Stock Exchanges Web site – www.fese.be.) These 'junior' stock markets offer all the benefits of their big brothers, such as higher public profile and access to capital, with a simpler entry structure.

NASDAQ

The NASDAQ stock market (www.nasdaq.com – see Figure 4.1) lists over 5,500 companies. NASDAQ provided the capital support for most of the dynamic and innovative high-tech companies in the United States, including Microsoft. It has two tiers: the National Market for medium size companies and the SmallCap Market, which has 1,200 smaller companies. All listed companies are required to meet certain standards of corporate governance, and a minimum set of SEC (US regulator) financial requirements.

NASDAQ's fees structure and financial requirements are listed on their excellent website. Basically, the fees comprise: a one-time *listing* fee ($5,000), an *entry* fee (under one million shares, $29,525) and an *annual* fee (under one million shares, $10,710) based on the number of shares.

The financial requirements vary, covering a combination of net

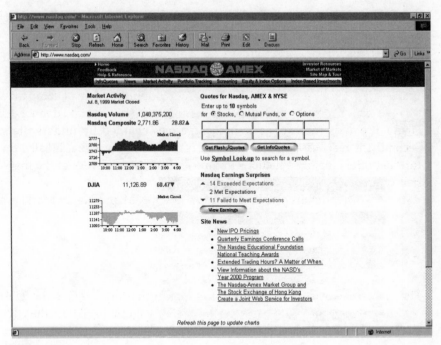

Figure 4.1

tangible assets (exceeding $6 million), market capitalization (ex. $75 million), shares (ex. 1.1 million), and shareholders (ex. 400), and so on. The application forms for listings are also available on NASDAQ's website.

EASDAQ

The EASDAQ stock market (www.easdaq.be – see Figure 4.2) operates across 14 European countries with one regulatory structure, one rulebook, and one trading and settlement system. The net worth of an applicant company should comprise total assets of at least 3.5 million euros and capital/reserves of 2 million euros. No minimum level of company profitability is required.

EASDAQ allows a number of forms of admission, from initial public offering (IPO) to dual listing with another exchange. The admission procedure starts with an informal presentation to EASDAQ. It finishes with the company, its financial advisors and EASDAQ agreeing the details of the offering, and arranging the settlement/clearance process.

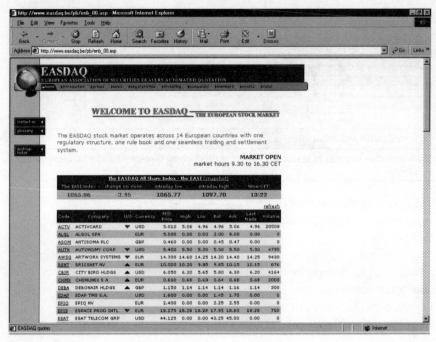

Figure 4.2

AIM

The London Stock Exchange's Alternative Investment Market (www.stockex.co.uk) targets small companies with a market capitalization of less than £30 million. Of the 271 AIM companies, 75 per cent of those raising capital at admission sought between £1 million and £10 million.

AIM has a simplified entry structure, placing no restrictions on company size, period of existence, or the percentage of shares in public hands. To obtain an AIM listing, a company must appoint a *nominated advisor* approved by AIM who will advise on the suitability of the placement, prepare the admission document and help the company comply with AIM's rules. Many financial people think AIM lacks liquidity.

Neuer Markt

The Deutsche Börse's Neuer Markt (www.neuer-markt.de) was launched on 10 March 1997 – as a new trading segment at FWB, the Frankfurt Stock Exchange. Companies typically listed on the Neuer Markt are based on

Table 4.1 Going public: advantages and disadvantages

Advantages	Disadvantages
Making money and realizing your investment.	Potential loss of founder control.
Funds to expand the business.	Increased scrutiny of decisions.
Acquisitions funded through share swaps.	'Short-term-ism': focus on short-term profits and dividends.
Enhanced status and public visibility.	Additional management overheads.
Share incentive schemes to motivate employees.	Unwelcome take-over bids for business.

industries with a strong future and above-average sales and earnings prospects, such as telecoms, biotechnology, multimedia or environmental technology.

Going public by seeking a stock market quotation has various advantages and disadvantages (Table 4.1). Marc Andreessen (Netscape) and Jerry Yang (Yahoo!) became instant millionaires when they floated their companies. In contrast, Richard Branson bought back Virgin because he regretted the hassle of dealing with the City in London.

Sources of help

AIM. (Alternative Investment Market). Old Broad Street, London EC2N 1HP, tel: 0171 797 1939, www.londonstockex.co.uk

British Venture Capital Association. Essex house, 12–13 Essex Street, London, WC2R 3AA, tel: 0171 240 3846, fax: 0171 240 3849, *www.bvca.co.uk*

Chapman, C (1998) *How the Stock Markets Work*, Century Business Books, London

EASDAQ (European Association of Securities Dealers Automated Quotation System.). Warwick House, 65–66 Queen Street, London, EC4R 1EB, tel: 020 7489 99 90 fax: 020 7489 88 80 e-mail: info@easdaq.be, *www.easdaq.be*

Lipman, F (1998) *Financing your business with Venture Capital*, Prima Publishing, Rocklin, CA

Moore, G, Johnson, P and Kippola, T (1998) *The Gorilla Games – an investor's guide to picking winners in high technology*, Capstone, Oxford

NASDAQ (National Association of Securities Dealers Automated Quotation System.). Durrant House, 8–13 Chiswell Street, EC1Y 4UQ, tel: 020 7374 6969, *www.nasdaq.com*

Neuer Markt (the German small company stock market). *www.neuer-markt.de*

Trapunski, E (1998) *The Secrets of Investing in Technology Stocks*, John Wiley & Sons, Toronto

Part 2

Launching *your* Start-up

---

5 Your Money-making Strategy

To quote Thomas Edison: 'Anything that won't sell, I don't want to invent.'

The majority of high-tech start-ups are based on the concept of working extremely hard for a couple of years, and then going public or selling out for a huge sum of money.

The three crucial factors for success are: firstly, you need an innovative idea; secondly, you need to really focus on the essentials; and thirdly, your business needs to be well managed. Any venture capitalist will tell you that good management can turn a borderline idea into a success, but borderline management can turn a good idea into failure . . . snatching defeat from the jaws of victory...

In this chapter we look at:

- ❑ what it takes to start a successful business – your idea, your product and you;
- ❑ how you go about thinking up a good idea;
- ❑ how you turn the idea into a product customers will kill for;
- ❑ making sure you have the personal characteristics and commitment to make it all happen.

Even when you have that brilliant idea, you must ask yourself if it has, realistically, all the ingredients to succeed. Has it the potential to make loads of money? Do you have the financial and human resources to launch the business? Do you have the mental discipline to focus on the essentials of your business? Have you the ability to manage the business well or do you need professional management? And are you persuasive; can you talk backers into investing and customers into buying?

Your brilliant idea

The first thing to recognize is that most entrepreneurs notch-up a few business failures before they hit on the winning business. As they say in the United States, 'you learn far more from your failures than your successes'. So it is important to get in the water and start swimming. For instance, many software and Internet entrepreneurs start off as *contractors*, building bespoke systems for clients. This is an excellent way to identify market opportunities and earn a little money, but you are most unlikely to earn a fortune from contracting.

So an important personal decision is: whether you are *trying for a fortune* or wanting to *work for yourself*.

Trying for a fortune

If you are trying for a fortune, you need to bear in mind the *Ten Golden Rules* in Chapter 1. In a nutshell – identify an idea for a market niche where you can totally dominate the global market. Create an integrated and glamorous image for your company, and promote it to the media and venture capital community. And realize your investment through a flotation or trade sale at the earliest opportunity:

So, from where does your idea come? A good business idea often comes from personal experience. That is why contracting is an excellent route in high-tech business. Often, good ideas take time to germinate and come into focus. Therefore, you will probably need a good flow of ideas.

When searching for ideas and opportunities, trawl through leading technical and business publications, especially American ones like *BusinessWeek* (www.businessweek.com), *Wired* magazine (www.wired.com) and *RedHerring* (www.redherring.com), the venture capital magazine.

Working for yourself

If you are looking to work for yourself, then the ground rules are somewhat different. What you want is a good revenue stream in a buoyant market. For instance, if you have unique expertise in JAVA or Media 100, you can apply your expertise in a whole range of areas, from finance and retail to media. In contrast, if you simply build websites for clients, you will find your market and charges under attack from many quarters – users programming their own pages, students working part-time, and major media companies building sophisticated sites for corporate clients.

Basically, you need to identify a profitable market and your business needs to be well managed. Sara Williams' *Small Business Guide* is a good introduction to traditional business techniques:

- ❑ *Your customers.* Obviously you need to be sure that people want to buy the proposed product or service, and that they will in fact buy *from you.*
- ❑ *Market buoyancy.* You need to estimate how long your market will remain profitable, or the life cycle of your product or service. When a new technology emerges, few people have the skills to service the market. Therefore you can charge high margins; but this encourages other suppliers, especially established companies, to move into the market.
- ❑ *Realistic prices.* You need to charge realistically high prices both to make a profit and to demonstrate to customers that you are a serious, professional business.

Then there are the elements of good management:

- ❑ *Controlling your business.* You need to plan how your business will develop. This covers not only technical and financial aspects, but also the life cycle of your product or service, and future technical developments. You also need profits for funding longer term growth. Many businesses never move beyond their first product, and many do not generate sufficient profits to expand.
- ❑ *Cash management.* In the short-term, you need to manage your cash flow to ensure you have enough cash to pay your bills. A surprising number of businesses fail simply because they run out of cash to pay their day-to-day bills.
- ❑ *Costs management.* I am tempted to say, 'run a tight ship'. Most successful managing directors are good at maximizing sales and minimizing costs.
- ❑ *Type of business.* Then you need to choose the correct legal form for your company. For most of us this will be a limited company.
- ❑ *Seeking advice.* Finally, no entrepreneur has all the skills required. Look at how other successful companies operate – their business

structures, marketing strategies, the look-and-feel of their products, even the design of their brochures. Also, seek the help and advice of friends and professionals.

When you are searching for ideas and opportunities, be aware that *The Sunday Times*, the *Financial Times*, *The Times* and *The Daily Telegraph* all publish weekly sections advertising other people's ideas and opportunities for small businesses. In addition, a number of organizations exist to put people in touch with business opportunities. For example:

- ❏ *The Business Exchange* is a 'marketplace' for buying and selling family-owned businesses in the range £800,000 to £15 million. It was set up by a number of leading accountants (tel 020 7930 8965, www.business-exchange-plc.co.uk).
- ❏ *European Business Centre Network* is a service for small and medium sized enterprises (SMEs) to contact similar SMEs in other European Union countries (tel 00 322 295 9421, www.citizen.be/ebn).

Remember, innovation does not just happen. It must be planned, managed and organized. It is worth noting that innovative high-tech enterprises like 3M allow R&D staff to spend 15 per cent of their time working on their own ideas, and have a company rule that 30 per cent of turnover must come from new products developed in the past five years.

Your product or service

When you start out, you need a good flow of ideas before a winner emerges. Sometimes, you will have a seemingly good idea, but deep down you know something is missing. When the winner emerges you will know it. Trust your 'gut feelings'. If you don't have absolute confidence in your product or the quality of your service, neither will your customers, and you will never get your business idea off the ground. So you need to perform a *reality check* on your 'brilliant idea', by asking yourself some hard questions.

Is it sound?

Ask yourself some hard questions:

❑ *Product.* What exactly is the product or service you are planning to offer? Remember, customers do not buy research; they want a 100 per cent complete offering.

❑ *Customers.* Why should customers buy your offering, rather than an existing product or service?

❑ *Response.* Will established competitors respond aggressively? If the market is such a lucrative one, all sorts of start-ups and established companies will want a slice of the action. And if competitors are not interested, are you deluding yourself?

Is there a market?

Next, ask yourself about the potential market:

❑ *Market size.* How many people are likely to buy the product or service in the UK, Ireland and principal overseas markets? And, more importantly, how many potential customers are likely to buy from you?

❑ *Profitability.* How many customers do you need to make a good profit, and is it realistic for you to expect to capture this percentage of the market?

❑ *Market share.* For your target market, what market share do established competitors already have and what share are they likely to have in the future?

❑ *Overseas competitors.* With areas like electronic commerce, will overseas competitors move into your UK marketplace and marginalize your offering? For instance, a number of UK companies established online bookshops, but now the US giants like Amazon.com (www.amazon.co.uk), Barnes & Noble (www.barnesandnoble.com) and Borders (www.borders.com) are offering a far superior service.

Then the feasibility of developing the product needs to be assessed.

Can it be built?

If your business centres on new technology, important questions relate to the feasibility of implementing the product or service in a reasonable time:

❑ *Resources.* Do the technical resources, such as equipment, exist to build and support the product?

❑ *People.* Are there reliable staff, contractors and suppliers who can do the work? For example, it is particularly difficult to recruit good C++ and JAVA programmers, and they are commanding increasingly high salaries.

❑ *Money.* Do the financial resources exist to fund the development? Investors are usually reluctant to fund the building of prototypes and it is very easy to fail simply by running out of money.

❑ *Management team.* Do you have a management team experienced in handling rapid growth, advertising, sales and global marketing? Remember that any investor will tell you that great management is far more important than a great idea.

Finally, prepare a so-called SWOT (strengths, weaknesses, opportunities, threats) analysis of your business concept (Figure 5.1).

...and you?

Now, most important of all, do you have what it takes? Are you a 'wannabe' or an entrepreneur?

Most entrepreneurs are brimming over with enthusiasm and confidence for their idea. But having done a SWOT analysis on the product and its market, you must next ask whether you have the personal attributes to make it all happen.

Strengths	Opportunities
'your business' strengths compared to your competitors'	'opportunities for your business in the marketplace, and potential to grow into new areas'
Weaknesses	**Threats**
'weaknesses in your business concept, management, technology and marketing'	'potential threats in the marketplace from competitors, customer trends and technology changes'

Figure 5.1 Prepare a SWOT analysis of your business

Your strengthens and weaknesses

- *Vision.* As an entrepreneur, do you have *the* vision of future trends? Most high-tech entrepreneurs are strong on *futurology*, and how technology and the marketplace will develop.
- *Discipline.* Whether you are driven to make your fortune or to change the world, do you have the self-motivation and discipline to make it happen?
- *Focus.* Can you focus on the essentials of the business, especially in the start-up phase? Most start-ups are remarkably 'unfocused', appearing reluctant to commit to a single idea. However, given your limited resources and time, focusing is an absolute priority.
- *Evangelism.* Do you have the ability to sell your idea to others – to investors, customers, staff and the media? In Silicon Valley, they now have a new meaning of CEO: *Chief Evangelist Officer!* Sounds wonderful, doesn't it?

Can you get it together?

Most high-tech entrepreneurs are confident of their ability (often bordering on arrogance), but weak at day-to-day management. Butterflies!

- *Leadership.* Can you build a team, and get them to turn your dream into a reality?
- *Finance.* Can you persuade investors to risk *their* money to finance *your* dream?
- *Sales.* Can you persuade large numbers of customers to buy?
- *Publicity.* Can you persuade the media to promote you and your company?

You can do all that, but can you organize your time effectively?

Time management for beginners

If you are going to achieve great things then you need to manage your time effectively. Plan ... *what* to do, *when* to do it, *where* to do it, and *how* to do it. And question *why* you need to do it at all. I always remember an American friend saying, *don't confuse effort with achievement.* Think of yourself as a general conducting a campaign.

❑ *Planning*. Plan your work by preparing 'to do' lists. These can be daily lists, weekly lists, possibly even monthly and yearly lists of things to do. Categorize each of the tasks into: A – essential, B – important, C – necessary, D – discard, and so on. Prioritize the tasks within category A1, A2, A3... . Then at the end of the day, re-evaluate your 'to do' list. It's surprising how much more you will achieve.

❑ *Executing*. At the beginning of each day start with A1 tasks, then A2, and so on. Strike out each completed task; that's an achievement. Always do the unpleasant tasks first, and do not be tempted into starting with the things you like or enjoy most. Do one thing at a time. Try to handle each piece of paper once. And – some advice given to me by a good businessman – dump as much as you can in the dustbin.

❑ *Meetings*. How many times have you sat in a meeting asking yourself, *how did I get talked into this?* Learn to say 'no'. Fix the length of a meeting in advance, and keep to the point.

❑ *Telephoning*. Make effective use of your telephone. Before you call people, plan your telephone calls. Quickly get to the purpose of the call, without being abrupt. Avoid being distracted by arranging for your telephone calls to be screened by a personal assistant, and in meetings keep your cellular phone switched off.

❑ *E-mail*. Electronic mail is one of the greatest scourges of modern society. Every organization seems to have one member of staff who feels it is their duty to answer every e-mail sent, and copy it to everyone in the company. (Good advice given to me by a director of a bank: *When you identify this person, go there and fire him immediately. It also serves as a warning to others!*) Have two sets of business cards, one with your e-mail address, one without; and be careful who you give them to.

❑ *Travelling*. Arriving late for meetings creates a very bad impression, so always allow plenty of time. Where possible, schedule a series of visits to optimize travelling. In addition, prior to affording your own chauffeur, use trains and planes to give yourself time to think and work.

Most of these time management suggestions are pretty obvious common sense.

Sources of help

Grove, A. (1998) *Only the Paranoid Survive,* HarperCollins, New York

Heller, R and Hindle, T (1998) *Essential Manager's Manual,* Dorling Kindersley, London

Hughes, V and Weller, D (1997) *Teach Yourself Setting up a Business,* Hodder-Stoughton, London

Williams, S (1999) *Small Business Guide,* Penguin Books, London

6 Market Research

To quote the British Army: 'Time spent in reconnaissance is rarely time wasted.'

Why bother with market research? You have a great idea, so why not just go for it? In fact, many high-tech businesses often identify a market need for a product or service, and test the market by selling the product to a 'real' customer. Then, fools rush in where angels fear to tread – and you will certainly need accurate market research if you are seeking to raise finance!

In this chapter we look at:

- ❑ market research to discover your customers and competitors;
- ❑ various types of research: *online* using the Internet, *desk* using published data, and *field* where a survey is conducted;
- ❑ how to segment your customers into purchasing groups;
- ❑ how to understand the market strategies of your competitors;
- ❑ how to prepare a market research plan;
- ❑ a comprehensive list of market research references and organizations.

The purpose of market research is to bring your customers, your competitors and the marketplace into sharp focus, and thereby to quantify them.

Types of research

Online research using the Internet

For high-tech businesses operating globally, Internet-based research is particularly good for searching for suppliers and potential competitors –

although the cynic might say that finding anything remotely useful on the Internet is a challenge indeed.

Internet research centres on so-called *search engines* that trawl the Net looking for useful data and accumulating it in massive databases. Some of the best known are Altavista (www.altavista.com), Excite (www.excite.com), Infoseek (www.go.com) and Yahoo! (www.yahoo.com – see Figure 6.1).

Search engines are becoming increasingly sophisticated. However, the skill is in choosing the list of *key words* to drive the search, given the billions of Web pages that are now online. Typically, search engines: (i) return the number of 'hits' – Web pages that may match the search; (ii) list the web pages in priority order; and (iii) allow you to either continue a modified search within the selected pages or initiate a new search.

In addition, there are also an increasing number of online business directories of companies, such as UK Companies House (www.companies-house.gov.uk), Dialog (www.dialog.com), Dow Jones (www.dowjones.com) and Hoovers (www.hoovers.com), with extensive financial details of US companies.

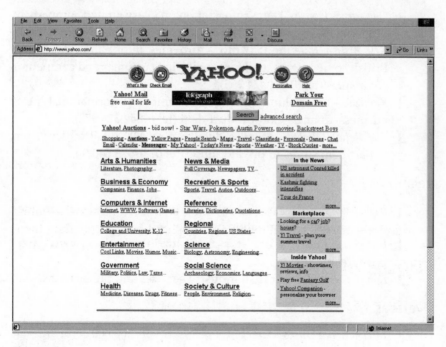

Figure 6.1

Desk research

Desk research involves the study of published information. When looking for information there is an almost endless list of sources: your local library, friends and professional advisors, government publications, newspapers, business magazines and trade journals, professional associations and trade bodies, chambers of commerce, competitors' catalogues, brochures and price lists, and even the telephone directory. This information falls into two broad groups, business directories and business statistics.

Business directories

There are some really comprehensive directories available giving company names, addresses and product information. These directories can be sub-divided into 'UK and Ireland' and 'overseas'. The following are some examples.

United Kingdom

- ❑ *Companies House* – keeps information on every limited company in England, Wales, Scotland and Northern Ireland (tel 029 2038 8588);
- ❑ *Key British Enterprises* (KBE) – provides information on 50,000 British companies; useful for monitoring customer and competitor companies (tel 01494 424 295);
- ❑ *Kompass* – four volumes giving basic company information, type of business, financial and product data (tel 01342 326 972);
- ❑ *The Retail Directory* – gives details of all UK retail outlets from department stores to private shops (tel 020 7973 6402)

Ireland

- ❑ *Irish Trade Board* – An Bord Tráchtála (www.irish-trade.ie) provides comprehensive information on trade;
- ❑ *Enterprise Link* – a 'one-stop-shop' for information (www.enter-prise-ireland.ie);
- ❑ *Kompass* – register of Irish industry services and publications.

Overseas

- ❑ *International Dun's Market Identifiers* – covers 500,000 companies in 143 countries (tel 01494 422 000);

❑ *Who Owns Whom* – lists of parent companies and subsidiaries in the principal countries and regions (tel 01494 424 295).

Business statistics – marketing and industry data by sector

United Kingdom

❑ *Annual Abstract of Statistics* – the basic source of UK statistics available from HMSO (tel 020 7873 0011);
❑ *British Rate and Data* (BRAD) – the advertiser's bible listing data on all newspapers and periodicals in the UK (tel 020 7505 8000 and 7242 3000).

Ireland

❑ *Central Statistics Office* – provides comprehensive information on trade (www.cso.ie);
❑ *Enterprise Link* – a 'one-stop-shop' for information (www.enterprise-ireland.ie).

Overseas

❑ *Economist Intelligence Unit* – economic reviews of 160 countries (tel 020 7930 8763);
❑ *European & International Marketing Data and Statistics* (Euromonitor) – two annual handbooks containing data on European and international markets (tel 020 7251 8024);
❑ *Industrial Market Research Reports* – worldwide data on 20 major sectors (tel 020 7730 3438).

A comprehensive list of market research information sources is given at the end of the book, together with contact details.

Field research

Field research involves interviewing people. This is a major business sector with leading companies such as MORI (www.mori.co.uk) and NOP (www.nop.co.uk). Rather than employ an expensive professional organization, with a little thought and planning you can conduct basic field research yourself, or hire some students. The most popular forms of field research are (see also Table 6.1):

❑ *Personal interviews.* These involve face-to-face interviews with a clipboard and questionnaire. This is a speciality for consumer market research.

❑ *Telephone surveys.* These involve interviews over the telephone, often driven by an on-screen questionnaire. The speciality is surveys of business markets.

❑ *Direct mail.* This involves postal surveys whereby a questionnaire is sent. It is used frequently for industry surveys.

❑ *Focus groups.* These are discussion groups composed of members of the public. This form of market research is popular in testing consumer and political trends.

❑ *Electronic questionnaires.* This involves e-mail, the Web and, in the near future, interactive television. Questionnaires are either sent/returned by e-mail or displayed as a Web page form. Owing to the ease and novelty value, this must be an area set for major growth.

Central to conducting good field research is the design of a questionnaire that is well thought out. Use the following list as a design guide:

❑ *Approach.* Think how you will greet the subject (eg 'Good morning, I am conducting...') and how you will identify yourself to the interviewee (eg show a student card).

❑ *Dress.* How will you dress to look professional without intimidating the interviewee?

❑ *Questions.* Prepare a list of questions, then review the list with the aim of minimizing the number of questions.

Table 6.1 Field research statistics

Research Technique	Speciality	Percentage
personal interview	consumer markets	55
telephone survey	company trends	31
direct mail	industrial markets	7
focus groups	consumer and political trends	7
electronic questionnaires	electronic commerce	–

❏ *Simplicity.* Review each question to ensure the text is clear, and unambiguous.
❏ *Answers.* If you actually plan to ask people the questions, keep them simple, ideally requiring the answers 'Yes', 'No' or 'Don't know'.
❏ *Segmentation.* Include a question that segments the respondent.
❏ *Exit.* Have an 'exit' question at the beginning for irrelevant respondents.

Having looked briefly at the three forms of market research, we now turn to how you can address your customer base.

Your customers

The principal question of this section is: 'Do you really understand your customers and what motivates them to buy your products or services?' There are a number of techniques being used to study customer behaviour systematically:

❏ *Data warehousing* – building a database of customer information, product sales and market research. Every time a customer pays for a product, uses a cash dispenser, orders something over the telephone, or uses the Internet, the information can easily be recorded for later analysis.
❏ *Data mining* – analysis of customer and product data, looking for relationships.
❏ *Market segmentation* – classification of customers into groups with 'similar' interests and behaviours; in particular, purchasing patterns.
❏ *Customer profiling* – analysis of individual customers' interests and behaviour.

Of these techniques, perhaps market segmentation is the most important because it attempts to divide customers into homogeneous groups. This segmentation can be done in a number of ways:

❏ *geographic* – customer preferences are grouped by geographic location;
❏ *demographic* – customer preferences are grouped by age, education or income;

- ❏ *geo-demographic* – customer preferences are a combination of geography and demography;
- ❏ *benefit* – customer preferences are grouped by perceived benefit of the product;
- ❏ *personal* – individual customer preferences are identified.

Dividing customers into a homogeneous group allows you to better understand their motivations, aspirations and purchasing behaviour, and then target your marketing appropriately. The most important questions related to segmentation are:

- ❏ *Size* – how many potential customers are there in the segment?
- ❏ *Targeting* – can you identify individual customers, and reach them with your marketing campaign?
- ❏ *Profitability* – what level of sales can you expect from a segment, what level do you need to be profitable, and is this realistic?
- ❏ *Competitors* – what is the level of potential competition in the market segment?

Your competitors

Gathering information on competitors and potential competitors is one of the most difficult tasks you will face – especially estimating their size and profitability. Your analysis needs to be accurate, realistic and thorough, especially concerning market share. If you have spotted a profitable gap in the market, competitors will certainly try to get a slice of the action.

Firstly, split competitors into *primary*, *secondary* and *potential*. This gives you a focus on the marketplace, and allows you to plan your research. The good news is that there is a considerable amount of information in the public domain, if only you can locate it:

- ❏ *Companies House.* The Companies Registration Office for the UK (tel 029 2038 0801, www.companies-house.gov.uk) and Ireland (tel 01804 5200) contains the annual accounts filed by each company. Information is available on microfiche at £1 per company, or can be photocopied at 10p per sheet.
- ❏ *Annual reports.* All public companies and most large/medium sized private companies publish an overview of their trading performance. Look at their Internet website, or telephone or visit their offices and ask for a copy of the annual report.

❑ *Business directories.* As discussed above, there are a number of excellent publications, such as *Kompass* (tel 01342 326 972) and *Kelly's Business Directory* (tel 01342 326 972), which give estimated sales volumes.

❑ *Commercial organizations.* Companies such as Extel European Companies Service (tel 020 7251 3333, www.extel.co.uk) will gather information on specific companies, for a fee.

❑ *Online information.* A number of online information services, some free and some by subscription, provide comprehensive information on companies. Well-known examples are Hoovers (www.hoovers.com), Reuters (www.reuters.com), Dialog (www.dialog.com), Gartner (www.gartner.com) and Forrester (www.forrester.com).

When preparing your analysis of competitors you should include the following:

❑ *List of competitors.* Split this into primary, secondary and even potential competitors.

❑ *Size of competitors.* Group these by assets, number of staff, global spread etc.

❑ *Profitability.* Analyse this by sales and profits, ideally split by subsidiary company and business unit.

❑ *Business strategy.* Gather marketing intelligence, such as product/service strategy, operating methods, distribution, location, etc.

❑ *Reputation.* What is the impact of competitors in the marketplace; brand recognition, customer loyalty, etc?

Research plan

Obviously, you will need to plan your market research. This is true whether you are considering a new business, launching a product, entering a new market or preparing a business plan to raise finance. It must cover the following:

❑ *Viability.* You need to prove, by detailed analysis, the viability of your business to yourself, to your partners and to potential investors.

❑ *Marketability.* You must demonstrate a realistic strategy for marketing your product based on detailed analysis of potential customers and competitors.

❑ *Profitability.* You need a detailed forecast of profitability, based on pricing, estimated sales and market growth.

Finally, you need to plan your method of approach to the customers or competitors.

❑ *Objectives.* What exactly do you need to know from the market research?

❑ *Target group.* List the market segment customers or competitors you will approach.

❑ *Locations.* List the geographical locations where the research will be conducted.

❑ *Sample.* How do you propose to select the actual set of customers or companies to sample, and how do you know that the sample is statistically meaningful?

❑ *Type of research.* What is the most appropriate method of market research – online, desk or field?

❑ *Analysis.* When you have collected the research data, how do you propose to analyse the data?

It's as easy as that! Finally, an excellent source of market research information is Colin Barrow's *The Complete Small Business Guide*.

Sources of help

Barrow, C (1997) *The Complete Small Business Guide. Sources of information for new and small businesses*, BBC Books, London

Central Office of Information. Hercules Road, London, SE1 7DU, tel: 020 7928 2345, email dgodfrey@coi.gov.uk, *www.coi.gov.uk/coi*

Crimp, M (1985) *The Market Research Process*, Prentice-Hall, London

Extel European Companies Service. Extel Financial Ltd, Fitzroy House, 13–17 Epworth Street, London, EC2A 4DL, tel: 020 7251 3333, fax: 020 7251 2725, *www.info.ft.com*

Guide to Official Statistics. Central Statistics Office, Cabinet Office, Information Department, House Guards Road, London, SW1P 3AL, tel: 020 7270 6363

Industrial Market Research Association. 11 Bird Street, Lichfield, Staffs, WS13 6WP

Market Research Society. 15 Northburgh Street, London, EC1V OAH, tel: 020 7490 4911, fax: 020 7490 0608, email: mrs@dial.pipex.com, *www.marketresearch.org.uk*

7 Preparing Your Business Plan

How many people do you know who would be prepared to risk $2.5 million on the basis of seeing a one-page business plan? Well, in 1968 Robert Noyce and his partner Gordon Moore, with a one-page plan written in two days, raised $2.5 million and launched Intel. The rest of us need to be a little more expansive.

Your business plan has two essential roles: firstly, it forces you to analyse rigorously the viability of your business and also document it; and secondly, if you need to recruit partners or raise finance you will need to communicate your money-making strategy to others.

In this chapter we look at:

☐ the structure of a *business plan*: an executive summary, business description, product/service, market and competition, business strategy, launch strategy, selling strategy, Internet strategy and financial projections, etc;

☐ the structure of a *marketing plan*: an executive summary, current market situation, market analysis, objectives of campaign, marketing strategy, action programme, budget, etc;

☐ the structure of a *technical plan*: an executive summary, technology description, product/service, product strategy, initial product offering, product workplan, project management, etc;

☐ *business plan software* available from the clearing banks.

Most high-tech start-ups need three plans:

☐ The business plan presents your business strategy, rigorously analyses its commercial viability, and sets out a financial roadmap.

❑ The marketing plan presents your marketing strategy for raising awareness of your product, attracting customers and ultimately building the valuation of your company.

❑ The technical plan presents your technology strategy, analyses its technical feasibility, and sets out a project schedule to develop the core technologies, focusing on being *first-to-market* with a product.

The business plan

When you consider that a venture capitalist may receive over 200–300 business plans a year, and make only 4–6 investments, you need to put a lot of effort into getting it right.

There is no universal structure for a 'business plan'. If your plan is clear and well organized, then it follows that your business is likely to be well run. Thus it should show the following features:

❑ *a quality document* – desktop published and printed to a high quality, but simply bound;

❑ *a focused business* – a market-led company with a single focus;

❑ *receptive customers* – evidence of customer demand, such as a sale to an 'early adopter';

❑ *exclusive rights* – ownership of intellectual property rights (eg copyright in the product)

❑ *accurate forecasts* – detailed and believable financial forecasts for the venture;

❑ *financial risk* – possible security to any loan, or shared risk with the entrepreneur.

You should aim for a 10–15 page plan, plus appendices. The common ingredients are listed in Figure 7.1.

Executive summary

The executive summary provides a complete overview of your proposed business venture, and might include a paragraph on each of the main sections listed above. Start with a mission statement – avoiding lofty goals – with hard facts and figures. You should also include paragraphs on the *objectives* of the *business*, the *management*, the *products or services*, the *technical plan*, the *marketing plan*, how you will *finance* the business, and possibly business *prospects*.

Section	Contents			
Executive summary (one to two pages)	Overview of the business	❏	The technical plan	❏
	The management	❏	The marketing plan	❏
	The products or services	❏	Financing the business	❏
The business (one to two pages)	Company background and mission	❏	Intellectual property rights (IPR)	❏
	Products and services	❏	Business prospects	❏
The management (one to two pages)	Management team	❏	Professional advisors	❏
	Your past employment/ record	❏	Weaknesses and solutions	❏
The products or services (one to two pages)	Simple product description	❏	Why the product is competitive	❏
	Competitor products	❏	Future developments	❏
The technical plan (one page)	Technical strategy	❏	Initial product offering	❏
	Key technical developments	❏	Technical risks	❏
The marketing plan (one to two pages)	Marketing strategy	❏	Competitors and their products	❏
	Size and growth of market	❏	Sales plans and team	❏
Operational details (one page)	Start-up strategy and key staff	❏	Usage of the Internet	❏
	Location of business	❏	Business controls	❏
Financial analysis (two to three pages)	Sales, cash flow & profits	❏	Financing the business	❏
	Any accounts	❏	Exit routes for investors	❏
Appendices (as needed)	Management team biographies	❏	Technical details	❏
	Professional advisors	❏	Audited accounts	❏

Figure 7.1 Business plan checklist

The business

This business section covers your new company's innovative idea, its background, and business strategy. State the focus of your business, its products, the principal market it addresses; give evidence that your customers want to buy your product or service, and that the timing of the launch of your business is correct. Support this with hard facts. Lastly, cover branding and also intellectual property rights (IPR) owned by the business.

The management

Your management team and its track record are essential to any business plan. Describe the experience and balance of your management team. You as the entrepreneur may be bursting with technical ideas, but investors and potential partners want to see a range of strengths covering technical, managerial, financial and sales. That is why companies have a *Managing* Director, a *Financial* Director, a *Sales* Director and *Technical* Director; each person with a proven track record, not just a placeholder.

The products or services

This section presents your products: what product or service you propose to market, what stage of development your product or service has reached, why it will be competitive in the marketplace, and future developments. Wherever possible, figures should be given to support your presentation.

The technical plan

High-tech start-ups are 'technology' driven, with the essential goal of being first-to-market. (This is referred to as 'first-mover-advantage'.) Present a summary of your technical plan. This should cover your research and development strategy, key technical developments, rollout milestones and deliverables, and an assessment of the technical risks.

The marketing plan

Likewise, high-tech start-ups are market driven, with the goal of building a $100 million company. This section focuses on your customers, your competitors, your marketplace, and summarizes the results of your market research. Even though your business may have the potential for leverage into many areas, for success it is essential to focus in the early stages.

Operational details

Your investors will be keenly interested in how you will control the business. So this section covers the set-up strategy and recruitment of key staff, the location of the business, together with day-to-day operational controls of finance, sales, technical developments, and staff.

Financial analysis

This section provides accurate, detailed and believable financial forecasts and how you intend to finance the new venture. The *forecasts* might include: sales, profit and loss, and cash flow forecasts, break-even and sensitivity analysis, and your financial assumptions. The *financing* should cover: current shareholders, usage of funding, anticipated gearing and interest, funding required and its timing, and, where appropriate, the 'deal on offer', plus 'exit route' for investors.

As a case study to illustrate the business plan, we will look at a real Internet start-up – *WotNot.net* – an *e-mail newsagent* where customers can subscribe to receive 'e-mail magazines'. WotNot.net is chosen because it was launched with minimal funding.

Case study: WotNot.net Ltd

WotNot.net is an Internet subscription service, inspired by Hotmail (www.hotmail.com), and launched by 23-year-old Damian Dutton.

WotNot.net has *subscribers* – who receive free e-zines; *publisher partners* – who publish e-zines; and *advertiser partners* – who pay to place adverts in specific e-zines. When choosing a brand name Damian found that the obvious ones such as 'Hotnews, Freenews, Newsline, .com, .net, etc' had already been taken. He chose *WotNot* as a catchy, easy to remember name akin to Yahoo! Initially, the service is being market-tested on university students in London. There are three million college students in the UK alone, most of whom have free access to the Internet. Once proved, the service will be expanded to other subscriber groups and to other European countries.

Below are outlined the sorts of information that might appear in WotNot's business plan.

❑   *Executive summary.* This starts with WotNot's mission of providing subscription, publishing and advertising services for e-mail magazines and newsletters. It then summarizes the technical and marketing strategies, and how the WotNot website is hosted.

❑ *The business.* This presents WotNot's mission, namely of being *the* e-zine publishing 'portal'. Next it describes how the business operates. The WotNot.net website allows subscribers (eg students) to register to receive a selection of e-zines. Publisher partners (eg students' unions, clubs and societies) are able to publish e-zines and have them delivered free by e-mails to subscribers. Revenue is from advertising (eg banks, travel agencies, entertainment), both banner ads and adverts inserted in e-mails.

❑ *The management.* This describes the company staff. Damian is the entrepreneur and handles all management and marketing functions. He employs a programmer with extensive commercial experience in building Web/database/e-mail systems for clients. (Note: a VC would probably like to see two founders: one marketing and the other with technology expertise.)

❑ *The products or services.* This describes the WotNot service. The core of WotNot.net is a Web-database system, where customers can subscribe (unsubscribe) online to receive specific e-zines. Registered publisher partners submit newsletters online. Advertiser partners also submit their ads online.

❑ *The technical plan.* This section describes the technical plan for rolling out the service. In particular, it describes how the Web-database and e-mail service supporting subscriber registrations and partner publishing/advertising is implemented and supported.

❑ *The marketing plan.* This sets out the marketing strategy, which is basically to market test WotNot on students in London and then roll it out to other colleges in the UK and Ireland. In parallel the service will be expanded to other subscriber groups, such as professional bodies, and other countries.

❑ *Operational details.* This covers how the business is run. In the launch phase, the marketing is handled by Damian, with initial office accommodation being in an Incubator unit in London.

❑ *Financial analysis.* This section covers the funding and cash flow forecasts etc. Pre-seed funding comprises £10,000 from family/friends and £10,000 from 'angel' investors, giving Damian 70 per cent of the company and the angels 30 per cent. This funding covers the nine-month launch phase. After this an outside investor will be sought to provide funds of £500,000 to expand the business into the United States and across Europe. There are two broad share strategies, the first being for the angel investors to sell their 30 per cent share holding (for instance, £50,000 going to the angels and £450,000 going to fund WotNot). Secondly the share division could be re-allocated: Damian 40 per cent, angels 15 per cent, new investors 25 per cent and future staff 20 per cent. In addition, it is important to make detailed sales and cash flow forecasts for the first 2–3 years.

❑ *Appendices*. In the appendices are detailed sales, cash flow and profit/loss forecasts for the first two years of the business, as well as biographies of the management team.

Marketing plan

Although a technical innovation may launch a high-tech start-up, for it to be successful it needs to be marketing led. So you need a marketing plan to set out what the business wants to achieve from its marketing, and how this will be achieved (see Figure 7.2; Chapter 30 covers each of the sections in detail).

The big problem when launching your start-up is how to run a successful marketing campaign with next to no money. You need customers to generate revenue, but at the same time you certainly do not want to attract competitors. You need to focus on the essentials – the four Ps:

❑ *product* – what you are going to sell initially (i.e. your initial product offering);
❑ *price* – basic price, discounts, credit and payment methods;
❑ *promotion* – how you reach your initial target market;
❑ *place* – where your customers will get your product.

Case study: WotNot.net Ltd

WotNot.net's big challenge in the launch phase is how to attract vast numbers of student subscribers, with only a small advertising budget of £5,000.

❑ *Executive summary*. This section sets out the objectives of WotNot's marketing campaign. This is to recruit 20,000 subscribers in

Section	Contents			
Executive summary (one to two pages)	Current market and analysis	❏	Target market	❏
	Objectives of the campaign	❏	Action programme	❏
Current market situation (two to three pages)	Market description	❏	Distribution review	❏
	Product review	❏	Business environment analysis	❏
	Competition review	❏		
Market analysis (one page)	Strengths	❏	Opportunities	❏
	Weaknesses	❏	Threats	❏
Objectives of campaign (as necessary)	Quantifiable	❏	Time deadline	❏
	Ranked in order of importance	❏	Realistic and achievable	❏
Marketing strategy (one page)	Target market	❏	Marketing mix	❏
	Positioning	❏	Marketing communication	❏
Action programme (one page)	What will be done?	❏	Who will do it?	❏
	When will it be done?	❏	How much will it cost?	❏
Budget (one page)	Budget for the campaign	❏	Projected sales forecast	❏
	Profit/loss statement	❏		
Controls (one page)	Sales analysis	❏	Customer research	❏
	Profitability	❏		

Figure 7.2 Marketing plan checklist

London to prove the concept and help raise venture capital for the rollout.

❏ *Current marketing situation.* This describes the target market, namely college students and societies, and organizations interested in advertising to students, such as banks, travel companies, retailers, and entertainment groups.

❏ *Market analysis.* This section gives a SWOT market analysis. *Strengths* – WotNot.net is first-to-market in the UK and is therefore establishing a 'first-move' advantage. *Weaknesses* – WotNot has very limited start-up capital. *Opportunities* – WotNot can leverage into any e-mail publishing for any subscriber group. *Threats* – the WotNot concept may be offered by many of the UK professional bodies, entertainment groups and ISPs.

❏ *Objectives of campaign.* This section states the short-term objectives. These are to recruit 10 student union publishing partners, five major advertising partners, and 20,000 subscribers within six months, and 20 publishing partners, 10 advertising partners and 200,000 subscribers within 12 months.

❑ *Marketing strategy*. This presents the initial marketing strategy. The target market is student unions, clubs and societies in the major colleges in the London area.

❑ *Action programmes*. This describes specific marketing actions. WotNot's marketing budget is being spent on: for students – A5 handbills to be distributed at the colleges and advertisements in student newspapers; for publishers – a 'publisher pack' of materials explaining the service; and for advertisers – an equivalent 'advertiser pack'.

❑ *Budget/controls*. The last section sets out the budget. This covers the budget for the marketing campaign (i.e. £5,000 for months 1–6), together with projections of subscribers, publishing and advertising partners to be recruited.

Technical plan

The role of the technical plan is to set out your technology strategy, analyse its technical feasibility, and set out a project schedule focusing on being first-to-market with your product (see Figure 7.3).

This plan is primarily to direct the internal technical work of the company during the launch stage. The aim is to focus all the technical staff on the same goal – the initial product offering:

❑ *Motivation*. The motivation for being first-to-market with a complete product has to be set out to motivate the technical staff.

❑ *Technical background*. The underlying technology needs to be stated to create a shared understanding and vision.

❑ *Product goals*. A series of products should be identified to act as milestones for the technical development.

❑ *Workpackages*. Technical development is divided into major 'workpackages' and subsidiary tasks.

❑ *Tasks*. Each task needs to be individually identified, the work specified and the responsible staff listed.

❑ *Project schedule*. A timetable of when each task is scheduled to start and finish (and its deliverables) needs to be set out.

Section	Contents			
Executive summary (one to two pages)	Overview of the new business	❑	Technology strategy	❑
	Initial product offering	❑	Technology management	❑
Technology and management (two to three pages)	Technical background	❑	Technical mission	❑
	Technical focus	❑	Initial product offering	❑
Product/service strategy (one page)	Research and development	❑	Initial product offering	❑
	Total product offering	❑		
Project workplan (as necessary)	Roles of partners and key staff	❑	Structure of the workplan	❑
	Effort per workpackage and task	❑	Timetable, milestones and products	❑
	Bar chart and/or PERT chart	❑		
Project management (one page)	Measurable objectives	❑	Internal management	❑
	External reporting	❑	Customer support	❑
Marketing strategy (one page)	First-to-market	❑	Early adopter	❑
	Niche market dominance	❑	Mass market dominance	❑
Technical controls (one page)	Technical specifications	❑	Integration	❑
	Testing	❑	Re-design and implementation	❑
Appendices (as necessary)	Detailed technical specifications	❑	Detailed technical data	❑

Figure 7.3 Technical plan checklist

❑ *Technical risk.* An assessment needs to be made of the technical risk of failing to complete a task.

The central part of the technology plan is the *project workplan*, covering the roles of staff, the technical task to be performed, and a schedule of work:

❑ *Roles.* Specify the work of key staff members, and outside contractors, on the project.

❑ *Workplan.* Specify the structure of the workplan, constituent workpackages and subsidiary tasks.

❑ *Effort.* Estimate the manpower effort of each workpackage and subsidiary task.

❑ *Timetable.* Specify a timetable, milestones and products (ie deliverables) for the work.

❑   *Chart.* Provide a task plan (using MS Project), a Gantt chart, and/or PERT diagram, of the work to be undertaken, with particular emphasis on the 'critical path'.

The Gantt chart is the most common way of showing tasks, milestones and target dates in a project plan. A Gantt chart shows time along the *x*-axis, the tasks as (grey) bars, and dependencies by arrows.

The PERT diagram, the alternative representation, uses boxes to show the tasks and arrows to show the dependencies. The critical path can then be highlighted by picking out the arrows in bold.

Case study: WotNot.net Ltd

WotNot.net's technical strategy centres on a Web-database and e-mail service supporting subscriber registrations, partner publishing and advertising. WotNot.net has two machines, one the server hosted by an ISP, and the other a development machine located at WotNot's premises. The website comprises the subscriber, publisher and advertiser databases, plus Web pages for each group to interact with the site.

ID	TASK NAME	3 Jan 2000	7 Feb 2000	6 Mar 2000	3 Apr 2000	1 May 2000	5 Jun 2000
1	Strategy						
2	Design						
3	Build						
4	Test						

Figure 7.4 Gantt chart for project planning

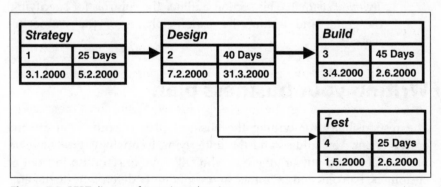

Figure 7.5 PERT diagram for project planning

- ❑ *Executive summary.* This sets out how Wotnot.net's service is supported, namely a Web-database and e-mail system using two machines, one the server hosted and the other a development machine.
- ❑ *Technology and management.* This section describes the system implementation. This is a website comprising standard Web forms, an SQL server database, and interface code written in JAVA for easy extensibility. The server and development machine both run Microsoft Windows NT and use Apache server software.
- ❑ *Product/strategy focus.* This section presents the technical details of the 'initial product offering'. Also covered is the status of the system, namely that it works for student unions, but will be enhanced for other professional bodies and organizations.
- ❑ *Project workplan.* This section sets out the technical development. This is divided into three phases. Phase one 'London students' is complete, and the code is in place for phase two when the service will be offered to student unions throughout the UK and Ireland. In phase three, a Yahoo!-like search engine and directory structure will be introduced to support a wide range of professional societies, arts/entertainment groups and large organizations.
- ❑ *Project management.* This section sets out a timetable for completing each stage of the rollout of the new services. The website enhancements are relatively straightforward.
- ❑ *Marketing strategy.* This section gives a summary of the marketing plan so the 'techies' know the objectives of their work, namely to market test the Wotnot.net concept in London and then roll out across the UK and Ireland.
- ❑ *Technical controls.* This section outlines the controls for specifying, designing and testing the various phases of the Wotnot.net website.

Writing your business plan

The responsibility for writing the business plan is yours. You are the entrepreneur. You understand the underlying technology, products and marketplace. And you are the one who will have to stand up in front of customers, bankers and investors, and confidently defend the statements and forecasts in your plan.

Having said this, you will certainly need to seek the advice of professionals. Consider the following:

❏ *Design and layout.* Business Links (tel 0845 756 7765, www.businesslink.co.uk), Enterprise Ireland (tel 01 857 0000, www.enterprise-ireland.com) and other small business organizations are prepared to help you with your business plan, often for free. You might also consider using MBA students from a business school, who need to prepare a business plan as part of their course.

❏ *Technical experts.* For businesses based on novel technology, you may need help from technical experts. A local university or college may provide free help.

❏ *Marketing professionals.* If you have a technical background, you may need professional advice in branding, advertising and sales. Again, a useful starting point is your local Business Link or Enterprise Ireland.

❏ *Financial analysis.* Your accountant will be able to help you prepare the financial analysis.

❏ *Corporate finance.* If you are raising substantial amounts of venture capital, you will need professional advisors, such as corporate finance specialists.

❏ *Specialist lawyers.* You will also need a specialist lawyer to check any venture capital agreements or other specialized investments.

Sources of help

Borrow, C, Barrow, P and Brown, R (1997) *The Business Plan Workbook*, Kogan Page, London
Business LINK. tel: 08457 567765, *www.businesslink.co.uk*
Johnston, A (1998) *A Hacker's Guide to Project Management*, Butterworth Heinemann, Oxford
Pattern, D (1998) *Successful Marketing for the Small Business*, Kogan Page, London

8 Setting Up Your Office

As soon as you launch your business, you will need an office, stationery, furniture, a computer system and all the other infrastructure of a credible business – even if your office is your bedroom and the computer system is your current PC.

In this chapter we look at:

- ❑ setting up your office;
- ❑ how to keep down costs by creating a virtual or mobile office;
- ❑ how to go about finding business premises;
- ❑ setting up the telephones, faxes, PCs, printers and other equipment;
- ❑ installing the necessary business software and administrative systems.

Even if you plan to work from home you need to create an office environment:

- ❑ *Office*. Dedicate at least part of a room, garage, or even shed, as your office.
- ❑ *Telephone*. Acquire a dedicated telephone for business usage.
- ❑ *Equipment*. Install basic office equipment and facilities: office furniture and filing cabinet, photocopier, computer equipment and business software etc.
- ❑ *Internet*. Set up a company website and e-mail facility.
- ❑ *Stationery*. Get stationery and business cards with your company name and contact details.
- ❑ *Routine*. Establish a routine for working, eg 8.00 am–6.00 pm.

Your requirements

When starting out, your type of business will largely dictate the most suitable types of office. The sort of questions to ask yourself are: (i) Will we work largely on customers' premises or will customers visit us? (ii) Will we need space for equipment, storage or manufacturing? (iii) What size premises will be needed both now, and in the immediate future? (iv) Do we need a prestigious address? (v) What telecommunications and other services will we require?

☐ *Consultant/contractor.* If you work largely at your customers' premises then you need little more than a mobile phone with a messaging service, a portable laptop PC and a company website and electronic mail service hosted by an Internet service provider (ISP). This is a virtual office.

☐ *Electronic retailing.* If you plan to sell information or digital media services, in theory you need to do little more than rent space on the computer of an ISP.

☐ *Consultancy/profession.* When two or more of you are working closely together, you need 'real' premises. The quality of the premises will be largely determined by the image you wish to give of your business. A programming company might choose modest offices near their clients, whereas a consultancy company may choose prestigious offices.

☐ *Mail order.* With 50–100 million customers having access to the Internet, a global mail order business becomes highly attractive. As we saw when we looked at Amazon.com in Chapter 1, many electronic commerce companies do not hold their own stock but farm out the orders to a so-called fulfilment house, who handles the delivery. So you could get by with modest offices but with excellent communications.

☐ *Shop.* If your business involves selling directly to the public and your customers need to visit your premises, then you probably need to open a shop in a location that is easily accessible.

☐ *Manufacturing.* If your business is involved in manufacturing, you are best advised to subcontract the work in the start-up stage of your business, to reduce cost and risk. Then look for premises in an area with a strong labour force.

So, you have decided on your business needs and your budget. Next you need to set up your office. Let's consider two types of 'office'.

A virtual office

Everybody expects a high-tech start-up to have the latest technology; at least a sophisticated website, e-mail and phone system. Therefore, turning necessity to advantage in the beginning, you can save money by setting up a mobile, virtual office. The components of a virtual office are:

- ❑ *Cellular phone.* Use a sophisticated cellular service with voice mail, a 'virtual' receptionist, and possibly fax facilities.
- ❑ *Laptop computer.* A portable laptop or notebook computer, with a modem that plugs into the cellular phone, will allow you to work anywhere.
- ❑ *Internet service.* A company website, e-mail, and soon videoconferencing, all hosted by an ISP, will allow your customers to be serviced 24 hours a day.
- ❑ *Personal organizer.* An electronic diary, such as a Psion (www.psion.com), holding your appointments and address book, and *ideally* communicating by infrared with your laptop PC, will allow you to manage your time effectively.

Premises

For many entrepreneurs their first office is their bedroom. But at some point you will want 'real' premises. There are a number of good sources of information on offices available to rent:

- ❑ *Your local library.* Libraries provide lists of premises, and directories such as the Business Location Handbook, etc.
- ❑ *Your local council.* Councils (www.open.gov.uk) often provide their own premises, especially for rental by new businesses, and also lists of business parks and industrial estates in their area.
- ❑ *Enterprise Agencies.* These are government agencies that offer advice for new businesses, and frequently have access to starter units at modest rents. A starting point might be the local Business Links (www.businesslinks.gov.uk).
- ❑ *Universities and colleges.* Leading academic institutions have

established incubator units (www.ukic.co.uk) and science parks (www.ukspa.gov.uk) close to their campuses.

❑ *Estate agents.* Many estate agents specialize in local business premises and, being specialists, have a detailed local knowledge. Their names and addresses can be found in your local library and also in local business directories.

Renting an office

Some key issues when renting an office are: (i) the rental price per square metre, (ii) the length of the lease, (iii) the deposit required, (iv) whether the cost of services such as heating and lighting are included, (v) whether services like receptionists and cleaning are provided and how they are charged for, (vi) the terms relating to maintenance of the building, and (vii) the usage regulations.

When you rent premises, certain services may be provided either as part of the rental or at an additional charge. These include cleaning, heating and light, reception, switchboard, mail in/out, and security. When you visit possible premises look around at the general state of tidiness and decor. Is the receptionist friendly and welcoming, does the environment give the appearance of being professionally run, and what about the other businesses nearby? All these issues will reflect on your business should you rent the property.

Obviously, once a company signs a lease it is committed to the specified length, but it is usually possible to sublet the lease to another company if you need to move. In turn, these 'tail-end' leases may be attractive to you. You can take over the 'tail-end' of someone else's lease for a month or two when you are starting your business and are unsure of success or even of the area.

Serviced offices

Setting up an office with all the support services can be a major distraction for any aspiring entrepreneur. One solution, especially if you need prestige premises, is a *serviced office* that provides every service including receptionist, switchboard, secretarial support, cleaning; even the office furniture and computer equipment. These premises are highly attractive for the 2–4 person consultancy or profession. You can literally move in and start doing business on day one. Regus is the world's leading serviced office company and they have an excellent website (www.regus.com), so check it out.

Business incubator units and science parks

Most local authorities and universities are keen to encourage the growth of small high-tech companies, and so many have established incubator units and science parks.

Incubator units are a cross between serviced offices and workshops, and some even provide modest seed funding. UK Business Incubation (www.ukbi.co.uk) is a good starting point for information.

Science parks are set in landscaped grounds and in close proximity to a university. A useful starting point in contacting them is the UK Science Parks Association (tel 0121 359 0981, www.ukspa.org.uk).

Table 8.1 summarizes the pros and cons of each type of premises.

Telecommunications services

The electronic services now offered by telephone companies and Internet service providers are becoming truly amazing. Remember your telephone system is the first contact potential clients will have with you, so it is important to create a good image. Most importantly you need to separate

Table 8.1 Choosing premises

	Advantages	Disadvantages
Working from home	• Cheap and flexible	• Distractions and interruptions
	• No travel costs	• Poor image
Renting an office	• Premises suited to type of business	• Cost
	• 'Tail-end lease' reduces cost	• Commitment to lease
Serviced office	• Prestige offices	• Expensive
	• Complete support services	
Incubator unit	• Cheap, starter premises	• Rudimentary accommodation
	• Business support + seed funding	• Possible poor location

your business telephone from your personal phone – not least for tax purposes.

When you are starting out in business it may be sufficient for you and your partners to each have a cellular telephone and a laptop computer with a modem. An answering service can be provided by the telephone company, and your ISP can support e-mail and your company website. As your office expands, and additional premises are added, so the telecommunications and data communications complexity will increase.

When planning your telephone, fax and communications services you need to consider the following:

❑ *Cellular phone system.* A mobile phone is essential, but make sure you can seamlessly integrate your mobile and office phone systems.
❑ *Office telephone and fax system.* Most offices will require at least three phone lines: the office telephone, the office facsimile machine and the Internet connection.
❑ *Receptionist and voicemail.* You will need an integrated receptionist and voicemail system that links your mobile and office phones, and operates 24 hours a day.

Telephones

When choosing your telephone system there are a number of facilities to consider:

❑ *Mute function.* A mute function allows you to have a conversation with a colleague without being overheard by the caller.
❑ *Intercom.* Where your business occupies a suite of offices, the phone system can be used as an intercom to talk to your colleagues in other offices.
❑ *Conference calls.* This facility allows multiple speakers to take part in the same call. It does this by joining together two or more telephone lines. Each speaker outside of your business premises will require a separate phone line.
❑ *Status lights.* These tell you which of the lines are in use, and whether someone is on hold.

Fax machine

There are two types of fax machine, based on the type of paper/printing:

☐ *Thermal paper.* These machines use heat-sensitive paper and literally 'burn' the image on to the paper. The paper comes in rolls and is distinguished by its shiny appearance and waxy feel.

☐ *Plain paper.* These machines print in a similar way to photocopiers, and can operate with standard A4 plain paper.

The advantage of plain paper fax is that its output is similar to that of a laser printer, but it costs more than the thermal variety. When choosing a fax the features to consider are:

☐ *Speed.* Since most machines exchange faxes at 9,600bps (bits per second), there is little point in paying extra for a higher speed device.

☐ *Resolution.* Choose a machine that automatically selects the best resolution for sending a document.

☐ *Auto-redial.* This is a useful facility, whereby if the destination fax machine is engaged there is automatic re-dialling of the number.

☐ *Document storage.* The more advanced machines will allow you to scan the fax into a memory. This is especially useful when you need to send the same fax to a number of recipients.

Receptionist and voicemail

As well as integrating your mobile and office telephone system, you need to integrate your electronic/real receptionist and voicemail. With a modern phone system you can seamlessly switch between a real and an electronic receptionist, forward calls automatically after so many rings, or automatically record a voicemail. That is a sophisticated 24-hour service. With a single 'direct dial' business number you can support the following:

☐ *Receptionist.* Modern cellular systems allow you to select between a real and electronic receptionist, both of which will try to locate you or route your message to a voicemail service.

☐ *Call forwarding.* This allows you to specify a phone number to which incoming calls are forwarded. *Programmable call forwarding* allows you to forward calls automatically and to turn the facility on or off. *Forward on busy* forwards the call when the phone line is busy. *Delay forwarding* forwards.the call after a specific number of rings.

❑ *Voicemail.* If you are unable to take a call, the system automatically offers to record a message to the call.

Telecommunications network

There are two basic choices of telephone line:

❑ *Twisted pair.* Most offices and homes are equipped with the traditional 'twisted pair' telephone line. This in fact comprises two lines but only one is normally in use. The cost of activating the second line is £50–100.

❑ *Integrated Services Digital Network.* ISDN allows one standard telephone line to be converted into three digital lines. Therefore, using a single telephone line, you can make phone calls, use a fax and also connect to the Internet. However, owing to BT's pricing policy, ISDN is expensive in the UK, and therefore is far less popular than in the USA and other countries.

Computers and software

Most businesses have at least one PC for each member of staff. You will need desktop PCs for the office and, if you need to make presentations to clients and work away from the office, more expensive laptops. One solution is to have a powerful office 'server' computer to hold company information, and a network into which you can connect your PC, either locally when in the office or remotely via the Internet.

Personal computers

Expect to pay at least £1,000 for a business PC. Pay more if you can afford it, to get as much main memory and hard disk storage as possible. This will 'future-proof' your systems. Check out the following:

- ❑ *Microprocessor speed.* The speed of the microprocessor (CPU speed) determines how fast the PC will execute your programs. Buy the fastest you can afford.
- ❑ *Main memory.* This is the high-speed memory used by the PC to execute programmes. Basically, the more you have, the faster programs run. You should get at least 32 megabytes (Mb).
- ❑ *Hard disk memory.* The hard disk is where all your programs and files are stored for immediate access. You should get at least 3 gigabytes (Gb). Buy as much as you can afford, because it fills up surprisingly quickly.
- ❑ *Monitor.* This is the display. Try to get at least a 15-inch screen rather than the now old-fashioned 14-inch.
- ❑ *Peripherals.* You will need a quality printer and possibly also a scanner. Although there are a number of printers available, based on different printing technologies, you are recommended to buy a *laser* printer that can handle all text and diagrams.
- ❑ *Tape storage.* You will also need 'backup' storage for archiving copies of all your files in case your PC fails. Losing all your business information is a disaster.

Business software

As your business grows you will need increasingly sophisticated business software, databases and networking. Here is a selection:

- ❑ *Office 2000.* Microsoft's latest version of Windows and Office 2000 will provide you with a basic 'windows' operating system and the standard suite of applications software for word processing, spreadsheets, databases, presentations etc.
- ❑ *Accountancy software.* Once you form a limited company you will need a basic accounting system such as Sage Instant Accounts (see Chapter 21), costing around £100 per licence, and as your business expands a more complex costing system.
- ❑ *Databases.* Office 2000 provides the Access database system, which is sufficient for modest database uses and can even be connected to a Web page for access over the Internet.
- ❑ *Lotus Notes.* Lotus provides a software system called Notes that allows all the files of a company's employees to be uniformly

accessible across the company, whether in a single building or across the world.

❑ *Networking software.* You will also need special software to inter-connect all your PCs and printers on a LAN (local area network), so they can exchange information.

❑ *Specialist software.* Media and other specialist companies frequently require specialist software such as Macro Media 100 and Adobe PhotoShop, which can be expensive.

❑ *Antivirus software.* Viruses are a real pain. You need good antivirus software, such as Dr Solomon (www.drsolomon.com), both to protect your own computers, and not to infect clients' systems. The latter is a real no-no!

Although a fair bit of software is available free for downloading over the Internet, software companies are becoming increasingly adept at 'encouraging' you to purchase the latest version of their software, which is an accumulating expense for new businesses.

Office equipment

Whether you run your business from your bedroom or rent premises in an incubator unit, you will need a range of office furniture and equipment:

❑ *Furniture.* Obviously you will need a desk and chair for each member of staff, chairs for visitors, filing cabinets etc. You may also need a conference table and chairs.

❑ *Essentials.* You will need desk lamps, a franking machine, filing baskets, fire extinguishers, a guillotine, hole punches, mouse pads, pens and pencils, Post-it notes, sticky tape, scissors, correction fluid, waste paper bins, etc. It all adds up! You will also require coffee and tea facilities: a kettle, coffee maker, refrigerator, mugs for the staff, cups for visitors, saucers, plates and spoons, a cup-board in which to keep them, and a dishwasher for when they are dirty.

❑ *Photocopier.* When deciding on a photocopier you need to estimate fairly accurately the number of copies you are likely to make in a year, and the facilities you will want: automatic sheet feeder, double-sided copies, reduction and enlargement etc.

Office equipment is becoming increasingly sophisticated, and multi-functioned. For instance, you can get a combined telephone, answering machine, fax and scanner for around £300, which is ideal for the 1–2 person business. However, for larger start-ups it is more cost-effective to buy individual pieces of equipment.

Sources of help

Barrow, C (1995) *The Complete Small Business Guide – sources of Information for new and small businesses,* BBC Books, London

English Estates. 120 Main Street, Burley In Wharfedale, Ilkley, West Yorkshire, tel: 01943 864585, *www.english-estates.com/*

Enterprise Zones DETR, Eland House, Bressenden Place, London, SW1E 5DU, tel: 020 7890 3000, *www.open.gov.uk*

Hughes, V and Weller, D (1997) *Teach Yourself Setting up a Business,* Hodder-Stoughton, London

Neely, M (1997) *Create your own Electronic Office,* Net.Works, Harrogate

Regus. Leading serviced office company. *www.regus.com*

UK Business Incubation Ltd. Aston Science park, Love Lane, Birmingham, B7 4BJ, tel: 0121 250 3538, fax: 0121 250 3542, email: info@ukbi.co.uk, *www.ukbi.co.uk*

UK Science Parks Association. 44 Oaks Road, Sutton Coldfield, West Midlands B74 2TL, tel: 0121 308 8815, *www.ukspa.org.uk*

9   **Business Documents**

Well-designed office stationery and documents are important to create the image of a professional, well-run business. Major companies spend a small fortune with design companies to create the right look and feel of their documents, and they are a good source of inspiration for your company stationery and brochures.

In this chapter we look at:

- ❏ the range of stationery you will need, such as headed notepaper, business cards and brochures;
- ❏ how to get your stationery designed and printed at minimal cost;
- ❏ the business forms you may need, such as invoices, receipt books and stock records.

The image your company conveys through its literature is crucial. You need a consistent professional design scheme reflected across the full range of your company literature:

- ❏ *stationery* – headed notepaper, compliments slips, and business cards;
- ❏ *brochures* – product descriptions, price lists and manuals;
- ❏ *financial documents* – estimates, quotations, orders, invoices, credit notes, statements, remittance advice, etc;
- ❏ *legal documents* – non-disclosure agreements, contracts, warranties, licences etc.

You can save yourself considerable sums by gathering good examples of company stationery, assembling the best ideas and preparing the artwork using a word processing package.

Remember the legal requirements. For instance, if your business is a limited company, all stationery and other business documents must carry the company's full name, its registration number, and the address of the principal office.

Letterheads, business cards and brochures

The basic stationery you will need from day one is headed paper, compliments slips and business cards. All the stationery should follow a uniform design with a common letterhead and layout. As an illustration, assemble the suite of stationery of a major company. You will need the following:

- ❏ *Headed paper*. For business letters (and invoices) you will initially need 500 sheets of 80 gram (weight) headed paper. Typically, the headed paper will carry your company's logo, full name, registered business address, and (if a limited company) its registered number plus a list of all (or none) of the directors.
- ❏ *Plain paper*. For continuation sheets get a supply of plain paper that is the same colour and weight as your headed paper.
- ❏ *Envelopes*. To create a good impression, get a supply of envelopes of the same colour and weight as your headed paper, but use cheap white or brown (manila) envelopes for unimportant correspondence to keep down costs.
- ❏ *Compliments slips*. These are miniature versions of your headed paper with the words *With compliments*, and of course your company name and address. Compliments slips are useful when sending out documents that do not require a formal letter.
- ❏ *Business cards*. Business cards are most important since they carry all your contact details. Have 500 printed as soon as possible, and carry some with you at all times.
- ❏ *Brochures*. To advertise your company's products and services you will at some stage need to prepare a brochure. The simplest brochure is an A3 sheet folded in half (into standard A4), perhaps with an advert on the front cover, technical details on the inside pages and contact details on the back.

Design and printing

Chapter 3 discussed the importance of 'branding'; getting your Internet domain name, company name and logo to be complementary and an advertisement for your business. Design of your stationery and documents, plus the colour and weight of the paper, are equally as important to match your company image.

To save money: (i) look at the stationery of established companies, (ii) seek the advice of a friendly printer, and (iii) if you can afford it, get some expert professional advice from a design consultancy. Then experiment with different designs. You can create your own logo, letterhead and business card layouts using Microsoft Word, print them out on a colour printer and, when satisfied, pass them to your print shop.

Smaller printers are often happy to give you advice and to undertake short runs such as 200–400 sheets. *Prontoprint* and other local photocopy franchises are a good place to start and may be able to supply you with a small-business 'stationery pack'. If you need a small amount of stationery fast, you can always photocopy your letterhead on to your plain paper, make a colour photocopy of your brochure, or print them on a colour printer. These options can be expensive, but can get you out of a jam.

Invoices, receipt book and stock records

The next set of documents will be largely determined by your type of business and how records are kept. For instance, a consultancy might require *estimates* and *invoices*, a manufacturer may require *stock records*, but an electronic commerce company might hold everything electronically.

Legal documents

The suite of legal documents required will be determined by your company's business. However, there are an increasing number of self-help packs of legal forms, such as *301 Legal Forms, Letters and Agreements*, that provide basic business forms. For a typical high-tech start-up they might include:

❑ *non-disclosure agreement* – a document signed prior to the release of

❑ confidential information, stating that the receiving party will not disclose or use for business purposes the information delivered;

❑ *heads of agreement* – a preliminary agreement between two parties to take forward a business collaboration;

❑ *contract* – a legal agreement between your company and another organization for the delivery of a product or service by a specific date and at an agreed price;

❑ *warranty* – an agreement to replace or compensate a customer should the product or service fail to perform adequately;

❑ *licence* – a legal document signed by you and your customer licensing a piece of software to be used (licensing does not transfer ownership, only the right to use the intellectual property);

❑ *online licence* – online agreements for the use of software or a service whereby the user formally acknowledges the agreement by 'clicking' on an on-screen button.

Sources of help

Hughes, V and Weller, D (1997) *Teach Yourself Setting up a Business*, Hodder-Stoughton, London

Law Pack Publishing (1997) *301 Legal Forms, Letters and Agreements*, London

Truman, M (1997) *Teach Yourself Book-Keeping and Accounting for your Small Business*, Hodder-Stoughton, London

10 **Recruitment**

As Bill Gates says about Microsoft, 'Take away the 20 best people at Microsoft and we would be a pretty ordinary company.' Employees can make an enormous contribution to your business if you choose them carefully.

In this chapter we look at:

- ❑ different types of people you will seek to recruit, such as an advisory board, professional managers, technical staff, and general staff;
- ❑ important procedures when taking on staff such, as non-discrimination, advertising and interviewing;
- ❑ payments, covering issues such as frequency and obligations;
- ❑ employment law, including the contract of employment and disciplinary procedures.

Before looking at the standard procedures for recruiting and employing staff, it is useful to discuss the broad types of staff required by a high-tech start-up:

- ❑ *An advisory board.* Rapidly growing high-tech start-ups, needing access to high-quality business advice, should consider appointing a part-time *advisory board* of senior people from outside the company. As your company expands, some of these advisors can become part-time non-executive directors of the company. Seek to appoint prestigious people with experience of the markets you are attacking, with networks of contacts, and who will enhance the reputation of your company. Look for potential candidates in client companies.
- ❑ *Professional managers.* High-tech entrepreneurs increasingly recognize the need to recruit professional management to grow their

company rapidly. However, finding 'successful' young dynamic managers with a track record is a real challenge. You need to seek these people out in already successful start-ups, and probably offer them share options to join you. Your venture capital partners are also a good source of contacts.

❏ *Technical staff.* Growth in high-tech start-ups is frequently limited by the difficulty of recruiting good technical staff; especially IT staff. In Silicon Valley, 'star' programmers are even starting to hire agents to manage their careers. So you need to search out good technical staff rather than placing an advert in the newspapers. One effective strategy is to recruit one or two summer students from prestigious universities and build a relationship with them.

❏ *General staff.* For all other types of staff you can use the traditional and well-tried methods of headhunting, advertising and selection, which are set out below.

Taking on staff

The best recruitment advice is to be well organized. Recruiting people will cost you time and money, so ask yourself if existing staff can in fact do the job. You must write the following:

❏ *a candidate profile* – a list of the elements that are essential, and those that are desirable, in the person you wish to employ;

❏ *a job description* – a summary of the main elements of the job and a schedule of duties that the employee must perform;

❏ *an application form* – a form for the applicant to complete listing their education and experience (Figure 10.1).

The application form should also contain space for you to make notes during the interview.

There are various laws you need to be aware of when advertising for staff.

Non-discrimination

In the recruitment process, the advertisement and application form, etc, an essential element is that they be 'non-discriminatory'. The law is very strict and there is now no limit on the compensation that you could be ordered to pay if you discriminate unlawfully against job applicants or employees.

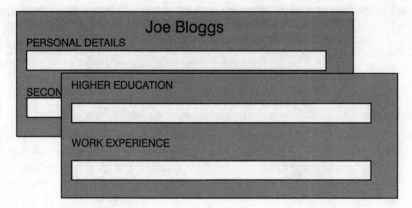

Figure 10.1 Application form

The potential areas of discrimination include race, sex, marital status, disability, trade union membership or non-membership. The Disability Discrimination Act 1995 also states that companies with 20 or more staff must modify their premises so as not to place disabled people at a disadvantage.

However, requirements can be selective if they are job-related and can be justified objectively. Advice and information can be obtained from the Equal Opportunities Commission (tel 0161 833 9244, www.eoc.org.uk).

Advertising

When producing your advertisement you should include: job title, brief description of job, special skills required, pay, whether it is full- or part-time, and how to apply. Be as specific as possible or you may be inundated with replies from unsuitable candidates. For senior candidates you may request their curriculum vitae (CV).

Next, you need to choose where to advertise: local press, national press, trade publications, the Job Centre or, increasingly, the Internet.

The Internet is a good place to search for staff, especially those with specialist technical skills. There are a number of excellent websites, ranging from general office sites such as Monster (www.monster.co.uk; see Figure 10.2) and Reed (www.reed.co.uk) to specialist sites like Jobserve (www.jobserve.com) focusing on IT.

Send the application form to all job applicants and ask them to fill

Figure 10.2

it in by hand. You can gain a lot by studying people's handwriting! You should also send the job description, as this encourages unsuitable candidates to drop out.

Selection

Sift the application forms and invite for interview the best three or four candidates matching your candidate profile. Reject immediately candidates who are clearly unsuitable. As a matter of courtesy and company reputation, you should reply to all applicants, even if it is only to say no to them.

Interviewing

Before the interview, prepare yourself. Allow at least one hour for each applicant. Prepare a list of general questions. Read through the application form, CV, job specification and candidate profile. Make notes of any specific questions you need to ask. Ensure the candidate matches your profile and look for any unexplained 'gaps' in their career history.

During the interview stick to the list of questions, make written notes of the answers, and file them away after the interview in case of any discrimination complaints. Remember to double-check answers on the application form, as most applicants will 'embellish' their answers. Finally, to assess the person's character, ask them about their leisure activities, interests and whether they have done any voluntary work.

For technical jobs you might ask the candidates to demonstrate their technical competence, for instance by writing a short program, or configuring software or a network system. It is also advisable, especially for more senior jobs, to have a series of interviews where you can thoroughly examine a candidate's professional competence, background and even personal situation.

Offer of employment

All offers of employment should be made in writing. They should cover the date when employment commences, the amount, method and frequency of payment, and whether the offer is conditional or unconditional. Basic terms include satisfactory references, a medical, a probationary period, and period of notice, etc. However, for a high-tech business you may wish to impose restrictions on what an employee can do after they leave. This is a very difficult area of law, and you are advised to get any employment contract drawn up by a specialist solicitor, because unreasonably stringent restrictions make the contract unenforceable.

Payment

At the job offer stage you will have agreed the amount of gross pay, and the method and frequency of payment.

Methods and frequency

You should agree the method of payment, such as into their bank account, and the payment frequency (weekly or monthly).

Tax, National Insurance, etc

You also have to make the statutory deductions of Pay As You Earn (PAYE) and National Insurance (NI). NI comprises two parts: the employee's contribution deducted from salary, and the employer's contribution, a percentage over and above the employee's salary.

You must also supply your employee with (i) a detailed salary slip showing gross pay and all deductions, (ii) an annual P60 showing the amount of tax deducted, and (iii) a P45 when a person leaves, showing tax deducted to date. This is covered in a later chapter on taxation.

Details of these statutory deductions are available from the Inland Revenue (www.inland-revenue.gov.uk), the Department of Social Security (www.open.gov.uk), and in Ireland the Revenue Audit-Guide for Small Business (www.revenue.ie). In addition, Job Centres have a useful leaflet called *Employing People in Small Businesses*, prepared by the Advisory, Conciliation and Arbitration Service (ACAS) (www.acas.org.uk), and the Labour Relations Commission also oversees the Industrial Relations Act 1990 and Unfair Dismissals Act 1977.

Statutory and non-statutory obligations

Statutory sick pay, maternity pay, working time directive, and health & safety are all *statutory* rights. Pensions, holiday pay and other sick pay provision are *non-statutory*, being at the discretion of the employer.

❑ *Statutory sick pay* (SSP). If an employee is sick for four or more days, you must pay them sick pay, which can be reclaimed from the government.

❑ *Maternity pay*. A pregnant woman has three statutory rights: (i) time off for antenatal care, (ii) statutory maternity pay (SMP) if she has worked at least 26 weeks for you, and (iii) the right to return to work after maternity leave. You can reclaim these payments from the government.

❑ *Working time directive*. Besides the traditional Christmas and bank holidays, there are upper limits on working hours and rules on entitlement to holidays (see Chapter 25).

❑ *Health & safety*. An employer is responsible for the safe working environment. This includes faulty wiring and equipment, inadequate lighting, badly designed furniture, etc, and covers both employees and third parties. You are strongly advised to take out employer and business liability insurance.

In contrast, there are no obligations for a company to run a pension scheme, or to provide holiday or sick pay, over and above the statutory ones.

Share options and incentives

They say in Silicon Valley that the 'oil' that makes things work is stock options – share options for all the staff.

It's very simple – when a high-tech business is starting up, good staff are difficult to recruit and money for salaries is tight. So the staff are given *share options*. In addition, once a business is well established, the pay of key employees, such as the CEO, needs to be tied closely to performance. Common schemes are *total shareholder return, long-term incentive plans* and *co-investment*.

❑ *Share options*. With options, staff have the opportunity (at some specified future date) to buy their company's shares and gain from the difference between current price and grant price. In Silicon Valley start-ups it is not uncommon for 26-year-old secretaries to become millionaires in this way.

❑ *Total shareholder return*. With TSR, for the executives to be rewarded, the company's share price needs to beat the median total shareholder return of the FTSE index, or another sector, by some percentage.

❑ *Long-term incentive plans*. Similar to TSR, 'Ltips' set relative performance hurdles for the company over a trading period; typically three years.

❑ *Co-investment*. With co-investment, the executives put their money into the company's shares alongside other investors, sharing in capital gains and losses.

Employment

Employing people carries with it a number of legal obligations covering the *contract of employment, period of notice* and *disciplinary procedures*.

Contract of employment

Legally you must provide to an employee, within 13 weeks, a written contract of employment. You and the employee should both sign two copies of the contract, and each should retain a copy. However, if you make someone an offer of employment in writing, and the employee gives a written acceptance, this too constitutes an employment contract. Figure 10.3 shows a schema for a contract.

EMPLOYMENT CONTRACT

THIS AGREEMENT IS MADE the _____ day of _____ 200__

BETWEEN (1) _____ of _____ (the "Employer")

and   (2) _____ of _____ (the "Employee")

1. **COMMENCEMENT AND JOB TITLE.** The Employer agrees ...
2. **SALARY.** The Employer shall pay the Employee ...
3. **HOURS OF EMPLOYMENT.** The Employee's normal hours ...
4. **HOLIDAYS.** The Employee shall be entitled to ...
5. **SICKNESS.** The Employee shall be paid ...
6. **COLLECTIVE AGREEMENTS.** No collective agreements are in force ...
7. **PENSIONS.** The Employee shall be entitled to join the Employer's pension scheme ...
8. **TERMINATION.** The Employer may terminate ...
9. **CONFIDENTIALITY.** The Employee ...
10. **NON-COMPETITION.** For a period of ___ months after the termination ...
11. **DISCIPLINE AND GRIEVANCE.** The Employer's disciplinary rules ...
12. **NOTICES.** All communications....
13. **GOVERNING LAW.** This agreement ... with the laws of England ...

IN WITNESS ...

SIGNED _____ (on behalf of the Employer)

SIGNED _____ (by the Employee)

Figure 10.3 Employment contract

Staff training

One of the frequently neglected areas in a company is staff training. This is about making people more effective. It can also build company loyalty.

❑ *Induction training.* All new employees joining your company should receive induction training – from the location of the coffee machine and toilet, through an introduction to colleagues, to a grounding in company procedures and regulations.

❑ *Staff development*. On an annual basis you should discuss with each staff member his or her *personal development* and a schedule of training should be agreed.
❑ *Specialist courses*. In a high-tech business, staff frequently need to acquire specialist skills. These should be planned and can be delivered in-house, at conferences and seminars, or through high-level external courses. These specialist courses can be extremely expensive, so care should be taken in selecting the right staff for the right courses.

Periods of notice

Employers and employees have broadly similar obligations regarding periods of notice. The minimum periods are:

❑ with less than one month's employment no notice is required;
❑ after one month to two years, one week's notice is required;
❑ over two years, one week's notice for every two years served is required.

However, most contracts normally specify longer periods.

Disciplinary procedures

You might think that it is virtually impossible to get rid of a bad employee. Well, a reasonable employer *can* get rid of an unreasonable employee. When you need to dismiss someone, you need to guard against a claim of 'unfair dismissal'. You need to show a substantial reason to justify the dismissal, and you need to have followed a 'fair' procedure.

It is wise to put in place both disciplinary and dismissal procedures. The disciplinary procedure might include the following:

❑ *Verbal warning*. At the first sign of trouble, the staff member is given a formal verbal warning, in the presence of another member of the senior staff.
❑ *Written warning*. If the trouble persists, the staff member is given a formal written warning of the consequences of his or her actions.
❑ *Final written warning*. If the trouble persists further, the staff member is then given a final written warning.

❑ *Dismissal notice.* The staff member is formally dismissed. Immediately prior to this the staff member should be barred access to all systems, to protect your company against damage. This is why financial services companies force dismissed staff to clear their desks immediately and escort them from the building, then paying them to sit at home.

In summary, the general principle with regard to recruitment and pay is 'fairness and equality'. Decisions on adverts, recruitment, promotion, training, fringe benefits, allocation of work, warning, disciplinary procedures, etc, must not be influenced by race, sex, marital status or disability. Equally, employees doing the same or equivalent work should broadly receive the same pay.

Sources of help

Association of British Correspondence Colleges. PO Box 17926, London, SW19 3WB, tel: 020 8544 9559, email: abcc@msn.com, *www.nationline.co.uk/abcc*

Barrow, C (1995) *Complete Small Business Guide – sources of Information for new and small businesses,* BBC Books, London

Clayton, P (1995) *Law for the Small Business,* Kogan Page, London

Croner's *Reference Book for Employers,* Croner House, London Road, Kingston-upon-Thames, Surrey, KT2 6SR, tel: 020 8547 3333, fax: 020 8547 2637 *www.croner.co.uk*

Head Start in Business. The Pepperell Dept, The Industrial Society, 48 Brynston Square, London, W1H 7LN, tel: 020 7262 2401, fax: 020 7706 1096

Industrial Society, The. 48 Brynston Square, London, W1H 7LN, tel: 020 7262 2401, fax: 020 7706 1096, *www.indsoc.co.uk*

Live Wire. Hawtron House, Forth Banks, Newcastle upon Tyne, NE1 3GS, tel: 0191 261 5584, fax: 0191 2611910

National Training Index, The.1st Floor, 25/6 Poland Street, London, W1V 3DB, tel: 020 7494 0596, fax: 020 7494 1268

Rapid Results College. Tuition House, 27/37 St George's Road, London, SW19 4DS, tel: 020 8947 2211, fax: 020 8946 7584

Training Access Points (TAP). Unit 5, AVEC, 1 Sidney Street, Sheffield, S1 4RG, tel: 0114 278 6101, email: sheftap@fdgroup.co.uk, *www.ourworld.compuserve.com/ homepages/ntics/sheffld.htm*

11 The Professionals

Many people who have launched a start-up company say that one of the biggest hurdles is finding out where to get good professional advice (and how to avoid paying for it!).

In this chapter we look at the following professionals:

❏ accountants and bookkeepers for financial management and taxation;
❏ bankers for financial forecasting, loans and investments;
❏ computer systems support for product development and installation;
❏ estate agents and surveyors for business premises;
❏ insurance brokers for business insurance;
❏ printers and designers for stationery and brochures;
❏ solicitors for all legal affairs and documents of a high-tech start-up;
❏ venture capitalists for investment, growth and professional management.

When you launch your high-tech start-up, and as it grows, you will need specialist professional services. These include a solicitor to set up your company, a printer for stationery, and an accountant for advice on tax and VAT. When you need professional services, ask for recommendations from other entrepreneurs or local business people, and if all else fails, look in the appropriate local listing in *Yellow Pages* or other classified directories and scan the local newspapers. The best option is obviously a personal recommendation from someone you know and trust. Your three most important professionals are probably your accountant, banker and solicitor.

The golden rule is: when you need professional help, get the best you can afford. Fortunately, British professionals are starting to follow their American counterparts by offering free services. For high-tech start-ups with the potential for spectacular growth, lawyers, accountants and even real-estate agents in the United States will donate $20,000 to $100,000 worth of free services in return for handling future work if the company is successful.

Alternatively, professionals might ask for 'sweat equity'. Again, they provide a free service to your high-tech start-up, but this time in return for a small percentage of shares in the company.

Accountants and bookkeepers

When you launch your business you may do the simple bookkeeping tasks yourself, but use an accountant for the more complicated tasks. Once you establish a limited company, an accountant is indispensable. Your accountant can provide the following services:

- [ ] preparation of annual accounts;
- [ ] bookkeeping;
- [ ] cash flow forecasts;
- [ ] investment and tax advice;
- [ ] tax returns for the Inland Revenue;
- [ ] VAT returns for HM Customs & Excise;
- [ ] venture capital advice.

A modern computer-based accounting system (see Chapter 21), such as Sage Instant Accounting 2000, will automate many bookkeeping tasks. This gives you better financial control over your business, optimizes your accountant's time, and equally importantly reduces their bills. You can then use your accountant for the specialist advice you need.

Bankers

All the major banks are keen to attract small business accounts. They offer a number of joining incentives, such as free banking during the first year of trading, a starter pack with advice on bookkeeping and banking procedures, and a small business advisor. Your banker can provide the following services:

- [ ] *a current account* – (i) cash withdrawals for petty cash, (ii) cheque payments, (iii) direct debits for monthly payments of National Insurance etc, and (iv) standing orders;

❑ *card accounts* – (i) cash cards for petty cash withdrawals, and (ii) credit cards for business expenses;
❑ *funding* – for investment;
❑ *an overdraft* – to ease cash flow;
❑ *Internet banking* – for daily access to your account.

There are a few basic things to consider when opening your business current account. Firstly, you need to deposit a sum of money in the account to activate it. Secondly, you need to decide who can legally sign cheques, and how many signatures are required on each cheque. In any case, sample signatures will be required from all signatories. Thirdly, if you arrange an overdraft facility, you will be charged an 'arrangement fee' and will pay interest on any overdraft. However, the interest rate is negotiable. Finally, ask the bank for a regular breakdown of service charges and how they are calculated.

Computer systems support

Even if you are a computer wizard, once your business is established you should concentrate on making money and not on maintaining your PC and communications software. You need either to employ a computer systems support person or use a part-time contractor. Systems support people can provide the following services:

❑ installing new software such as applications packages;
❑ installing new hardware such as printers and servers;
❑ networking such as Internet connections;
❑ creating new user accounts, etc;
❑ maintaining your company website;
❑ writing bespoke software, such as Web-database systems.

One excellent source of help is students, who are happy to maintain your company system, on a part-time basis, and for a relatively modest fee.

Estate agents and surveyors

Estate agents and surveyors can give you specialist advice on premises. Certain estate agents specialize in business premises. When you have located a property it is wise to get a professional survey done. Estate agents and surveyors provide the following services:

- recommending the optimal size of premises for your business;
- suggesting suitable locations;
- the availability of properties in a locality;
- advising on local planning and usage restrictions;
- arranging a structural survey of potential premises;
- drawing up plans when seeking planning permission.

If you are intending to rent an office in an area you already know well, all you will probably need is the going rental per square metre for your target areas, and the length of the lease you will be asked to sign. However, if you are planning to purchase a property or modify its layout, then clearly you will want a structural survey and planning advice. Also, check with the planning department of the local council about the type of trading allowed from the premises.

Insurance brokers

Insurance brokers arrange your insurance needs. Although the insurance companies pay them for their intermediary role, they are required by law to give you the 'best, impartial advice'. Insurance brokers provide the following types of insurance:

- premises (buildings and contents);
- vehicles;
- personal (life and health);
- liability (public, employer's and professional negligence, covering lawyers, accountants, etc.)

Insurance brokers will also identify and arrange special insurance needs, such as 'keyman' insurance and goods in transit.

Printers and designers

High-quality stationery and business documents are an important advertisement for your business. When you launch your company, you will probably keep down costs by seeking inspiration from the stationery of established companies (but remember the copyright laws – see Chapter 27), and by preparing your own 'artwork' using, for example, Microsoft Word or Publisher.

Once you have prepared the artwork for your stationery and business documents you can transmit the files to your printer either on a floppy disk or as an e-mail attachment. Most printers accept MS Word files and can produce the necessary colour separations to print your business literature. In addition, you may want to employ a designer to create your company logo.

Your print and design consultancy can provide the following services: design advice (layout, size, colour, quality, quantity), artwork and printing.

Initially order a small amount of letterheads, envelopes, business cards, compliments slips and brochures. For instance, 500 sheets of headed notepaper should be sufficient, which you can get from a small printer or even the local photocopy shop. This is pragmatic because you may want to change your logo, and possibly even your address, a few times before you are settled.

Solicitors

The first professional you hire will probably be a solicitor to set up your limited company. Most legal firms handle the basic aspects of setting up companies. However, you are advised to seek out specialist firms when you need advice in areas such as high-tech intellectual property rights, contract law and litigation (court work). A solicitor provides the following types of service:

- ❏ company registration;
- ❏ contracts (employment, non-disclosure agreements, service);
- ❏ conveyancing;
- ❏ intellectual property rights (copyright, trademarks, patents);
- ❏ litigation advice;
- ❏ partnership agreements;
- ❏ rental, leasing and letting agreements.

Legal advice and representation can be very expensive. However, a solicitor should be able to give you a reasonable estimate of the cost of a given piece of work. In addition, the American practice of lawyers working for *free*, for a *success-fee* or for *sweat equity* is on the increase in Britain. So, if your business looks like becoming the next Yahoo!, try offering your solicitor the future business or some shares in return for free legal work.

Venture capitalists

Most UK entrepreneurs, as opposed to US entrepreneurs, fail to appreciate the help that the right venture capital firm can give them (see Chapter 17). While an entrepreneur should be extremely wary of any individual or firm wanting to 'hitch a free ride', a good VC will give you informal advice, and later arrange funding to accelerate growth, find good people to help manage the company, and arrange introductions and partnerships. You need to ask yourself if you want 100 per cent of a £1 million company, or 50 per cent of a £100 million company. The big problem in the UK is 'poverty of ambition'.

A venture capitalist and investment banker provides the following types of service:

- [ ] arranging investment, both from their own funds and from other VCs;
- [ ] finding key staff for the company (managing director, finance director, marketing director);
- [ ] arranging new joint ventures and partnerships;
- [ ] arranging a stock market flotation;
- [ ] dealing with trade sales.

The UK has a highly developed venture capital industry. However, only a small number of firms and funds specialize in high-tech start-ups. One specialist high-tech fund is Amadeus (www.amadeus1.com). Another recommended source is the list of 'business angels' published by the British Venture Capital Association (www.bvca.co.uk). In Ireland the recommended VC source is O'Hurley Blair Irwin Chartered Accountants and 'experts in venture capital' (see www.obi.ie).

Sources of help

Institute of Management Consultants. 5th Floor, 32–33 Hatton Garden, London, EC1N 8DL, tel: 020 7242 2140, fax: 020 7830 4597
Lawyers for your Business. PO Box 61, London NW1 7QS, tel: 020 7405 9075, fax: 020 7611 6968, *www.lfyb.lawsociety.org.uk*
Williams, S (1999) *Small Business Guide*, Penguin Books, London

Part 3

Business *on the* Internet

12 Putting the Internet to Work for You

The Internet should be an integral part of your business. Electronic mail to communicate with your customers, the World Wide Web for marketing your products and for sales, and (soon) videoconferencing for customer support.

In this chapter we look at:

- [ ] the process of going online with a PC, modem and browser;
- [ ] how to use electronic mail (e-mail) effectively;
- [ ] how the World Wide Web ('the Web') operates;
- [ ] how to use file transfer protocol (FTP) for moving files between computers;
- [ ] how to use the Internet for telephoning and videoconferencing.

Going online

The major advantages of the Internet for business are cost and flexibility. For information-based products and services, adverts, orders and product delivery are tied together and can be processed in seconds, 24 hours a day. Setting up a *virtual shop* merely involves renting £500-worth of disk storage on a computer connected to the Internet. This is ideal for 'road testing' your new business with minimal risk. More importantly, customers can be serviced from anywhere in the world with advertising, online sales and customer support targeted at the individual. The big challenge is advertising your presence to potential customers.

What is the Internet?

As we know, the Internet is a network of computer networks, broadly similar to the telephone network but with computers at the ends of the wires. Just as each company and telephone in the world has a number, so each Internet computer and accessible file has a textual address (eg www.microsoft.com), and corresponding unique Internet address (eg 207.46.131.13) used to access it. For instance, all Microsoft addresses contain 'microsoft.com' – the organization is called 'Microsoft' and it is a company ('com'). E-mail addresses are '<person>@microsoft.com', Web pages are 'www.microsoft.com/<directory>/<file>...' and FTP archive documents are 'ftp.microsoft.com/<directory>/<file>...' The Internet grew out of an amalgam of academic and military computer networks, and the private networks of large corporations. In fact, you will come across three 'internet' terms:

- ❑ The *Internet* – the linkage of many computer networks throughout the world, using agreed rules and protocols for exchanging information.
- ❑ *Intranet* – 'closed' computer networks that are developed privately and operated within an organization, but which use Internet standards and protocols.
- ❑ *Extranet* – collaborative 'business-to-business' networks that use Internet technology to link businesses to their suppliers and other businesses.

The Internet and its ancestors have been around for 25 years. For most of this time the Internet has been used by computer people to send and receive electronic mail and to access remote computers (Telnet). All this changed in the past few years with the so-called World Wide Web.

Electronic mail, the Web etc

Today, the major Internet facilities available to support your business are as follows:

- ❑ *Electronic mail* (e-mail). A message, possibly with an attached document, is sent to one or more specific destinations, world-wide, in a matter of seconds.

❏ *World Wide Web.* This is a massive online electronic library of inter-linked documents containing text, graphics, audio and video, that can be retrieved from anywhere in the world.

❏ *Newsgroups* (Usenet). These are electronic noticeboards, each devoted to a specific topic or interest, where you can browse messages or post your own. There are around 20,000 newsgroups, on almost every conceivable topic.

❏ *File transfer protocol* (FTP). This allows online documents and computer programs to be moved between your personal computer and a remote computer; 'downloaded' directly to your PC's local disk store, or 'uploaded' from your disk to the remote computer's disk.

❏ *Lotus Notes* (Notes). This is a library of electronic documents that appear as a shared 'file-store' to a group of individuals, usually in the same organization but geographically dispersed.

❏ *Videoconferencing.* Two or more people can use the Internet as a telephone service or videoconferencing service. This requires your PC to be equipped with a microphone, sound card, speakers, camera and video card.

Your computer, modem and browser

To access the Internet you need three items: a personal computer, a modem to connect your PC to the telephone network, plus a browser to access Web pages and send/receive e-mails.

Personal computer

When you buy your personal computer you basically have three choices – well, 2½ really – depending on how you want to use the PC. It is a bit like choosing between a stereo system, 'ghetto blaster' and a Walkman.

A desktop PC lives on a desk or table and costs around £1000. All PCs have a *microprocessor* (eg Intel Pentium), and four types of memory. *Main memory* is composed of microchips that store programs and data during processing; its capacity is typically 64–128Mb (megabytes). A *hard disk* provides a 'library' of progams and data. A *floppy disk* is a removable read/write disk typically of about 1.4Mb. A *CD ROM* is a removable disk of 640Mb capacity.

Figure 12.1 Palmtop (reproduced with kind permission of Sony IT Group UK)

When purchasing a PC, the best advice is to buy as fast a micro-processor, and as much memory, as you can afford, to 'future proof' your PC. Also, expect your PC to come with a *modem* for connecting to the Internet, *stereo speakers* for playing audio, a *microphone* for input, and possibly a *video camera* for videoconferencing.

A laptop PC is for mobile computing. It will be more expensive, around £1500, because the manufacturer has to shoe-horn the electronics into a smaller box. *Main memory* should be at least 32–64Mb, otherwise your programs will run slowly. Also, manufacturers find it difficult to get the floppy disk and CD ROM in the same box – so check what is involved in swapping these two bits of equipment over. Expect your laptop to come with a *modem, speakers* and *microphone*.

A palmtop PC is a baby laptop, costing about £800. A palmtop is highly portable, but with minimal specification – hence the 2½ choices.

Modem

To access the Internet, your computer needs a device that connects to a network and allows it to access other computers. The simplest form of connection is a *modem* that connects to your standard telephone line and allows your computer to dial other computers with modems. There are three basic types of modem: *internal, external* and *card*. A typical speed is 56kbps (56,000 bits per second) and costs around £90.

Alternatively, if you expect to make heavy use of the Internet or to connect a number of computers, you can use ISDN or leased lines, or cable modems. These are covered in Chapter 13.

Browser

The final item you need to get online is an Internet browser, such as Netscape's Communicator or Microsoft's Internet Explorer. These browsers let you view any Web page on the Internet, as well as send and receive e-mail. Basically, browsers and upgrades are available free – from your Internet service provider, on the Windows CD, on many of the free CDs distributed with magazines, or downloadable from the Internet.

Choosing a service provider

To use the Internet you must subscribe to a so-called Internet service provider (ISP). This is similar to renting a telephone service from BT or Cable & Wireless.

The service provider sends you software on a CD, or floppy disks, for you to load into your PC. When you want to use the Internet, you run this software. The software uses the computer's modem (which you connect to the telephone line) to dial and connect to the service provider's computer. Your computer passes the address of, say, Tesco's page to the service provider's computer. It then asks Tesco's computer for the page. The service provider's computer then passes this page back to your computer, which displays it on its screen.

Service providers are either free, or charge £5–10 per month to connect you to the Internet. The service provider pays for dedicated national and international lines. So it costs you the same – the cost of a local telephone call – to access an Internet page on a computer in London, Paris, New York or Tokyo.

There are basically two ways to get on-line (see also Figure 12.2).

Internet service provider (ISP)

ISPs such as BT Internet (www.btinternet.com), Virgin Net (www.virgin.net), Demon (www.demon.com), and Dixon's FreeServe (www.freeserve.com) provide you with a basic link to the Internet. Businesses pay a subscription of around £5–10 a month, but for domestic customers increasingly the service is free, so all you pay is the cost of the telephone call while you are connected. In Ireland there are Ireland-On-Line (www.iol.ie) and Telecom Eireann (www.tinet.ie).

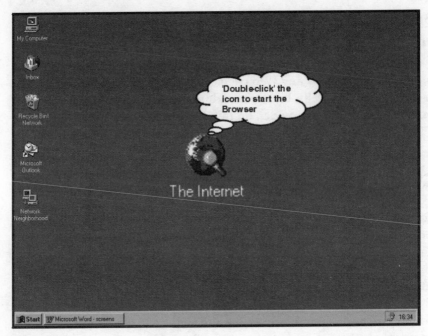

Figure 12.2

Online service provider (OSP)

OSPs such as CompuServe (www.compuserve.com) and AOL (www.aol. com) provide you with an Internet link, but in addition they provide access to their own extensive databases and other online resources – akin to an 'Internet within the Internet'. For these services you may pay the cost of the local telephone call while connected, together with a charge for the proprietary databases accessed. However, various payment packages are on offer, including a fee that incorporates the telephone charge.

Connecting to the Internet

We will look first at how to dial and connect to an ISP, and then how to find and subscribe to an ISP. The dial-up (subscription and software installation) is broadly the same for all providers. As an illustration we will here use BT Internet.

To start the browser, double-click the icon in the normal way (Figure 12.2). Starting the browser automatically starts the 'dial-up connection' software that uses your PC's modem to dial the ISP's computer.

Table 12.1 ISP versus OSP

	ISP (free service)	ISP (business service)	Online Svc. Providers
Telephone access	local access nationally	local access nationally	local access world–wide
Charging	free connection	fixed monthly subscription	variable, based on connect time and services accessed
High-speed connections	not usually supported	supports ISDN and leased lines	not usually supported
Extra Options	none	own domain name and website	proprietary databases and forums
Service appropriate for	domestic customers	business with major usage; business with own website	international travellers; business researchers

The connection software will then ask you to confirm your 'user name' and password, and the phone number of the ISP (Figure 12.3). When you have done that, click on 'Connect'.

The software then dials the ISP, connects, and the ISP's computer verifies your user name and password.

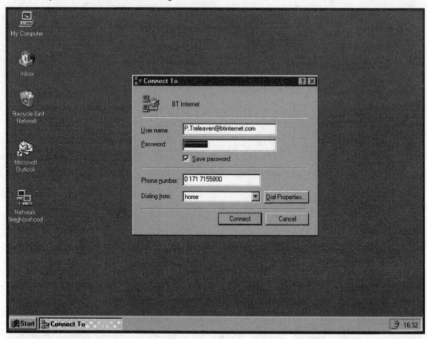

Figure 12.3

Once connection is established, the so-called 'home page' is displayed (Figure 12.4). A Web page can then be retrieved by 'clicking' on the address line, and typing its Web address. For e-mail services, 'double-click' the Mail icon in the toolbar. Closing the browser should disconnect you from the ISP automatically.

Subscribing to an Internet service provider

Finding an ISP could not be easier – there are over 100 in the UK. Go to your local newsagent and buy one of the excellent Internet magazines, such as the one shown in Figure 12.5. Usually at the back you will find a comprehensive list of service providers, the areas they serve, their costs and reliability. You have a choice between *national* service providers serving the whole country (such as BT Internet, Demon, Virgin Net) and *local* providers serving a particular town, city or region. (The location of the ISP determines the cost of telephone calls when you connect to their computer.)

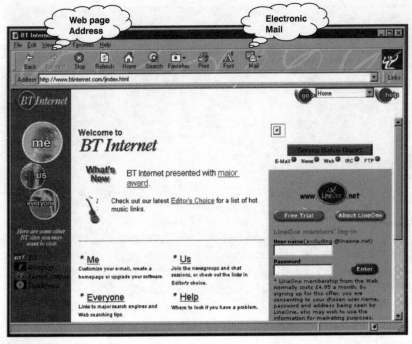

Figure 12.4

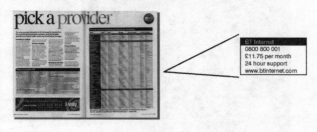

Figure 12.5

For instance, telephone BT Internet's call centre on 0800 800 001. They will take your name and address and send you their Internet software on CD ROM or floppy disk.

Load the CD and installation should start automatically. If nothing happens, follow the instructions on the installation guide sheet. This involves clicking on the Windows *Start* button, selecting *Settings*, then *Control Panel*. Then click on *Add/Remove*, and then select *Install*. If all else fails you can always call the BT Internet Helpdesk on 0345 77 66 66.

The first screen you see is shown in Figure 12.6. Step through the tutorial screens, the loading of the Internet browser and the online registration, until you are successfully registered with the ISP.

An alternative is to go into any branch of a store selling computers or accessories and ask for a free Internet CD.

Although e-mail, the Web and FTP will be familiar to many readers, the topics will be introduced briefly here for completeness.

Electronic mail

Electronic mail is fast and cheap. If you send 1000 business letters by first class post in the UK, the cost of stamps will be at least £260, and the letters will take 1–2 days to reach their destinations. This ignores all the stationery and secretarial costs of printing, folding and inserting the letters in envelopes, and 'licking' the stamps. In sharp contrast, by electronic mail, it may cost as little as £5 to send 1000 messages winging around the globe in a few seconds. What is more, the contents could be a simple letter or a whole product catalogue.

Electronic mail programs are probably the simplest of all computer

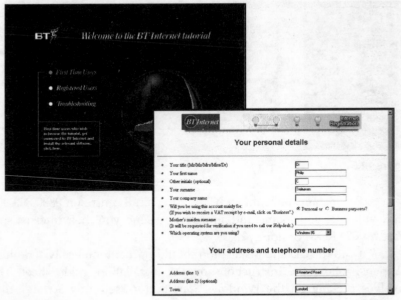

Figure 12.6

applications to use. When you load the e-mail software, it accesses the Internet computer that connects you to the 'world', downloads any new mail messages, and lists them in the *In* mailbox (the actual name depends on the software used) (see Figure 12.7). Each message entry lists *who* sent the message, the *date* and the *subject*. There is a corresponding *Out* mailbox listing all the messages you have sent.

Two extremely useful e-mail facilities for any business are:

- ❑ *alias lists* – a distribution list of recipients to receive a copy of the message;
- ❑ *attachments* – being able to attach a file containing a document to a message.

A circulation or *alias* facility allows you to give a name to a group of e-mail addresses. When you type the alias in the *To*: line, everybody will receive a copy of the message. For instance, in the Eudora software, click on the *Address Book* button, then on the *New* button. Type the alias 'nickname', and then list the e-mail addresses on the circulation list.

An *attachment* facility allows you to attach a document to your message. Again in Eudora, click on the *Attach File* button and specify the

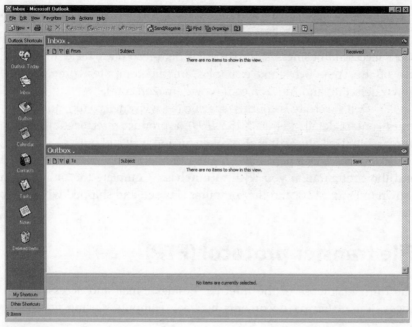

Figure 12.7

file to be attached. Then click on *Open* and the file is listed as attached to the e-mail.

The World Wide Web

The Web (for short) is an amazing source of online information open 24 hours a day. However, a cynic might add that the great challenge *is finding anything remotely useful in this morass of information*. To visualize the Web, imagine the world's largest 'living' document – billions of text, graphic, audio and video pages interlinked throughout the world – and being able to move easily between these pages using a 'browser'.

The Web provides your business with four basic services:

- ❑ *Information*. Online information on your company, and its products and services, is available 24 hours a day.
- ❑ *Ordering*. Online ordering of your products and services is, again, available 24 hours a day.
- ❑ *Delivery*. There is online delivery of information-based products and services, within seconds, anywhere in the world.

☐ *Market research.* You can do a wealth of online market research on customers, suppliers and competitors.

Most successful businesses, in particular high-tech ones, make maximum use of the Web. Two good examples are the computer company Dell (www.dell.com) and Amazon.com (www.amazon.com).

Dell's website is country-specific (eg www.dell.co.uk), and it provides contact details (tel 0872 152 4699), a product directory and online purchasing (Dell Store). It is also colourful and well laid out.

To buy a Dell personal computer online, simply select the product and the configuration you wish to purchase. Complete the online form shown in Figure 12.8, and the computer is boxed and shipped within two days.

File transfer protocol (FTP)

The third major use of the Internet, besides e-mail and accessing Web pages, is transferring documents between computers using *file transfer*

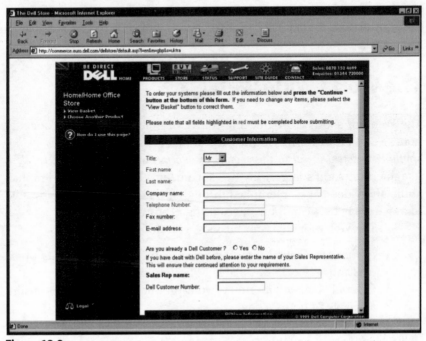

Figure 12.8

protocol. Most software companies distribute software and upgrades to products via their Internet site.

The simplest way to 'download' a file is to use a standard Internet browser, such as Microsoft's Internet Explorer. When the browser encounters an 'unknown file type' it displays a dialog box, from which you can store the file on your local disk.

The UK academic archive HENSA (www.hensa.ac.uk) illustrates how this FTP concept works. To access the software, enter the Internet address into the browser. Once the HENSA home page is displayed (Figure 12.9), click on the *Search* icon to load the search page. Then enter the name of the software you wish to download – in our case WinZip (compression software). The results of the search are displayed. Double-click on file.zip to download the software. The system then displays another dialog box. Click on the *Save to Disk* button (Figure 12.10) to save the file to your local disk.

Many FTP archives hold files in a compressed (or zipped) format. Such files have a suffix '.zip' and are 'unzipped' using a program such as WinZip (www.winzip.com).

The alternative way to transfer files between computers is to use special FTP programs. These are particularly useful to transfer files between your laptop and the company computer system. The FTP soft-

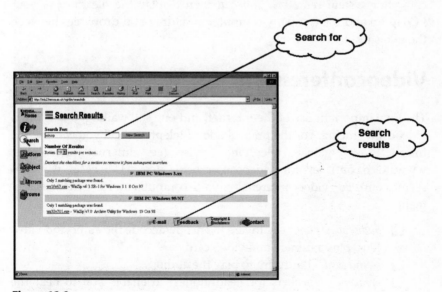

Figure 12.9

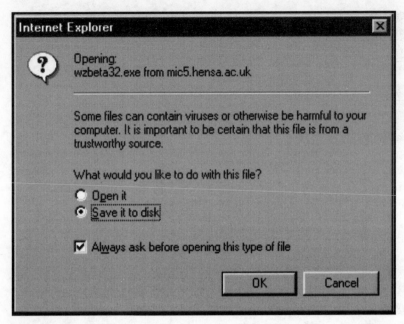

Figure 12.10

ware (CuteFTP) (see Figure 12.11) allows you to log on to your company's computer system remotely. You can then display the file store of your PC/laptop and the company computer and 'drag-and-drop' files between the two sites.

Videoconferencing

The final important use of the Internet, and one still waiting to take off, is videoconferencing. For the price of a local telephone call you can use the Internet for global telephone calls (eg Internet Telephone, www.itelco.com), or for videoconferencing (eg CU-SeeMe, www.cu-seeme.com). For videoconferencing your computer needs certain equipment:

- [ ] *audio/video player* – software to encode/decode the audio and video files, plus a camera and video card;
- [ ] *sound card* – hardware to play the audio;
- [ ] *speakers* – speakers (or headphones) to enable you to hear the audio;

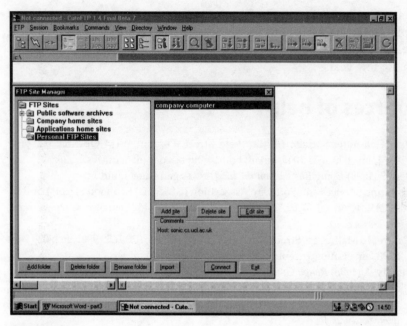

Figure 12.11

❑ *microphone* – to input audio;
❑ *high-speed line* – a fast Internet line (eg ISDN) to receive and send video.

Most personal computers, even laptop PCs, now come with a sound card, speakers and a microphone, and *player* software, like RealAudio. You can also download RealAudio (www.realaudio.com) for free from the Internet. However, to achieve an acceptable 'frame rate' for videoconferencing you will need a high-speed Internet line, for example ISDN, with a capacity of 64–128kbps, or a cable modem (see Chapter 13).

A number of companies support teleconferencing over the Internet. For example, Vocaltec (www.vocaltec.com) sell software for about $50, which supports both audio and video teleconferencing. Having paid your $50 and installed the software, you, and the person you wish to speak to, both log in to Vocaltec, whose server connects you together.

Using an analogy with the telephone, Internet teleconferencing is currently at the stage of development where you needed to get the operator to connect you if you wished to make a long distance call. However, many people believe that Internet telephony will be one of the biggest applications (a 'KillerAp') of the Internet. So expect some startling advances both in the underlying technology and the applications in the coming few years.

Sources of help

British Computer Society. 13 Mansfield Street, London W1M OBP, tel: 020 7637 0471, fax: 020 7631 1049, email: bcshq@hq.bcs.org.uk, *www.bcs.org.uk*

Collin, S (1998) *Doing Business on the Internet,* Kogan Page, London

Computing Services and Software Association (CSSA). 20 Red Lion Street, London, WC1R 4QN, tel: 020 7397 6700, fax: 020 7404 4119, email cssa@cssa.co.uk, *www.cssa.co.uk*

E-Centre. 10 Maltravess Street, London WC2R 3BX, tel: 020 7655 9000, fax: 020 7681 2290, email info@e-centre.org.uk, *www.e-centre.org.uk*

Kennedy, A (1998) *Rough Guide to the Internet,* Rough Guides Ltd., London

National Computing Centre. Oxford House, Oxford Road, Manchester M1 7ED, tel: 0161 228 6333, fax: 0161 242 2400/2171, email: webster@ncc.co.uk, *www.ncc.co.uk*

TradeUK. *www.tradeuk.co.uk*

Yahoo! *www.yahoo.com*

13　Getting an Internet Presence

So you have a wonderful idea for a company. The next task is to establish your company's presence in the electronic marketplace. In fact, most high-tech entrepreneurs will start with their Internet address, referred to as the *domain name*.

In this chapter we look at:

- [ ] how to register your company's Internet domain name;
- [ ] how international domain names are organized;
- [ ] how to advertise the presence of your domain name;
- [ ] how to set up your Internet site;
- [ ] various options for connecting to the Internet, such as modems, ISDN and ADSL.

Domain name registration

The importance of good branding cannot be over-emphasized. Ideally, your company name, your website and e-mail address should be complementary (see Chapter 31). Microsoft, Amazon.com, Hotmail, eToys, e-trade, are all good examples:

- [ ] *Company name* – Amazon.com
- [ ] *E-mail address* – info@amazon.com
- [ ] *Web address* – www.amazon.com

Domain names

How are Internet domain names or addresses composed? Well, an address comprises three basic parts: *user@host.domain*, usually pronounced as 'user' at 'host' 'dot' 'domain'. The *user* portion can be anything, such as 'info', 'sales' or 'feedback', but most typical is a person's name or their 'login' on the host system: for example, b.gates (or bill.gates, or bgates). In fact, most mail systems will allow a user to be reached by a small number of different, common *aliases*, typically b.gates@microsoft.com, bill.gates@microsoft.com, and bgates@microsoft.com.

The *host* is the organization, typically 'company', 'division' 'dot' 'company', 'university' or 'department' 'dot' 'university'; examples are microsoft, virgin, games.virgin, ucl and cs.ucl.

Lastly, *domain* covers the type of organization and country, apart from global names and United States companies that are '*.com*' '*.net*' etc (see Figure 13.1).

The good news is that, when choosing your Internet name, you have considerable flexibility subject to a few provisos. Firstly, you need to find out whether any other organization has already registered your intended Internet domain name. Secondly, you are strongly advised not to try to register a domain name of a well-known brand. Even if you succeed you will certainly have the name taken off you. Thirdly, the domain needs to reflect your business: '.co' or '.com' are appropriate for any sort of

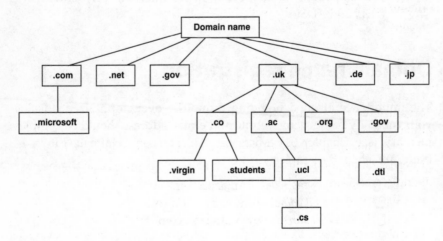

Figure 13.1 Internet domain names

company, '.org' is appropriate for a non-profit organization, '.ac' or '.edu' for an educational institution. Fourthly, your company or organization should be actively intending to use the Internet domain name within the country specified by the domain.

However, because domain names need to be exact, two different companies can register two broadly similar names (eg www.company.com and www.company.net). The bad news is that most good Internet addresses have already been registered. But you might be lucky!

Let us assume you have named your high-tech company NewCo Ltd. To trade globally you might want to register *newco.com*, or, if that is already taken, *newco.net*. Even if both of these are taken, you could still try to register *newco.co.uk*. In fact, if they are all available, NewCo Ltd might register the lot just to protect its brand. The last one, newco.co.uk might then be reserved for providing specialist information on its UK subsidiary.

You can check online whether your preferred Internet domain name has already been registered, using one of the domain name registration companies, such as Tabnet (www.tabnet.com) in the US, or NetNames (www.netnames.co.uk) in the UK.

Name registration

Global Internet 'domain' names – those ending in .com and .net – are administered in the United States by an organization called *InterNIC* (www.internic.net). InterNIC provides an online search and registration facility.

All other countries, the United Kingdom (.uk), Germany (.de), Japan (.jp), and Australia (.au), handle their national registration. UK Internet names – those ending in .co.uk and .org.uk – are handled by the company Nominet (www.nic.uk). Typically, to register a domain name, the organization needs either to already be doing business in the country, or intends to establish a business.

The simplest way to register a domain name is to use one of the Internet name companies such as Tabnet or NetNames, who for a fee will handle all registration details for you. The process of registering a name was described in Part 1 on page 31.

Registration is instantaneous, but sorting out the details seems to take about two days. The registration company will also set up an Internet site for you. This can be merely a 'dummy' site as part of your name registration, or they will provide you with a Web page for your company and an e-mail facility. You now 'own' the registered Internet name, as long as you continue to pay the fees every two years. You can move it to another computer at a later date if you so wish.

Later, when you get your own Internet server, it will be allocated an Internet (IP) address to identify it. An IP address identifies a single computer on the Internet, and is represented by four numbers from 0 to 255, separated by dots (eg 123.4.56.789). (This IP address is similar to a telephone number.) So-called *routing tables* of national servers are then reset to link your website to the new IP address of your computer.

Advertising your domain name

As with any business, once you have registered your domain name and set up your company Internet site, you need to advertise your presence. This ranges from placing your Internet address on company stationery, to ensuring your address is known to key Internet sites so that it can be located easily by *search engines*. Here is a checklist:

- ☐ *Company stationery.* Place your e-mail and Web addresses on all stationery; business cards, compliments slips, notepaper, brochures and advertisements, etc.
- ☐ *E-mail.* You could send an announcement e-mail message to any *alias* lists of potential customers. This should be used with extreme caution, since the Internet community considers junk e-mails very bad form.
- ☐ *Newsgroups.* Choose the most relevant newsgroups for your business and place an announcement for potential customers. Two websites that help you find the appropriate newsgroups are DejaNews (www.dejanews.com) and TileNet News (www.tilenet.news.com).
- ☐ *Online directories.* Register your domain name with online directories like the international business directories, BigBook (www.bigbook.com) and BizWeb (www.bizweb.com); UK electronic yellow pages (www.yell.co.uk); the export site for British business, TradeUK (www.tradeuk.com); and any specialist sites providing 'hotlists' of relevant businesses.
- ☐ *Search engines.* You should also register your address with the

leading search engines. These are online directories, built by special programs that continuously search the Web for new sites. You can 'short-circuit' the process by registering your site with them. Popular search engines are AltaVista (www.altavista.com), Excite (www.excite.com), Infoseek (www.go.com), Lycos (www. lycos.com), Magellan (www.mckinley.com) and Yahoo! (www. yahoo.com).

❑ *Domain name servers.* These are key computers that store the addresses of every computer on the Internet.

For online directories and search engines, you could register your domain name with each directory individually. As an alternative you can use a special registration program that will automatically send a summary of your website to up to 200 hundred directories. Two companies that provide this service, for a fee, are Exploit (www.exploit.com) and Submitit (www.submitit.com; see Figure 13.2).

Marketing your presence on the Web is covered in more detail in Chapter 15.

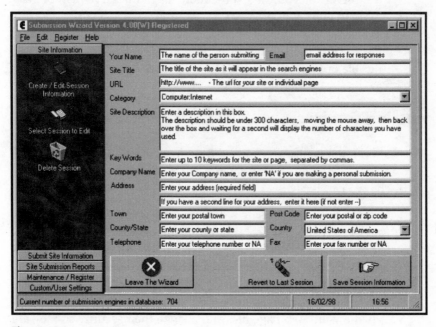

Figure 13.2

Setting up your Internet site

In the start-up phase of your business, rather than trying to manage your own Internet server, it is probably a good strategy to let an Internet service provider (ISP) 'host' your website for you.

Choices

You have three basic alternatives:

❑ *Renting Web space from an ISP*. The ISP provides file space for your website, transparently services requests for Web pages, and provides facilities for sending and receiving e-mails, just as if they were hosted on your own server.

❑ *Having an ISP host your server*. You locate your own Internet server at the ISP's site. The ISP connects the server to their high-speed communications link, thereby giving fast access, and also manages the server for you. At a subsequent stage the server can be relocated to your own premises.

❑ *Managing your own server*. You install a computer connected 24 hours a day to the Internet at your own premises. This is the most flexible option, but also the most expensive.

Hosting services

The best option for most start-ups and Internet users is to rent resources from an ISP. Changing your information on the 'hosted' site is straightforward. The typical steps are:

1. Connect to your ISP, using a dial-up connection.
2. Run file transfer protocol (FTP) software on your computer to link to your storage area on the ISP's system.
3. Use the FTP software to transfer the files from your hard disk to the ISP's file store.
4. Run 'Telnet software' to 'log on' remotely to the ISP's computer.
5. Rename your Web page files and change their security so they are accessible by any Internet browser.

6. Disconnect from your ISP.

Your own Internet server

To set up your own Internet server you need the following:

❑ *A dedicated computer server*. This should be a high-performance PC with a large hard disk capable of running 24 hours a day.

❑ *An operating system*. This must be a suitable operating system for running the server software, such as Microsoft Windows NT or Unix.

❑ *Internet server software*. This software manages the Web pages on your site and fetches Web pages when requested by a browser. Popular Internet server software includes Apache (www. apache.com) which runs under Unix, Microsoft's IIS (www. microsoft.com/iis) running under NT, Netscape's Enterprise Server (www.netscape.com), and O'Reilly's Web Server (www. ora.com) software.

❑ *Database tools*. These tools connect a website to a company database, so that queries entered on a Web page can interrogate or enter information into a database, and the response be returned. Popular Web-enabled databases include Microsoft's SQL Server (www.microsoft.com/sqlserver) and Oracle (www.oracle.com).

❑ *Server management tools*. These increasingly important tools allow you to monitor usage of your website and analyse usage logs.

❑ *Security (eg firewall) tools*. These high-security tools allow you to connect your Internet server to your office network safely, and stop hackers gaining access to your computers. The best known firewall company is Check Point (www.checkpoint.com).

❑ *High-speed connection*. If your server is located on your own premises you need a high-speed connection and an adapter/router to link your server to the ISP. For a small site with few visitors you could use an ISDN line, with a 'dial-up' connection being established when needed. An ISDN line costs around £200 per year, plus the additional call charges, giving an overall annual running cost of say £2,000. For larger sites or frequent accesses, a permanently open leased line is required. A leased line costs around £4,000 a year, but does not incur call charges.

Table 13.1 Advantages and disadvantages of using ISP

	Advantages	Disadvantages
Website hosted by ISP	• ISP sets up domain name, website, e-mail • Uses ISP's equipment • Low rental cost • High-speed connection to Internet, 24 hours a day • ISP manages server, including backups	• Charges increase as usage increases • Need to use FTP and Telnet to update files • Cannot link to company database
Server hosted by ISP	• Uses your equipment • High-speed connection to Internet, 24 hours a day • ISP manages server, including backups	• Need your own dedicated server • Need to use FTP and Telnet to update files
Own server	• Size of site can be increased without extra rental cost • Link company database directly to website • More control over secure payment facilities • Full control over subscribers and personal information on users	• Far more expensive than ISP hosting • Need your own dedicated server • Need dedicated staff to manage the site • Need a high-speed link to your ISP

A summary of the advantages and disadvantages of choosing between a hosted or your own server is given in Table 13.1.

Next, we shall look at some of the communications terminology you will meet when choosing an Internet connection.

Digital communication terms

For completeness, the common 'digital' terms will be listed first. Do not feel insulted!

Digital measures

The units of digital information are: *bit* – the fundamental unit of information, either 0 or 1; *byte* – an eight-bit unit of information, equivalent to one character; *multiples of bytes* – KB (kilobytes), MB (megabytes), GB (gigabytes), TB (terabytes).

Capacity and bandwidth

The capacity and bandwidth of a communications link are often used synonymously in computing, but they are in fact different:

❑ The *capacity* of a communications link defines how much information can be transmitted through the medium in a given time; it is expressed in bits per second (bps), kilobits per second (Kbps), megabits per second (Mbps), gigabits per second (Gbps) and terabits per second (Tbps).

❑ The *bandwidth* is the range of signal frequencies that can pass through a communications medium.

Internet connection and installation

When connecting to the Internet you have two basic decisions, the service provider and the type of line.

The service provider

Britain's excellent Internet magazines provide a comprehensive list of UK ISPs, their charges and their performance. Well-known ISPs are BTInternet (www.btinternet.com), Demon (www.demon.co.uk) and VirginNet (www.virgin.net). When you subscribe to an ISP they will send you a CD ROM or a set of floppy disks, containing the software that connects you to their Internet computer.

The type of connection

Next, you need to decide on the type of link to the ISP. You have a number of choices, as shown in Table 13.2.

When you are starting out, your company's website might be hosted by an ISP and all you need is periodic access to the ISP to send or download e-mails. A dial-up link may be sufficient; a modem for your laptop PC and possibly an ISDN link for the office, especially if you transfer large graphic files. As the business expands, and you may have your own server, then a leased line open 24 hours a day will give fast access between your server and the Internet.

Two additional choices are appearing. ADSL gives you a digital line that can send at 64Kbps and receive at 6Mbps. Secondly, cable modems use the cable TV network and hence can transmit at up to 500Mbps.

Modem

A modem is a 'MOdulator DEModulator' used to convert digital information into analogue signals for transmission through the telephone network. A modem at the ISP's computer converts the information back into digital form. There are three basic types of modem: a modem (PCMCIA) *card* for a laptop PC, an *internal* (board) modem in a desktop PC, and an *external* modem that can be used for any type of PC. The typical modem at present has a transfer speed of 55.6Kbps. However, modems are *asymmetric*, sending at 33.6Kbps and receiving at 55.6Kbps.

ISDN

ISDN stands for Integrated Services Digital Network. The phone company connects two digital lines into your home, each having a capacity of 64Kbps and together 128Kbps. To connect a computer to an ISDN line you need an ISDN *terminal adapter* (TA) in place of a modem.

Table 13.2 Internet connections

Connection	Definition	Speed	Cost	Comment
Modem	MOdulator DEModulator	55.6Kbps	£100 pa +calls	dial-up
ISDN	integrated services digital network	64–128Kbps	£2,000 pa	dial-up
Leased line	dedicated line between two points	2Mbps	£6000 pa	dedicated line
ADSL	asymmetric digital subscriber loop	64Kbps–6Mbps	–	experimental
Cable Modem	connection to cable TV network	500Mbps	–	experimental

Leased line

Leased lines are fixed connections between two points. This is like having a 24-hours-a-day, permanently open telephone line. Analogue leased lines are like normal telephone lines but can bypass the exchanges to give you up to 128Kbps. Digital leased lines can give you up to 2Mbps. With leased lines you pay only a fixed (but expensive) line rental costing from £500 to £2,000 per month, depending on the type of line.

ADSL, cable modem etc

There are various experimental forms of high-speed digital communications:

- ❑ *ADSL* (asymmetric digital subscriber loop) is a digital line available from telephone companies. As implied by the name, ADSL is able to send at 64Kbps but can receive at 6Mbps.
- ❑ *Cable modems* are special modems for connecting your PC to the cable network, to provide up to 500Mbps capacity.
- ❑ *Frame relay* is a technology with a variable capacity depending on requirement, but transfer speeds up to 50Mbps are possible.
- ❑ *ATM* (asynchronous transfer mode) is a technology with capacity varying between 1.5Mbps and 500Mbps.

Cable seems to be ideal, unless the cable companies price themselves out of the market.

Sources of help

Exploit. *Submits your domain name to search engines, www.exploit.com*
Fluckiger, F (1995) *Understanding Networked Multimedia*, Prentice-Hall, London
InterNIC. *International Domain name registration, www.internic.net*
NetBenefit. *UK name registration service, www.netbenefit.co.uk*
NetNames. *UK name registration service, www.netnames.co.uk*
Nominet. *The United Kingdom domain name registration service, www.nic.uk*
Submitit. *Submits your domain name to search engines, www.submitit.com*

14 Your Company Website

It is well within the capability of most entrepreneurs to design and program a simple set of Web pages to advertise their company's products and services. For more sophisticated sites providing customer support, online ordering and online payment, a Web-database system is required. When you are starting out and money is tight, a practical solution is to use students to build an initial site and possibly also maintain the site.

In this chapter we look at how to create:

- ❏ the various options for your company website, such as contact information, product brochures, online sales and customer support;
- ❏ your company Web pages using Internet Assistant or the hypertext mark-up language (HTML);
- ❏ an online catalogue using a database such as Microsoft's Access.

Company website

Your company's website is your online shop window to the world. The first decision is what you want the website to achieve for your company.

Types of site

The five basic categories of website are as follows:

❏ *Marketing site*. This provides basic information on your company, its mission, the types of products and services, and contact information. For instance, it is surprising how many companies fail to provide their postal address and telephone number online.

❏ *Corporate catalogue*. This is an online version of your company catalogue, listing details and prices of all products and services, together with ordering details and distribution network.

❏ *Online retailing*. This interactive site allows customers to browse the company database, and purchase products online with a secure form of payment.

❏ *Customer service and support*. Here you have a site with customer service information together with an e-mail facility or Web-form for customer interaction.

❏ *Intranet/extranet site*. This is a site accessible only by company staff, providing access to sales, marketing and product information.

Once you have decided the role of your company website, you next have to decide how much you are prepared to spend. Sophisticated multimedia sites like CNN (www.cnn.com) probably cost over $10 million to implement and maintain. IBM typically charges $1 million to implement a secure, online retailing site. A professional Web programming company might charge between $50,000 and $100,000 for a company site. In contrast, a group of students might charge as little as $1,000, even for an interactive site; that is a good option for launching your business.

Web design considerations

Let us start with some definitions:

❏ *Hypertext mark-up language* (HTML). This is the textual language describing the way a Web page is to be displayed by a browser.

❏ *Web page*. This is a single page displayed by a browser, comprising the HTML file containing the text and links to other pages, plus graphic, sound and video files containing elements of the page.

❏ *Website*. This comprises all the company's Web pages and related files.

❏ *Home page*. This term describes the first page of a company's website, from which all other pages are accessed.

❑ *Web server*. The computer that supports and services the company website.

When designing your first Web page, browse the Internet looking for good ideas. In fact, most people teach themselves Web design and programming by 'grabbing' other people's pages and modifying them.

For instance, if you want to learn how Yahoo! is implemented, first load the Web page (see Figure 14.1). Click on *View* in the menu bar, then click on the *Source* entry in the drop-down menu. This will display the HTML source in a separate window. If you save a Web page, it is this HTML text specification that is actually saved in the file.

Web page programming

A Web page is made up of several files:

❑ The *HTML file* contains the textual description of how the Web page is to be displayed, together with links to other Web pages.

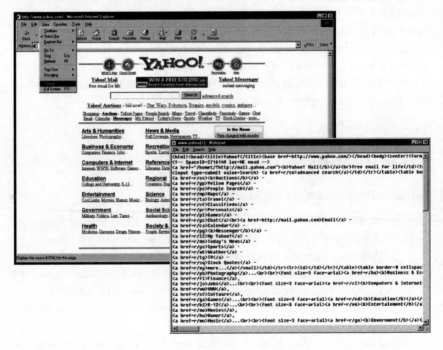

Figure 14.1

For instance, a page title is specified by enclosing the text between two HTML 'tags': <TITLE>NewCo Home page</TITLE>.

❑ *Graphic files.* These contain picture images, background page patterns, and photographs for insertion in the page. These images are typically encoded in either the 'gif' or the 'jpeg' graphic file formats.

❑ *Scripts.* These are small programs that let you add functions to your Web pages.

❑ *Database files.* These contain databases, such as product and customer information, that are accessible via the Web page.

❑ *Sound and video files.* These provide sound and video functions for the Web page.

Before describing some of the ways to create an HTML specification of a Web page, we will look briefly at the language.

Hypertext mark-up language

HTML is pretty simple once you get over the shock of seeing the computing hieroglyphics! HTML is a textual language comprising 'tagged' information, describing the layout of the Web page. Each tag is delimited by angle brackets, as in <tag>, and each command typically has a start tag, <tag>, and an end tag, </tag>.

The layout of a simple <HTML> ... </HTML> Web page is shown in Figure 14.2. It comprises a header, <HEAD> ... </HEAD>, and a body, <BODY> ... </BODY>. Within the body is a level-one heading, <H1> ... </H1>.

You have two basic options to create the HTML for your company Web page. You can either use an authoring tool such as Internet Assistant (part of MS Word), or you can type the HTML text into a file using a text editor program such at Notepad.

Microsoft's Internet Assistant

Internet Assistant is Microsoft's simple 'tool' that allows you to create basic Web pages. Internet Assistant provides an HTML editor and also a simple Web browser. Its two major advantages are, firstly, that it involves no

```
<HTML>
<HEAD>
<TITLE> NewCo Home Page </TITLE>
</HEAD>
<BODY>
<H1> Welcome to NewCo </H1>
. . .
</BODY>
</HTML>
```

Figure 14.2 Simple HTML specification of a Web page

additional cost; and, secondly, that it is integrated with MS Word. (In fact, Internet Assistant 'add-ons' are provided for a number of Microsoft products, including Excel, PowerPoint and Access.) Internet Assistant appears in Word as an HTML template, which loads additional Web menu entries and toolbar icons.

To create your simple company Web page, load the HTML template as follows:

1. Click on *File* in the menu bar, then click on *New*.
2. Click on the tab *Web Pages* to display the HTML templates (Figure 14.3).
3. Click on *Blank Web Pages* and the template is loaded, together with the Web menus and icons. The HTML commands (or tags) are now part of MS Word.
4. Next insert the company name. To do this, click on the down arrow adjacent to *Normal*. Scroll down to the H1 and click on the entry. Then type the name 'Welcome to NewCo Ltd' (without the quotation marks) (Figure 14.4).

That is the basic procedure for inserting text into the Web page. But what about art? To insert a picture:

1. Either click the 'picture' icon in the Web page toolbar, or click on *Insert* in the menu bar. The *Insert Picture* dialog box is displayed (Figure 14.5).
2. Select the file to be inserted and finally click on the *Insert* button.

Figure 14.3

Figure 14.4

Figure 14.5

When you have completed your company Web page, click on the *File* entry in the menu bar in the normal way for Word documents and give the file a name. Word saves the file with the suffix '.html', signifying it as an HTML document.

Programming in HTML

Alternatively, you can type the HTML text directly into a file using the Notepad text editor. To load Notepad, click the Windows *Start* button, select *Programs*, followed by *Accessories*, and then Notepad (see Figure 14.6).

When you have finished, you save the file in the normal way but with the suffix '.html'.

Web page authoring tools

Besides Internet Assistant, whose main (some would say only) advantage is being integrated with Microsoft Word, there are a number of excellent

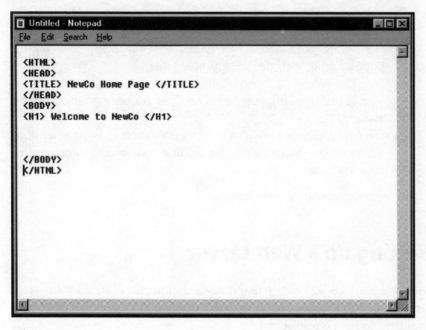

Figure 14.6

Web page design tools and programming languages. Some of these tools/languages will be listed briefly, and the Web addresses where you can find further information if you are interested:

- ❑ *Active server pages* (ASP). ASP (www.activeserverpages.com) is server-based software that assembles complex and dynamic Web pages on the server before sending them to the client.
- ❑ *ActiveX.* This (www.microsoft.com/activex) is a programming language from Microsoft for extending HTML.
- ❑ *Applets.* These so-called plug-ins (java.sun.com/applets) are simple programs often generated by scripting languages (see below) that are downloaded separately from a Web page and run independently on the user's computer.
- ❑ *Cookies.* A cookie (www.cookiecentral.com) is a file stored on your computer by an accessing Web page, allowing it to save settings like page display options. Cookies are a powerful but controversial technique.
- ❑ *Dreamweaver.* Macromedia's Dreamweaver (www.macromedia. com/support/dreamweaver) is a set of professional Web tools.

- ❏ *FrontPage*. This (www.microsoft.com/frontpage) is Microsoft's combined Web design tool, Web management and server product.
- ❏ *Hot Metal*. SoftQuad's Hot Metal (www.sq.com) is a highly popular set of website development tools.
- ❏ *Java*. This (www.sun.com) is Sun's – some would say revolutionary – programming language based on C++ for programming online systems.
- ❏ *Shockwave*. Shockwave (www.macromedia.com) is another tool produced by Macromedia for adding multimedia functions to your Web page.

There are some very nice tools around.

Setting up a Web server

Setting up a Web server is straightforward. You can even do it on your laptop, as a prototyping aid. There are a number of good server packages available, so here is a selection:

- ❏ *Apache*. Apache (www.apache.com) is one of the most popular Web server software applications available, as it runs under the UNIX, NT or Mac operating systems.
- ❏ *FrontPage*. This well-known package from Microsoft includes the server software that comes with FrontPage and the IIS server product that works with Windows NT.
- ❏ *Netscape*. Netscape's principal product is the excellent Enterprise Server software.

Having set up your website, you will obviously want to know who is using it.

Monitoring site usage

There are a variety of tools available for monitoring site usage. These range from simple *counters* of the number of users that access your site, to sophisticated programs for analysing the *log files* that record user information.

Counters

Most Internet service providers will provide you with a CGI script to count the number of visitors to your site. An alternative is to use a commercial system such as WebCounter (www.digits.com).

Analyzing access logs

Each time someone accesses your site, most servers record information about where they came from, in your log file. You can browse this information manually or use one of the log analysis tools such as Hit List (www.marketwave.com).

Sources of help

Apache. *www.apache.com*
Collin, S (1998) *Doing Business on the Internet*, Kogan Page, London
Fluckiger, F (1995) *Understanding Networked Multimedia*, Prentice-Hall, London
FrontPage. *www.microsoft.com/frontpage*
Marketwave. *www.marketwave.com*

15 Internet Marketing

There is a classic cartoon. One dog is sitting in front of a computer and saying to another dog: *'On the Internet, nobody knows you're a dog'*. Equally, however, if your website is a 'dog', everybody will assume that *you* are, too.

Internet marketing is becoming increasingly sophisticated. Only a few years ago, 'marketing' seemed to consist of a picture of the chairman and a hypertext link to the company accounts. Presumably it helped the career of the website manager!

In this chapter we look at:

- ❏ the comprehensive function of Internet marketing;
- ❏ the design and promotion of websites and domain names;
- ❏ advertising using banner adverts and swapping of ads with other companies;
- ❏ downloads of audio/video, screen savers and Web casting;
- ❏ Internet mail shots using e-mail and fax;
- ❏ encouraging customers to subscribe, and personalization of content.

To put Internet marketing in perspective, it is part of the broader domain of *electronic marketing*.

Electronic marketing

This spans all forms of electronics-based marketing:

- ❏ *Telemarketing* is marketing via telephones, faxes, and even pagers.
- ❏ *Database marketing* is the building of customer profiles in a database, and using this information to identify customers precisely and to market to them in a highly individual manner.

Data warehousing is the electronic collection of customer data from point-of-sales (PoS) terminals, bank teller machines (ATMs) and the Internet, and its storage in databases. *Data mining* is the computer analysis of customer and product data looking for useful relationships. *Mail shots* are direct mail sent to customers by post, faxes and electronic mail.

❏ *Broadcast marketing* is the broadcasting of advertising information to customers, via radio programmes, via one-way broadcast television, or via films and videos.

❏ *Interactive marketing* is a mechanism whereby the customer and the marketer can interact in real time. *Magnetic storage* uses high-volume CD ROMs and DVD storage to support multimedia marketing. The *Internet*, of course, allows online interaction using the Web or e-mail. In addition, *electronic kiosks* are interactive booths covering shopping kiosks in stores, ticketing kiosks in stations, information kiosks, and even bank teller machines (ATMs). *Interactive digital TV* will allow two-way interaction, either two-way via cable, or receiving via broadcast TV with a response via the telephone line.

So, electronic marketing is any *method* of marketing that uses electronic devices and technologies. The above list is obviously only illustrative, with the devices and technologies continuously being combined and modified. The remainder of this chapter will focus on Internet marketing.

Internet marketing

Obviously you need a comprehensive strategy for Internet marketing, whether you are an electronic commerce start-up relying totally on the Internet, or merely the online channel of a more traditional company. Internet marketing is concerned with every aspect of your company, its product or service from its inception until it finally reaches the customer, and the provision of after-sales service.

The company website

Your website is your *electronic* shop window. It needs to look inspiring, and needs changing regularly to keep it fresh.

❑ *Domain name.* Your domain name is your *brand*; easy to remember, self-explanatory and easy to find with a search engine.

❑ *Web page design.* Your home page needs to be well structured and customer-oriented, providing all required information.

❑ *Search engine 'hits'.* You need to program your website so that search engines place it near the top of the search list. (The latest trend is for search engines to charge for this privilege!)

Advertising

This covers both advertising your own website and making money by selling advertising space (banner ads) on your site.

❑ *Traditional.* The easiest way to promote your site is to place the Web address on business cards, stationery and on all traditional forms of advertisements.

❑ *Search engines.* You should also register with the leading search engines.

❑ *Banner adverts.* Buy space on websites where potential customers may be browsing, and sell Web space on your own site.

❑ *Ad swapping.* Swap hypertext links and banner adverts with complementary websites.

Subscriptions

Encourage your customers to enter their names and addresses into your website by offering them something free in return. Newspapers offer free access to back issues, and many sites now offer free e-mail services. As Hotmail (www.hotmail.com) and ICQ (www.icq.com) have shown, each subscriber is worth a notional $25–250 on your market capitalization.

Mail shots

Create mailing lists and a database of customers, and send them selective promotional offers. But be very, very careful, because customers are easily annoyed by 'junk' mail shots. Where possible, persuade them to subscribe to the mailing list and make it easy for them to 'unsubscribe'.

❏ *E-mail.* All e-mail systems allow you to set up simple mailing lists and aliases, and broadcast messages to groups of customers. It is also relatively straightforward to build a database of e-mail addresses, and from them generate e-mail messages automatically.

❏ *Faxes.* Likewise, the more sophisticated fax systems allow you to build fax lists and to generate fax mail shots from databases.

Personalization

It is also increasingly desirable to customize Web pages for the person accessing the site, to give the electronic equivalent of personal service.

❏ *Advertisements.* The simplest form of customization is search engines changing the banner ad based on the keywords being used in the search.

❏ *Newspapers.* Many news organizations provide a customized newspaper service; you enter your interests and the site automatically generates you a bespoke newspaper. This is an excellent way of building a customer profile.

❏ *Personal greetings.* Companies like Amazon.com, who hold the names, addresses and purchase history of customers, match this information to the IP address of the computer used to access the site. Recognizing the IP address, they can then give you a personal greeting: '*Welcome back Dr Treleaven*'.

Downloads

Many sites offer free 'downloads' of software. This includes audio and video adverts, screen savers, and *webcasting*, which regularly downloads free information, such as the price of your favourite stocks.

❏ *Audio/video.* Free downloads and also 'streaming' of sample music and video clips are popular with the media industries.

❏ *Screen savers.* Attractive adverts, like the famous Guinness screen saver, can be downloaded and installed on your PC quite easily, but are surprisingly difficult for the novice to remove.

❏ *Webcasting.* So-called *push* technology is based on screen savers that, once installed, will regularly update themselves by pulling information over the Internet and displaying it on your PC. The good one can provide a really useful update service; almost your own personal TV channel.

The company website

The starting pointing for Internet marketing is your company website, so Web page design is crucial.

Web page design

Basically, a customer should be able to get the same information and service from your website as if they had stepped into one of your offices. This includes online brochures and catalogues, online ordering, contact details and after-sales service.

A good illustration is the Internet site of Regus (www.regus.com; see Figure 15.1), the world's leading serviced office company. The home

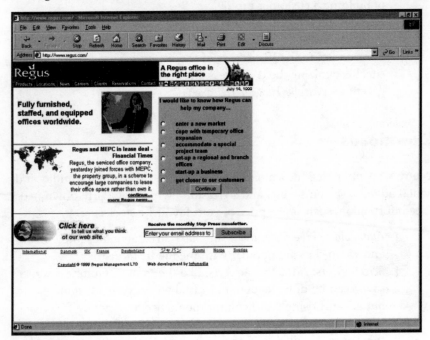

Figure 15.1

page is attractive, simply laid out and provides hypertext links to all key information. In fact, the only information missing that might be found on a US company's website is 'Investor information'.

The domain name

Two marketing issues are important for your domain name. Firstly, consider its potential as a major, valuable brand (this is discussed in detail in Chapter 31). Secondly, make sure that the domain name is easy to find by search engines. Special Internet marketing sites, like Exploit (www.exploit.com; see Figure 15.2), SubmitIt (www.submitit.com) and Submissions (www.submissions.com) will distribute your website address and description to hundreds of online search engines – for a small fee.

Search engine hits

Obviously, if you are McDonalds.com, you and your customers would like to have your website listed by search engines before the personal Web

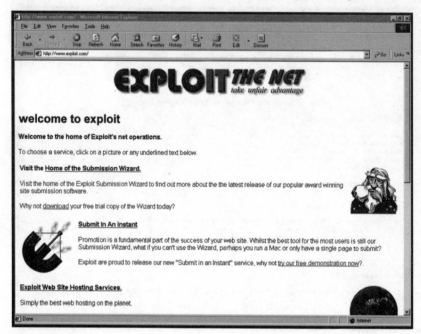

Figure 15.2

pages of every member of the McDonald clan. Equally, you would like your company's page to be listed ahead of your competitors.

It's a game. Search engines use increasingly sophisticated and secret algorithms to rank sites. There are, however, various ways to promote the 'ranking' of your website:

❑ *List keywords*. Make a list of all the 'keywords' that users of search engines may think of to locate the products and services offered by your website.

❑ *Embed keywords*. Incorporate the selected keywords into the headings, text and 'hidden files' of your website. This is important for your site to interface with the search engines.

❑ *Address submission*. Register your website with the seven leading search engines: Yahoo! (see Figure 15.3), Go/Infoseek, Excite, Lycos, HotBot, Alta Vista and Webcrawler. Also submit it using a service like Exploit, SubmitIt or Submissions.

❑ *Test*. Each week, test the search engines to see that your submissions have been accepted, that their description of your website is acceptable, and that the keyword you have used gets your website

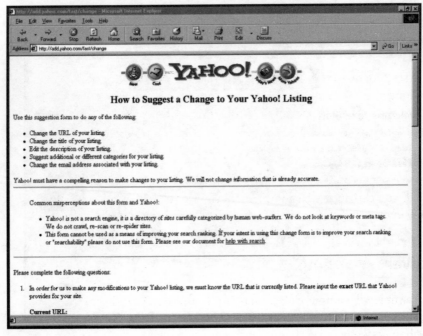

Figure 15.3

a 'top 20' ranking in one or more search engines. There is even a service called Position Agent (www.positionagent.com) to show you how high on the search engines you rank.

❏ *Redo*. Re-program your website, re-submit it and re-test it.

Website hits

The other vital piece of market research is: 'who is accessing your website'. As discussed previously, each time someone accesses your site, information is recorded in your log file. You can browse this information manually, or by using one of the log analysis tools such as 'Hit List' (www.market-wave.com).

Advertising

Realistically, the best way to advertise your Internet site is still through the traditional channels.

Traditional channels

The starting point for advertising is to place your Web address on business stationery and brochures, and in your traditional advertising. Most firms now list their website address on their billboard poster.

Banner adverts

Next, you can approach complementary Internet sites and get them (possibly even pay them) to display your banner advert.

Advert swapping

A number of commercial sites operate a scheme for exchanging your advertising banner with those of other sites. One example is Internet Link Exchange (www.linkexchange.com; see Figure 15.4).

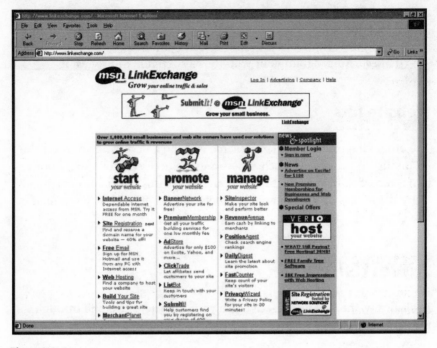

Figure 15.4

Advertising networks

Advertising network companies, such as DoubleClick (www.doubleclick.net), provide software for measuring online advertising and plan online marketing strategies for clients. These companies aim to centralize planning, execution, control, tracking and reporting for online media campaigns.

Subscriptions

Companies go to great lengths to capture information on their customers. In retail a popular strategy is *loyalty cards* that allow retailers to tie together point-of-sale data with customers' names and addresses. With the Internet, subscriptions for free services are becoming a major paradigm. Companies like Hotmail, ICQ and Dixon's FreeServe have increased their market capitalization by approximately $25–250 for every new subscriber. Fantasy land!

Getting customers to 'subscribe' to your service, whether free or not, is becoming increasingly popular with newspapers and the travel industry.

Mail shots

Electronic mail shots are a powerful tool both for *direct marketing* – contacting individual customers directly, and *customer care* – sending individual customers information on the status of their order or on after-sales service. The two principal technologies are e-mail and fax.

Electronic mail

For electronic mail there are a number of excellent packages, such as Qualcomm's Eudora (www.eudora.com) and Pegasus' software (www.pegasus.com), as well as the e-mail facilities in Microsoft's Internet Explorer (www.microsoft.com) and Netscape Communicator (www.netscape.com). Most modern packages support mailing lists and also interface with popular database packages.

To create a mailing list, simply 'click' on the address book facility, create a 'nickname', and enter all the associated e-mail addresses. Then, create an e-mail and type the nickname in the *To:* field and a copy of the message is sent to everyone in the address book entry.

Unfortunately, with some packages, everybody who receives the message is listed in the *To:* field, which blows confidentiality. One solution is to generate separate e-mail messages and pull the addresses from a database.

Facsimile

Most PC fax packages also support mailing lists, and the more advanced ones interface with database packages. The example in Figure 15.5 is from the popular WinFax package, showing how to create a new group fax list. Click on the *Phonebook* entry in the toolbar, then select *Phonebook Group*, and create a new entry.

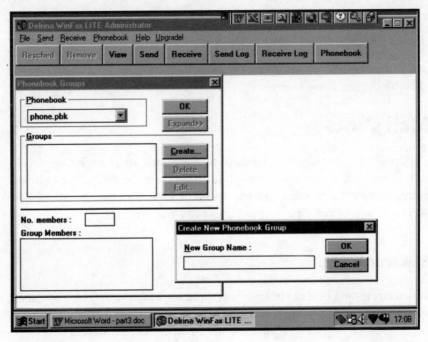

Figure 15.5

Personalization

Next we look at 'personalization', one of the major paradigms of direct marketing. The Internet (and interactive television) is an ideal one-to-one marketing medium. The goal is to develop personal empathy with customers on a one-to-one basis. The simplest level on the Internet is a search engine switching the banner ad to reflect the interest of the customer. More advanced systems analyse a customer's shopping profile to produce propositions and advertisements 'on the fly'.

Advertisements

Typical of the companies personalizing their Web pages is Amazon.com. They do this in a number of ways:

❑ *personal greeting* – matching the IP address of your computer with your registered name and address, to give you a personal welcome;

❏ *propositions* – compiling a personalized list of newly published books that may be of interest to you, based on your previous purchases;

❏ *mail shots* – offering to notify you of new books based on your specified list of interests.

You can expect customer profiling and personal propositions to become increasingly sophisticated as artificial intelligence and agent technology mature.

Newspapers

This is another area in which personalization is proliferating. An increasing number of news services offer to construct bespoke newspapers in response to your stated interests. (Do you really want them to know?) Obviously, this is a slick market research ploy and a major one-to-one news service. An early example of such a news service is offered by CNN (www.cnn.com; see Figure 15.6).

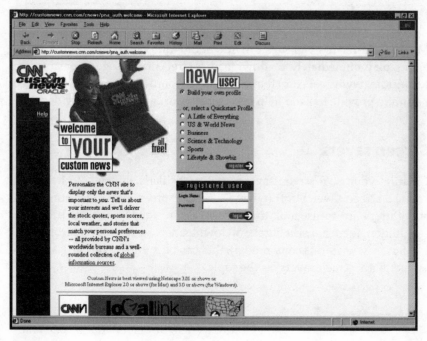

Figure 15.6

Virtual communities

Where do we go next? The Internet is moving from so-called *customer profiling* to *psychographic profiles* of customers. An interesting marketing service was Firefly. Firefly attempted to harness the power of peer recommendations or word-of-mouth marketing to build detailed psychographic profiles of customers, based on their answers to scores of questions. On the basis of these profiles, Firefly identified other individuals who appeared to have similar shopping patterns and then recommends products and services based on what 'psychographic neighbours' have reportedly liked.

Downloads

The Internet is the ultimate source of free information. Marketers have turned this to their advantage by allowing you to download entertaining advertisements.

Audio/video

Most media-related websites provide audio and video clips that you can either play immediately or download for repeated usage. Websites like RealAudio (www.real.com) that offer 'player' software for audio and video naturally provide tools to help you create your own audio and video.

Screen savers

Creating your own screen saver is not particularly difficult. To help you create a screen saver, Slsoft (www.slsoft.com/sunscr) provide a number of straightforward-to-use tools that do not require you to be able to program. In addition, there is a vast library of downloadable screen savers from sites, like Sirius (www.sirius.com/ ratloaf), that can be found by running a search engine with 'screen savers' as the topic.

Webcasting

Finally, we look at webcasting, which is based on screen saver technology.

Figure 15.7

To get information from the majority of websites, you need to connect to the Internet and explicitly 'pull' the information. In contrast, webcasting uses so-called 'push' technology, based on screen savers. To use webcasting, you download and install the associated program, and customize it to fetch specified information. As with other screen savers, when your PC is idle the program is run and updates itself by pulling information over the Internet and displaying it on your PC. Two of the best-known webcasting companies are Pointcast (www.pointcast.com; see Figure 15.7) and Marimba (www.marimba.com).

Sources of help

Collin, S (1998) *Doing Business on the Internet,* Kogan Page, London
DoubleClick. *Leading service provider of network advertising, www.doubleclick.net*
Exploit. *Leading service for placing your URL on search engines, www.exploit.net*
Peterson, R (1997) (ed) *Electronic Marketing and the Consumer,* Sage, London

Point Cast. *Leading producer of web casting software, www.pointcast.com*
RealAudit. *Leading producer of audio and video software, www.real.com*
Slsoft. *Slsoft produces screen saver software, www.slsoft.com/sunscr*

16 Electronic Commerce

Electronic commerce is much more than doing business with personal computers on the Internet. Its about interacting with your customers electronically, via PCs, interactive television, electronic kiosks, personal digital assistants and increasingly sophisticated telephones – all connected uniformly to the so-called *information superhighway*.

In this chapter we look at:

❏ the *totality* of electronic commerce and the information superhighway;
❏ the opportunities offered by smart phones, the Web, kiosks and interactive TV;
❏ a case study – e-commerce companies serving the travel sector;
❏ commercial strategies for electronic commerce.

E-commerce opportunities

Although Internet commerce is well established, *electronic commerce* is really getting started. Companies such as Amazon.com (www.amazon.com) have built global businesses, and have also forced their major competitors such as Borders (www.borders.com) and Barnes and Noble (www.barnesandnoble.com) to respond. However, interactive digital television is still very much in its infancy, and mobile information through smart telephones is only on the horizon. In fact, many argue that electronic commerce in Europe and Japan will really take off only when interactive television is widely available – the argument being that whereas the United States is a *PC society*, Europe and Japan are *TV societies*.

Therefore, when establishing your electronic commerce business you need to keep in mind the wider picture of interactive television and

Internet-enabled telephones. You should also bear in mind that, having launched an e-commerce business, you might wish to introduce traditional channels such as paper catalogues and shops! Figure 16.1 attempts to capture this 'big picture'.

As an e-commerce case study we shall be looking at the travel industry. The radical changes under way in the travel industry serve to illustrate the limitless opportunities for e-commerce. Already in France, 75 per cent of holidays are booked using their Minitel service. Forester Research, the US business analyst, predicts that by 2002 more than 65 million holidays will be bought online, with £1 billion of business being done in the UK alone. In fact, the travel industry is a microcosm of the larger e-commerce industry:

❑ *Telephone services.* The motoring organizations have long supplied travel information over the telephone. Now, the cellular phone companies have the technology to locate a mobile phone within one metre (www.uswireless.com). The market for personal mobile information services (such as the location of the nearest hotel, restaurant or cash dispenser) will be enormous.

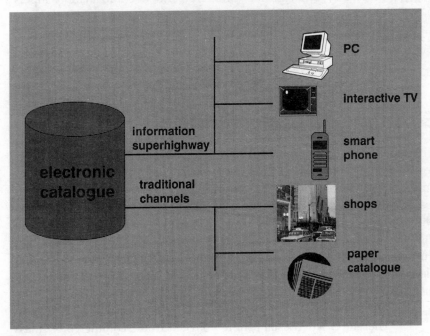

Figure 16.1 'Total' electronic commerce

❑ *Internet websites.* Travel company websites, such as that of British Airways (www.ba.com), are already selling tickets online. Already 57 of the 75 largest airlines, hotels and car-hire companies take online bookings. Likewise, *intermediaries,* such as Travelocity (www.travelocity.co.uk/), will search for bargains for you.

❑ *Electronic kiosks.* An increasing number of touch-screen information and ticketing kiosks are appearing in railway stations and in travel agents, such as Thomas Cook.

❑ *TV channels.* The Travel Channel on UK cable focuses on travel documentaries. Such television channels should be major beneficiaries of interactive digital television.

It is noticeable, as Bill Gates has frequently pointed out, that a pioneering company in one generation is succeeded by a new 'gorilla' in the succeeding technology generation (see Table 16.1).

Commercial strategies

So what are the commercial strategies for e-commerce? Even a cursory glance at the Internet shows a small number of money-making strategies being replicated from business sector to business sector. Here are a few examples:

❑ *Portals.* A 'portal' is the name given to a major gateway to the Internet: directories like Yahoo!, search engines like Infoseek, and online stores like Amazon.com. Being a portal allows you to sell, make money from banner adverts, and also expand into new markets.

Table 16.1 Traditional and electronic commerce companies

Sector	Sales Force	Retail	Direct (telephone)	Online (Internet)
Books	Britannica	WH Smith	–	Amazon.com
Travel	–	Thomas Cook	British Airways	Travelocity.com
Computers	IBM	Compaq	Dell	Dell.com
Directories	–	Yellow Pages	BT	Yahoo.com
Finance	–	Barclays	First Direct	E-Trade
Betting	Littlewoods	Ladbrokes	–	National Lottery

❑ *Online retail channels*. Most major retailers, like British Airways (www.ba.com), Freemans (www.freemans.com) and Tesco (www.tesco.co.uk), have established online sites to complement their traditional sales channels such as shops, catalogues and direct telephone sales. In many ways they are now forced to do so by customer expectations.

❑ *Customer care*. After-sales service and customer support is expensive, so companies are increasingly turning to the Internet for 24-hour customer support. One example is the courier DHL (www.dhl.com; see Figure 16.2), who allow you to track parcels via the Internet.

❑ *Intermediation*. The Internet is in many ways *the* ideal low-cost intermediary for bringing together buyers and sellers. One of the hottest companies in the area, Ebay (www.ebay.com), provides a marketplace for individuals to buy and sell.

❑ *Subscriber bases*. An increasingly popular way of making money (by boosting the valuation or market capitalization of your company) is to provide a free service and have subscribers register with you. Hotmail's Web-based e-mail service (www.hotmail.com), ICQ (www.icq.com) and Dixon's FreeServe (www.freeserve.co.uk) are classic examples.

❑ *Banner advertising*. Banner ads are another source of revenue for many popular sites. However, advertisers are increasingly looking for 'click-thru' or evidence that the viewer actually reacted to the advert rather than just paying for 'hits' to the hosting website.

Portals

Portals are the principal gateways (or on-ramps) to the Internet, and as such have major revenue potential for advertising, market capitalization and leverage into new businesses. They are all the big brand names: Yahoo!, AOL, Amazon.com etc. Portals are by definition *gorillas*. The main portal classes are:

❑ *Browsers*. Netscape Communication and Microsoft Internet Explorer are the first thing you see when accessing the Internet.

❑ *Service providers*. AOL (www.aol.com) is the dominant online service provider.

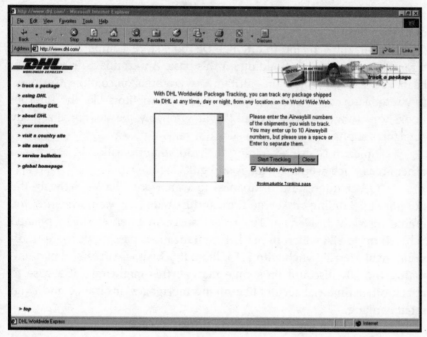

Figure 16.2

- ☐ *Directories.* Yahoo! is the most visited site on the Internet.
- ☐ *Search engines.* Major players are Yahoo!, Go/Infoseek, Altavista, and Excite etc.
- ☐ *Online stores.* Amazon.com and Charles Schwab (www.schwab.com) are the gorillas of the online book business and share trading.
- ☐ *Intermediaries.* EBay (www.ebay.com) is the major intermediary for buyers and sellers.
- ☐ *Free services.* Hotmail and FreeServe (www.freeserve.com) have major subscriber lists.

E-commerce gorilla

My favourite *gorilla* is Amazon.com. In many ways it is classic e-commerce: electronic catalogue, online ordering, 'customer care' messages that track your purchases, personalized welcome messages, notification of relevant new releases, searching for out-of-print books, etc. If you have a good idea for online customer service, Amazon.com have probably already thought of it. Wonderful!

Amazon's major traditional US bookstore competitors are left scrambling to catch up. Building on this base, Amazon is now setting up bespoke foreign sites in Britain (www.amazon.co.uk), Germany (www.amazon.co.de) and elsewhere. Local competitors like the Internet Bookshop (www.bookshop.co.uk) will probably be marginalized by Amazon's sophisticated site and slick delivery.

Amazon is also leveraging their dominant position in books into other areas, such as music, videos and gifts. Where next?

Other interesting companies to watch are Charles Schwab, the dominant US online brokerage firm, and E-Trade (www.e-trade.com), the online discount brokerage. The recent surge in Internet stocks pushed Schwab up to $26 billion in market capitalization, passing its more traditional rival Merrill Lynch with $25 billion. If Schwab is successful in dominating the UK discount brokerage market, this might give it a base to attack other financial sectors like online mortgages, insurance and even retail banking.

The lesson for other aspiring British e-commerce businesses is: if you want to survive, you have to be the US gorilla.

Online retail channels

Four trends are currently sweeping the retail industry:

- ❑ *Catalogues.* Most of the major retailers are introducing catalogues and home delivery, even if this is restricted to specific product ranges like flowers and wine.
- ❑ *Direct sales.* Many major retail companies have call centres taking orders by telephone for home delivery.
- ❑ *Websites.* Most of the progressive retailers have Internet sites where their products can be purchased online.
- ❑ *Interactive digital TV.* Retailers are scrambling to establish their own TV shopping channels, similar to QVC (www.qvc.com).

Image is everything. If you are a major retail brand, your customers now expect you to have a catalogue, a website with online ordering, and soon they will expect to see you on TV. If you don't have these prerequisites you will appear to be falling behind in the technology race.

Progressive retail companies with a strong presence in e-commerce include Gap (www.gap.com; see Figure 16.3), Freemans (www.freemans.com) and Tesco (www.tesco.co.uk).

These sites mostly follow the classic e-commerce retail organization. Customers browse the electronic catalogue, placing purchases in the electronic shopping basket/kart. When they have finished shopping they proceed to the checkout. If a returning customer, he or she 'signs on' by entering an e-mail address and password. The system then charges the person's credit card number and dispatches the goods to the registered address, both of which are securely stored in the system – all very simple and safe.

Customer support

Customer support includes giving online technical support for consumer products, such as computers; and giving customers information on their

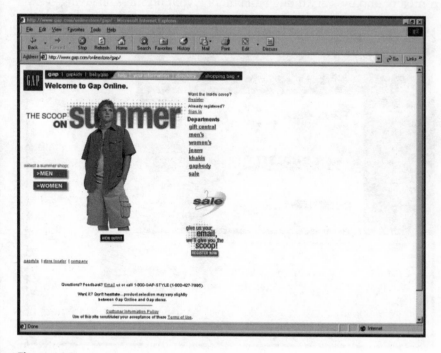

Figure 16.3

purchases, such as tracking delivery. Obviously, the information is available 24 hours a day and is cheap to provide. The sites are becoming increasingly more 'intelligent'.

Dell, which has a major market share in the direct and online sale of computers, has a highly effective site for providing customer service (see Figure 16.4).

My first experience of online customer care was from Amazon.com, who send you e-mail messages thanking you for your order and informing you when it is dispatched, and also notifying you of new publications that may be of interest. I certainly felt cared for! In contrast, I was shocked to receive a terse e-mail message from a UK book site saying 'order rejected'! Needless to say, I have parted company with them.

Free services

Traditionally, revenue growth has been the yardstick of any successful company, and the very thought of building your business on giving every-

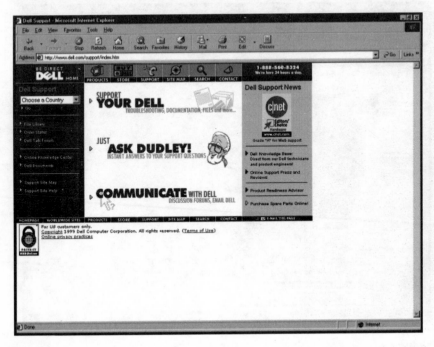

Figure 16.4

thing away free is anathema. E-commerce has changed the ground rules. You get customers to subscribe to a free service. And, because you have this potentially enormous audience for advertising and shopping, the valuation or market capitalization of your company soars.

Pioneers of this 'free service' e-commerce strategy are Hotmail, for its free e-mail service, ICQ, a chat service, and FreeServe, the free Internet service provider. Hotmail (see Figure 16.5) recruited 5 million customers and was sold on the back of this to Microsoft for $400 million. ICQ built its customer base to five million and was bought by AOL. Dixon's FreeServe has 450,000 users and a market capitalization of over £1 billion.

The Israeli company Mirabilis' ICQ is a revolutionary, user-friendly Internet tool that informs you who's online at any time and enables you to contact them at will. No longer will you search in vain for friends or associates on the Net. ICQ does the searching for you, alerting you in real time when they log on. The need to conduct a directory search each time you want to communicate with a specific person is eliminated. With ICQ, you can chat, send messages, files and URLs, play games, or just hang out with your fellow 'Netters' while still surfing the Net. It's simple.

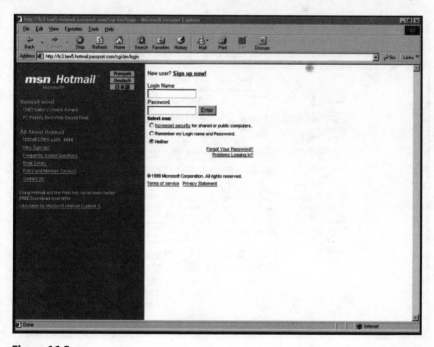

Figure 16.5

When you install ICQ, the program asks you to register at a server, which is connected to a broad network of servers spanning the Internet. At the time of registration, you receive a unique UIN (Universal Internet Number). In addition, ICQ gives you the option of entering personal information along with your UIN. This allows other ICQ users to recognize you when you log on.

Intermediaries

Finally, we look at eBay (www.ebay.com; see Figure 16.6), one of the hottest e-commerce companies currently around.

eBay is a person-to-person Internet trading community, in which users buy and sell personal items in an auction format. Product items in more than 1,000 categories include antiques, dolls, collectibles, coins, computers, stamps, memorabilia, trading cards and jewellery. Sellers pay a fee to have their items placed on the company's website, where potential

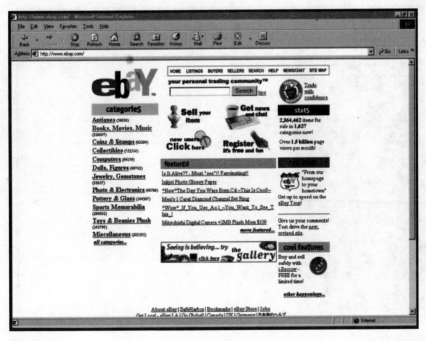

Figure 16.6

buyers browse and make bids on merchandise. If an item sells, eBay will charge the seller a percentage of the closing price.

Now let us look at the online travel industry and the various types of website open for business.

The (e)-travel industry

Holidays, flights, hotels, car hire, weather, maps – you name it, and someone has implemented a website for it. Hundreds of thousands of holidays can be booked online using a credit card. Websites search for the cheapest available scheduled flight and also allow you to book charter flights up to a few hours before departure. There is information on hundreds of thousands of hotels world-wide, including pictures of facilities, availability and discounts of up to 40 per cent. Sites find you the best deals for car hire at a specific location and provide customized maps and directions. Other sites provide five-day weather forecasts for any city worldwide, and live pictures of tourist destinations. Others provide daily health information, including recommending jabs, tracking outbreaks of epidemics, and listing government warnings. Short breaks, flights and hotels are now being auctioned at the last minute for remarkable knockdown prices. Travel companies encourage you to register for up-to-the-minute bargains notified by e-mail, and provide a free portable (Hotmail style) e-mail address to allow you to keep in touch while you are travelling.

Now let's take a tour (excuse the pun) of the travel industry by 'business strategy'.

Portals

Travel – even more so than financial services – is ideally suited to electronic commerce. The typical customer often knows more than the travel representative and is happy to pay online by credit card; and the tickets and receipts can simply be put in the post or picked up at the departure counter. The Internet provides a vast interactive library of information and resources. In fact, just about everybody engaged in the travel business realizes they need a website. Microsoft's Expedia (www.expedia.com), or its UK version (www.expedia.msn.co.uk), is the principal portal for the travel industry, encompassing flights, hotels and travel guides (see Figure 16.7).

```
                    www.100hot.com/travel
               (The world's most popular travel sites)

   1.  www.expedia.com
       This popular site searches for the cheapest scheduled fares available.

   2.  www.travelocity.com
       Searches for cheap flights using the travel agents' SABRE system.

   3.  www.city.net
       A comprehensive city travel guide and restaurant listing.

   4.  www.mapquest.com
       Creates customised maps of hundreds of cities world-wide.
```

Figure 16.7 www.100hot.com, listing the world's popular travel sites

Next, we look at the 'niche gorillas' that have established them-selves in each of the travel sectors.

Niche gorillas

Each business sector in the travel industry has spawned major specialist online companies. Leading niche gorillas in airline tickets are Travelocity (www.travelocity.com) who specialize in cheap scheduled flights, and the Co-op's Travelcare (www.co-op-travelcare.co.uk), building a niche in the charter flight market.

Once companies like Travelocity have established a global pres-ence, the trend is to then establish local UK sites.

Arguably, the hotel and car-hire sectors have yet to see a gorilla emerge. However, there are major players such as Hotels & Travel (www.hotelstravel.com), with 100,000 properties in 120 countries, the Hotel Guide (www.hotelguide.com), with 60,000, and Travlang (www.travlang.com), with 30,000. Naturally, the established companies are responding.

Online retail channels

All leading travel companies, airlines, hotel chains and car-hire firms have websites and accept e-mail reservations; for example, Thomas Cook (www.thomascook.co.uk), British Airways (www.ba.com), Holiday Inn (www.holiday-inn.com) and Hertz (www.hertz.com). Their addresses can be located using any search engine such as Yahoo!. Business companies, especially, take it for granted that they can make a world-wide reservation by telephone, by fax, through a website, via e-mail, and (in the future) through interactive television.

Subscriber bases

The travel companies have not been slow to jump on the 'subscription' bandwagon. To use many of these travel sites you must typically register first as a member, and receive a user name and password. This is now a standard e-commerce business strategy. Firstly, it allows the site to build a trading profile of its customers, which can be used to target advertising and offers. Secondly, each 'registered user' increases the company's market capitalization.

In the US, Expedia offers subscribers a fare tracker service that will inform them when it finds a flight to a specific destination at or below the maximum price the customer is prepared to pay.

Intermediaries

Whether it's bums-on-airline-seats or filling vacant hotel beds, online auctions are a major growth area. Obviously the Internet is in many ways a perfect medium for matching sellers and buyers world-wide. Two hotel-related intermediaries, www.lastminute.com and www.holiday-rentals.co.uk, auction luxury hotel beds and ski accommodation, respectively. Typically you are asked to register and make a bid, and the winners are notified the next day and asked to pay by credit card. Virgin and Lufthansa, and many of the airlines, auction their seats.

Customer care

This section is rather a catchall, listing many of the other online, travel-related ideas people have had to make money:

- ❏ *Online guides.* A whole library of online guides exist, from Rough Guides' description of 4,000 destinations (www.roughguides.com/travel), to Condé Nast's interactive holiday finder (www.epi.curious.com).
- ❏ *Online video.* Major tourist destinations are starting to provide online, real-time video feeds of their popular vistas, as a tourist lure.

❑ *Maps*. Never again will you need to arrive disoriented at your destination. A number of sites, such as QuickAID (www.quickaid.com) and Tripquest (www.tripquest.com), print out bespoke maps showing you how to get between two points. One can also locate subway maps (metro.ratp.fr:10001/bin/cities/english), bank teller machines (www.visa.com/atm), road signs (www.travlang.com/signs), and even speed-traps (www.speedtrap.com/speedtrap).

❑ *The weather*. A number of sites, such as CNN (www.cnn.com), will give you four-day weather forecasts covering 6,100 cities worldwide, while others, such as Complete Skier (www.complete-skier.com), cover the ski resorts.

❑ *Exchange rates*. Yes, someone – O&A Converter (www.oanda.com/converter/classic) – has even thought of an online converter for any two foreign currencies. It produces a conversion table and takes account of the 2% commission charges.

After this review of the spectrum of e-commerce business ideas for the travel industry, all you need do now is find a quiet backwater which e-commerce has yet to reach and transmute one of the business strategies.

Sources of help

Collin, S (1998) *Doing Business on the Internet,* Kogan Page, London

E-Trade. *The online discount brokerage, www.e-trade.com*

Expedia. *Microsoft's travel industry portal, www.expedia.com*

Kennedy, A (1998) *Rough Guide to the Internet,* Rough Guides Ltd. London

Lawrence, E et al (1998) *Internet Commerce – digital models for business,* John Wiley & Sons, Australia

TradeUK. *The online directory of UK companies, www.tradeuk.com*

Travelocity. *The travel intermediary specialising in discount scheduled flights, www.travelocity.com*

Part 4

Financial
Management
for
Small Business

Part 4

Financial
Management
for
Small Business

17 Raising Money

How Hotmail – the free Web-based e-mail service sold to Microsoft for $400 million – raised its first money is legendary! As the story goes, its founders went to a venture capital firm for investment in a different idea, but the VC was unconvinced of the viability. As they were leaving, the VC happened to ask if they had any other ideas. They mentioned Hotmail, and the VC bit. And as we say, 'the rest is history'!

This chapter focuses on finding money for your technology-based start-up and small firm. Most books (and most people's concept) on starting a business centre on the *venture-capital* model. In this model you identify an opportunity in a large and growing market, hire a complete team of experienced and successful managers, raise a million dollars of venture capital, and spend it to accelerate your business development.

However, VC investors rarely provide money to brand-new companies at the 'idea' stage. The alternative is the *low-risk* model. You raise a small amount of money from friends, family or other entrepreneurs, and slowly expand your business, learning management skills as you go. In fact, the optimum approach is to use the low-risk model to start your company, then, once your business is established, use venture capital to accelerate growth. This also ensures that you retain a much bigger share of your company.

In this chapter we look at:

❑ the various types and sources of funds – grants, debt, and equity;
❑ getting money from friends and family – so called *love money*;
❑ grants from local, national and European government organizations;
❑ getting money from clearing banks and merchant banks;

❏ how the venture capital industry works, so you know when to approach them;

❏ various other sources such as hire purchase, leasing and factors.

Below we look at a 'roadmap' for raising money. A good introduction is Kate Lister and Tom Harnish's *Finding Money: The Small Business Guide to Financing*.

Sources of funding

Before you raise any money you obviously need to quantify how you will spend it, how much money you need and for how long, and what security, if any, you can offer for the money. Running out of money and asking for more is a real no-no! Your business plan and cash flow forecasts will help identify how much, and the planned usage will help identify appropriate funding sources. In fact, there is rarely a shortage of money; what is missing are good, small business propositions from entrepreneurs.

What you spend it on

Your business needs two types of funds, called fixed and working capital:

❏ *Fixed capital* is money to fund items the business will keep for a long period, such as buildings, equipment and vehicles.

❏ *Working capital* is money to fund day-to-day operations, such as renting premises and communications links, purchase of raw materials, payment of staff, running costs and other overheads.

Types of money

Usage of the funds will typically dictate the financing source. Broadly, there are three types of money a start-up can access:

❏ *Grants* – money that does not have to be repaid, given by your family, a public body, charity or individual for some worthy objective.

❏ *Debt* – money borrowed from a financial institution or individual that is repayable in the future, during which time interest is paid on the loan. Debt obviously covers loans and overdrafts, but might also include hire purchase and leasing that must also be repaid.

❏ *Equity* – money put in and left by investors in return for shares in the company. Investors can sell their shares, and will also expect to be paid a small proportion of any profits (called a dividend).

Where it comes from

Financing sources, reviewed below, fall into the following categories:

❏ *Founder, family, friends.* So-called love money, covering funds from the founders, family and friends (other private investors are called *business angels*). When raising money, you may have little in ready cash, but you may have valuable assets such as a house, or family who can afford to bankroll you.

❏ *Business partners.* Businesses, especially *early adopters* of technology, frequently fund developments in start-ups so as to get new technology for competitive advantage.

❏ *Government.* Encouraging high-tech start-ups is a government priority at local, regional, national and European levels. Thus, numerous grants and loans are available from government and non-profit organizations. A comprehensive list of sources is given in Part 7.

❏ *Banks.* For most of us, raising money is synonymous with visiting the bank manager. This might be a clearing bank for a term loan or overdraft, or an investment bank for help in raising venture capital. However, many US entrepreneurs simply use their credit cards.

❏ *Venture capital.* A broad definition 'is any form of high-risk investing, where the investor receives shares in the company'. This covers investments by specialist venture capital firms and funds (VCs), company investments (corporate investors), large investment banks (merchant banks), small, specialist investment banks (boutiques), and private individuals ('angels').

❏ *Others.* Various other financial organizations provide investment. This spans credit unions, local exchange trading systems (called LETS), leasing companies, hire purchase and factors; all covered below.

And, if you are really desperate, you can always try contacting the Mafia (I'm only joking!).

Interestingly, by far the largest source of funding for start-ups (70–75 per cent) is *founder, family and friends*.

Founder, family and friends

Surveys of successful start-ups in Britain and the United States show that most are funded by love money, and grown by profits. A survey by Coopers & Lybrand (see *Finding Money* by Lister and Harnish; and Table 17.1) found that 71 per cent of businesses in the USA launched with love money. The survey also reveals that, of successful US companies, 25 per cent started with less than $5,000, and 50 per cent with less than $50,000.

Love money is appropriate for certain types of start-up but not for others. We can divide them into two categories:

❑ *Soft starts* are high-tech businesses, such as consultancies, software and media companies, requiring minimal product development and modest investment. Lead times are short, front-end costs are low, and revenue flows quickly. Here, the primary source is love money.

❑ *Hard starts* are high-tech businesses, such as biotechnology and electronics, requiring a large investment over a long period to get going. Here, term loans and venture capital are a necessity.

Software and Internet start-ups are typical soft starts following the low-risk, organic-growth strategy. A typical software start-up generates funds by consulting and contracting. When a potentially successful product is identified, the company either funds development from its own resources or finds a so-called early adopter client to fund the product. Likewise, an Internet start-up registers its domain name, builds its website and then

Table 17.1 Start-up funding (source: Lister and Harnish, *Finding Money*)

Founder, Family, Friends	71%
Investors (eg Angels)	13%
Bank Loans	8%
Alliances (eg business partners)	8%

hosts the site at a commercial Internet service provider (ISP). Once the service is generating revenue, the Internet start-up can establish a 'real' office and install its own Internet server.

Business partnerships

A business partnership with a major company is another source of 'free money'. It is also a stamp of approval on both your product and your company. Three sources are:

❑ *Early adopter client*. Customers are frequently keen to get new technology to obtain competitive advantage. They will often pay you to develop a bespoke system, which you can later turn into a general product, provided you have protected your intellectual property.

❑ *Joint venture client*. Customers can be encouraged to 'bank-roll' your development of a new product by offering them royalties on future sales or some other joint venture arrangement.

❑ *Licensing*. Many large companies see start-ups as a source of new and innovative products that they can sell under their own label. These companies prefer to buy or license a 'packaged' product.

Government and charities

Yet another good source of 'free money' are government agencies, and, to a lesser extent, charities. Local authorities, the UK and Irish governments, and the European Commission have a vast range of grants, adding up to £1–2 billion a year. Before you get too excited, these funds are often targeted at rural and depressed areas that may be totally inappropriate for your business.

As a starting point for advice on available government grants, try the following: Business Links (UK), Enterprise Ireland (Irish Republic), or the European Commission (EU) – the contact details are in Part 7.

The principal sources of grants, *soft* loans and guarantees are:

❑ *Local agencies*. Local authorities and local enterprise agencies have business advice units that often provide small grants, especially for establishing business premises.

❑ *Regional agencies*. Organizations like Scottish Enterprise, the Welsh

Development Agency and the Rural Development Commission provide grants to promote business in specific areas.

❏ *UK government.* The government, through the Business Links (www.businesslink.co.uk) and the Department of Trade and Industry (www.dti.gov.uk), offer a range of grants.

❏ *Irish government.* The Irish Republic is particularly well organized to help start-ups. Enterprise Ireland (www.enterprise-ireland. com/el) and Industrial Development Agency (www.idaireland. com) are good sources of help and advice.

❏ *European Commission.* The Commission (www.europa.eu.int) provides a number of generous grants applicable to high-tech start-ups.

❏ *Charities.* Grants are also available from a number of charities and trusts, such as The Prince's Youth Business Trust, especially to help young people and the unemployed.

There are so many different agencies and grants – the collective noun must be *'a confusion of ...'* – that we can merely scratch the surface here. The addresses, telephone numbers and websites of the various agencies are listed in Part 7.

Local agencies

The principal local sources of funding are local authorities and local enterprise agencies:

❏ *UK local authorities.* Most authorities (www.open.gov.uk), especially those in disadvantaged areas, provide finance and advice for business start-ups, and premises at subsidised rents.

❏ *UK local enterprise agencies.* Over 400 local enterprise agencies and trusts exist across the UK to help new businesses, including the financing of running costs.

❏ *Irish county enterprise boards* (CEBs). City and county enterprise boards and APCs (area partnership companies) offer a range of grants, including for feasibility studies.

UK regional agencies

At the regional level in the UK, the principal contact points for funding are the Business Links in England, and the regional enterprise boards in

Wales, Scotland and Northern Ireland. In addition, funds are available from the Crafts Council, the Tourist Boards, and the Rural Development Commission (RDC):

❑ *Business Links*. These are intended as 'one-stop-shops' for advice and finance for small businesses (www.businesslink.co.uk; see Figure 17.1).

❑ *Development agencies*. The Welsh Development Agency, Scottish Enterprise and the North Ireland Local Enterprise Development Unit (LEDU) provide a range of grants, low-interest loans, and equity funds.

UK government

Below are listed a few of the schemes operated by the UK Department of Trade and Industry (www.dti.gov.uk; see Figure 17.2):

❑ *Small Firms Merit Award for Research and Technology* (SMART). This is an annual competition open to small businesses with fewer than

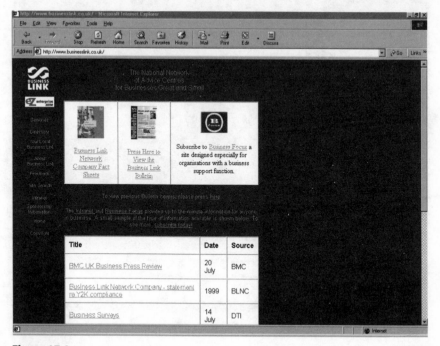

Figure 17.1

50 staff for funding technology-based products. An initial grant of up to £45,000 is followed by second-stage funding up to £60,000.

☐ *Support for Products Under Research* (SPUR). This scheme targets high-tech companies with up to 250 staff, providing a fixed grant of 30 per cent of eligible development costs, up to £150,000.

☐ *Small Firms Loan Guarantee Scheme* (SFLGS). This provides banks and other financial institutions with loan guarantees of 70–85 per cent, up to £250,000.

☐ *Enterprise Investment Scheme* (EIS). This provides income tax relief and investment benefits up to £1 million per company per year, with a minimum holding period of five years, in UK unquoted trading companies.

☐ *Overseas Trade Services* (OTS). This provides a wide range of financial assistance and advice to small firms in entering overseas markets.

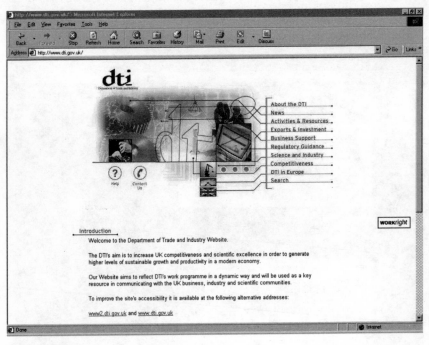

Figure 17.2

Irish government

The Irish Republic has a world-class organization for supporting entrepreneurship and start-ups. Information on government help for start-ups is available from Enterprise Ireland (www.enterprise-ireland.com/el; see Figure 17.3). Support is provided by the county enterprise boards and also by the Industrial Development Agency (www.idaireland.com) through its Small Business Programme and Enterprise Development Programme.

☐ *ACT Enterprise Fund*. ACT and Forbairt jointly provide funds of between £100,000 and £250,000 for early-stage SMEs.

☐ *Bank of Ireland Entrepreneurs Fund*. BoI have a £10 million early-stage fund investing between £100,000 and £500,000.

☐ *Business Expansion Scheme* (BES). This is a form of venture capital intended to help small businesses obtain additional capital.

☐ *Business Innovation Centres* (BICs). These are backed by the Irish government and European Union, providing early-stage venture capital for start-ups.

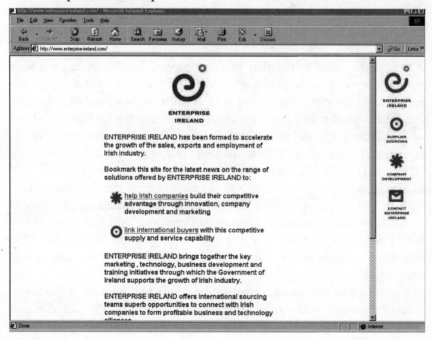

Figure 17.3

- ❑ *County Enterprise Boards.* From a fund of £12 million, CEBs provide grants for preparing business plans (up to £5,000) and covering start-up costs (up to £50,000).
- ❑ *Enterprise Development Programme.* This scheme encourages senior managers to join with others to launch start-ups.
- ❑ *Irish Science & Technology Agency* (EOLAS). This agency funds research and development of science and technology in companies and universities, both to develop new products and to raise expertise.
- ❑ *Revenue Commissioners.* The Seed Capital scheme repays income tax to people leaving employment to start their own businesses.
- ❑ *Small Business Programme.* This provides grants of up to £425,000 for start-ups covering R&D, employment and equipment grants, and loan guarantees.
- ❑ *Udaras na Gaeltachta* and *Shannon Development.* Covering their respective counties, they provide grants for feasibility studies (up to £5,000), R&D (up to £100,000), employing skilled workers (£3,000–9,000), capital grants and even interest subsidies.

European Commission

It is probably true to say that the European Commission has a pot of money for every new business need. When hunting for money, two people are important: firstly, the person in Brussels who looks after the pot, and secondly, the government person in London or Dublin, whose job it is to help you get the money. Once you find them they are incredibly helpful (well, it isn't their money). Just ring the DTI Information Service (tel 020 7215 5000) in the UK or the Irish Enterprise Link (tel 1850 35 33 33) and say you want help to get a grant from the European Commission. An excellent booklet called *Funding from the European Union* is available from the London Chamber of Commerce and Industry (tel 020 7489 1992). And if you like a real challenge, you can browse the CEC websites – www.europa.eu.int and www.cordis.lu – both are pretty impenetrable.

Another interesting organization funded by the CEC is the European Community Business and Innovation Centres (EC-BIC). EC-BIC is a network of CEC-funded agencies that provide comprehensive help, including funding to new businesses.

Charities

A number of charities provide support for start-ups, especially in deprived areas:

❑ *UK Prince's Youth Business Trust* (PYBT). Each year the PYBT spends £2.5 million on grants and £6 million on loans to help around 3,000 young people to launch start-ups.
❑ *UK National Lottery*. 'It could be you' with the right business proposition.
❑ *Irish Liffey Trust*. This gives advice on all aspects of launching a business, what grants are available, and also provides office space.
❑ *Irish Bolton Trust*. This provides incubator facilities for start-ups.

Banks

When Willie Sutton, the infamous US bank robber, was asked why he robbed banks, he is reputed to have replied: 'Because that's where the money is'. Like Willie, when we need a loan, the first thing we think of is a visit to the bank manager. There are four main sources of debt funding from banks:

❑ *Credit cards*. In the USA a surprising number of entrepreneurs use their credit cards for access to 'instant loans'. Maybe this will catch on in the UK.
❑ *Clearing banks*. These principally provide overdrafts and short- to medium-term loans, at both fixed and variable rates of interest.
❑ *Merchant banks*. These are intermediaries organizing medium- to long-term loans and advising on the terms and price of share issues. The loans are usually for larger amounts of money than provided by the clearing banks. Small merchant banks ('boutiques') put together loan and venture capital deals; whereas large investment banks prefer to handle 'going public' and management buyouts (MBOs) where the commissions are larger.
❑ *Finance houses*. These also provide loans as well as various forms of instalment credit ranging from hire purchase to leasing.

Clearing banks

Banks make their profits by 'renting' money to individuals and companies. It is a highly competitive business, so it pays to shop around for the best deal. We distinguish here between four types of bank loan:

❑ *Credit card overdraft*. Each time you use your credit card you are effectively taking out a simple loan. If you pay the account on time, it is free. Otherwise, you pay a variable annual rate of return (APR) of 14–21 per cent, tied to bank base rate.

❑ *Current account overdraft*. Your bank will arrange an overdraft facility for a given period, and up to a specific amount. For this, it charges a fee, plus interest on the amount actually borrowed based on APR.

❑ *Consumer loans*. These cover all short-term personal loans, either unsecured or covered by second mortgages, etc. Rates are negotiable and can be fixed or variable depending on how you believe the Bank of England will set bank base rates over the coming period.

❑ *Commercial loans*. Business loans are short- to medium-term, usually secured with liens on company and personal assets. Your home will often be taken as additional collateral on such loans.

Start by talking to your local bank manager, but remember to shop around. Table 17.2 illustrates typical charges on a 'loan' of £1,000 for a year.

Merchant banks

Merchant banks organize medium- to long-term loans and advise on share issues. The fees charged are based on a percentage of the amount raised;

Table 17.2 Comparison of charges on £1,000 loan

Loan	Fees	Interest Rate	Interest	Total Charges
Credit Card (full payment)	–	–	–	£0
Credit Card Overdraft	–	14%–21%	£200	£200
Bank Overdraft	£85	10%	£100	£185
Fixed Rate Loan	1%–2% of loan	11%	£110	£125
Variable Rate Loan	1%–2% of loan	7%BBR + 3%pt	£100	£115

typically 2–5 per cent for debt and 3–10 per cent for equity. They will normally also ask you for a retainer of £500–1,000, which should be partially refundable if you are unsuccessful. Your accountant and lawyer will also help you find money, and usually charge their hourly rate.

Loan evaluation

So, how do bankers work out your credit risk? For decades, bankers have evaluated loan requests informally, on what is called the *five C's of credit*. Recently, they have used more scientific methods, called *credit scoring*:

❑ *The five C's of credit.* The informal credit checks are: *character* – will you pay?; *capacity* – can you pay?; *collateral* – what if you do not pay?; *capital* – how much do you personally have at risk?; and *conditions* – what might happen to you, your company, the economy, to stop you paying?

❑ *Credit scoring.* Originally developed as a scientific method for 'scoring' the risk of consumer credit, credit scoring is increasingly being used for commercial loan risk for amounts under £150,000. Basically, the bank assesses your business and personal information, adding or subtracting points for each factor, to give an overall credit score.

❑ *Credit rating agencies.* Specialist credit reporting agencies, such as Experian (www.experian.com) and Equifax (www.equifax.co.uk), can usually provide an assessment on your creditworthiness.

Venture capital

Next we look at venture capital, known colloquially as *vulture capital*. Venture capital, to quote the British Venture Capital Association (www.bvca.co.uk; see Figure 17.4), 'provides long-term, committed, risk sharing equity capital, to help unquoted companies grow and compete'.

Like most industries, venture capitalists (VCs) have their own set of jargon, which any aspiring entrepreneur needs to know. In terms of the amount of funding, the lexicon contains the following:

❑ *Sweat equity.* Lawyers, accountants and other professionals will often work for free for a start-up in return for handling their business, if successful, or for a small equity stake. Hence the term

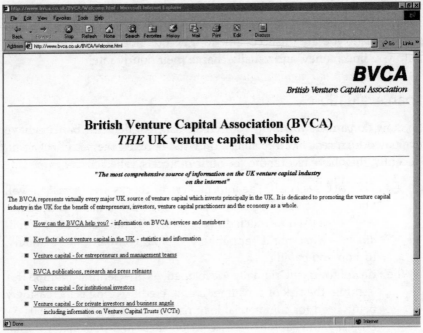

Figure 17.4

'sweat (for) equity'. This is common in the US but rare in the UK and Ireland.

☐ *Pre-seed funding.* This is the earliest stage of funding (typically less than £10,000). It allows an entrepreneur to explore an idea and prepare a business plan. Some universities provide pre-seed funds to their students.

☐ *Seed funding.* This early-stage funding (£10,000–100,000) allows the entrepreneur to prepare a prototype of the product, and assemble a management team. Seed investors expect to provide business advice and possibly even office facilities.

☐ *Start-up funding.* This entails the commitment of significant funds (£100,000–1,000,000) so the business can complete product development and start initial marketing. Soft starts need to demonstrate a product with a competitive advantage. Hard-start companies, like biotech, need to show impressive research. Start-up investors usually provide help in recruiting key personnel and customers for the business.

❏ *Development funding.* This is financing provided to companies that have completed product development and are commencing operation and sales. Investors will closely monitor the cash flows and head count, against sales revenues.

❏ *Mezzanine funding.* This refers to later-stage financing that typically combines debt and equity, and is typically used just prior to an IPO.

❏ *Expansion funding.* This is capital provided for the growth and expansion of an established business. Investors expect to monitor financial performance but do not expect to be actively involved in solving problems.

❏ M&A, MBO, MBI. These abbreviations describe late-stage financing covering *mergers and acquisitions* (M&A) of additional companies, *management buy-outs* (MBO) of a product line or business, and external *management buy-ins* (MBI) into a business.

When negotiating with you, the three key VC considerations are:

1. What is the value of your business?
2. What will be the *rate of return* of the investment?
3. What is the so-called *exit strategy*?

Valuing your business

The value of your business before the investment is called the *pre-money*, and the value after is called the *post-money*. Your pre-money and post-money valuations determine how much equity you have to give up to outside investors (this is the motivation for launching your business by the low-risk model and then, when established, using venture capital to accelerate growth). For example, if the pre-money value of your business is £4 million and outside investors are injecting £1 million, then they will expect around 20 per cent of the equity:

$$\frac{\text{£1 million}}{\text{£4 million} + \text{£1 million}} = \frac{1}{5} = 20\%$$

In fact, most venture capitalists calculate the post-money value of your business at the projected exit date, and then discount that figure back to the present. Using this figure they then calculate the equity percentage they require for the proposed investment.

There are a variety of methods for calculating the value of your company:

❑ *Company comparisons*. It can be compared with similar companies quoted on a stock market, or purchased through a recent trade sale.
❑ *Discounted cash-flow method*. This uses valuations based on discounting future cash flow projects, using various formulas such as the *capital asset pricing model*.
❑ *Registered subscribers*. For Internet companies, like Yahoo! and Hotmail, a value (eg $25–250) is given for each registered subscriber, giving 'fantasy' valuation, some would say.

For a complete discussion of valuing your company, refer to Lipman's *Financing Your Business With Venture Capital*.

Internal rate of return (IRR)

The IRR is central to the VC's decision on whether to invest, because it is the estimated return on the investment (see Table 17.3). IRR takes account of the risk, length of time the money is tied up, even the potential for a trade sale or float. VCs are typically looking for IRRs of 50 per cent per annum. On face value this might look greedy. However, for every ten businesses that a VC invests in, one might be a major success (returning 10 times the investment), two or three might return 30–50 per cent, another two or three might return 10–30 per cent, and one or two might be a total loss.

For a description of how to calculate the IRR for an investment

Table 17.3 Internal rate of return (rule of thumb)

Stages of venture capital	IRR %
Seed	80–100
Start-up	60–80
Development	50–60
Expansion	40–50
Mezzanine	30–40
M&A, MBO, MBI	20–30

(and programs to help you), type 'Internal Rate of Return IRR' into an Internet search engine.

Exit strategies

The exit strategy defines how and after what length of time the investors take their profits. VCs typically look to exit in three to five years, in various ways:

- ❏ *trade sale* – selling your business to another company or individual;
- ❏ *going public* – obtaining a public quote on a stock exchange, such as NASDAQ, AIM or EASDAQ;
- ❏ *repurchase* – having your company buy back the VCs investment;
- ❏ *refinancing* – having another company (possibly a longer-term investment institution) purchase the interests of the VC.

Sources of venture capital

The principal sources of venture capital are:

- ❏ *Business angels.* Private individuals who typically commit between £10,000 and £100,000 of their own money on an investment. The BVCA (www.bvca.co.uk) and the leading banks publish lists of UK business angels.
- ❏ *Corporate investors.* Companies that invest in an external business both to make money and increasingly to track the technology of the start-up. This form of investment is popular with large companies like Microsoft, Reuters and WPP, who have the option of importing the technology or buying the company if it is successful.
- ❏ *Venture capital firms.* These firms manage funds or investment trusts, and raise their capital from pension funds, insurance companies, banks, corporate investors and private individuals. Some VCs are independent, others are subsidiaries of larger financial institutions. The majority of UK venture capital firms prefer established companies seeking capital above £1,000,000. As a guide, the average VC deal size in 1996 was £2.3 million.

For a complete list of UK venture capital firms and also business angels, contact the British Venture Capital Association.

Commercial groups

Many other specialist financial institutions provide money to start-ups:

☐ *Trade credit*. Supplier companies will often advance you 'trade credit' once you have established creditworthiness.

☐ *Hire purchase companies*. HP is used to spread payments on most types of business assets, especially equipment. On completion of payments you own the asset.

☐ *Leasing companies*. With leasing you rent the asset from the lessor, who will probably also maintain it. This is a popular way to get vehicles, plant and even computer equipment without paying the full cost up front. However, the asset returns to the lessor on completion. Contact the Finance and Leasing Association (tel 020 7491 2783).

☐ *Factors*. The factoring company takes on responsibility for your invoices, both issuing and collecting, and advances money to you against these invoices. Contact the Association of British Factors and Discounters (tel 020 7930 9112).

☐ *Discount houses*. These are specialist financial institutions providing a 'bill of exchange' facility to smooth your cash flow. Once you have delivered goods to a customer, a Bill is drawn up whereby, for a fee paid to the discount house, you receive payment immediately, and the customer agrees to meet payment at a specific date in the future.

And at the 'poor end' of the market:

☐ *Credit unions*. These provide cheap and convenient alternatives to banks and building societies for people on low incomes. Contact the National Federation of Credit Unions (tel 0191 257 2219).

☐ *Local exchange trading systems*. LETS allow people to exchange skills or services, at an agreed hourly rate without money changing hands. Contact Letslink (tel 01985 217871).

Finally, if you have valuable assets and wish to borrow against them, you can always head for a pawnbroker. The proprietor will lend you a small amount of money based on the second-hand value of your treasured asset. You can then redeem it later, paying interest on the amount borrowed. Not recommended.

Sources of help

Arundale, K (1996) *A Guide to Venture Capital,* British Venture Capital Association, London

Barrow, C (1997) *Complete Small Business Guide – sources of information for new and small businesses,* BBC Books, London

British Venture Capital Association (BVCA). Essex house, 12–13 Essex Street, London, WC2R 3AA, tel: 020 7240 3846, fax: 020 7240 3849, www.bvca.co.uk

Business Angels – now known as 'Lenta Ventures'. National Business Network, 4 Snow Hill, London, EC1A 2BS, tel: 020 7236 3000, fax: 020 7329 0226, email: sbda@lenta.demon.co.uk

Development Agencies and Boards. Welsh Development Agency, Principality House, The Friary, Cardiff, CF10 3FE, tel: 01686 626 965, *www.wda.co.uk* ; Scottish Enterprise 120 Bothwell Street, Glasgow, G2 7JP, tel: 0141 248 2700, fax: 0141 221 3217, *www.scotent.co.uk* ; Northern Ireland Local Enterprise Development Unit, LEDU House, Upper Galwally, Belfast, Northern Ireland, BT8 6TB, tel: 02890 491 031 www.ednet.ledu-ni.gov.uk/

European Business Centre Network. Rue D'Arlon 80, 1040 Brussels, Belgium, tel: 00 322 2959421, fax: 00 322 2962572

European Commission (CEC). CEC funding programmes, www.europa.eu.int or www.cordis.lu

European Venture Capital Association. *www.evca.com*

Financing your Business. Irish Department of Enterprise, Trade and Employment, Davitt House, Adelaide Road, Dublin 2, tel: 01 661 4444

Funding from the European Union. Available from the London Chamber of Commerce and Industry, tel: 020 7489 1992

Garage.com *www.garage.com*

Irish Republic Business Information Centre. Central Library, Ilac Centre, Henry Street, Dublin 1, tel: 011 873 3996, fax: 011 872 1451

Irish Republic Industrial Development Agency (IDA). Regional offices Co. Kerry: 57 High Street, Killarney, Co. Kerry, tel: 0164 34133, fax: 0164 34135, *www.idaireland.com*

Lipman, F (1998) *Financing your business with Venture Capital,* Prima Publishing, Rocklin, CA

Lister, K and Harnish, T (1995) *Finding Money – the small business guide to financing,* John Wiley & Sons, New York

Red Herring magazine. Principal venture capital magazine. www.herring.com

18 Financial Management

In 1980, when Microsoft hired its first professional book-keeper, the latter was appalled that a company approaching $8 million dollars in annual revenue was keeping track of its money in hand-written ledgers. Microsoft was forced to computerize its book-keeping, though it used only a small Radio Shack TRS-80 to do the job. There is a lesson in there somewhere.

Obviously, your business, and every other, needs to keep records of each business transaction in order to manage the finances. Properly maintained books give you a current, accurate picture of your finances, but can also be used for estimating future sales and liabilities. This is important for a number of reasons: (i) managing your company's finances, (ii) raising a loan from a bank or investor, (iii) satisfying the Inland Revenue that your tax liability and national insurance have been calculated correctly, and (iv) managing your VAT returns for Customs & Excise.

In this chapter we look at:

- ❑ the important records such as cash books and ledgers;
- ❑ the accounts: the balance sheet, P&L account and cash flow;
- ❑ the business documents needed: invoices, receipt book, etc;
- ❑ getting your accounts audited.

First we shall look at the business records and statements you need to deploy.

Business records

Figure 18.1 illustrates the range of records and statements that a typical company uses. They are reviewed below, including, for completeness, the basic ones such as cheque book and bank statements.

Banking

Banking statements and records cover all business payments and receipts of cheques and cash, referred to as cash transactions. This includes:

❑ *Cheque book.* Most payments by small businesses to suppliers are still usually made by cheques similar to those for a personal account, but typically counter-signed by two directors. Other forms of payment documents are 'bankers draft', 'bill of exchange' and (with the rise of online banking) 'direct payment'.

❑ *Paying-in book.* The paying-in book supplied by your bank is used to record all cheques and cash paid into your business bank

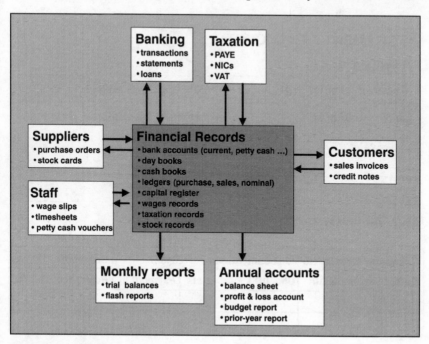

Figure 18.1 Financial statements

accounts. Obviously it is essential to keep this up to date so that you can reconcile your accounts.

❏ *Bank statements.* The statements from your bank detail all payment and receipt transactions through an account (Figure 18.2). You can get the bank to send statements monthly or weekly. Ideally, you will use online banking (see Chapter 21) and have 24-hour instant access. Bank statements are typically terse; Chapter 20 looks at deciphering the entries.

❏ *Cash book* – the record of all cheque and cash payment and receipt transactions (Figure 18.3). Traditionally these transactions were recorded on an A3 sheet, with the left part recording payments (*payments out*) and the right part recording receipts (*payments in*).

❏ *Petty cash book and vouchers.* The petty cash book records all small payments in notes and coins which may be regarded as sundry or incidental expenses (Figure 18.4). Petty cash payments can be recorded in a variety of ways: filling in a 'voucher' and placing it in the cash box each time a sum is spent, or using a 'sheet of paper' or 'petty cash book' to record payments.

STATEMENT OF ACCOUNT
NewCo Ltd

Account number	01234567		Sort code	01 23 45	
Date	**Details**		**Payment**	**Receipts**	**Balance**

Figure 18.2 Bank statement

Company NewCo Ltd		Account number 01234567				Sort code 01 23 45	
Date	Payments out	Chq. no.	Total	Date	Payment In	Reference	Total

Figure 18.3 Cash book

Cash received	Date	Details	Receipt number	Total	Postage	Phone	Travel	Stationery
£				£	£	£	£	£
100.00	1 April	Stamps		20.00	20.00			
	2 April	Telephone card		10.00		10.00		
	3 April	Taxi		5.00			5.00	
				35.00				
		Balance		65.00				
100.00				100.00				

Figure 18.4 Petty cash book

Customers ('Sales')

The primary sales documents are invoices, advice and delivery notes, and the receipt book:

❑ *Sales invoice.* This document records a sale to a customer. As shown to the right of Figure 18.5, the invoice lists the company name, invoice number, date, VAT registration number, the quantity, details, and cost.

❑ *Advice note.* Broadly similar to the invoice, this advises the customer of the delivery details.

INVOICE
NewCo Ltd.

VAT REG NO
123-4567-89

Date _____
Invoice No. ABC/123/99

Quantity	Details	£	£

Figure 18.5 Invoice

```
┌─────────────────────────────────────────────────┐
│                                                   │
│   RECEIVED WITH THANKS        Date _____      │
│                                                   │
│   From _____                   │
│                                                   │
│   Cash                              _____        │
│   Cheque                            _____        │
│   Discount                          _____        │
│   Total                             _____        │
│                                                   │
│   Signed _____                         │
│   For    NewCo Ltd.                               │
│                                                   │
└─────────────────────────────────────────────────┘
```

Figure 18.6 Receipt

- ☐ *Delivery note.* This document, similar to a sales invoice, keeps a record of receipt of the goods and is signed by the customer.
- ☐ *Receipt book.* This is a memorandum book, usually in duplicate or triplicate, used to provide a record of the money (cash or cheques) received for both the customer and supplier (Figure 18.6).
- ☐ *Sales day book.* This is the initial record of every sales transaction occurring in the business.

Suppliers ('Purchases')

The primary purchase documents are purchase orders and stock records:

- ☐ *Purchase order.* This document records a purchase from a supplier. It may simply be a copy of the supplier's sales invoice, or could be a separate purchase invoice.
- ☐ *Stock records and cards.* These show the receipts, issues and the amount 'in stock' of all stock items. A stock card records the particulars of a specific item.
- ☐ *Internal and store requisition.* This records a request to supply goods and services internally within a company, authorized by an agreed procedure.
- ☐ *Purchase day book.* This is the initial record of every purchase transaction occurring in the business.

Staff data

Most high-tech companies pay staff 'salaries' into bank accounts, with staff only using timesheets to allocate their time to specific projects or clients. Three records are essential here:

❑ *Payroll sheet*. The traditional way of recording employment details is by using a 'payroll sheet' or 'wages book' listing hours worked, gross pay, deductions, net pay and the employer's National Insurance payments.
❑ *Timesheets*. These record when, and for how many hours, an employee worked on a project or for a particular client.
❑ *Expense claim*. This records the money spent by an employee while working for the business. This includes travel, meals, accommodation, etc.

Monthly reports

Now we look at the principal financial reports used to manage a business. Obviously, the final accounts for a business are produced and audited on an annual basis. However, information from the *ledgers* (financial records) is used to produce interim monthly reports of the financial 'health' of the company. The main reports are the trial balance and flash reports:

❑ *Trial balances*. These are the reports produced each month by totalling every page in the principal, *nominal* ledger of a company.
❑ *Flash reports*. These are the monthly financial reports drawn from all the ledgers, showing the financial 'health' of the business.

A trial balance, as shown in Figure 18.7, sets out the expenses and profits comprising the recurring *revenue* aspects of the business, together with the assets and liabilities reflecting the longer-term *capital* aspects.

Annual accounts

The three principal reports forming the annual accounts are the balance sheet, profit and loss (P&L) account, and the cash and funds flow forecasts:

❑ *The balance sheet* is a statement of the assets owned by a business

Trial balance					
NewCo.Ltd				01 March 2000	
		Revenue		Capital	
Account	Ledger	Debit	Credit	Debit	Credit
		£	£	£	£
Cash	Cash Book			100.00	
Bank				1000.00	
	Purchase				200.00
	Sales			200.00	
TOTALS					

Figure 18.7 Trial balance

and the way in which they were financed, at a particular *point* in time.

❑ *The profit and loss account* monitors income and expenditure over a particular *period* of time.

❑ *Cash flow* is the money received by a business, *minus* the money spent by the company, over a particular period of time.

Taxation

Finally, financial statements are concerned with taxation, which is the subject of Chapter 23. Taxation covers:

❑ *pay-as-you-earn* (PAYE) – the tax you as employer are responsible for deducting from an employee's wages;

❑ *National Insurance contributions* (NICs) – payments notionally towards the employee's state pension;

❑ *value added tax* (VAT) – the tax paid by a business when it buys goods from someone, and the tax charged when selling them on to a customer, the difference being handed over to the taxman.

Accounting conventions

We all know that a business' financial position subdivides into liabilities and assets:

- ❏ *Liabilities* are where the money came from or claims made by people outside the business.
- ❏ *Assets* are what the money has been spent on, or, in accountancy terms, valuable resources owned by the business.

However, there are a number of conventions used in accounting with which you should be familiar.

Balance sheet conventions

- ❏ *Conservatism.* By convention, accounts are always presented from the most pessimistic viewpoint.
- ❏ *Asset ranking.* Assets are listed in terms of 'permanence', for instance starting with buildings and finishing with cash.
- ❏ *Cash terms.* Only items that can be measured in monetary terms are entered in a balance sheet, not intangibles (although this is changing).
- ❏ *Cost value.* Assets are entered at their cost value, rather than the 'worth' or perceived value of the asset.
- ❏ *Viability.* The balance sheet value of assets assumes that the business is a 'going concern' and will continue trading.
- ❏ *Duality.* For completeness you need to show both the money received and, correspondingly, how that money was used. NB: capital = assets – liabilities!
- ❏ *Consistency.* In your balance sheet, choose the best accountancy method of showing your company's financial performance, and stick to that method.

Profit and loss conventions

- ❏ *Realization concept.* In accounting, income is usually recognized as having been earned when the products or services are delivered and the invoice dispatched.

❏ *Accrual concept*. An item is included in the accounts for the period it accrued rather than was paid.

The two axes of accounting

So accounting, in simple terms, has two axes. The first axis is things you own (*assets*) and things you owe (*liabilities*). The second are long-term and short-term positions. This is illustrated by Figure 18.8. On the right are listed the company's assets; basically this is what has been done with the money obtained. On the left is listed where the money came from to pay for the assets. This is the basis of a company balance sheet.

In Figure 18.8, on the left side we have the liabilities and claims against the company, subdivided into long-term liabilities and short-term current liabilities (under a year). On the right side are the company assets, subdivided into long-term fixed assets and short-term current assets. The finances are laid out in this form to show clearly both the long- and short-term financial positions.

Balance sheet

Figure 18.9 shows how a company's financial position is presented in a *real* balance sheet.

	Liabilities		Assets	
Long term (over a year)	Liabilities	£	Fixed assets	£
Short term (under a year)	Current liabilities		Current assets	
Totals	Total liabilities		Total assets	

Figure 18.8 Company's financial position

Balance sheet (on 31 December 200x)		
	£	£
ASSETS		
Fixed assets (long-term)		
Property	_____	
Equipment	_____	
TOTAL FIXED ASSETS (A)		_____
Current assets (short-term)		
Cash	_____	
Stock	_____	
Debtors	_____	
TOTAL CURRENT ASSETS (B)		_____
TOTAL ASSETS (A)+(B)		_____
LIABILITIES AND CAPITAL		
Liabilities (long-term)		
Loans	_____	
Current Liabilities (short-term)		
Tax payable, including VAT	_____	
Creditors	_____	
TOTAL LIABILITIES (C)		_____
Capital		
Shareholders' Capital	_____	
Profit (and Loss)	_____	
TOTAL CAPITAL (D)		_____
TOTAL LIABILITIES AND CAPITAL (C) + (D)		

Figure 18.9 Balance sheet

The first difference to note between Figures 18.8 and 18.9 is the introduction of a number of new terms. A balance sheet gives you the following:

❑ *Net assets employed*. Put in simple terms, what has the business' money been spent on? Examples are the buying of fixed assets, money tied up in working capital, and money that has been invested.

❑ *Net current assets*. This is the working capital, calculated by subtracting the *current liabilities* from the *current assets*.

❑ *Financed by*. This lists where the money came from and typically comprises the *share capital* (or owner's capital), *profits* generated by the business and *loans* from outside organizations.

The balance sheet shows the financial health of your business at a particular moment in time. The corresponding profit and loss account monitors your business' income and expenditure over a period of time. It gives you what you are most interested in; your net profit (or loss)!

Profit and loss account

As with any accounting report, the profit and loss account should be prepared in the best form for your particular business. A typical P&L account, whether for a high-tech start-up, service organization or consultancy, is likely to comprise the following entries:

❑ *Sales*. This is the revenue from operating the business.

❑ *Cost of sales*. This records the direct expenses incurred in producing the products or service, such as purchasing stock.

❑ *Gross profit*. This is the difference between 'sales' and 'cost of sales'.

❑ *Operating expenses*. These are the indirect expenses incurred, such as selling, administration, etc.

❑ *Operating profit*. This is the difference between the gross profit and the operating expenses.

❑ *Non-operating revenues*. There may be revenue additional to that generated by sales, such as interest on investments or rental of property.

❑ *Profit before tax*. Obviously, untaxed profits.

❑ *Provision for tax*. This should cover both income tax and VAT.

A simple P&L account containing a number of these items is shown in Figure 18.10.

Cash flow

One of the greatest problems facing successful high-tech start-ups is 'rapid growth'. Often the growth is too rapid, from being two or three friends working for a single client, to a sizeable business with customers in Europe and the United States. Obviously, you need to monitor your cash and funds flow, so you have the money to service the new business. (Taking on more business than you have the cash to finance is called *overtrading*.) Cash flow and funds flow are different:

Profit and loss account (1 January 200x to 31 December 200x)		
	£	£
SALES (A)		
Less cost of sales		
Purchases		
Labour		
Other direct costs		
TOTAL (B)		
GROSS PROFIT (C)=(A) - (B)		
Less overheads		
Rent & rates		
Heating & lighting		
Telephone		
Employee costs		
Professional fees		
TOTAL (D)		
Miscellaneous Income (E)		
NET PROFIT (F)=(C) + (E) - (D)		

Figure 18.10 Profit and loss account

☐ The cash flow statement looks at the movement of 'cash' in and out of the business. An example is shown in Figure 18.11.

☐ The funds flow statement looks at the movement of both 'cash' and 'credit' in and out of the business.

Audited accounts

The legal requirements for preparing your company's annual accounts depend on whether you are a sole trader, in a partnership, or a limited company.

Monthly cash flow statement (1 January 200x to 31 December 200x)										
	Jan	Feb	Mar	Apr	...	Oct	Nov	Dec	TOTAL	
Opening bank balance (A)										
Receipts										
Cash from sales										
Cash from debtors										
Sale of assets										
VAT (net receipts)										
TOTAL RECEIPTS (B)										
Payments										
Cash purchases										
Suppliers payments										
VAT (net payments)										
Rent/rates										
Heating/lighting										
Telephone										
Employee costs										
Tax (PAYE, NICs)										
Professional fees										
TOTAL PAYMENTS (C)										
CLOSING BANK PAYMENTS (A)+(B)-(C)										

Figure 18.11 Cash flow statement

Sole trader or partnership

As a sole trader or partnership, by law your annual accounts must show 'a true and fair picture' of trading. However, the exact format of the accounts is not specified. This means you are not obliged to produce a balance sheet or to get your accounts officially audited.

Limited company

For a limited company, the form of accounts is specified by the Companies Acts, and the accounts need to be audited by a professional accountant. In addition, accounts must be filed with the Companies Registration Office, where any member of the public can inspect them.

However, the rules provide simplified procedures for small limited companies. To be counted as small, a company must meet two of the following conditions: sales no more than £2.8 million; balance sheet total no more than £1.4 million; 50 or fewer employees. A small company can file a simplified balance sheet and auditor's report, and a company with sales of less than £350,000 is not required to have accounts audited.

Sources of help

Barrow, C (1995) *Financial Management for the Small Business*, Kogan Page, London

Institute of Chartered Accountants in England and Wales (ICA). Chartered Accountants Hall, Moorgate Place, London, EC2P 2BJ, tel: 020 7920 8100, fax: 020 7920 0547, *www.icaew.co.uk*

Institute of Chartered Accountants in Ireland. 87–89 Pembroke Road, Dublin 4, Republic of Ireland, tel: 00 01 680 400, *www.icai.ie*

Institute of Chartered Accountants in Scotland. 27 Queen Street, Edinburgh, EH2 1LA, tel: 0131 225 5673, *www.icas.org.uk*

Starting your own business? Form CWL1, Board of Inland Revenue, Somerset House, Strand, London, tel: 020 74386420, *www.inlandrevenue. gov.uk*

Truman, M (1997) *Teach Yourself Book-Keeping and Accounting for your Small Business*, Hodder & Stoughton, London

Williams, S (1999) *Small Business Guide*, Penguin, London

19 Forecasting and Pricing

If you want to make your fortune, you need accurate planning, forecasting and costing of your products and services. Two of the most common reasons for the failure of small businesses is, firstly, running out of cash, and secondly, pricing their products and services at too low a value.

In this chapter we look at:

- ❏ forecasting your sales, cash flow, profit or loss, and balance sheet;
- ❏ pricing your products and services to make a healthy profit;
- ❏ calculating the 'break-even point' of your business.

Forecasting

Forecasts should be the basis of all your business decisions: raising money, hiring more staff, taking on additional business. Frequently they are not. Fortunately, computer-based spreadsheets and modern accounting packages are excellent tools for forecasting balance sheets, profit and loss (P&L) accounts, and cash flows. Having said this, it must be acknowledged that some of your financial figures will be pure 'guestimates'. Let's start with sales.

Sales forecasting

When estimating future sales, existing businesses have a distinct advantage. They have actual trading records on which to base their predictions.

Start-ups must grope in the dark, and avoid the natural tendency of being over-optimistic about potential sales volumes.

Two popular techniques used in forecasting sales are *sales trends* predictions and *gap analysis*:

❏ *Sales trends*. For a business with a sales history, future sales can be predicted by plotting a graph of the previous sales volume *by quarters*, fitting a trend line and then extrapolating this into the future.

❏ *Gap analysis*. Having plotted your sales trend, you can then plot the *sales objective*. The difference between the two lines is the so-called *sales gap* (Figure 19.1).

This sales forecast will form the major input to your P&L forecast, discussed below.

When making forecasts, it is good practice to break down sales into market segments, product and service classification, geographic areas, distribution channels and other divisions (Figure 19.2).

Cash flow forecasting

The cash flow forecast estimates when you will receive cash into your business from customers and when you will have to pay it out. Prior to launch, a monthly cash flow forecast for six months and one year is probably necessary. For managing the business longer term you will need monthly forecasts of one and possibly two years, and yearly forecasts for 3–5 years. Your forecasts should coincide with your accounting year (eg 1 January to 31

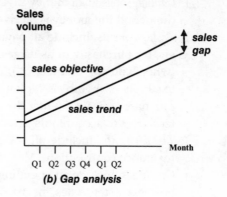

(a) Sales trend   *(b) Gap analysis*

Figure 19.1 Forecasting sales

217

Monthly sales forecasts (1 January 200x to 31 December 200x)									
	Jan	Feb	Mar	Apr	...	Oct	Nov	Dec	TOTAL
By market segment									
Number of units									
Price per unit									
TOTAL SALES									
By product and service									
Number of units									
Price per unit									
TOTAL SALES									

Figure 19.2 Monthly sales forecasts

December). Also, be realistic, possibly even pessimistic, about when and if you will receive cash.

The financial figures to be included are as follows:

- ❏ *Opening bank balance.* This shows how much money you have in your account, or the level of overdraft, at the start of the period.
- ❏ *Cash receipts.* Include estimates of all cash received by the business, including all sales and even VAT net receipts. Typically, 'cash' is subdivided into 'cash from sales' (where you are paid there and then), 'cash from debtors' (where you are paid in response to an invoice), 'sale of assets' (excluding products and services) and 'VAT' (net receipts).
- ❏ *Capital.* Include all money invested in the business and enter it in the period the money is received.
- ❏ *Cash payments.* Include all payments plus VAT, whether to suppliers, for purchases, or as wages. This includes 'cash for purchases' (where you pay 'on the spot'), 'cash for creditors' (paid in response to suppliers' invoices), 'capital expenditure' (enter any assets to be purchased), 'wages' (enter the wages/drawings), and 'professional fees' (fees to accountants, lawyers etc).
- ❏ *Tax payments.* Include all tax payments such as PAYE, National Insurance contributions, VAT, income tax and corporation tax.
- ❏ *Overheads.* Include all operating expenditure in the running of the business – rent/rates, heating/lighting, telecommunications and general expenses, such as postage and travel.

❑ *Bank payments.* Enter interest charges, all bank charges, interest on overdrafts and repayments on loans.

❑ *Closing bank balance.* Finally, calculate the closing bank balance for the period, by adding the opening bank balance and the total receipts, and subtracting the total payments.

Profit and loss forecasting

The financial figures to be included are as follows:

❑ *Sales.* Enter the sum of the invoices you expect to send out during the period, which will not necessarily be the cash you will receive.

❑ *Cost of sales.* Enter your estimate of all costs attributable directly to sales. Remember to vary these costs over the period, as sales volume goes up (or down), and the levels of cost move correspondingly. Include purchases, labour and other direct costs.

❑ *Overheads.* Include all estimated operating expenditure in the running of the business, which should be spread over the year. Include rent/rates, heating/lighting, telecommunications, professional fees, asset depreciation, employee costs, drawings, and other expenses.

Balance sheet forecasting

The annual balance sheet shows your financial 'health' (what you are owed and what you owe) on a given day. Thus, a balance sheet *forecast* is

Monthly profit and loss account (1 January 200x to 31 December 200x)									
	Jan	Feb	Mar	Apr	...	Oct	Nov	Dec	TOTAL
SALES (A)									
Less cost of sales (B)									
GROSS PROFIT (C)=(A)-(B)									
Less overheads (D)									
Plus misc. income (E)									
NET PROFIT (F)=(C) + (E) - (D)									

Figure 19.3 Monthly profit and loss forecasts

your estimate of what the business will look like on a given day in the future. A standard balance sheet is shown in Figure 19.4. The financial figures to be included are:

❑ *Fixed assets.* Include all semi-permanent assets, such as equipment, furniture, vehicles and buildings, which are purchased in the period. But remember to use the depreciated value of the asset at the end of the period rather than the purchase cost. For instance, computer equipment typically depreciates by a third of its cost per year.

❑ *Current assets.* The main current assets are cash (in the bank), debt owed by customers, and any stock held to produce your products and services. Also, if you are VAT registered, remember to include VAT in figures where appropriate.

❑ *Capital.* Include in the capital entry all capital invested, and the profit (and loss) figures from your P&L forecast.

❑ *Long-term liabilities.* Include loans from financial institutions, where repayment is longer than a year.

❑ *Current liabilities.* Include overdrafts, and income tax and VAT to

Balance sheet forecast (on 31 December 200x)	£	£
ASSETS		
Fixed assets (long-term) (A)		
Current assets (short-term) (B)		
TOTAL ASSETS (A)+(B)		
LIABILITIES AND CAPITAL		
Liabilities (long-term) (C)		
Current liabilities (short-term) (D)		
Capital (E)		
TOTAL LIABILITIES AND CAPITAL (C) + (D) + (E)		

Figure 19.4 Balance sheet forecast

be paid, etc. The tax is calculated from any profits estimated in the P&L forecast.

❏ *Creditors*. Include money you owe to suppliers.

Pricing

Having made all your forecasts, there are four ways in which to increase profits: cut costs (see Chapter 22), change the marketing mix (Chapter 30), sell more (Chapter 34), and/or increase your prices. Clearly, your aim at start-up should be to price your products and services so as to give you the highest possible profit.

As previously noted, one of the major reasons why small businesses collapse is that they fail to value their products or services accurately. Many rely simply on knowing and charging 'the market rate'.

In calculating your prices, the main ingredients are:

❏ *cost price* – the cost of producing the products based on the total costs of the business;

❏ *sales price* – the charge to the customer so as to produce a profit for the business;

❏ *profit* – the sales price minus the cost price;

❏ *mark-up* – the percentage profit based on the *cost price* (sales price minus cost price, divided by the cost price);

❏ *margin* – the percentage profit based on the *sales price* (sales price minus cost price, divided by the cost price).

So the answer to the pricing question appears deceptively simple: add up all the *cost components* to get the *cost price*; then add on some mark-up percentage to get a *sales price*. Unfortunately, costs are frequently unpredictable. For example, a full-time member of staff is a fixed cost, whereas a telephone has a quarterly charge that is a fixed cost, but a cost per unit usage charged, which is a variable cost.

Price considerations

Cost is just one of a number of marketing factors to consider when setting the price of a product. The others include the following:

❏ *Market position*. The price of your product needs to reflect the target market position. Do you want to be a prestige brand or the cheapest? Clearly, if you are the market leader (ie the 'gorilla') you may be able to charge a premium price.

❑ *Competition.* How will your product compare with the competition? What is its unique selling proposition (USP)? What might customers be prepared to pay, and in what volumes?

❑ *Life cycle.* Where in its life cycle is your product compared with the rest of the marketplace. Is it new and unique, or entering a well-established market?

❑ *Price sensitivity.* If you raise or lower your prices, how will this affect your customer base? Will you retain existing customers or attract new customers while increasing profits?

❑ *Product presentation.* What brand image does your product convey to the marketplace? If your packaging, presentation and delivery are superior to your competitors, you may be able to charge a premium price.

❑ *Valuation.* For many high-tech start-ups, valuation and market capitalization (if listed on a stock market) is more important than short-term profits. Hotmail, Yahoo! and Virtual Vineyards are examples.

Figure 19.5 lists some of the pricing considerations when comparing (through the eyes of potential customers) your product against competitive offerings.

Pricing strategies

Pricing is a paradox! By selecting a price for your product you are sending a message to your potential customers (see Table 19.1). Pricing of high-tech products, and especially online services, is even more difficult. For many high-tech start-ups, market share (ie the number of customers), and hence valuation, is more important than revenue (income) and profitability.

The pricing dichotomy is this: you are unlikely to build a major business offering low quality at high prices (unless your product is unique), but you could be throwing away profits by offering high quality at low prices (unless your goal is grabbing market share).

✓	Assess the position of your product in the marketplace
✓	Assess the impact of any planned changes to your product
✓	Assess the threat of the competition to your business
✓	Decide on a pricing strategy; highest, average, lowest, free
✓	Assess the impact of a range of potential prices on sales and profits
✓	Choose an optimum price and test its impact on a small market segment

Figure 19.5 Pricing considerations

Table 19.1 Pricing strategies

Pricing	Strategy	Advantages	Disadvantages
High	Price near the top of the range	Market leader, prestige product, unique offering	High price demands high quality and attracts competition
Average	Price at the going market rate	Ensure reasonable profitability	Competitors lower their prices and improve quality
Low	Price near the bottom of the market	Strategy for grabbing market share	Low price implies low quality and savages profits
Free	Valuation and revenue more important than profits	Aggressive strategy for grabbing market share	Severe cash flow problems

Costs

Understanding costs, and how to control them as the business changes, is the key to survival. There are several types of cost:

❏ *Fixed costs* are the costs that must be met, irrespective of the level of business activity. Operating fixed assets such as equipment, and employing people, are two examples.

❏ *Variable costs* are those that are related to the level of business activity. Examples are the price paid for bulk components from suppliers, customer disk space from an Internet service provider, or the rental of additional office space.

❏ *Semi-variable costs* are those having a fixed part and a variable part. For example, you may pay a fixed cost for rental of telephone equipment, plus a variable cost per minute for usage.

❏ *Start-up costs* are those associated with the launch phase of the business. This so-called 'burn rate' is one of the main reasons start-ups fail in the early stages.

The break-even point

Having determined your costs you next need to calculate the break-even point (BEP) for the product. The BEP is where 'real' profits start to be made.

As shown in Figure 19.6, the trick is to visualize the total costs by starting the variable costs from the fixed-costs line. The break-even point formula is:

$$BEP = \left(\frac{\text{Fixed costs}}{\text{Unit selling price} - \text{variable cost per unit}} \right)$$

So, if you are a software company with fixed costs of £100,000, a selling price of £100 per package, and variable costs of £20 per package, then the break-even point will be: £100,000 divided by (£100 – £20), which is 1250 units.

However, when costing products and services, your ideal starting point is working backwards, so-to-speak, from the 'desired profits'. This is achieved by amending the BEP to a BEPP (break-even profit point) formula:

$$BEPP = \left(\frac{\text{Fixed costs} + \text{Desired profit}}{\text{Unit selling price} - \text{Variable cost per unit}} \right)$$

So, continuing the above example, if the profit objective is £50,000, then the break-even profit point now becomes: (£100,000 + £50,000) divided by (£100 – £20), which is 1875 units.

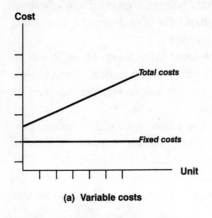
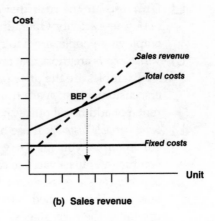

Figure 19.6 Break-even point (BEP)

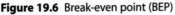

The BEPP formula can be used for a variety of 'what if. . .?' business calculations, from costing special orders that may be unprofitable, to spending start-up capital of the new business.

In conclusion, the selling price should provide a suitable margin to produce a profit for the business. Obviously, the selling price, as discussed above, needs to reflect what your competitors are charging in the marketplace, but the profit must also be adequate to cover fluctuations in the market as well as investment for the future. However, using the BEP and BEPP equations, the unit cost for products and services can be calculated with reasonable precision.

Sources of help

Barrow, C (1995) *Financial Management for the Small Business*, Kogan Page, London
Bolt, G (1994) *Marketing and Sales Forecasting: A Total Approach*, Kogan Page, London
Williams, S (1999) *Small Business Guide*, Penguin, London

20 Book-keeping and Accounting

A cynic might say that 'double-entry' book-keeping is the technique used by villains to hide cash from the taxman! In fact it is a thoroughly respectable accounting procedure.

If you have found introductions to book-keeping and accounting difficult to follow, and full of jargon (double entry, ledgers, journals etc), the reason is very simple. They are written primarily for students taking examinations in accounting suited to large businesses. This chapter introduces the basics of book-keeping and accounting from the viewpoint of the entrepreneur launching a small business.

In this chapter we look at:

❑ understanding your business bank statement;
❑ recording payments and receipts in a cash book;
❑ handling wages, PAYE, National Insurance and VAT;
❑ understanding double-entry book-keeping;
❑ types of day books and ledgers;
❑ monthly 'flash reports' on the financial health of the business, and the year-end balance sheet.

For simplicity, book-keeping and accounting are here divided into:

❑ *Basic book-keeping* – recording payments and receipts, VAT, wages, PAYE and National Insurance. Most accountants recommend such basic financial records for the sole trader and small business.
❑ *Double-entry book-keeping* – the standard accounting method recording both where money came from and what was done with it. This maintains the essential accounting relationship 'assets =

capital + liabilities'. Double-entry book-keeping is suitable for both small and large companies.

❏ *Company accounts* – the year-end accounts, comprising a balance sheet, profit and loss account, and cash flow statements.

Use whichever method of book-keeping with which you feel the most comfortable.

Basic book-keeping

Basic book-keeping for a typical, small, high-tech business centres on the business bank account, recording receipts and payments, and calculating tax on behalf of the government. Suppliers are paid by cheques drawn on the account. Customers' cheques are paid into the bank account. Staff wages are drawn on the account, tax paid. All payments and receipts are reconciled.

The four principal financial records for your small business are:

❏ *cheque book* – recording all payments made by cheque to suppliers;
❏ *paying-in book* – recording all cash and cheques paid into the business;
❏ *bank statement* – giving a brief listing of all payments and receipts, and the balance of the account;
❏ *cash book* – a 'spreadsheet' where details of all payments and receipts are recorded.

The bank account

The layout of a bank statement is the same for a business or personal account. However, for your business account it is far more important to understand the terse information in the statement.

The statement of account will list the company name and address, and the account number and sort code. Below this will be a list of the transactions, starting with the balance brought forward from the previous statement, and finishing with the current balance to be carried forward to the next.

Each entry records a date, details, an entry in the payment or receipt column, and account balance. The details are cryptic, but need to be understood to reconcile the accounts. Receipts comprise cheques or cash paid into a branch, and bank transfer from one account to another through the automated clearing system, CHAPS. Payments comprise cheques drawn on the account, direct debits from the account, and standing orders whereby your bank regularly pays an amount. The final item is the charges levied by the bank for managing your account (see Figure 20.1).

Because of the brevity of the information in your bank statement, it is necessary to keep comprehensive records of transactions in what are called 'cash books'.

The payments and receipts cash book

A simple cash book records details of all payments and receipts associated with your business account. In designing the cash book for your business, it is recommended that the layout follow that of a bank statement (date, details etc), with the columns based on the categories used by the Inland Revenue in the self-assessment tax return.

In a cash book, as illustrated by Figure 20.2, the two principal sets of entries are payments and receipts. The cash book comprises the following entries. At the top of the page is the name of the company, bank account number and sort code, plus the date the new page was started. Then, starting on the left, the first column records the *date*. The next set of columns record the payments, listing the details (ie *payments out*), *totals*,

STATEMENT OF ACCOUNT NewCo Ltd					*Commentary*
Account number 01234567		**Sort code** 01 23 45			
Date	*Details*	*Payments*	*Receipts*	*Balance*	
1 April	Balance b/f			1000.00	balance brought forward
2 April	Cheque 987654		100.00	1100.00	cheque paid in
3 April	Cash		100.00	1200.00	minimal details on cash paid in
4 April	Bank credit		100.00	1300.00	electronic payment
5 April	Cheque 123456	100.00		1200.00	payment by cheque
6 April	DD ABC Ltd	100.00		1100.00	direct debit payment to ABC Ltd
7 April	SO J. Bloggs	100.00		1000.00	standing order to J. Bloggs
8 April	Bank charges	10.00		990.00	bank charges for cheques etc
9 April	Balance c/f			990.00	balance carried forward

Figure 20.1 Layout of a bank statement

Company NewCo Ltd.		Account number 01234567				Sort code 01 23 45		
Date	Payments Out	Chq. No.	Total	Date	Payment In		Reference	Total
1 April	Balance b/f		1000.00					
2 April				2 April	Cheque 987654			
3 April				3 April	Cash			
4 April				5 April	Bank credit			
5 April	Cheque to XYZ Ltd	123456						
	Cash for stamps							
	Credit card for petrol							
6 April	DD ABC Ltd for …							
7 April	SO J. Bloggs for …							
8 April	Bank charges							

Figure 20.2 Layout of a cash book

and a series of analysis columns. The final set of columns on the right records the receipts, listing the details (ie *payments in*), *totals*, and again a series of analysis columns. The sum of the entries in the analysis columns must be the same as the amount in the *totals* column.

Following the Inland Revenue self-assessment form, and dependent on the type of your business, the analysis columns might be as shown in Figure 20.3.

Wages, PAYE and NICs

The above has covered all the basic entries a small business needs to make in its records. However, you also have to work as an unpaid tax collector for the government, and this requires additional entries in your cash book. The next part of the cash book concerns wages, and the calculation of PAYE and National Insurance contributions (NICs).

Put in simple terms, the Inland Revenue issues a code number for each employee, based on their tax position. Using this code number, the

- **Cost of sales** (expenses in preparing your product)
- **Employee costs** (salaries and payments)
- **Premises costs** (rent, heat, insurance etc)
- **Repairs** (for premises and equipment)
- **General administration expenses** (stationery, telephones etc.)
- **Motor expenses** (fuel and servicing)
- **Travel and subsistence** (fares etc)

- **Advertising** (all promotions, but not entertainment)
- **Legal and professional fees**
- **Interest** (on loans)
- **Other finance charges** (bank charges)
- **Drawings** (expenses, like entertainment, not allowed by the Inland Revenue)
- **Purchase of equipment** (such as computers)

Figure 20.3 The analysis columns

employee's earnings and tax paid to date for the current tax year, and tables supplied by the Inland Revenue, you calculate the amount of tax to be deducted from this week's or month's pay. The balance of the salary is then paid over to the employee. PAYE and NIC details should be included in the cash book.

Value added tax (VAT)

It is mandatory to register for VAT once your turnover in products and services that are liable to VAT exceeds the registration limit in a given year. Once registered, a business must charge VAT on taxable supplies, but can also claim back VAT paid on products and services purchased. The main purpose of this short section is to illustrate how VAT is recorded in the cash book of a book-keeping system.

For a business accounting for VAT, the records need to identify VAT paid on all products and services purchased by the company, and the VAT charged on all products and services sold by the company. When 'keeping the books' the main thing to remember is that VAT is 'owned' by HM Customs & Excise, and therefore should be accounted for separately. VAT should be subtracted from sales income, and the real cost of purchases is the VAT-exclusive price. As shown by Figure 20.4, VAT is recorded by including an additional 'VAT' column in the analysis section of payments out and payments in. These VAT columns are 'totalled' just like the other analysis columns.

Double-entry book-keeping

We now move on to 'grown-up' accounting, commonly known as double-entry book-keeping. The name is derived from the system of writing up every entry twice, one as a debit entry and once as a credit, so as to cross-

Company NewCo Ltd.			Account number 01234567					Sort code 01 23 45		
Date	Payments Out		Employee Cost	PAYE	NI	VAT		Payments In		VAT
1 April										
2 April										
3 April										

Figure 20.4 Layout of a cash book (including tax)

check entries and minimize the chance of errors. Although double-entry book-keeping can be used for any size of business, it is complicated to learn, and novices frequently make mistakes in entering transactions.

To keep a complete record of every business transaction, you need to know both where money came from and what has been done with it. Double-entry book-keeping thus implies two entries for the same transaction in your accounting system. The term comes from the traditional double-entry format of a paper ledger – on the left the 'debit' entries and on the right the 'credit' entries. For any given transaction:

❏ debit the account receiving the money;
❏ credit the account giving the money.

For example, if you sell something for cash, you must credit your sales account and debit your bank account, which will ultimately receive the money. However, when the sale is on credit, you credit your sales account, but debit your debtors account. This may seem slightly confusing, but your bank and business are separate, you being the 'customer' of the bank. So, when you pay the money into the bank it will be entered as a credit entry.

Recall, a balance sheet 'balances' because it shows all the assets owned by the business (eg cash, equipment, etc) less the money owed to creditors. It also shows who owns what. The basic cash book (Figure 20.5) 'balances' because on the payments side the totals are the credits and the analysis columns are the debits, and vice versa for the receipts.

Next, we look briefly at the principal ledgers.

Payments					Receipts				
	Credits	Debits				Debits	Credits		
Details	Totals	Analysis			Details	Totals	Analysis		

Figure 20.5 Double-entry book-keeping

Bank accounts

There are several different types of bank account in use, and when you set up your business you may establish a number of accounts, and these will be mirrored in your accountancy system:

- ☐ *Current account.* This is the day-to-day account for receipt and payment of invoices, usually settled by cheque but in the future by electronic banking.
- ☐ *Petty cash.* This is a subdivision of your current account, managing a small amount of cash used for miscellaneous purchases such as tea, coffee and office stationery.
- ☐ *Deposit account.* This is most used by individuals rather than businesses, to accumulate interest on surplus money.
- ☐ *Credit card account.* This can be used to pay miscellaneous business bills, particularly travel, entertainment and accommodation.

Day books ('journals')

Day books, sometimes called 'books of original entry', are used for the initial recording of daily transactions. Each one caters for a specific type of transaction. The principal daybooks are:

- ☐ *Cash book.* This records all payments and receipts by cheque.
- ☐ *Petty cash book.* This records all transactions in notes and coins.
- ☐ *Sales day book.* This records sales on credit.

Sales (customer) ledger

The sales ledger maintains customer records, invoices and credit notes. The three basic sales transactions are:

- ☐ *Cash sales.* Goods and services are paid for straight away, so you must debit the bank account and credit the sales account.
- ☐ *Credit sales.* A customer invoice is raised stating the amount to be paid, a credit entry is created in the sales account and a debit entry in the debtors account (recall, double-entry book-keeping).
- ☐ *Credit notes.* These are notes issued to customers to cover goods and services paid for but not properly delivered.

Purchase (supplier) ledger

The purchase ledger maintains supplier records, invoices and credit notes (see Figure 20.6). As above, the three basic transactions are:

❏ *Cash purchases.* This is the record of goods and services purchased for cash.

❏ *Invoices received.* This is the record of invoices received from suppliers for goods and services on credit.

❏ *Credit notes received.* These are the notes issued by suppliers to cover goods and services paid for but not properly delivered.

Debit				Credit			
Date	*Details*		*Amount*	*Date*	*Details*		*Amount*

Figure 20.6 Purchase ledger

Nominal (general) ledger

The nominal, or general, ledger brings together all of the information from the 'primary' ledgers (eg sales and purchasing) and is usually kept by your accountant.

Capital (asset) register

By law, all limited companies must keep a capital or asset register recording all capital items owned. This includes equipment, vehicles, buildings and land. The register records the cost at date of purchase, cumulative depreciation and any disposals.

Company accounts

Finally, we come to the monthly and yearly reports.

Trial balance

As a confidence check on the financial figures, every month each page of the nominal ledger is totalled. The sum of all the left-hand totals is compared with the sum of all the right-hand totals to check they are equal.

Flash reports

To monitor the business's performance, each month a 'flash report' is generated to show an interim profit and loss account, the balances from the cash book, and how much money the business owes and is owed from the purchase and sales ledgers. In addition, many of the control ratios on liquidity and profitability can be generated.

Balance sheet

The balance sheet is a statement of the company's financial position at year-end, showing the assets of the business and where it got the money to finance those assets. This and other statements (eg P&L, cash flow) are covered in Chapter 18.

Sources of help

Barrow, C (1995) *Financial Management for the Small Business,* Kogan Page, London

Institute of Chartered Accountants in England and Wales (ICA). Chartered Accountants Hall, Moorgate Place, London, EC2P 2BJ, tel: 020 7920 8100, fax: 020 7920 0547, *www.icaew.co.uk*

Institute of Chartered Accountants in Ireland. 87–89 Pembroke Road, Dublin 4, Republic of Ireland, tel: 00 01 680 400, *www.icai.ie*

Institute of Chartered Accountants in Scotland. 27 Queen Street, Edinburgh, EH2 1LA, tel: 0131 225 5673, *www.icas.org.uk*

Piper, A (1997) *Teach Yourself Bookkeeping,* Hodder & Stoughton, London

The VAT Guide. Notice 700, HM Customs and Excise, March 1996

Truman, M (1997) *Teach Yourself Book-Keeping and Accounting for your Small Business,* Hodder & Stoughton, London

21 Accounting Software

Many small businesses continue to 'keep the books' in the traditional way, using large A3 sheets of paper ruled into columns and rows. Unbelievable! Obviously, any self-respecting high-tech start-up, even a sole trader, will make use of online banking, spreadsheets, personal financial software and accounting packages.

In this chapter we look at:

❑ traditional methods of book-keeping using 'paper';
❑ spreadsheets to build your own day books and ledgers;
❑ online banking to monitor your accounts and transfer money;
❑ personal financial software;
❑ powerful but simple accountancy packages.

Financial software for the small business falls into five basic categories:

❑ *Spreadsheets* – providing basic 'electronic' ledger and book-keeping facilities. Well-known packages include Microsoft's Excel (www.microsoft.com/excel) and Lotus' 1–2-3 (www.lotus.com).
❑ *Online banking* – software for managing your bank accounts via the Internet: checking balances, monitoring transactions, moving money between accounts and paying bills. Most high-street banks now provide Internet banking services.
❑ *Personal finance* – providing a suite of tools for managing one's personal finances, including chequebook, mortgages, bills, investments, online banking, etc. Examples include Money and Quicken.
❑ *Accountancy packages* – providing tools for business book-keeping, including sales ledger, purchase ledger, VAT, invoicing, etc. The UK market-leader is Sage.

❏ *Discount brokerages* – low-cost, online services for trading shares.

Book-keeping on paper

The traditional 'software' for keeping the books is obviously paper. Payment and receipt transactions are set out in an A3 'cash book', obtainable – as they say – from most good stationery shops. It is worth looking at the paper-based method because it can easily be transferred to a spreadsheet package.

Cash book

A typical cash book layout is shown in Figure 21.1. There is space at the top for a sheet heading together with a heading for each column. On the left, the first column is designed to hold the date, the second wider column details of the transaction, and a possible third column (referred to as the *folio* column) records a cheque number. These are followed by 32 additional columns for recording the cash amounts.

Payments and receipts

In a 'cash book', at the top of the page is the name of the company, bank account number and sort code, plus the date the new page was started. Then, as we saw in Chapter 20, the two principal types of entries are *payments* (payments out) and *receipts* (payments in). Starting on the left, head the first column *Date*, then *Payments out*, *Cheque no.*, *Total*, and so on. In fact, list the following 'payment' columns in the order they appear on the tax

Company NewCo					Bank account	01234567		Sort code 01 23 45			
1 Date	2 Payment out	3 Chq no.	4 Total			22 Date	23-25 Payments in	26 Ref	27 Total		32
1	1 April	Balance b/f									
2											
3											
	TOTALS					TOTALS					

Figure 21.1 A cash book double page

return. Finally, at the foot of the page, write *Totals* in the *Details* column. Next, the receipts are recorded starting in column 22. Head this column *Date*. Then, over the next three columns (23–25), write *Payments in,* leaving space to record details of the transaction. Column 26 is headed *Reference* and records details such as the number of the bank paying-in slip. Title the next column *Total,* and so on.

Start the cash book at the beginning of the financial year to ease tax calculations. (Start a new sheet at the beginning of each month.) The first entry is the bank account balance brought forward (b/f). If the balance b/f is positive (you are in credit), enter the amount in column 27; the *Total* of 'payments in'. If you are overdrawn, enter the amount in column 4; the *Total* of 'payments out'. This will ensure the figures balance when totalled up. Easy and straightforward.

Next we shall look at software systems for 'keeping the books', starting with spreadsheet packages, which can be used to automate cash books and ledgers.

Spreadsheets

When you are starting out in business, a spreadsheet package like Microsoft's Excel, or personal finance software like Microsoft's Money or Intuit's Quicken, are perfectly adequate for managing your accounts and chequebook. In fact, the cash book is nothing more than a series of spreadsheets, which you can easily set up yourself.

Your computer will undoubtedly have one of the 'office suites', such as Microsoft Office or Lotus Smartsuite, already installed when you buy it. These suites provide spreadsheet packages such as Excel and Lotus 1–2-3 respectively.

Creating a spreadsheet 'cash book' is straightforward. Simply lay out the spreadsheet as you would a paper-based cash book. Start at the top of the sheet with title and date. Then, starting on the left, enter the columns for the payments, followed by the columns for the receipts (see Figure 21.2).

Since you will need to start a new cash book sheet each month, the best approach is to create a standard spreadsheet containing all the headings etc, which can be saved on to your hard disk as a 'template' for each new month's spreadsheet. When you create your cash book template, remember to set the currency fields to two decimal places, and to show brackets when amounts are negative (see Figure 21.3).

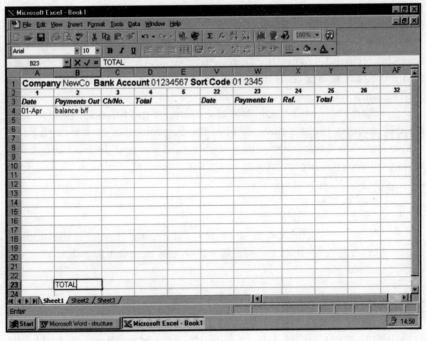

Figure 21.2 Spreadsheet cash book

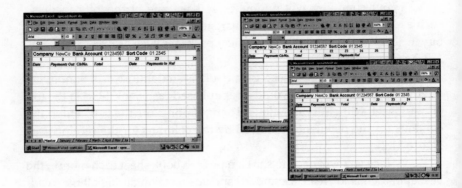

Figure 21.3 Monthly cash books

To check the accuracy of calculations, you should include row and column totals, and specify 'ranges' on the values that can be placed in cells.

Finally, if you make each month of the financial year a separate spreadsheet you can link them into a 'master spreadsheet' which will calculate the overall totals.

Online banking

Online banking is a natural progression from direct, telephone banking. The demand for online banking is rising rapidly, especially from small businesses, owing to the ease of access and the availability of data 24 hours a day. In addition, online banking is increasingly being integrated into other financial packages such as personal finance and accountancy software.

Basic facilities

Online banking provides a range of everyday services such as checking account balances and transactions. All you need is a PC with an Internet connection. The online services come in two *flavours*:

❑ *PC banking* uses special PC-based software (from the bank), or Microsoft's Money, to provide a full online banking service: check your account balances, view recent transactions, transfer money between your accounts, and pay bills. The software being resident in your PC provides an additional level of, and therefore more, security than general access via the Internet.
❑ *Internet banking* allows you to access your bank accounts from any PC with an Internet browser. You can check balances and recent transactions, transfer money, but for reasons of security you often cannot pay bills.

These online banking services are either free or carry a small administrative charge of typically £10–15 a year. For these fixed charges you can use the services as often and for as long as you wish. As an illustration, look at the websites of Barclays Bank (www.barclays.co.uk) or the Bank of Ireland (www.boi.ie), and click on 'Internet banking'.

Software packages

Most high-street banks provide online services, just as they do direct telephone banking. Online banking software also connects to personal financial software like Microsoft's Money and Intuit's Quicken.

Personal financial software

Personal financial software provides you with all the tools to manage your personal finances. These tools can just as easily be used for managing the accounts of a small business. The two leading packages are Microsoft's Money (www.microsoft.com/money) and Intuit's Quicken (www.quicken. com). Both provide a comparable suite of facilities for setting up and maintaining an integrated set of accounts for bank, building society, assets and investments; paying bills and writing cheques; handling standing orders and direct debits; and downloading financial data and news from the Internet.

However, once your business becomes a limited company, with premises, staff, suppliers and customers, and a significant number of invoices and accounts to service, then you need a 'grown up' accountancy package such as Sage's Instant Accounting.

Accountancy packages

We start by looking at setting up an accountancy or book-keeping system for your business.

Basic facilities

In simplistic terms, we can think of accounting software as comprising two parts: the *ledgers* (databases) and the *reports* (programs). Book-keeping software packages provide programs for all the major reporting procedures listed in Figure 21.4.

Software packages

There are a number of easy-to-use and powerful packages that will carry out the book-keeping and accounting functions of a small business. Your

Ledgers		
Bank accounts	*Current*	Principal bank ledger listing payment and receipts by cheque
	Petty cash	The ledger listing all cash transactions
	Deposit	
	Credit card	
Ledgers	*Purchase*	Ledger containing supplier information
	Sales	Ledger containing customer information
	Nominal	Ledger integrating the 'primary' cash, purchase and sales accounts
Registers	*Capital*	Records all the company's assets, such as equipment, vehicles and buildings, etc
Reports		
Weekly-monthly	*Wages*	
	Audit trail	A 'scrollable' list of all transactions, starting with the most recent transaction
	Trial balance	Report of totals of all debit and credit balances within the nominal ledger
	Flash reports	Monthly report from accounts on state of business
Quarterly	*PAYE, NI*	Prepares the 3-monthly tax returns for the Inland Revenue
	VAT return	Prepares the 3-monthly VAT returns for Customs & Excise
Year-end	*Balance sheet*	Reports the assets and liabilities at the end of the financial period
	P&L account	Shows how the business has performed financially in a given period
	Budget report	Reports on financial indicators: gross and net ratio, debtor and creditor ratio ...
	Prior year report	Shows sales, purchases, direct expenses and overhead accounts

Figure 21.4 Accounting ledgers and reports

major commitment once the package is installed is to keep the information up to date. That aside, the range of financial information available for reports and forecasting is significantly better even than a spreadsheet system.

SAGE's Instant Accounting

The Sage Group (www.sage.com) produce some excellent packages. Examples are Instant Accounting 2000, the entry-level product for small businesses, and Line 50 and Line 100 for larger businesses requiring stock control and networked usage etc. These are remarkably straightforward to use, and have similar screens and structures. The products are 'Internet ready' with built-in browser software for connecting to the Internet.

Instant Accounting provides a comprehensive set of facilities:

□ A sales (customer) ledger creates and maintains customer records, and prints invoices, credit notes and statements, etc.

□ A purchase (supplier) ledger creates and maintains supplier records, and enters batch invoices and credit notes, etc.

□ A nominal ledger is maintained.

□ Current, cash and credit card accounts are maintained.

□ Financial reports are produced, including trial balance, VAT returns, balance sheet and profit and loss accounts.

Each of these facilities is accessed via its corresponding icon in a toolbar (see Figure 21.5).

Setting up your accounts

To install Instant Accounting, place the CD ROM in the drive and the software will install automatically into a directory c:\Instacc. Load the application in the normal way by clicking the Windows *Start* button and then on Instant Accounting 2000. There is a tutorial available from the menu, and

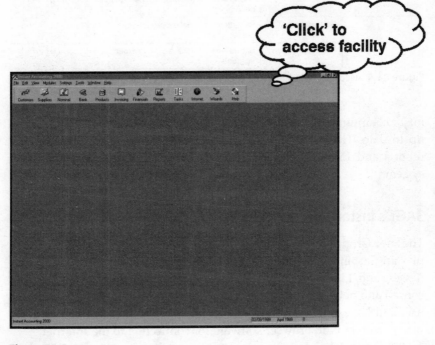

Figure 21.5

an easy-step 'wizard' that loads automatically the first time you use the system and helps you set up your basic accounts. Keep clicking the *Next* button to navigate through the screens.

The first set of screens request 'company information', such as name, address and telephone. Subsequent screens ask for details of your financial year, tax codes and VAT registration, etc. Next, a set of screens request 'customer information', including the ageing period for payments, account terms, and actions when invoices are posted. This is followed by a similar set of screens for 'supplier information'. Finally, the software announces that you have successfully configured the accounting system.

You are now ready to enter your customer and supplier information into their respective ledgers. These are accessed via the icons on the toolbar.

Instant Accounting is an excellent product, which is both powerful and straightforward to use. In fact, it is a good case study for any aspiring software designer. Well done, Sage!

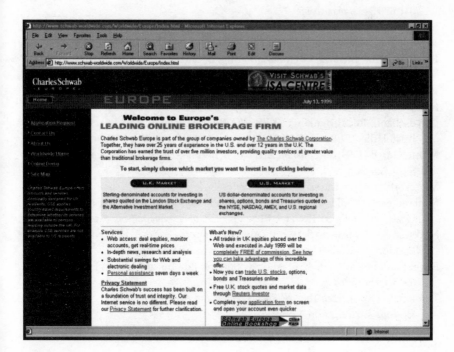

Figure 21.6

Online discount brokers

When you have made your money, you will of course want to invest it wisely. So it is worth mentioning the new US online discount brokerage firms such as Charles Schwab (www.schwab-europe.com; see Figure 21.6) and E-Trade (www.e-trade.com). Discount brokers execute share trades at far lower commissions than traditional 'full-service' brokers. The Internet is obviously highly suited to online brokerage.

Just as Amazon.com is taking increasing trade from traditional UK booksellers, such as WH Smith and Waterstones, look out for Schwab and E-Trade to attack the business of UK banks.

Sources of help

Allied Irish Bank. 12 Old Jewry, London, EC2R 8DP, tel: 020 7606 4900, fax: 020 7606 4966, email: aibtoday@aib.ie, *www.aib.ie/global*

Bank of Ireland. Head Office, Lower Baggot Street, Dublin 2, tel: 011 661 5933, fax: 011 676 3493, *www.boi.ie*

Bank of Scotland. PO Box 12, Uberior House, 61 Grassmarket, Edinburgh, EH1 2JF, tel: 0131 4427777, fax: 0131 243 5948, *www.bankofscotland.co.uk*

Barclays Bank. Business Sector Marketing Department, PO Box 120, Longwood Close, Westwood Business Park, Coventry CV4 8JN, tel: 02476 694242, *www.barclays.com*

Intuit Quicken. *www.quicken.com*

Lloyds Bank. Retail Banking UKRB, PO Box 112, Canon's House, Canon's Way, Bristol, BS99 7LB, tel: 0117 9433138, *www.lloydstsb.co.uk*

Mantovani, B (1999) *Sage Instant Accounting in easy steps*, Bill Mantovani, Computer Step, London

Microsoft Money. *www.microsoft.com/money*

Midland Bank. Midland Enterprise, Ground Floor, Courtwood House, Silver Street Gead, Sheffield, S1 1RG, tel: 0114 2529037, *www.midlandbank.co.uk*

NatWest. Small Business Services, Level 10 Drapers Gardens, 12 Throgmorton Ave, London, EC2 N2DL, tel: 020 7920 5966, *www.natwest.com*

Royal Bank of Scotland. 42 St Andrew Square, Edinburgh, EH2 2YE, tel: 0131 556 8555, *www.rbs.co.uk*

Truman, M (1997) *Teach Yourself Book-Keeping and Accounting for your Small Business*, Hodder & Stoughton, London

22 Controlling Your Business

To quote Derek Bok, President of Harvard University: '*If you think knowledge is expensive, try ignorance.*' In the 'adrenaline rush-hour' of launching your start-up, probably the last thing that concerns you is analysing the financial performance. However, even though you might be in 'hyper-growth', you can still simply run out of cash to finance your daily business.

In the preceding chapters on financial management we have looked at how to prepare financial reports and set up an accounting system. To control your business effectively you must be able to analyse and interpret this information.

In this chapter we look at ways to control:

❑ finance and operations in a successful business;
❑ working capital and ratios for analysing liquidity;
❑ fixed assets, the capital register and payback period;
❑ customers, covering invoices, credit controls and payment;
❑ stock and suppliers.

A good introduction to the subject of business controls is Colin Barrow's *Financial Management for the Small Business*.

Business controls

Traditionally, any discussion of business controls focuses on financial controls. However, we will take a more comprehensive view spanning financial controls and operational controls, covering: *cash, assets, customers, suppliers, stock* and *staff*. For these business controls, the main analysis tools are called *ratios*. A ratio is simply a means of expressing an item as a proportion of some other item to give an indication of its behaviour.

To summarize the major areas of business controls:

- ❏ *Cash*. This covers working capital (called liquidity), making a satisfactory return on investment and avoiding any unnecessary financial risks. Important ratios to be considered are: liquidity, return on capital employed (ROCE), and internal rate of return (IRR).
- ❏ *Assets*. This covers long-term assets such as land and buildings, vehicles and equipment. Important ratios include: average return on capital employed (ARCE), payback periods, present value and profitability index.
- ❏ *Customers*. This covers credit controls, credit terms, control of invoices, and chasing payments (agencies, factoring).
- ❏ *Suppliers*. This involves checking the risk of suppliers, such as proof of viability.
- ❏ *Stock*. This covers methods of monitoring stock levels
- ❏ *Staff*. Staff need to be monitored for the efficient operation of the business, to ensure they are paid appropriately and to stop fraud.

Cash control

With cash control, all businesses have two common objectives: firstly, to monitor the cash coming in and going out of the business, and secondly, to make a satisfactory return on investment. You, your bank manger and your investors need this information to monitor the financial health of the business, to make investment decisions and to measure the rate of return on investments. There are a number of standard techniques for doing this analysis.

Monitoring cash

A surprising number of new businesses are poor at managing their cash. *Cash-rich* start-ups leave it in current accounts and lose potential interest. *Cash-poor* start-ups fail simply because they run out of cash to fund their daily operations. You need to monitor your cash and make it work for you. Here are two tips:

❑ *Business bank accounts.* Keep sufficient cash in your current account for daily operating expenses, but no more. Move surplus cash into a high-interest account. Make a comparison of bank charges before you open a business account, and check each month that charges are correct. Use a credit card to defer payments on small items and reduce bank charges.

❑ *Control system.* Monitor cash balances on a weekly basis. Use online banking software (see Chapter 21) to get a weekly (or even daily) bank statement and to monitor the account balances. Set aside a specific day each month for paying bills. Any bills missing the deadline are then forced to wait until the next payment day. Make monthly forecasts of receipts from customers and payments to staff and suppliers.

During the launch phase of your business cash will be tight, so you need to monitor your cash more closely for three reasons. Perhaps you are not meeting your projected sales (forecasting problems); or your costs are too high for the sales generated (costing problems); or you do not have enough cash to fund an increase in debtors and stock (growth problems).

Liquidity and gearing

The financial resources employed in a business are called *capital*. The principal measures associated with capital are liquidity and gearing:

❑ *Liquidity* (or working capital in the business) is typically measured in terms of the *current ratio*:

$$\text{current ratio} = \frac{\text{current assets}}{\text{current liabilities}}$$

❑ *Gearing* is the measure of money (ie debt) borrowed by a company; broadly the ratio of debt to equity in a company's capital structure:

$$\text{gearing (debt to equity)} = \frac{\text{long term liabilities}}{\text{total capital}}$$

For example, Figure 22.1 shows the calculations of liquidity, current ratio and gearing based on equity of £48,000, long-term liabilities of £25,000, current assets of £36,000 and current liabilities of £15,000.

Working capital	£	£
ASSETS		
Fixed assets		
= property	45,000	
+ equipment	7,000	
TOTAL FIXED ASSETS		52,000
Current assets		
= cash	1,000	
+ debtors	10,000	
+ stock	25,000	
TOTAL CURRENT ASSETS		36,000
TOTAL ASSETS		88,000
LIABILITIES AND CAPITAL		
Long-term liabilities		
= loans		25,000
Current liabilities		
= overdraft	5,000	
+ creditors	10,000	
TOTAL CURRENT LIABILITIES		15,000
Capital (equity)		
= shareholders' capital	30,000	
+ profit	18,000	
TOTAL CAPITAL		48,000
TOTAL LIABILITIES		88,000
Working capital (liquidity)		21,000
Current ratio		2.4
Gearing		0.5

Figure 22.1 Liquidity and gearing

Measures of profitability

Central to controlling any business is analysing the levels of sales activities and resulting profits.

Sales

'Sales' is the actual money coming from selling the product; it is the basis of all 'profitability' calculations. 'Cost of sales' is the materials and labour costs of producing the goods/services, but not the selling expenses and financial charges. (It is useful to express the 'cost of sales' as a percentage of sales to identify trends in rising or falling costs.)

Profit

Profit is a main measure of sales activity, but there are various ways of expressing it:

❏ *Gross profit* is derived by deducting the cost of sales from the sales revenue.
❏ *Trading/operating profit* is derived by deducting expenses from the gross profit.
❏ *Net profit* is derived by deducting all financial charges (apart from tax) from the gross profit.
❏ *Profit margin* is derived by dividing the various profit measures by 'sales' to obtain the ratios required.
❏ *Gross profit percentage* is obtained by deducting the cost of sales from the sales, and expressing the result as a percentage of sales.
❏ *Trading profit percentage* is obtained by deducting the cost of sales from the sales, deducting business expenses (to derive the operating profit), and expressing the result as a percentage of sales.
❏ *Net profit before tax* is derived by deducting all finance charges from gross profits.

Return on investment

It is said that we must speculate to accumulate. Each investment of capital must provide: (i) the *investors* with a good return and at an acceptable risk, (ii) the *business* with enough profit to fund future growth, (iii) the *financial incentive* for future investors and lenders to provide money for the business, and (iv) the *reserves* to maintain the capital base of the business. Two important ratios used to evaluate investments are:

❏ *Return on capital employed* (ROCE). The return on capital employed is the *net profit* divided by the *capital employed*, as illustrated in Figure 22.2. It is usually expressed as a percentage.
❏ *Return on shareholder capital* (ROSC). This is a measure of the increase in worth of the funds invested by the shareholders. To obtain the ROSC ratio, divide the net profit by 'shareholder capital + profits retained in the business'.

Sales		Capital employed	
	£		£
Sales		Working capital	
= revenue	200,000	= current assets	10,000
– cost of sales	100,000	– current liabilities	5,000
= gross profit	100,000	= capital	5,000
– operating expenses	50,000	+ fixed assets	20,000
= trading profit	50,000	= capital employed	25,000
– tax, bank charges etc	10,000		
= net profit	40,000		
ROCE			
= Net profit ÷ capital employed		= % return on capital employed	160%

Figure 22.2 Return on capital

Assets control

A headache for all new businesses is the management of fixed assets, such as buildings and equipment. A major question is whether to buy or to rent. Once an asset is newly introduced into the business, it must be utilized effectively. For a future asset you need to assess the likely impact on the business of the investment made in it.

Asset control centres on three areas:

❑ *Capital register*. Limited companies have to keep a register of all capital assets they own, showing the cost at the date of purchase.

❑ *Current fixed assets*. A good measure of how well assets are being utilized is the ratio of sales to fixed assets; that is, the total sales revenue is divided by the total value of the assets.

❑ *Capital investment*. A number of methods exist for evaluating planned new capital investment. These include *payback period, discounted cash flow* and *average return on capital employed*.

Current fixed assets

One method of assessing the contribution of a given asset to your business is the so-called *fixed asset pyramid*. As illustrated by Figure 22.3, start at the top with the total sales and total value of all fixed assets. Next decompose the fixed assets into component parts, repeating this until you reach the individual asset items, such as specific computers.

This concept of 'an asset pyramid' can be extended to include equipment utilization, downtime and even repair costs, in its contribution to sales.

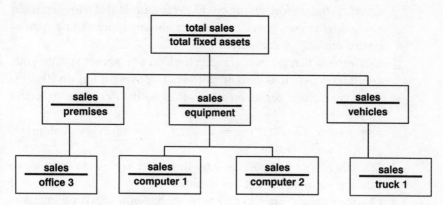

Figure 22.3 Fixed asset pyramid

Capital investment

Next we look at the tools available to analyse proposed capital investments in new fixed assets and the replacement of existing assets. Techniques for the evaluating of capital investments include:

- ❏ *Payback period.* This technique calculates the period of time over which the investment will be paid back. For example, a personal computer purchased for £1,500 and producing £1,000 net profit per year will have a payback period of 1½ years.
- ❏ *Average return on capital employed* (ARCE). The ARCE is calculated by taking the average net profit over the working life of the asset and dividing it by the total capital used to purchase the asset. For example, a personal computer purchased for £1,500 and with a working life of three years produces an average £1,000 net profit per year; this will give an ARCE of 67 per cent (1,000/1,500, expressed as a percentage).

For a complete discussion on these techniques, including discounted cash flow, look at *Financial Management for the Small Business,* by Colin Barrow.

Customer control

Very few businesses are lucky enough to have 'ideal' customers, namely those that pay their bills as soon as the product is delivered. But there are a few simple precautions you can take to ensure you get paid promptly:

❑ *Credit control.* Before giving credit to customers and allowing them some time to pay, check out their creditworthiness and payment record with other companies.

❑ *Credit terms.* Having run a credit check on a customer, specify your credit terms, such as cash on delivery or payment within 30 days. Print your credit terms on all invoices so they are known to the customer.

❑ *Keep records.* Detailed records of the status of every customer's account are essential.

❑ *Invoices.* Never delay in sending these out. If you do so you are offering your customers free credit.

❑ *Chasing payment.* Start to chase the money you are owed immediately at the end of the agreed credit period.

We will take a closer look at each of these items in turn.

Credit controls

A bad customer is probably worse than no customer. For example, you sell a customer a £10,000 piece of software that costs you £5,000 to produce, but after one year they have still not paid. This might cost you a bank charge of £500 on an overdraft at 10 per cent, plus say £500 of your own time and £1,000 on legal fees in chasing the debt. That comes to a total of £7,000 if you fail to get paid, so it pays to check out potential customers.

Credit checks on customers clearly depend on your type of business. If yours is an electronic commerce company and your customers pay by credit card over the Internet, then the card company will already have checked the customer's creditworthiness and will ensure you are paid. If you have a retail business then customers probably pay 'cash on delivery'.

For the rest, you need to check them out to some degree before offering them credit. Given the potential sales to the customer are large enough, you have a number of options:

❑ *Visit the customer.* Arrange to visit the prospective customer and meet the directors to get a personal 'feel' for their creditworthiness.

❑ *Bank reference.* Ask the customer for a bank reference.

❑ *Trade references.* Ask the customer for two or more trade references from established companies.

❑ *Credit agency*. Pay a credit reporting agency, such as Experian (www.experian.com) or Equifax (www.equifax.co.uk), to give you a credit rating on the customer.

❑ *Annual accounts*. Ask for a copy of their annual balance sheet and profit and loss accounts.

If a prospective customer does not warrant this level of attention you can always restrict the credit terms offered.

Credit terms

Again, credit terms will vary depending on the type of business you are engaged in and how well you know the prospective customers. For example, if you are building a software system for a client, you can typically ask to be paid as you meet regular contractual deadlines, or even be paid in advance if you are in the start-up phase of your business.

Possible terms you may offer a customer are:

❑ *Cash with order* (CWO). This is basically payment in advance.

❑ *Cash on delivery* (COD). Payment is received on delivery of the product – no money, no delivery.

❑ *Weekly credit*. For goods and services delivered this week, payment is required by a specific day next week. There is also something called 'net 7', which means 'payment within seven days'.

❑ *Monthly credit*. For goods and services delivered this month, payment is required by a specific day next month.

❑ *60 days' credit*. Payment is actually due 30 days after delivery, but many large companies force their suppliers to wait 60 days for payment.

Invoices

You can encourage early payment of bills by sending invoices promptly. Your billing needs to be well organized:

❑ *Records*. Good credit control centres on good records: an historical record of invoices and payments for each customer, the date an invoice was sent, how much you are owed, etc.

☐ *Prompt invoices*. Good credit control also means sending out your invoices promptly. Failure to do so will give the impression you are happy to wait for payment.

☐ *Cash discounts*. Offer a cash discount of, say, 1–5 per cent for payment initiated within seven days.

☐ *Late payments*. Small companies (fewer than 50 employees) can now charge interest on money owed by large organizations. Specifically, where there are no agreed credit terms, after 30 days from the date of the invoice interest can be charged at eight percentage points above bank base rate.

Chasing payments

While you cannot ring up a customer and threaten to 'send round the Heavies and the Alsatians', there are a number of ways of encouraging payment. One of our students was having trouble getting paid by an Internet company, so he planted some 'time-bombs' in the server code. As soon as the system shut itself down the payment miraculously appeared!

Have a system of chasing to encourage payment, such as the following:

☐ *Fax request*. As soon as a bill is outstanding, fax and post a 'polite' request for payment.

☐ *Recorded Delivery*. After seven days without response, check all the details of the invoice to verify they are correct and then send a letter by Recorded Delivery requesting immediate payment.

☐ *Phone*. Telephone the customer (specifically the accounts department) to ask the reason for non-payment. Also find out if the customer has a weekly or monthly cheque run, and whether your cheque is in the current run. There may be a number of legitimate reasons for non-payment, but do not be fobbed off.

☐ *And phone again*. If the money still fails to appear, call the managing director, ideally very early in the morning, and try to extract a promise for payment. Keep calling. You might also consider going to the customer's premises in person and saying you will not leave until you have been paid. However, be aware that you may have no right to be on the customer's premises.

☐ *Solicitor's letter*. Get your solicitor to write to the customer threatening legal action to recover the debt, winding-up proceedings against the company, or the use of a debt collection agency.

❏ *Debt collection agency*. After 2–3 months you could appoint a debt collection agency to pursue the debt. The main agencies, such as the Credit Protection Association Ltd and Graydon UK Ltd, are listed in *Yellow Pages* (www.yell.co.uk/), or go to www.golden-pages.ie.

❏ *Factoring*. This is an arrangement whereby you can receive up to 80 per cent of the money due from your customers. The factoring company buys your trade debts and takes over the day-to-day work of invoicing and chasing customers.

Supplier control

For high-tech start-ups whose business is knowledge-based, 'suppliers' can mean little more than buying software over the Internet or renting services from an ISP. However, for many small traditional businesses, obtaining credit from suppliers is a significant source of finance.

To juggle payments to suppliers you need to keep good records. For each supplier you need to know how much you owe, and from when; the credit terms; and a record of all previous invoices and payments.

With regard to your own creditworthiness, expect to be asked by suppliers for exactly the same information as you would want from a prospective customer: a bank reference, two or more trade references and annual accounts, etc.

There are two acceptable techniques for conserving cash in your business. Firstly, introduce a monthly payment schedule whereby cheques are sent out only on a specific day each month; any invoice missing the deadline must wait until the following month. Secondly, pay your bills at the end of the credit term's period. But remember, if you get a reputation for 'playing games' with your suppliers, they may refuse to work with you.

Stock control

If yours is a manufacturing or retail business, you need to introduce a control system to monitor the levels of stock and to re-order items when they fall below a certain level. Keeping good stock records will also protect you against staff pilfering. Stock control information includes:

❑ *Stock records*. Computerized stock records need to be kept, showing receipts, issues and the amount for every item of stock.

❑ *Stock cards*. A card is used to keep a record of each particular item of stock.

❑ *Advice notes*. These are a notification from a supplier that goods will be delivered in response to an order. File them.

❑ *Delivery notes*. These come with the goods when they are delivered. Again, file them.

❑ *Stores requisition notes*. These request someone to issue a certain amount of goods from stock.

❑ *Stationery*. Well, everyone has stolen the odd pencil from work, but if you do not want to supply the local population with free stationery, you need to introduce some workable stock controls.

Staff control

Staff are the single most important asset of any high-tech business, and good staff controls can help the business run efficiently. Listed below are some of the 'controls' you will need for staff:

❑ *Contracts of employment*. Each member of staff is entitled by law to a contract of employment. It can also set out what you expect of them.

❑ *Job descriptions*. These describe the roles of the members of staff in the business.

❑ *Reporting*. Once your business starts to grow you will need a system of management reporting. Consider weekly verbal reports of work in progress and objectives for the coming week. You might want monthly written reports by your major groups covering what has been achieved in the previous month, and group objectives for the coming month.

❑ *Employee timesheets*. In knowledge-based businesses, such as computing, media, consulting and professional services, you need to control how staff allocate their time, especially if this is the basis for charging customers. Therefore, it is often appropriate for staff to complete weekly timesheets.

❑ *Telephones*. Phone calls are a big expense, especially international calls. To keep down costs and to ensure that calls made by staff are legitimate, make sure all are logged, and possibly monitored, and that staff know this.

Staff controls need to be effective but fair. Many US chief executive officers (CEOs) – including Gates – fly tourist class inside the United States to keep down company travel costs. So did the legendary investor Warren Buffet until he bought his own plane! Your staff expect to be treated fairly, but they also expect people who fail to pull their weight to be taken to task.

Sources of help

Barrow, C (1995) *Financial Management for the Small Business*, Kogan Page, London

Institute of Chartered Accountants in England and Wales (ICA). Chartered Accountants Hall, Moorgate Place, London, EC2P 2BJ, tel: 020 7920 8100, fax: 020 7920 0547, *www.icaew.co.uk*

Institute of Chartered Accountants in Ireland. 87–89 Pembroke Road, Dublin 4, Republic of Ireland, tel: 0001 680 400, *www.icai.ie*

Institute of Chartered Accountants of Scotland. 27 Queen Street, Edinburgh, EH2 1LA, tel: 0131 225 5673, *www.icas.org.uk*

Williams, S (1999) *Small Business Guide*, Penguin, London

23 **Taxation**

In Taiwan, the government is so keen to encourage new businesses that high-tech start-ups do not have to pay tax for the first three years. Wonderful! But, unless you are planning to move to Taiwan, read on. This chapter covers income tax, pay as you earn (PAYE), value added tax (VAT), and local business rates (UBR).

In this chapter we look at:

- [ ] registering your business with the Inland Revenue, Contributions Agency and Customs & Excise;
- [ ] tax assessment for sole traders, partnerships and limited companies;
- [ ] income tax, capital gains tax and corporation tax;
- [ ] deductible tax allowances such as business expenses and car benefits;
- [ ] taxes related to employment, such as PAYE, NICs and pensions;
- [ ] value added tax – VAT.

Whether or not your tax affairs are in order, the Inland Revenue may investigate your tax returns, the Contributions Agency can check your employment records, and Customs & Excise, responsible for value added tax, may question your VAT returns. If you fail to declare income, or are even unable to provide supporting documentation, you face hefty fines. Basically, you need to know how the tax system works, what you need to disclose and the allowances to which you are entitled, so you can keep the appropriate records and handle self-assessment.

Having a professional tax advisor to help you with your tax calculations and presentation of the returns is essential. Online sources of information are the UK Taxation Directory (www. uktax.demon.co.uk), UK

Inland Revenue (www.inlandrevenue.gov.uk) and the Irish Revenue Commissioners (www.revenue.ie).

The tax inspector

UK taxation is administered primarily by the Inland Revenue, through a unified structure of *Taxpayer Service Offices* – handling PAYE coding, allowances, assessments and preliminary collection work; *Taxpayer District Offices* – handling business accounts, corporation tax, PAYE audit and tax recovery; and *Taxpayer Assistance Offices* – handling enquiries and providing forms. In Ireland, taxation is handled by the Revenue Commissioners.

UK and Irish business taxation is broadly similar. For a good introduction to Irish taxation, see *Starting Your Own Business* by Ron Immink and Brian O'Kane.

When you first set up your business you need to inform four organizations: the Inland Revenue (Figure 23.1), the Contributions Agency, HM Customs & Excise and the local authority (summarized in Table 23.1).

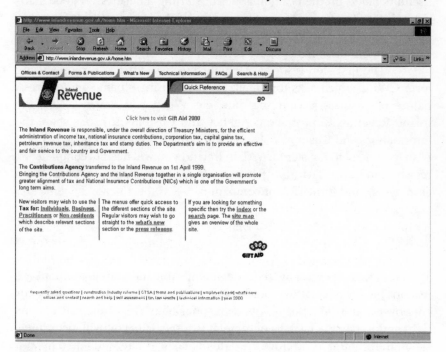

Figure 23.1

Table 23.1 UK taxation agencies

Agency	Taxation	Contact point
Inland Revenue	Income tax Capital gains tax Corporation tax	Inland Revenue Information Centre Bush House, Strand, London WC2 Tel: 020 7438 6420 www.inlandrevenue.gov.uk
Contributions Agency *(now handled by the Inland Revenue)*	PAYE NICs Pensions	Contributions Agency Department of Social Security Tel: Directory Enquiries for one near you. www.dss.gov.uk/ca
Customs & Excise	VAT Import duty	HM Customs & Excise (VAT) Enquiries (see *The Phone Book*) www.hmce.gov.uk
Local authorities	Business rates	Local authority (see *The Phone Book*) www.open.gov.uk

These agencies provide helpful information services with a number of useful booklets on the taxation issues of starting a business. A good starting point is *Starting Your Own Business,* booklet CWL1, available from any of the agencies. For the Irish Republic the main contact point is the Revenue Commissioners (Figure 23.2).

The first step is to register your business for tax purposes using form CWF1, which asks for details of your business name and address, nature of business, accounting date, etc. When you return CWF1, the Inland Revenue, Contributions Agency and Customs & Excise share the information, and Customs & Excise will write to you to ask whether you wish to or need to register for VAT. In Ireland you will need to complete tax registration form TR1 (for persons other than companies and PAYE employers), and form TR2 for companies.

Taxes

The tax system operates by 'self assessment'. You and your accountant are responsible for calculating your business tax, the PAYE and NIC for your employees, and VAT. But it is your responsibility to get the calculations right and to pay the tax bills on time. If you pay late, you will incur interest on the amount owed from the date the tax was due, and you may also incur fines for late payment. The main taxes are summarized below.

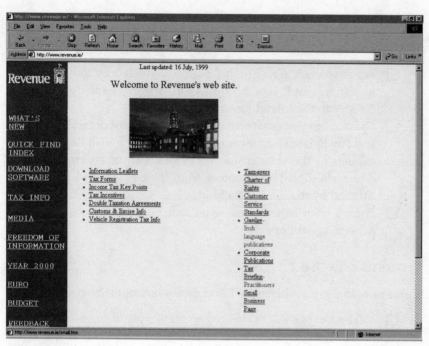

Figure 23.2

Inland Revenue

The UK Inland Revenue and the Irish Revenue Commissioners handle taxes associated with trading profits:

❑ *Income tax.* This is a tax paid by sole traders and partners on trading profits, based on bands of profits (eg 40 per cent above £28,100 for 1999/2000).

❑ *Capital gains tax.* This is a tax paid by sole traders and partners on the sale of major assets, such as buildings and equipment (eg 40 per cent above £28,100 for 1999/2000). The tax is charged on the disposal of all assets, gains and losses, being calculated on each individual asset.

❑ *Corporation tax.* Limited companies are charged this tax based on their profits. It covers all sources of income and capital gains world-wide.

Contributions Agency

The CA handles taxes associated with employment:

❏ *Pay-as-you-earn* (PAYE). This is a tax deducted by limited companies from employees' and directors' wages or salaries. It is paid directly to the Inland Revenue.

❏ *National Insurance contributions* (NICs). Payment of NICs in the UK, and Pay Related Social Insurance (PRSI) in the Irish Republic, contributes to the state pension schemes. Part of an employee's or director's contribution comes from their salary and part is contributed by the limited company.

❏ *Pension contributions.* Tax relief can be obtained on additional pension contributions.

Customs & Excise

Customs & Excise administer VAT, and duties on imported goods:

❏ *Value added tax.* VAT is charged on the supply of goods and services within the UK and Ireland, as well as on the import of goods and certain services.

❏ *Excise duty.* Duty is payable on goods (eg beer, wine, spirits, mineral oils and tobacco) and betting services (bingo, casinos, gaming machines, pool betting, lottery).

❏ *Business rate.* Businesses pay a uniform business rate based on the rateable value of their premises. If a property changes hands, the new owner is entitled to the existing rate, and empty properties attract only half the normal rates bill.

The tax timetable

The Inland Revenue, Contributions Agency and Customs & Excise operate to separate timetables. The following is a guide to this maze.

Inland Revenue

There are various important dates in the self-assessment timetable:

❏ *31 January.* This is important for three reasons. Your completed personal tax return for the previous tax year must be received by this date. It is also the deadline for paying the final tax instalment for the previous year, and the date for the first instalment of tax for the current year.

❑ *April*. The tax return form for the current year is sent to you from the Inland Revenue.

❑ *31 July*. The second instalment of the tax bill for the previous year is due; generally it is half the tax you paid in the previous year.

❑ *30 September*. This is the deadline for submission of your personal tax return to the Inland Revenue if you wish them to calculate your tax.

Contributions Agency

For the CA the important dates for PAYE and NICs etc are as follows:

❑ *Month-end plus 14 days*. Within 14 days of the end of each month you must send employees' income tax and NIC deductions to their PAYE office.

❑ *April*. You will receive from the Inland Revenue a return form asking for details of all pay and benefits for employees.

❑ *31 May*. One copy of the form is given to each employee (P60), and the others are returned to the Inland Revenue.

Customs & Excise

VAT forms and payments are typically processed quarterly, although you can request monthly or annual returns if your situation warrants it:

❑ *Quarterly*. Every three months you need to return the Customs & Excise form declaring VAT.

❑ *Quarterly plus one month*. Payment of any VAT owed must be forwarded to Customs & Excise.

❑ *Annually*. Relatively small businesses can opt for an annual VAT return.

Local authority

The uniform business rate (UBR) is paid on an annual basis, but can be paid by monthly instalments with the agreement of the authority.

Employment status

Of major concern to the Inland Revenue is the employment status of you and the people you employ. This distinction of whether you and your staff are employed or self-employed is important in deciding whether PAYE and employees' National Insurance contributions should be deducted from payments (and the employer's NICs paid); what business expenses may be claimed; whether you should be registered for VAT; and your income tax status.

Table 23.2 offers guidance on the employed/self-employed dichotomy, although it has to be said that at the time of writing some of these issues are still being discussed by the government and the Inland Revenue. If you can answer 'yes' to the questions in one of the columns, you are likely to be judged to have that status for tax purposes. The table is from booklet IR56/N139.

Taxation for a sole trader or partnership

Sole traders and partnerships are taxed as self-employed.

Sole trader

If you are a sole trader you are taxed on the profits you make in a specific tax year. You are assessed annually and pay your tax bill in two instalments, in January and July, rather than through the PAYE system.

Table 23.2 Taxation: employed or self-employed?

You are employed	You are self-employed
• Do you do the work rather than hiring someone else?	• Do you have the final say in how the business is run?
• Can someone tell you what to do?	• Do you risk your own money in the business?
• Are you paid by the hour, week or month?	• Are you responsible for meeting the losses as well as taking the profits?
• Do you work set hours?	• Do you provide the main items of equipment?
• Do you work at the premises of the person you work for, or at a place they decide?	• Are you free to hire other people on your own terms?
	• Do you have to correct unsatisfactory work in your own time and at your own expense?

Perhaps the most important decision is choosing your business' accounting year. If you choose what is called *fiscal accounting* – to make your accounting year coincide with the tax year (6 April to 5 April), this simplifies tax calculations, but gives you very little time to meet the self-assessment deadlines. If you choose a year-end early in the tax year, you can delay the payment of taxes on profits and give yourself additional time to prepare your return, but at the expense of 'overlapping profits'.

Calculation of taxable profits

❑ *Trading income*. Calculate the basic profits made on sales.
❑ *Deductible expenses*. Deduct from the profits any allowable business expenses, capital allowances and losses.
❑ *Asset sales*. Add in any balancing charges from the sale of assets.
❑ *Non-trade income*. Deduct any income that is not part of your trading (such as bank interest and dividends); these are taxed separately.

Additional taxes you will pay include:

❑ *National Insurance*. If you are a sole trader you need to pay NICs at a weekly rate, for which you will receive a quarterly demand.
❑ *Capital gains tax* (CGT). You will have to pay CGT on the sale of major assets, such as buildings and equipment, although sales of stock are exempt.

Partnership

If you are in a legal partnership, you are treated in a similar way to a self-employed sole trader, and taxed on the profits you make in a specific tax year. For tax purposes, profits are divided between the partners according to their partnership agreement, and each partner is taxed accordingly. Likewise, tax from any investment income to the partnership is calculated according to the partnership agreement.

In April the Inland Revenue sends tax return forms to the partnership and to each individual partner. The partnerships' return consolidates the total tax return for the partnership and includes sales income, investment income, deductible expenses, etc.

Capital gains tax

Capital gains tax applies when chargeable assets are disposed of, with the actual gains and losses being calculated on an asset by asset basis. For an individual, sole trader or partner, for the tax year 1999/2000, the first £7,100 was exempt – with the balance being charged at income tax rates as if it were the top slice of the taxpayer's income. The amount of 'gain' is worked out by taking the total costs of buying, improving and disposing of it, and deducting this from the sale price.

In general, all forms of property are chargeable (unless exempt) and disposal of a chargeable asset naturally gives rise to a taxable gain or loss. Fortunately, if you win the National Lottery, you will be pleased to know that the prize is exempt!

National Insurance

You have to pay NICs for yourself and every employee, whether you are a sole trader or partner. There are two classes of contribution:

- ❑ *Class* 2. Everyone is charged a fixed-rate weekly contribution (£6.55 in 1999/2000), unless their income is below the exemption level (£3,770 in 1999/2000).
- ❑ *Class* 4. If your earnings are above a certain amount (£7,530 in 1999/2000), an additional contribution is made at 6% of profits, up to a set limit (£26,220 in 1999/2000). Class 4 contributions are worked out and collected with your income tax.

It is not uncommon for a sole trader or partner to be also an employee of a limited company, and therefore have to pay a combination of class 1, 2 and 4 contributions in a given tax year (class 1 being the rate for an employed person).

Taxation for a limited company

Taxation of limited companies is significantly different from both sole traders and partnerships. For instance, income tax and capital gains tax are rolled into one, and called *corporation tax*.

Calculation of taxable profits

❑ *Trading income*. Calculate the basic profits made on sales.
❑ *Capital gains*. Include so-called *chargeable gains*, which are profits on the sale of major assets, such as buildings and equipment.
❑ *Certain investment income*. Include income from rents, interest and dividends from unit trusts.
❑ *Deductible expenses*. Deduct from the profits any allowable business expenses, capital allowances and losses.

But, do not include:

❑ *Dividends*. Dividends and distributions from UK companies are treated differently for tax purposes.

Corporation tax

Corporation tax is charged on the world-wide profits of UK-registered limited companies. Your company's taxable income is computed broadly using income tax rules, as discussed below. In computing your company's trading profits, capital allowances are deducted as trading expenses, and balancing charges are treated as trading income. For a limited company, 'capital gains' are calculated on chargeable gains rules, but are then charged to corporation tax, as opposed to capital gains tax. The only sources of income that escape corporation tax are dividends or other distributions from UK-resident companies.

In Ireland there are currently three rates of corporation tax: *reduced rate* – 30 per cent on the first £50,000 of a company's income; *standard rate* – 38 per cent on the balance of income over £50,000; and *manufacturing rate* – 10 per cent on income arising from manufacturing.

PAYE and National Insurance

As an employer with a limited company you have to act as tax collector for the government. On each pay day you have to deduct the correct amount of tax and NICs from each employee's pay, including your own, and send it to the tax collector. The following is a guide:

❑ *On taking on your first employee*. Inform your own tax office, who will notify you of your PAYE office as an employer. The PAYE office will then send you the appropriate tax and NIC tables for calculating deductions.

☐ *On taking on a new employee.* When the person starts work you should ask him or her for form P45 from the previous employer. Complete part 3 of the form and forward it to your tax office. If the new employee does not have form P45, ask him or her to complete form P46, and send this to the tax office.

☐ *On each pay day.* Calculate the tax and NICs for each employee. Fill in the Deductions Working Sheet (form P11) for each employee.

☐ *At month-end plus 14 days.* Send the Deductions Work Sheet, and the PAYE and NI deductions, to the PAYE accounts office.

☐ *At tax year-end.* At the end of each tax year (5 April) the Inland Revenue will send you a return form requesting the details of pay and benefits for each employee. One copy of the return (form P60) is given to the employee and two others are sent back to the Inland Revenue.

National Insurance for each employee of a limited company is paid as part of the PAYE system. *Class 1 contributions* are paid in part by the employee and in part by the company. The actual amounts are related to the levels of earnings and are calculated from tables supplied by the PAYE tax office.

At the end of the tax year there are several PAYE/NIC forms you need to complete for each employee:

☐ *Form P14.* For the tax office, complete a form for each employee, listing their total earnings, tax and NIC deductions.

☐ *Form P60.* Give all employees a copy of their total earnings, tax and NIC deductions.

☐ *Form P35.* For the tax office, you need to complete a statement of total PAYE and NIC deductions.

When an employee leaves, you must complete the four-part form P45 listing their total pay and tax deductions for the year. Send part 1 to the tax office. Give parts 1A, 2 and 3 to the employee; 1A for their records, and 2 and 3 for their future employer.

Income tax rates and personal allowances change yearly. The UK Inland Revenue's and Irish Revenue Commissioners' websites (see Figures 23.1 and 23.3) show the changes following each budget. There are different bands of taxable income, and it is necessary to check which bands you fall into. The UK Inland Revenue provide a *Quick Guide to PAYE and NIC* (called the CWG1 card), and provide an employer's helpline for queries (tel 0345 143 143).

Deductible allowances

Claiming all your deductible allowances against your tax bill is one area where timely professional advice is essential.

Business expenses

You are entitled to deduct legitimate business expenses from the profits of your company. Basically, the expense must be 'allowable', and incurred 'wholly and exclusively' for the business. However, with an office at home and a car used for both business and pleasure, you can claim a proportion of the running costs. As a rough guide, Table 23.3 lists typical items that are allowed or not allowed.

Table 23.3 Tax-deductible business expenses

Allowed	Not allowed
General expenses	
• Raw materials and goods bought for resale • Rates and rental of business premises • Office expenses: lighting, heating and cleaning • Stationery and books • Computer software • Maintenance and repairs • Proportion of home and car expenses for work	• Computer equipment • Private use of car
Staff costs	
• Wages, salaries, bonuses, redundancy • Employer's National Insurance contributions • Pensions to employees • Travel, subsistence and gifts • Subscriptions to professional or trade bodies	• Your own income and living expenses • Travel between home and work • Not your own NIC • Business entertainment (except staff)
Financial and legal expenses	
• Fees for accountancy, advertising, etc. • Bank charges on business accounts • Interest on loans and overdrafts for business • Business insurance • Legal charges such as preparing contracts • Fees for IPR registration such as trademark	• Tax (except NIC and VAT) • Bank charges on personal account • Legal expenses on forming a company

Capital allowances

Capital allowances relate to the purchase of equipment and even know-how. Although the initial cost of capital equipment is not allowed as a business expense, you can claim a capital allowance on the depreciation cost of equipment (see Table 23.4).

In calculating the allowance on a piece of equipment, in the first year you use its cost price, and in subsequent years you use its depreciated value. For example, with a personal computer, bought for £1,000 and depreciated over three years, the successive values are: £1,000, £667, £333.

Losses

When you launch your new business, in its start-up phase you may spend more money than the business actually generates. To help you, the Inland Revenue and Revenue Commissioners give special treatment for losses in the first four years of your business. These 'losses' may be treated as deductible allowances against tax over the four years. Depending on the circumstances, you can use a combination of the following:

❑ *Deducting loss from other income or capital gains.* You can deduct the loss either from other income and capital gains in the current tax year, or from income and gains in the previous year.

❑ *Carrying the loss forward.* Alternatively you can carry losses forward and deduct them from future trading profits, apart from capital gains.

Table 23.4 Capital allowances (subject to yearly change)

Capital Item	Allowances
Computer equipment	40% in first year
Plant and machinery	40% in first year
Vehicles	25% up to £3,000
Buying a patent	25%
Buying know-how	25%
Undertaking scientific research	100% in first year

If you want to use losses to offset your tax bills, you need to do so within two years of the year the trading loss occurred.

With all deductible allowances, negotiate with your tax inspector and seek their advice on what is acceptable.

Enterprise Investment Scheme

To encourage investment in start-ups, the UK government's *Enterprise Investment Scheme,* and similar schemes in the Irish Republic, give tax concessions to private individuals who invest in unquoted companies. With the reinvestment scheme, individuals who sell their shares and then reinvest in a new private company can delay paying capital gains tax. Agreement of the Inland Revenue is required to gain EIS qualification.

Value added tax

Of all the taxes levied, VAT causes the most difficulty on a day-to-day basis. It is a tax on goods and services supplied, but a VAT-registered company can claim back the VAT on all legitimate business expenses. By law, all VAT-registered companies must show their nine-digit registration on all stationery, in particular on invoices and receipts. Obviously, only VAT-registered businesses can charge VAT.

The threshold for VAT registration is currently an annual turnover of £49,000, but it is probably worth registering your company (and recording VAT charges) if your turnover is below this figure because you can recover VAT retrospectively. (The recording of VAT is discussed in Chapter 18.) The form for VAT registration is illustrated in Figure 23.3, and registration enquiries are handled by an automated telephone system (tel 0345 112 114).

VAT returns are made quarterly to UK Customs & Excise (www.hmce.gov.uk) or the Irish Collector-General (www.revenue.ie/vatinfo). You list the gross values charged to customers for goods and services, the values of goods and services for which you have paid suppliers, and the total tax you owe to the government, or the total claim if VAT is owed to you.

Surprisingly, it is a *person* who is registered for VAT and not a *business*, and each registration covers *all* business activities of the registered

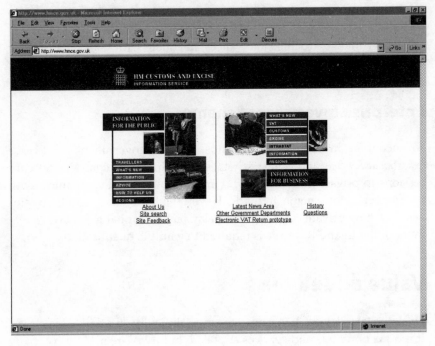

Figure 23.3

person. However, the person registered can be a sole trader, a partnership, a limited company, or a charity.

The system works as follows. Each person in the chain from first supplier to final consumer is charged VAT on taxable supplies to him/her (called *input tax*) and charges VAT on taxable supplies made by him/her (*output tax*). You pay over to UK Customs & Excise or Irish Collector-General the excess of output tax over input tax, or recover the difference. The broad result is that businesses are not affected by VAT, except that they are required to administer it; the main burden falls on the consumer.

UK Customs & Excise publish an excellent guide to VAT, obtainable from your local VAT office.

Uniform business rate

In the UK, a local authority receives revenue from three sources: *central government grants*, the *uniform business rate* levied on local businesses, and the *council tax* levied on residential properties.

The uniform business rate is based on the 'rateable value' of a non-domestic property – broadly, the rental the property could have commanded in 1993. There are two rate bands for business, depending upon whether the rateable values are over or under £10,000 (£15,000 in Greater London). For 1998/99 these rates (called the uniform poundage) were 47.4p and 46.5p respectively. The rate bill is calculated by multiplying the rateable value of the property by the uniform poundage (eg £10,000 multiplied by 0.474/£ = £4740 due).

Sources of help

Armstrong, K (1994) *Taxes on Business,* Kogan Page, London

Capital Taxes Office. (England & Wales) Ferrers House. PO Box 38, Castle Meadows Road, Nottingham, NG2 1BB, tel: 0115 974 2400 www.inlandrevenue.gov.uk

Chartered Institute of Taxation. 12 Upper Belgrave Street, London, SW1X 8BB, tel: 020 7235 9381, fax: 020 7235 2562, *www.tax.org.uk*

Homer, A and Burrows, R (1997) *Tolley's Tax Guide 98–99,* Tolley Publishing Co. Ltd., Croydon, Surrey

Irish Collector-General (Taxes). Sarsfield House, Francis Street, Limerick, tel: 061 310 310, fax: 061 410 311

Irish Revenue Commissioners. Dublin Castle, Dublin 2, tel: 01 679 2777, *www.revenue.ie*

Starting in Business. Form CWL1, Board of Inland Revenue, Press Office, Somerset House, Strand, London, *www.inlandrevenue.gov.uk*

Taxguide Web site. *www.taxguide.co.uk*

UK Customs and Excise. King's Beam House, 39–41 Mark Lane, London, EC3R 7HE, tel: 020 76201313, www.hmce.gov.uk

UK Inland Revenue. Public Enquiry Room, West Wing, Somerset House, London, WC2R 1LB, tel: 020 7438 6420, *www.inlandrevenue.gov.uk*

Williams, S (1999) *Small Business Guide,* Penguin, London

Part 5

Law
for
Small Businesses

---

24 **Forming a Company**

To quote J P Morgan: 'I don't want a lawyer who tells me what I can't do. I hire a lawyer to tell me how I can do what I want.'

In the next few chapters we shall be looking at law for the high-tech start-up. This covers setting up a company, company law requirements, legal forms such as software contracts, and intellectual property rights. This chapter specifically follows *English* law, although Irish and Scottish company law are similar.

In this chapter we look at:

- ❑ options for the type of company you want to launch (ie the method of trading);
- ❑ the duties of company staff, whether directors, shareholders or employees;
- ❑ how to go about forming a limited company.

You need to choose the correct legal form for your company. This is important for a number of reasons: the costs of registration, issues of taxation, and your legal liabilities if things go wrong.

An excellent introduction to the subject is Patricia Clayton's *Law for the Small Business*. Other good sources of help and advice are your local Chamber of Commerce, Consumer Advice Centre and Citizen's Advice Bureau. For Irish law, I recommend *Starting your own Business* by Ron Immink and Brian O'Kane.

Methods of trading

A number of options exist for launching your business, ranging from a fully registered limited company to 'moonlighting' in the black economy, which is definitely not recommended! During the course of your business career you are likely to utilize a number of different types of 'company'. Many entrepreneurs start in business as a *sole trader*, undertaking part-time work, maintaining someone's computer systems or developing Web pages, and then as their business grows they register as a partnership or limited company. The methods of trading are (see also Table 24.1):

❑ *Sole trader.* If you are a one-person business, your best option is probably to operate as a sole trader. All you need is some stationery with your name and address on it. You don't need to register with any official body, but you do need to inform the Inland Revenue and Department of Social Security (DSS) that you are self-employed. You don't have to have your accounts audited, but you are liable personally for all debts incurred by the business.

❑ *Partnership.* If two or more of you are planning to work together, you can operate as a partnership. The ground rules are essentially the same as for a sole trader. Your stationery must show your names and address. Again, you need to inform the Inland Revenue and DSS that you are all self-employed. Most importantly, all partners are collectively and individually liable for any debts. Although you are not required by law to have a formal partnership agreement, it is wise to do so.

❑ *Limited company.* A limited company must have a minimum of one shareholder, and two officers who act as director and company secretary, and the company must be formally registered with the Companies Registration Office in the UK, or the Registrar of Companies in Ireland. Your stationery must show the company's name, address and place and number of registration. It can either show the names of all directors or none. Accounts must be professionally audited, annually, and lodged with Companies House in the UK, or Companies Office, Dublin.

❑ *Co-operative.* A co-operative is a business owned jointly by its 'members'; at least seven people. A co-operative has to be registered under the Industrial and Provident Societies Acts. However, this is not a simple task and you are advised to seek advice from the Co-operative Development Agency (21 Panton Street, London SW1 4DR), or, in Ireland, the FAS Co-operative Development Unit.

❑ *Registered charity.* Certain types of educational, artistic and religious business can be incorporated as a registered charity with the Charity Commissioners. The tax advantages can be quite considerable, broadly giving exemption from income tax, capital gains tax, corporation tax and inheritance tax. Naturally, the trustees of the charity may not profit from their positions, but they can receive a salary.

❑ *Franchise.* With a franchise, you trade under the brand name of the franchisor, who helps you set up in business. You pay a one-off franchise fee, and an ongoing management fee of around 10 per cent of turnover. The type of company formed to run the franchise could be a sole trader, partnership or more likely a limited company.

❑ *Part-time employment.* Many people choose to work part-time as contractors or consultants. You do not need to inform the Inland Revenue and DSS that you are self-employed, but you do need to declare these earnings in your annual income tax return. Like a sole trader you are responsible for any debts and for liability. The Inland Revenue is interested only when your total income is more than £4,335 per year (1999/2000 figure).

Table 24.1 Methods of trading, and obligations

Method of trading	Registration	Professionally Audited Accounts	Liability	Taxation	PAYE/NI
Sole Trader	no	no	personal	income tax	NI
Partnership	no	no	personal	income tax	NI
Limited Company	yes	yes	company	corporation tax	PAYE/NI
Co-operative	yes	yes	company	corporation tax	PAYE/NI
Registered Charity	yes	yes	company	basically exempt - except for VAT	PAYE/NI
Franchise	no	yes	company	corporation tax	PAYE/NI
Part-time Employment	no	no	personal	income tax	no

Sole trader

If you plan to be a one-person business, trading from your home as a contractor or consultant, for example, then being a sole trader is one option (see Table 24.2). Setting up is easy and straightforward:

- ❑ display your name and address on your stationery;
- ❑ if your trading name is different from your own name, check it is legal;
- ❑ inform the Inland Revenue and DSS you are self-employed;
- ❑ check with the local Planning Office that your place of work is suitable;
- ❑ consider whether you need to register for VAT.

As a sole trader you are totally responsible for all business transactions and debts. So you will need also to check with your solicitor about your business liability – and the best ways of covering yourself. Lastly, although you are not legally obliged to have your accounts audited professionally, it is wise to have your accounts and tax returns prepared by an accountant specializing in small businesses.

Partnership

A business partnership is an association of between two and 20 people trading together as one firm and sharing the profits (see Table 24.3).

The partnership operates under broadly similar rules to a sole trader. You need to show the names and address of the 'partners' on the stationery, inform the Inland Revenue that you are self-employed, check any made-up business name for legal objections, and register for VAT

Table 24.2 Advantages and disadvantages of being a sole trader

Advantages	Disadvantages
• Start trading immediately	• Unlimited personal liability
• No registration; minimal formalities	• Low business status
• No set-up costs (eg lawyers)	• Limited access to investment capital
• No annual audit or audit fees	• Higher tax rates than a limited company
• No disclosure of trading information	• Limits on pension contributions

Table 24.3 Advantages and disadvantages of forming a partnership

Advantages	Disadvantages
• Start trading immediately	• Unlimited personal liability on all partners
• No registration; minimal formalities	• Partnership ceases on death of a partner
• No set-up costs (eg lawyers)	• Limited access to investment capital
• Optional annual audit	• Partnership agreements can be costly
• No disclosure of trading information	

when your turnover exceeds the VAT threshold. Setting up as a partnership is relatively straightforward:

- ❏ display your names and business address on the stationery;
- ❏ check the name under which you trade is legally acceptable;
- ❏ draw up a legally binding partnership agreement;
- ❏ take out life insurance on each partner to protect the partnership;
- ❏ inform the Inland Revenue and DSS you are self-employed;
- ❏ check with the local Planning Office that your place of work is suitable;
- ❏ consider whether you need to register for VAT;
- ❏ consider whether to form a limited (liability) partnership.

It is wise to draw up a partnership agreement setting out the roles of each partner in the business, their share of the profits, and how each partner's share is to be valued should they wish to withdraw from the partnership.

In addition, you should note that upon the death of a partner, that partner's share of the business becomes part of their estate, and the partnership itself officially ceases.

The main drawback of a partnership is that all partners are collectively liable for any debts incurred by the business.

Limited company

The big advantage in setting up your business as a limited company is that, if things go wrong, it is the company that is liable, not you having to pay debts from your personal savings (see Table 24.4). To set up one, the simplest procedure is to buy an 'off the shelf' company (discussed later in this chapter).

Table 24.4 Advantages and disadvantages of forming a limited company

Advantages	Disadvantages
• High business status	• Company has to be formally registered
• Company carries the liability	• Professional annual audit required
• Access to investment capital	• Public disclosure of trading information
• Possible flotation on stock market	• Director's duties and obligations
• Business has life independent of founders	
• Lower tax rates	

A limited company must be registered officially with the Companies Registry, and have a *certificate of incorporation*. The basic requirements of a private limited company are:

❏ At least one shareholder is required, together with a director and a company secretary.

❏ Companies House requires various documents: *Memorandum of Association*; *Articles of Association*; *Form 10* – directors and registered address; *Form 12* – declaration of compliance; *Form 117* – sent before trading; *Registration fee* (currently £20).

❏ The company name must be displayed outside of the office premises.

❏ The company name, address and registration must be displayed on stationery

❏ The Inland Revenue must be informed.

❏ The local Planning Office must confirm that your place of work is suitable.

❏ The company accounts must be audited professionally and lodged annually.

There are two basic classes of 'company': limited and public. With a limited company (Ltd) the liability of the owners is limited to the amount outstanding on the share capital. A public company (Plc) is one whose shares can be traded freely. A public company can also be a listed company whose shares are traded on a stock exchange.

To form a public company you must have share capital of at least £50,000 and at least one-quarter must be paid-up on each share. In addition, a public company must have at least two directors plus a company secretary.

Co-operative

A co-operative is a business owned jointly by its members, which must be seven or more people, who share the profits and vote on management decisions. People are attracted to co-operatives for the greater level of involvement in decision-making in the workplace, rather than for great financial benefits (see Table 24.5).

As discussed below, there are a number of formalities when establishing a co-operative. Typically you need to (i) recruit at least seven members; (ii) approach a 'sponsoring body' such as the Industrial Common Ownership Movement (ICOM); (iii) adopt ICOM or other model co-operative rules; and (iv) apply for registration under the Industrial and Provident Societies Acts (I&PS) 1965–76.

To meet the legal requirements, a co-operative must conform to the following basic rules:

- ❑ *Benefit*. The members (ie the workers) must be the primary beneficiaries of the business, rather than the investors.
- ❑ *Membership*. This must be open to anyone satisfying the membership rules, and must comprise at least seven people.
- ❑ *Management*. The management must be under the control of the members, with each member having equal control.
- ❑ *Voting rights*. The members must have an established voting system for decision-making.
- ❑ *Profits*. Any profits must be retained in the business or shared amongst the members.
- ❑ *Payments*. These are basically restricted to loans, with specific limits on payment.
- ❑ *Disbanding*. The co-operative can be disbanded only with the agreement of the members.

Table 24.5 Advantages and disadvantages of forming a co-operative

Advantages	Disadvantages
• Members are the primary beneficiaries	• Complicated registration procedure
• Each member has equal control	• Limited financial incentives
• Profits are shared amongst the members	• Limited access to investment capital

Setting up a co-operative is not a simple procedure, so you should seek the advice and sponsorship of ICOM (tel 0113 246 1737). They will provide you with model rules and guide you through the registration process.

Registered charity

If you are not trying to make your fortune but setting up a business associated with education, the arts or religion, then you may be able to register as a charity (see Table 24.6). However, it is a fairly complicated procedure to register. Typically, (i) seek the advice of your solicitor on the registration procedure; (ii) set up a company *limited by guarantee*, as an initial step; and (iii) contact the Charity Commissioners and request application forms.

The tax advantages of being registered as a charity are quite considerable, with relief or exemption on rates (ie 50 per cent rates relief), income tax, capital gains tax (no CGT on gifts), corporation tax (exemption in most cases) and inheritance tax (exemption on gifts).

However, before you try to register yourself as a charity, you should broadly know the rules governing the operation of a charity. They are obviously strict, otherwise every Tom, Dick and Harriet would try:

- ❑ *Charitable status.* The organization must be 'charitable'; eg relief of poverty, beneficial to the community, educational organization, arts organization or a religious organization.
- ❑ *Company limited by guarantee.* Where a 'charitable' company is limited by guarantee, its objectives must be acceptable to the Charity Commissioners.
- ❑ *Trustees.* The trustees must not profit from their position, but they may receive remuneration.

Table 24.6 Advantages and disavantages of forming a registered charity

Advantages	Disadvantages
• Encourages donors to donate money	• Complicated registration procedure
• Major taxation advantages	• Negotiation with Charity Commissioners
• Suitable for arts, education, religion	• Strict rules to follow
	• Trustees cannot benefit financially
	• Annual submission of accounts

❏ *Accounts*. The charity must keep and register accounts with the Charity Commissioners.

Obtaining charitable status is quite difficult, for obvious reasons, and therefore you should seek professional help if you wish to apply to the Charity Commission (tel 0870 3330123; www.charity-commission.gov.uk).

Franchise

Franchises are an increasingly popular way for a *franchisor* to expand and for a *franchisee* to launch a new business. The benefits are:

❏ *Franchise*. The brand and business organization being replicated benefits from broad nation-wide advertising, brand recognition and bulk purchasing.
❏ *Franchisor*. The owner of the business and brand can expand rapidly, nationally or globally, with far lower investment required.
❏ *Franchisee*. The purchaser of the 'franchise' benefits from the knowledge, branding, advertising and support of the franchisor.

Below, we look briefly at franchising from the perspectives of the franchisor and the franchisee.

A franchisor guide

The requirements for becoming a franchisor are: (i) a distinctive brand image; (ii) a proven business format suitable for franchising; and (iii) high enough profits for the franchisees and yourself. To become a franchisor:

❏ Seek the advice of the British Franchise Association (BFA).
❏ Approach existing franchisees and the franchisor to see how they operate (obviously you could pretend to be interested in becoming a franchisee).
❏ Find a solicitor affiliated to the BFA to advise you on the structure of your franchise business and to draw up the necessary contracts.
❏ Talk to the franchise unit of your clearing bank to seek their advice on the financial aspects of the proposed franchise business.

In most high-tech areas the concept of franchising remains largely unexploited. As a starting point, the British Franchise Association (tel 01491 578050, www.british-franchise.org.uk) publish a guide for prospective franchisors.

A franchisee guide

To become a franchisee, you need: (i) a successful franchisor; (ii) a distinctive brand image; (iii) a proven business format; and (iv) high enough profits for yourself. To become a franchisee:

- ☐ Approach the BFA for help in identifying a list of suitable franchises.
- ☐ Identify a suitable franchise, and then visit existing franchisees to assess the business potential and also the level of support of the franchisor.
- ☐ Talk to the franchise unit of your clearing bank to seek their advice on the financial aspects of the proposed franchise.
- ☐ Find a solicitor affiliated to the BFA to advise you on the franchise, any restrictions, and how the franchisor will make money from you.

If you want to work for yourself, then franchises have a number of advantages. These, and the disadvantages, are summarized in Table 24.7.

The franchise industry claims that starting in business as a franchisee gives you a much greater chance of surviving because you are buying into a well-known brand with a proven business formula. However, you need to determine that the franchise is 'right for you', that the franchise is in fact successful, and that the franchisor can be trusted.

Table 24.7 Advantages and disadvantages of taking up a franchise

Advantages	Disadvantages
• You are trading under a well-known name	• Strictly controlled method of trading
• You receive advice, help and training	• Charged a franchising fee
• Access to bank loans via the franchisor	• Often a large start-up investment required
• Nationwide advertising campaigns	• Charged an ongoing management fee

Roles of directors

An entrepreneur friend said that the most worrying thing he recalls is taking on his first employee. *He* was worried about moral obligations; but you also have to comply with employment law, strewn with regulations, fines and penalties.

The directors are responsible for the management of a limited company. Their powers and responsibilities are set out in the company's Memorandum and Articles of Association.

Types of director

A director is anyone occupying a senior executive position. High-tech companies, influenced by the United States, increasingly use the terms chief executive officer (CEO) for the managing director, chief financial officer (CFO) for the director in charge of finance, and chief technical officer (CTO) for the research and development director. (My favourite is chief evangelising officer – CEO? – for the director responsible for promoting a new business innovation!)

The appointment and removal of directors must be reported to the Registrar at Companies House.

Directors' obligations

With directors' powers come wide responsibilities:

- ❑ *Company interest.* Decisions must be in the best interests of the company (and shareholders) as a whole, rather than employees, customers, the directors, or a specific shareholder.
- ❑ *The law.* They must ensure that the company does everything it is obliged to by law. This includes employment, industrial training, health and safety legislation, and taxation.

Forming a limited company

Most high-tech start-ups begin by forming a *private* limited company. Basically there are two ways of doing this.

An off-the-shelf company

The fastest route to registering is to buy an 'off-the-shelf' company from a lawyer, registration agent or Companies House. Existing shareholders then have to resign in favour of your shareholders, and you can change the company name later. The registration currently costs between £100 and £250, plus a £50 fee if you change the name.

A company from scratch

Submit the necessary forms and documents (see below) to the Registrar of Companies at the Companies Registration Office, either yourself or through a solicitor. A useful website to visit is that of Companies House (www.companies-house.gov.uk). In the Irish Republic, contact the Registrar of Companies (tel 011 804 5200).

Registering the company

To register a limited company with Companies House in the UK or the Companies Office in Ireland, you need to file the following information:

- ❑ *Company name.* Choose a name that is different from those already appearing in the Index of Names of the Registrar of Companies, otherwise you could be challenged for 'passing-off'. In addition, there are certain 'restricted' names that could be misleading (eg those containing the words 'bank', 'government', 'international', 'royal', 'charity', etc), and those that could be considered offensive. Once permission is granted for the name, it is *reserved* pending a special resolution for its adoption by 75 per cent of the shareholders.
- ❑ *Memorandum of Association.* The Memorandum sets out your company's basic constitution and its powers and duties as a legal 'person'. This includes: (i) the company name; (ii) its registered address; (iii) the objectives for which the company was formed; (iv) a statement that the liability of the members is limited; (v) the amount of nominal capital; and (vi) the names of the *subscribers* (ie the first 'parents' of the company).

❏ *Articles of Association.* The Articles deal with your company's internal organization and its relationship with its shareholders. This includes: (i) types of shares; (ii) restrictions on the issuing of shares; (iii) restrictions on share transfers; (iv) names of the directors and their powers; and (v) any general provisions such as notice of meetings, etc.

❏ Statement of director(s) and secretary, and the intended situation of the registered office. Form 10 gives details of the company's officers, and a signed declaration by the first director and secretary of agreement to act for the company.

❏ *Declaration of compliance with the requirements on application for registration of a company.* This is 'form 12' signed by the company officers or their solicitor.

To register a business name in the Irish Republic you must complete form RBN1B and send it with a fee (currently £25) to the Registrar of Companies.

Business capital

Registering as a limited company means your high-tech start-up is structured for growth, whether through issuing shares or borrowing. Your company's capital structure subdivides into corporate capital and company borrowings.

Corporate capital

This is the money put into the business by shareholders, and is of two types:

❏ *Nominal capital.* This is the total amount of share capital that the Memorandum authorizes the company to issue, in contrast to paid-up capital that defines the *actual* amount of money invested.

❏ *Additional capital.* New capital can be raised by issuing additional shares, which can be ordinary shares or preference shares whose rights must be met before the ordinary ones.

Company borrowings

This is all the money borrowed by the company. There are three main types:

- *Mortgage.* The company can lodge its own shares or its business assets as security on a loan.
- *Loans.* These can be raised from an individual, bank or other institution.
- *Debentures.* Loans can be raised also by issuing a financial instrument to the 'debenture holder' as evidence of a mortgage or charge on the company assets.

Types of shares

- *Ordinary shares.* The standard share is referred to as an 'ordinary share', and each one has equal voting rights and claim on income.
- *Preference shares.* These are new shares issued to shareholders who are given 'preference rights' over the ordinary shareholders, whereby they are paid before any ordinary share dividend is paid.
- *Share options.* Often staff in start-ups are given share incentives, namely the right to buy or sell a number of shares at a specified price before a specified deadline.

Sources of help

Charity Commissioners. Harmsworth House, 13–15 Bouverie Street, London, EC4Y 8DP, tel: 0870 3330123, *www.charity-commission.gov.uk*

Clayton, P (1994) *Forming a Limited Company*, Kogan Page, London

Companies House (England and Wales). Crown Way, Maindy, Cardiff, CF4 3UZ, tel: 012920 388 588, *www.companies-house.gov.uk*

Companies House (Scotland). 37 Castle Terrace, Edinburgh, EH1 2EB, tel: 0131 535 5800, *www.companies-house.gov.uk*

Companies Registry (Northern Ireland). IDB House, 64 Chichester Street, Belfast, BT1 4JX, tel: 01232 234 488

Immink, R and O'Kane, B (1997) *Starting your own Business*, Oak Tree Press, Dublin

IOD (1995) *Director's Liabilities and Guidelines for Directors*, Institute of Directors, 116 Pall Mall, London, SW1Y 5ED, tel: 020 7242 1222, *www.iod.co.uk*

Law Pack (1996) Do-it-yourself Limited Company, Law Pack Guide, London

Registry of Business Names. Parnell House, 14 Parnell Square, Dublin, tel: 011 804 5200

25   Company Law Requirements

Here we look at the legal requirements of running your business:

- ❑ the annual accounts and the returns required by Companies House;
- ❑ company officers, specifically the roles and responsibilities of directors;
- ❑ employment law, the contract of employment, and statutory rights;
- ❑ insurance for premises, personal indemnity, and public liability;
- ❑ premises, including planning law, leases and the health and safety at work act;
- ❑ some laws affecting trading.

This chapter is based on *English* law, but Scottish and Irish law is broadly similar. A good introduction to all these areas is *Law for the Small Business* by Patricia Clayton.

Accounts

Accounts play an important role in a limited company. They must conform to the Companies Acts, must be audited professionally, and must be submitted annually.

Requirements

By law, the company accounts must include the following:

- ❏ *Director's report*. This is a summary of the trading performance of the company in the previous financial year.
- ❏ *Profit and loss account*. This monitors the income and expenditure over the accounting period.
- ❏ *Balance sheet*. This shows the financial position of the company at the end of the accounting period.
- ❏ *Auditor's report*. The auditor's report must be supplied to shareholders and Companies House.

Exemptions

Companies House exempts 'small businesses' from a full audit and submission. The conditions are:

- ❏ *Turnover under £350,000*. These companies, with a balance sheet value of no more than £1.4 million, may dispense with an audit.
- ❏ *Medium-sized companies*. Qualifying companies may submit an abbreviated P&L account.
- ❏ *Small companies*. Qualifying companies may submit an abbreviated balance sheet.

Timetable

The timetable for producing the accounts is important:

- ❏ *Financial year*. This is the period covered by your accounts – typically 12 months.
- ❏ *Accounting reference date*. This is the date that your financial year ends.
- ❏ *Approval*. The accounts must be approved by the board, and the balance sheet signed; likewise the directors' report.
- ❏ *Circulation*. The accounts must be formally considered by the annual general meeting, and a copy sent in advance to every shareholder and debenture holder.
- ❏ *Submission*. The accounts and annual return must be submitted to Companies House within seven months of the accounting reference date.
- ❏ *Annual return*. A 'shuttle' return containing information held on the Companies House database is sent annually. This needs to be checked and amended and returned within 28 days.

Importantly it is the responsibility of each director to ensure that the accounts are prepared and circulated to shareholders, and submitted on time to Companies House.

Company officers

The principal officers of the company are the directors, the company secretary and the auditor. The directors (by whatever title they are known) are responsible for the management of the company:

❑ The chairman is the director responsible for chairing board and general meetings and for signing the minutes of the meetings.

❑ The managing director (or chief executive officer, to use the US term) has no specific powers under the Companies Acts, but is empowered by the Memorandum and Articles to 'manage' the other directors.

❑ Companies typically have a director with special responsibility for financial matters; called the finance director (UK) or chief financial officer (US).

❑ High-tech companies usually have a director with special responsibility for technology and product development, called the technical director (UK) or chief technical officer (US).

❑ A director may appoint an alternative to carry out his or her duties during an absence.

❑ Shadow directors are anybody 'who in effect acts as a director'. This might be a major shareholder or someone in accordance with whose wishes the board/company is accustomed to act.

In addition, every company must have a company secretary – the chief administrative officer – who can be a director but not the sole director. The company secretary has important duties and obligations, such as convening company meetings, taking minutes, keeping the statutory books (see Chapter 24), and filing all information with Companies House.

A qualified auditor must be appointed or reappointed annually by the general meeting, to audit the accounts as required by the Companies Acts.

When a new director is appointed, form 288a must be completed and returned to Companies House. The director in question must consent to act by signing the form. On the whole anyone can be a director, with the exception of: (i) someone formally disqualified for previously failing to carry out their obligations as a director; (ii) an undischarged bankrupt; and (iii) those not meeting certain age constraints, such as being under 16 in Scotland or over 70 in Northern Ireland. When a director retires, is removed or disqualified, form 288b is completed and sent to Companies House.

Data protection

If you hold computer data containing personal details of customers, suppliers and employees, then you need to be aware of the provisions of the Data Protection Act and register your information with the Data Protection Registrar (tel 01625 545 745; www.dpr.gov.uk). The Irish counterpart is the Data Protection Commissioner (write to info@dataprivacy.ie). Forms are available from Post Offices, and a three-year licence is around £75.

The purpose of the Act is to control the storage and use of information about individuals on computers. There are a few logical exceptions. For example, certain computer-based information is excluded:

❑ information used within the company for the purposes of the payroll;
❑ names and addresses used only for distribution of information (ie a mailing list).

The Data Protection Act is discussed in more detail in Chapter 28.

Employment Law

Chapter 10 looked at the process of taking on staff. This section will review the legal requirements associated with being an employer.

The main requirements

As an employer you have basic obligations to treat job applicants and employees fairly. This covers discrimination, pay and working conditions, and procedures for dismissal. The following are the main requirements.

When advertising for and interviewing new applicants, the job should be described accurately, and you should avoid terms implying sex and age of intended applicants. Do not discriminate in terms of ethnic origin, sex, marital status or disability. However, you can employ men and women for specific jobs. If you have more than 20 employees, 3 per cent of your workforce must be registered disabled.

The basic offer of employment should set out the agreed amount of payment, together with a brief specification of the job. Men and women should be given equal pay for similar duties. Do not insist on any employees working for more than 48 hours a week.

After one month in employment, staff should be paid even if there is no work. They are entitled also to minimum notice periods.

After 13 weeks of employment, make sure that every new recruit has a written statement setting out the terms of employment. After three months (in other words, roughly the same period), give employees a minimum of three weeks paid holiday a year. After six months, female employees are entitled to statutory maternity pay.

When someone has been employed continuously for two years, their rights change significantly. They are entitled to a payment for redundancy if necessary, and disciplinary procedures must be followed rigorously.

The contract of employment

The contract of employment is a legally binding agreement between you and your employee. Given the increasing strength of employment legislation, it is important for the contract to be accurate.

The document should contain details of the parties, the payments, the job and statutory entitlements. Dismissal provisions cover those who have worked for more than two years, or less if the dismissal is for various 'inadmissible' reasons such as pregnancy or trade union membership. An employee can be dismissed instantly for serious unacceptable behaviour such as theft or violence, which amounts to gross misconduct.

If an employee is not actually dismissed but is placed in such an untenable position that he or she is forced to resign, that is 'constructive dismissal'. It is illegal and leaves you open to a claim for damages.

Payment

❑ *Method and frequency.* The contract of employment will set out the full remuneration entitlements of the employee.

❏ *Tax and National Insurance*. You as the employer are responsible for deducting PAYE and NICs from each employee's salary and forwarding these deductions to the Inland Revenue.

❏ *Statutory obligations*. As an employer you have various statutory obligations, including: maternity pay, minimum wages, and overtime restrictions (under European employment law, employees cannot be forced to work more than 48 hours per week).

❏ *Non-statutory obligations*. There are non-statutory obligation areas where you have discretion. For example, you have discretion about sick pay. However, employees off sick for at least four consecutive days are entitled to Statutory Sick Pay (SSP). You do not have to make contributions to pension schemes.

Insurance

With insurance, as with betting, you can get cover for just about any future (abnormal) eventuality. So Lloyds of London and Ladbrokes are in the same business, more or less. Most risks can be covered if you are prepared to pay the premium, but riot, war and acts of God are usually excluded.

If you get into a dispute with an insurer, you can contact the Insurance Ombudsman Bureau (tel 08456 006 666; www.theiob.org.uk). In the Republic of Ireland the contacts are ombudsman@ombudsman.irglov.ie and www.irglov.ie/ombudsman.

Conditions, cover and terms

Central to the legal binding of insurance contracts is that 'contracts are of the utmost good faith'. This means that both parties must disclose all information related to the risks, and that any misrepresentation may invalidate the insurance policy.

The 'cover' specifies the period of the policy and the extent of the coverage of risks. The 'terms' of the contract – the so-called small print – embrace exclusions, valuations, replacing 'new-for-old', etc.

Types of insurance

Failing to get the right insurance with the right levels of cover could mean the collapse of your business. It comes down to a trade-off between prudence and pragmatism. In simple terms, insurance cover falls into three areas:

❑ *Legally required*. You are required by law to be insured for certain risks. Examples are employer's liability, motor vehicle cover, and so on.

❑ *Necessary*. Some insurance cover is not required by law but is nevertheless a necessity for most businesses. Examples are buildings insurance, theft, director's liability and professional indemnity insurance.

❑ *Optional*. This is insurance that, based on the nature of your business, it would be wise to have, such as goods-in-transit, product liability, legal expenses, etc.

Below are listed some common instances of insurance.

Insurance of assets

This covers all your company assets, such as buildings, vehicles and equipment:

❑ *Motor vehicles*. Just as with privately owned vehicles, you must have at least third-party cover against liability to others.

❑ *Buildings*. Even with leasehold premises it is prudent to have insurance to cover the contents, loss of business and any repairing covenant in the lease, resulting from accidental damage.

❑ *Engineering equipment*. Certain potentially dangerous equipment must be inspected regularly, and this can be combined with insurance covering potential risk.

❑ *Burglary*. This covers you against theft or damage to the contents of your business premises. Theft of money and theft by employees are usually covered by separate policies.

❑ *Money*. Depending on whether you handle considerable amounts of cash and cheques, you can get insurance to cover theft from both your business premises and home.

Insurance of goods

Insurance of goods in transit covers damage or theft while they are being delivered to customers. Also, as with household insurance, you can get cover for breakage on your premises. However, defective goods are discussed below under liability insurance.

Liability insurance

Liability claims are on the increase, so it is wise to get liability insurance, whether your business involves products, services or consultancy. There are various types:

- ❑ *Public liability*. This provides general cover for any injury to customers, visitors or the general public caused by your business.
- ❑ *Product liability*. This provides liability cover for risks related to your products and services. You need to make a value judgement on the potential risks of your products and services, but damages can be enormous in countries like the United States.
- ❑ *Professional indemnity*. This provides insurance cover against claims of negligence, where your business involves giving professional advice.
- ❑ *Employer's liability*. If you have staff, you are required by law to have a valid policy of employer's liability insurance to cover injury.

People insurance

'People' insurance covers both professional and personal risks:

- ❑ *Personal accident and sickness*. To cover against the risk of not being able to work, you (and your family) may need health insurance, life insurance and a pension plan.
- ❑ *Directors' indemnity*. Although limited companies have 'limited liability', directors can still be sued for negligence in certain circumstances. It is therefore advisable for you to insist that the company takes out directors' indemnity insurance to cover such risks.
- ❑ *Key persons*. If the death of any 'key person' in your business will

cause significant financial loss, you are able to take out a special life policy.

❏ *Fidelity bonds.* To cover against theft by employees, and also breach-of-confidence and fraud, you can get so-called fidelity bonds.

Trading insurance

Insurance for trading activities includes:

❏ *Credit insurance.* Debts are usually covered by an *indemnity*, whereby the debt is transferred to the insurer, and you are paid some percentage of the debt.
❏ *Legal expenses.* You can insure against legal expenses caused by employment problems and contractual disputes.

Premises

The law affecting premises covers two areas: taking on the premises and ensuring a safe working environment for your staff.

Taking on premises

Taking on premises is an expensive and major long-term commitment. It is important to seek legal advice and to ensure you are legally entitled to conduct the type of business you wish from the premises:

❏ *Planning permission.* Check with the Planning Department of the local authority whether local laws permit the current business use, your proposed use, or your intended alteration of use.
❏ *Lease.* It is important to study the conditions. They include the length of time the lease has to run, and what say the landlord has in the alterations or change of use, both for your business and co-located businesses. A very important term will be the obligation to carry out or pay for repairs to the property and responsibility for making good any dilapidation during the term of the lease. Also consider the rules for renewal of the lease, which may be subject

to strict formalities and time limits. (See the Landlord and Tenant Act 1954.)

❑ *Charges.* Get advice on any charges associated with the building, such as maintenance of the common areas and the building itself.

Health and Safety at Work Acts (HASAWA)

Employee obligations

Clearly, employees must follow reasonable health and safety instructions as set out and displayed by the company.

Employer obligations

By law you have to provide a safe environment for your employees, independent contractors, the general public, and even trespassers. Your employees are entitled to work in reasonable safety and comfort, and the catering and toilet facilities you provide must be hygienic and safe.

You should inform the relevant *health and safety inspector* of your company name and address. This might be the Environmental Health Department of your local authority or the Health and Safety Executive Area Office (www.hse.gov.uk). The corresponding contact in the Republic of Ireland is the Health and Safety Authority (www.hsa.ie). Other requirements are:

❑ *Liability insurance.* Take out employer's liability insurance and display the certificate.

❑ *Policy.* If you employ more than five people, you must display the health, welfare and safety procedures, as well as a written policy on management and employees' responsibilities.

❑ *Poster.* You must display the Health & Safety Law poster.

❑ *Training.* You must provide employees with information and training to protect their health and safety at work.

❑ *Accident book.* If you have ten or more employees, by law you must keep an accident book and record accidents at work.

❑ *First aid.* A first-aid kit of the approved type should also be available.

Further information on health and safety at work, including a number of useful booklets, is available from the Health and Safety Executive (tel 08701 545 500; www.hse.gov.uk).

Trading

Briefly, we now look at company law requirements associated with trading:

- ☐ *Public liability*. This covers liability to employees and the general public for compensation for injury, damage and accidents caused by defective goods.
- ☐ *Product liability*. Manufacturers and suppliers are responsible for all defective products, which includes supplying proper instructions for use and checks to minimize health and safety hazards.
- ☐ *Sale of Goods Act*. Goods sold for cash are governed by the 'sale of goods' legislation, which sets down standards of quality. Goods should be free from even minor defects.
- ☐ *Misrepresentation*. Misleading descriptions of goods covers a number of areas: (i) misrepresentation of goods for which damages can be claimed; (ii) false trade descriptions – FTDs; and (iii) misleading adverts. This is 'policed' by the Director General of Fair Trading (www.oft.gov.uk).
- ☐ *Consumer Credit Act*. This Act governs all buying and selling on credit arrangements for sums between £50 and £15,000.

Sources of help

Ashton, H (1995) *The Company Secretary's Handbook*, Kogan Page, London
Clayton, P (1995) *Law for the Small Business*, Kogan Page, London
Companies House (1996) *Companies and their Directors*, Companies House
Immink, R and O'Kane, B (1997) *Starting your own Business*, Oak Tree Press, Dublin
Law Society, The. 113 Chancery Lane, London, WC2A 1PL, tel: 020 7242 1222, fax: 020 7831 0344, *www.law-soc.co.uk*
Office of Fair Trading. Field House, Breams Building, London, EC4A 1PR, tel: 020 7242 2858, *www.oft.gov.uk*
Selwyn's *Law of Employment*, Butterworth Bookshop, 35 Chancery Lane, London, WC2A 1EL, tel: 020 7405 6900

26 Contracts and Legal Forms

All trading of products and services is based on a commercial *contract*. Legally, a contract is defined as a promise or set of promises enforceable by law. Common sense and prudence dictate that most business agreements, ranging from forming a company to the sale of a business, must be written in precise language.

In this chapter we look at:

- ☐ the legal definition of a contract;
- ☐ international issues affecting contracts;
- ☐ the formation of contracts;
- ☐ the conditions of business relating to contracts;
- ☐ the different types of contract;
- ☐ specifically, contracts of employment and litigation.

In English, Scottish and Irish law, a contract must contain three elements: an *offer*, an *acceptance* and a *consideration*. Most foreign commercial law is derived from English law and therefore also embraces these three elements. In addition, the parties must have the legal capacity to make a contract and the intention to enter into a legal agreement.

Contracts

A contract is an agreement between parties who promise to deliver products or services in return for a promise to pay. Contract law dictates the remedies for non-performance. In law, most contracts are equally enforceable whether written or oral. However, some business contracts and leases must be supported by written evidence and signed by the parties whose obligations are being enforced; referred to as *evidenced in writing*.

Definitions

Legally, a contract must contain the three essential elements:

- ❏ *offer* — a promise to supply a product or service;
- ❏ *acceptance* – a promise to receive a product or service;
- ❏ *consideration* – some benefit passing between the two parties.

Because of the 'consideration' element, a simple promise to do something does not, necessarily, create a binding contractual relationship.

Specific business contracts have additional elements:

- ❏ Some agreements, such as a deed, must be signed by the parties to execute it.
- ❏ For signatures requiring witnesses, typically one witness is sufficient unless signing on behalf of a company, when two witnesses are required.
- ❏ Agreements such as deeds must be handed over to execute them, and be witnessed.

International issues

To understand contract formulation, you need to be aware that across the world there are broadly four types of legal system:

- ❏ *Common law*. Every activity is deemed legal unless specifically proscribed by law (eg in the UK and US). Here the law is built up from custom, precedent (decided cases) and statute.
- ❏ *Civil law*. Every activity is deemed legal unless specifically proscribed by law (eg in France). Here the law is laid down in a set of codified rules.
- ❏ *Scandinavian law*. This is a mixture of common law and civil law (eg in Sweden).
- ❏ *European Community law*. Directives are laid down by the European Commission requiring member states to pass legislation that then becomes national law. It prevails over the national laws of EU members.

These four types of legal system are important because they affect contract formation and the fundamental principles of contract law. This is especially true for computer-based industries and electronic commerce, which naturally have an international dimension.

Additional international issues are:

- ☐ *Jurisdiction.* A contract should state which law it has been agreed should govern it (eg by English, Scottish or Irish law). Otherwise the courts may need to decide jurisdiction.
- ☐ *Property.* Even if a contract is governed by English law, for instance, it can be enforced in a foreign court. This is necessary when there are no assets available to satisfy a claim within the English jurisdiction.
- ☐ *Consideration.* In a civil law jurisdiction, it is usual for the law not to require a contract to have an element of 'consideration'; i.e. benefit passing between the two parties.
- ☐ *Privity of contract.* In common law only the actual parties to a contract are able to enforce the contractual obligations arising under the contract. This limitation does not apply in civil or Scandinavian law.

Contract formation

The 'manner' in which a contract is created is critically important. It determines: (i) the time and place; (ii) the exact terms and conditions; and (iii) the jurisdiction and national law applicable.

Formalities

Common law contract law is dictated by the practical needs of commerce. Hence, a contract is usually enforceable whether or not it is written and signed, as long as it contains an offer, acceptance and consideration.

However, the law recognizes that certain types of contract, such as a guarantee obligation or a contract dealing with land (called 'real' property), must be 'evidenced in writing and signed by the party to be charged'.

Conditions of business

Most commercial organizations draw up standard conditions of business relating to their trading:

❑ *Standard conditions*. These specify the provisions for normal trading. They usually cover: (i) interpretation of the contract; (ii) supply of the relevant products or services; (iii) price to be charged; (iv) intellectual property rights in any materials created; (v) passing of risk; (vi) passing of title (ownership); (vii) warranties and liabilities issues; and (viii) length of agreement and provisions for terminations.

❑ *General conditions*. These typically cover exceptions: (i) exclusion of other terms; (ii) notice; (iii) waiver of enforcement; (iv) acts of God called *force majeure*; (v) consequences of un-enforceability; (vi) procedures for arbitration; and (vii) the applicable law and jurisdiction.

In addition, the law introduces a number of 'operating conditions' that determine which parties' conditions take precedence.

❑ *Competing conditions* – known as the 'battle of the forms'. This covers situations where there is a potential conflict of conditions: (i) buyer's terms versus seller's terms; (ii) a situation where an offer is followed by a counter offer; and (iii) the 'last is the winner' situation for determining which terms take precedence.

Terms and conditions of business are important because the seller and the buyer may have completely different ideas about quality, delivery, warranty, liability and termination of agreements. Also important is precedence of terms and conditions. For instance, a customer may send you an order (an offer) with accompanying terms and conditions. You may respond with an acknowledgement (*acceptance*) with your accompanying terms and conditions.

These 'competing conditions' often exercise the court. In addition, arbitration conditions in a contract may be of little use since they form part of the contract. A good source of information on 'arbitration' is the Centre for Dispute Resolution (tel 020 7600 0500; www.cedr.co.uk). The corresponding contact in the Republic of Ireland is the Labour Relations Commission (www.ire.ie).

Types of contract

When you need a contract to be legally watertight, prudence suggests using a lawyer. However, there are an increasing number of self-help law packs, such as *301 Legal Forms, Letters and Agreements*, that provide basic business forms:

The Internet is a good online source of legal forms, though primarily for the United States. Sites include the Internet Legal Resource Guide (www.ilrg.com) and AV Limited publications (avlimited.com/legal-forms). Examples of the types of contracts are shown in Figure 26.1. Below are listed some of the business contracts relevant to high-tech start-ups:

❑ *Collaboration agreement*. This covers where two or more organizations undertake a business collaboration, and agree on the rules for ownership and exploitation of intellectual property rights associated with the collaboration.

Basic Agreements		Intellectual property	
Agreement	❑	Non-disclosure agreement	❑
Waiver of liability and assumption of risk	❑	Release of confidential information	❑
Breach of contract notice	❑	Royalty contract	❑
Business		**Leases and tenancies**	
Contract/subcontractor agreement	❑	Rental agreement	❑
Joint venture agreement	❑	Commercial lease	❑
Share certificate	❑	Notice to terminate tenancy	❑
Buying and selling		**Loans and borrowing**	
Contract for sale of goods or services	❑	Guarantee	❑
Purchase order	❑	Loan agreement	❑
Quotation	❑	Security agreement	❑
Credit and debt collection		**Partnership**	
Credit information	❑	Partnership agreement	❑
Demand for payment	❑	Assignment of partnership interests	❑
Remittance advice	❑	Valuation of share of partnership	❑
Employment		**Transfer and assignments**	
Contract of employment	❑	Assignment of contract	❑
Employee confidential agreement	❑	Assignment of option	❑
Notice of dismissal letter	❑		❑

Figure 26.1 Types of business contracts

❏ *Confidentiality*. This covers the protection of confidential information.

❏ *Employment*. This is the contract of employment between the employer and employee.

❏ *Intellectual property rights*. This covers the ownership and rights to intellectual property.

❏ *Licences*. This covers the issuing of licences to allow use of copyright material, such as software.

❏ *Partnership agreements*. This is the legal agreement covering all aspects of a business partnership.

❏ *Sale of goods*. This agreement covers the sale of products and services.

❏ *Venture capital*. This is an agreement signed with a venture capital fund covering all aspects of their investment in a business.

❏ *Warranty*. This agreement covers the quality and operation of a product or service.

We shall next look at some of these agreements in more detail.

Collaboration agreements

Often high-tech companies (and universities) collaborate on the research and development of new technologies. Their roles, responsibilities and ownership of intellectual property are set out in a collaboration agreement (see Figure 26.2).

The collaboration agreement typically starts by listing the *participants* ('between'). Then, as with any legal document, there is a set of *definitions* to be used in the collaboration agreement. A statement follows this on how the collaboration will be *conducted*, the *duration* and the *management* of the work. Next, the important issues of intellectual property rights are set out in terms of: *background* – intellectual property rights (IPR) owned at the start of the collaboration by one of the partners, and *foreground* – IPR results generated by the partners during the collaboration, plus their ownership, exploitation and royalties.

The agreement then sets out the rules for protecting the confidentiality of information about the collaboration, and procedures for obtaining agreement for dissemination of information to third parties outside the collaboration. Next, the agreement addresses issues of *withdrawal* from the

---

COLLABORATION AGREEMENT

BETWEEN	- the list of participants
IT IS NOW HEREBY AGREED AS FOLLOWS	
1. **Definitions**	- list of definitions used in the collaboration agreement
2. **Conduct of Collaboration**	- how the work will be conducted
3. **Duration**	- the length of the collaboration
4. **Management**	- how the collaboration will be managed
5. **Use, ownership and exploitation of intellectual property**	- ownership of IPR
6. **Confidentiality**	- agreement to keep information secret
7. **Dissemination of information**	- rules for the dissemination of information to third parties
8. **Withdrawal and termination**	- procedures for formal withdrawal from the collaboration
9. **Arbitration**	- procedures for arbitration of disputes
10. **Force majeure**	- acts of God
11. **Warranties**	- accuracy of information supplied
12. **General**	- general conditions of the collaboration agreement
13. **Law**	- the contract governed by English law
14. **In witness ...**	
SIGNED FOR AND ON BEHALF OF	- signatures of all the partners.

Partner .... Name .... Position .... Signature .... Date ....

Figure 26.2 Collaboration agreement

collaboration, *arbitration* of disputes, and *general* contract conditions. Finally, the *signatories* of the agreement are listed.

Confidentiality

Details of business and technical activities may be commercially highly valuable. For your employees there is an implied duty of confidentiality, usually backed up by terms implied or expressed in their contracts of employment.

What do you do with non-employees, such as self-employed independent consultants? To negotiate a business venture you will frequently need to share confidential information that should not be disclosed to a competitor. You should therefore ask visitors to sign what is called a non-disclosure agreement (NDA) or confidentiality agreement (Figure 26.3).

NON-DISCLOSURE AGREEMENT
with
NewCo, London WC1E 6BT

PERMITTED PURPOSE

I ....(name)

of ....(business address)

acknowledge that all confidential information I receive is made available to me for the purposes of

(i) ....

(ii) ....

I AGREE

(i) ....

(ii) ....

RELEASE

(i) ....

(ii) ....

DATED ....

SIGNATURE ....

FULL NAME ....

WITNESS ....

FULL NAME ....

ADDRESS ....

Figure 26.3 Non-disclosure agreement

The NDA sets out the name of the person to whom the information is to be given, the nature of the information, the scope of its use and the procedures for release from the NDA. If the person signing your NDA breaches the contractual obligations, he or she can be sued for damages, both (i) for breach of contract and (ii) under the law of tort.

Employment contracts

As discussed in Chapter 25, under employment legislation you as an employer are obliged to supply, within 13 weeks of the commencement of a contract of employment, a written notice setting out the main terms and conditions of the employment.

The employment contract sets such conditions as normal working hours, holiday arrangements, illness, pensions, obligations regarding confidentiality of company information and non-competition should the employee leave the company, ownership of intellectual property created

---

CONTRACT OF EMPLOYMENT

THIS AGREEMENT IS MADE the ....day of ....20....

BETWEEN (1) .... of ....(the "Employer")

and   (2) .... of .... (the "Employee")

This document sets out the terms and conditions of employment which are required to be given to an employee under section 1 Employment Rights Act 1996 and which apply at the date hereof.

1. COMMENCEMENT AND JOB TITLE
2. SALARY
3. HOURS OF EMPLOYMENT
4. HOLIDAYS
5. SICKNESS
6. COLLECTIVE AGREEMENTS
7. PENSIONS
8. TERMINATION
9. CONFIDENTIALITY
10. NON-COMPETITION
11. DISCIPLINE AND GRIEVANCE
12. NOTICE
13. SEVERABILITY
14. ENTIRE AGREEMENT
15. GOVERNING LAW

IN WITNESS OF WHICH ....

Employer .... Signature .... Date

Employee .... Signature .... Date

Figure 26.4 Contract of employment

by the employee, and procedures for disciplinary proceedings and for resolving disputes (Figure 26.4).

In a high-tech company, you will obviously be worried about employees gaining valuable knowledge of your business that could be of enormous benefit to a competitor. Clearly, during the period of the employment contract the employee can be prohibited contractually from divulging such information. You can also protect yourself by including restrictive covenants such as a 'non-competition' clause that stops the employee from working for named competitors, both during and for a reasonable period after the end of the contract. Here, two principles of law must be reconciled:

❑ *Employer freedom to contract.* As an employer you may wish to prevent an employee from working for a competitor for a period of time after the contract terminates.

❑ *Employee freedom to exploit skills.* Equally, the courts are vigorous in protecting the rights of an employee to exploit their professional skills.

The degree of enforceability of employment contract restrictions hinges on whether the court considers that the extent of the restrictions imposed are *in all the circumstances* reasonable for the protection of your legitimate business interests.

Litigation

What does one do when things go wrong? When legal action is inevitable, letters of demand (eg for debts) should be carefully worded, setting a time limit for compliance. This should be done by a solicitor, ideally one specializing in such litigation.

Before you take any actions you are strongly advised to weigh up your chances of obtaining payment, compensation and costs. Even if you win you could be massively out of pocket. The actions available are:

❏ *Letter before action.* Before issuing proceedings through the courts you should send a standard 'letter before (legal) action' on which you can take proceedings (see Figure 26.5).

DEMAND FOR PAYMENT

Date ....

To   ....
     ....
     ....

Dear ....

Your account is overdue in the amount of £ .... We have tried on several occasions to secure payment of your overdue account but it remains unpaid.

This is the final notice. Unless we receive cash or your cheque for .... pounds (£ ....) within seven (7) days, we will refer your account to our solicitors for collection who will be instructed to commence proceedings without further reference to you.

Please note that immediate payment is in your best interests as it may save you further interest and legal costs, and help preserve your credit rating.

Only if the outstanding sum has been paid in the past few days can you afford to ignore this letter.

Yours sincerely,

Figure 26.5 Letter before (legal) action

- ❏ *Starting an action.* Commercial litigation is dealt with by the civil courts, namely the small claims court (for up to £5,000), county courts (for up to £25,000), and the High Court (over £15,000 but thereafter unlimited).
- ❏ *Criminal proceedings.* Crime is the responsibility of the police, Crown Prosecution Service, magistrates, and the crown courts. Private prosecutions are available but compensation is typically low.
- ❏ *Civil proceedings.* The civil courts deal with contract and business disputes, and claims in tort (the old French word meaning 'wrongs'). Contractual claims cover written and oral agreements. Tort claims cover negligence, damages for personal injury and a number of other wrongs.

And the result is:

- ❏ *Costs.* The costs of a court case comprise the court fees, witness expenses and allowances, solicitors' costs, plus the amount awarded for damages. Note that you can expect to recover from the other party only approximately three-quarters of what it actually costs you.
- ❏ *Judgement.* If you win the case you end up with a judgement in your favour. You then have to use the courts again to enforce the judgement if the other party does not pay up.

Sources of help

Clayton, P (1995) *Law for the Small Business,* Kogan Page, London

Irish, V (1994) *Intellectual Property Rights for Engineers – The legal protection of innovation,* Institution of Electrical Engineers, London

Law Pack Publishing (1996) *301 Legal Forms, Letters and Agreements,* Law Pack Guide, London

Law Society, The. 113 Chancery Lane, London, WC2A 1PL, tel: 020 7242 1222, fax: 020 7831 0344, *www.law-soc.co.uk*

Lipman, F (1998) *Financing your business with Venture Capital,* Prima Publishing, Rocklin, CA

Office of Fair Trading. Field House, 15–25 Bream Buildings, London, EC4A 1PR, tel: 020 7211 8000, *www.oft.gov.uk*

Siberstein, S (1994) *Consumer Law,* Sweet and Maxwell, London

27 Intellectual Property Rights

Intellectual property rights (IPRs) is the general term for legally protecting your ideas, work and products. There are five basic categories of IPR: patents, design rights, trademarks, copyright and confidential information. A product could be protected by all five IPRs during its life cycle – concept, design, production and marketing – but this would be unusual.

In this chapter we look at:

❏ the protection, ownership and licensing of intellectual property;
❏ patents for protecting the uniqueness of technical innovations;
❏ design rights for protecting the 'look and feel' of manufactured products;
❏ trademarks for protecting brand names and commercial labels;
❏ copyright for protecting literary and artistic works, broadcast media and computer software.

For the high-tech start-up there are a number of good sources of information on IPR, including *Intellectual Property Rights for Engineers: The Legal Protection of Innovation* by Vivien Irish.

The Patent Office website (www.patent.gov.uk; see Figure 27.1) provides an online introduction to all intellectual property issues in the UK, covering patents, registered designs, trademarks and copyrights. It also allows you to search online for registered intellectual property (IP) in the UK. However, for a comprehensive search you are still recommended to employ a professional search agency.

GGMark (www.ggmark.com) is a useful American website that provides online information on IPR in each of the American states, the European Union, and around the world.

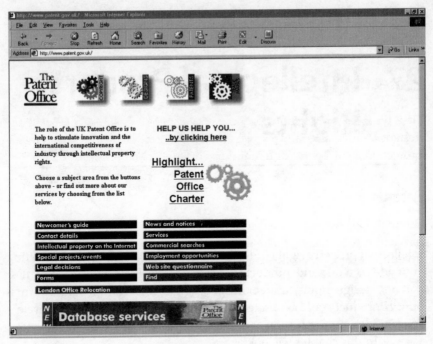

Figure 27.1

Intellectual property

So, what is 'intellectual property'? Basically, IP covers innovation in branding, design, media, products, services or industrial processes. The different forms of IPR stop your competitors exploiting your innovation without consent. The principal forms of intellectual property rights are:

- ❏ *Patents* give protection to unique technical innovations, such as products and manufacturing processes superior to their predecessors.
- ❏ *Designs* give protection to the appearance of manufactured products.
- ❏ *Trademarks* give protection to signs, brand names and commercial labels that distinguish products and services.
- ❏ *Copyright* gives protection to literary, artistic and musical works, broadcast media and software.
- ❏ *Confidential information* gives protection to commercial and technical information where an undertaking to keep secret the information is obtained.

In considering your intellectual property rights, three issues are important: *protection, ownership* and *licensing*.

Protection

First, we look at protection and how you go about obtaining it for patents, designs, trademarks and copyrights. Figure 27.2 illustrates the possible protection available for different types of intellectual property.

Patents

Patents (see also below) cover hardware or process inventions. The essential action is to file a patent application before any information on the invention is disclosed publicly in any way whatsoever.

Designs

Design rights fall into three classes: *design* rights, *registered* designs and *topography* rights. Design rights protect the appearance of mass-produced articles or products. Registered designs protect the external appearance of a product. Topography rights protect the layout pattern of semiconductor chips.

IP	Patent	Designs	Trademark	Copyright	Confidential information
Business proposal				✓	✓
Technical report				✓	✓
Technical specification	✓			✓	✓
Engineering drawing	✓			✓	✓
Screen design	✓			✓	✓
Computer program	✓			✓	✓
Hardware	✓	✓			
Industrial process	✓				
Consumer product		✓			
Product name			✓		
Logo			✓		

Figure 27.2 Protection of IPR

315

Trademarks

Trademarks cover signs, brand names and commercial labels that distinguish a company, product or service, such as Virgin, McDonald's, Windows 98, or the red triangle for Bass beer (the first trademark ever registered and therefore Trade Mark no. 1).

Copyright

Copyright applies to a wide range of written, drawn and computer-generated material, such as reports and specifications, drawings whether artistic or engineering, Web pages and screen shots, and computer programs. If you wish to deter others, you should mark the material with the copyright symbol ©, the owner's name and the date the material was first created; for example: © Owner's name, 2001.

Confidential information

Confidential information applies to your valuable company data, drawings, specifications and documents that need protection. It is the most difficult of the five types of IPR to quantify, because there is no statute law; it is all defined by legal cases stretching back more than 100 years.

Ownership

Your ownership of an intellectual property right is not as straightforward as it might seem, and depends on whether you created the IP as an 'employee', as a 'contractor' commissioned to do the work, or as the 'instigator' who commissioned the IP (see Figure 27.3). Here we shall consider three situations:

☐ *You are an employee.* You are bound by a contract of service and are paid regularly by the company; and your IPR obligations may be stated in your contract. Employees have obligations to their company, so any IPR generated as 'normal duties' is likely to be the property of the company. However, any IPR you generate outside of work (and unrelated to normal duties) will typically reside with you.

IPR	Patent	Designs	Trademark	Copyright	Confidential information
Employee	✓				
Contractor (see contract)				✓	
Instigator/employer	✓	✓	✓	✓	✓

Figure 27.3 Ownership of IPR

❑ *You are a contractor.* You are commissioned to deliver products and services to a company. You will typically own the IPR unless the commissioning company specifies ownership in the terms of the contract. This is clearly important if you wish to develop similar products and services for different clients.

❑ *You are the instigator.* You (or your company) cause the IPR to be generated and hence own the IPR. For instance, with copyright, important examples include the producer of a film, and the owner of a computer, producing computer-generated work. Otherwise, ownership depends on the terms of the contract.

Licensing

When starting out you may have a brilliant idea but no resources to exploit it. The solution is to license the IPR to other companies. You issue an IP licence to the company that allows them to use your IPR in return for payment to you. A start-up company or university frequently does this to get a return on its R&D investment, because it is not in a position to make the product and sell it.

Basically, you can issue an IP licence for any or all of the IPR classes that you own: patent, trademark, copyright etc. This can be for specific regions, and on a non-exclusive, sole or exclusive use basis:

❑ *Non-exclusive licences* may be granted to any number of competing companies.

❑ *A sole licence* is granted to a single company, but the IPR owner may still compete with the company granted the licence.

❑ *An exclusive licence* is granted to a single company and the IPR owner undertakes not to compete with the company.

Payment is typically in two forms: an initial *lump sum* and a continuing *royalty* payment. The royalty level is usually set either as sum per item sold, or as a percentage of sales, but not profits made. In fact, it is normal in a licensing agreement for the IPR owner to include a *performance clause,* such as minimum sales and royalty payments, below which the licence agreement comes to an end and the rights revert to the licensor.

Now we will look at patents, designs, trademarks, copyrights and confidential information in more detail.

Patent

A patent protects an 'invention' through an application filed with the Patent Office (www.patent.gov.uk). Of all the IPRs, patents are the most expensive, costing around £3,000 per country to register.

There are three key elements to a successful patent application. It must be *genuinely new and non-obvious* (ie more than the application of known principles), it must contain an element of *creativity*, and it must be capable of *industrial application*.

Types of patent

The scope of patent registration is continually expanding from the original 'tangible' product or item, to new ways of operating equipment and processes. We can identify four types:

- ☐ *Products* covers any item capable of industrial application in the broadest sense, such as a chip.
- ☐ *Materials* covers a new material, such as a semiconductor device used to make a chip.
- ☐ *Processes* covers a new method of manufacturing an item, such as the lithography to etch a chip.
- ☐ *Operation* covers new algorithms for routing information, such as controlling the flow of information through the chip. This is an expanding area given the increasing importance of computing and communications.

Items that specifically cannot be patented are: (i) discoveries, theory or mental concepts; (ii) literary and artistic works (protected by copyright); (iii) items deemed immoral. Computer programs are also explicitly excluded by the Patent Acts. However, owing to the potential value of 'software patents', applicants are finding ways round the rules, and they are being issued by the European Patent Office (www.european-patent -office.org).

Filing a patent

A patent application passes through eight stages:

1. *Initial search*. An optional initial search can be carried out by the Patent Office or a commercial firm prior to submission of an application to access originality.
2. *Initial application*. An outline of the invention is submitted and is given a priority date, the official date of receipt, and a number.
3. *Complete application*. The complete application, which must be filed within 12 months of the priority date, gives a comprehensive specification of the invention. This is to allow for development of the invention.
4. *Preliminary examination*. The preliminary examination is carried out by the Patent Office to test the validity of the patent application, such as searching for similar existing patents in the area.
5. *Search report*. A search report is prepared by the Patent Office, listing the results of the search, which are sent to the applicant, who can decide to proceed or not.
6. *Substantive examination*. A substantive examination is then carried if the applicant wishes to proceed.
7. *A-specification*. The so-called A-specification is published 18 months after the priority date, unless the application is withdrawn. This is the first time that the invention is described publicly.
8. *B-specification*. The B-specification listing the complete details of the application is published sometime later, if granted.

All these stages must be completed within 54 months of the priority date. If successful, the applicant is issued with a patent that lasts for 20 years from the priority date, provided annual fees are paid.

The first step in registering a patent is to prepare a specification describing the invention. This forms the basis of discussion with your Patent Agent, who will file the application, together with the official forms and fee, with the Patent Office (e-mail: enquiries@patent.gov.uk).

As shown in Figure 27.4, the official form includes a title, a short

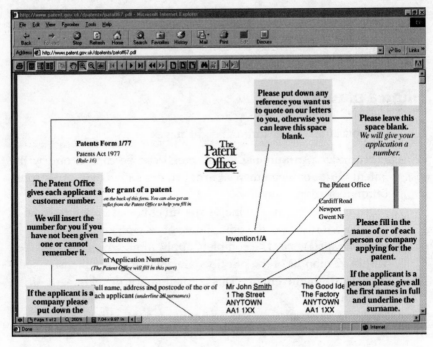

Figure 27.4 Online patent application form

abstract, the applicant's name, etc. The accompanying specifications typically comprise: (i) background – the current technical state of the invention's field and existing patents; (ii) the problem being addressed; and (iii) a technical summary of the invention, including drawings and diagrams, describing how the invention works. An indicative list of fees is shown in Table 27.1.

Table 27.1 Typical patent charges

	Registration Fee	Agent's Charge
Initial Search	£130	£150
Initial Application	–	£1220
Complete Application (after 12 months)	–	£850
Substantive Examination	£70	£190
Patent Renewal (fee increase annually)		£70
Total (approx.)		**£2680**

Given the cost (nearly £3,000) and complexity of filing a patent application, you are strongly advised to use a Registered Patent Agent, or 'Patent Attorney'. Either consult *Yellow Pages* or contact the Chartered Institute of Patent Agents (tel 020 7405 9450; www.cipa.org.uk).

Design rights

Design rights apply to tangible objects, whether artistic or engineering. The key attributes are: *new* – the design must be original, and *not commonplace* – the design should not be similar to two or more pre-existing designs from different sources.

Types of design rights

The scope of each type of design right is as follows:

❑ *Design rights*. The article must be a tangible three-dimensional object of any size, with IPR covering the shape and configuration of the object, both internal and external.

❑ *Registered design*. This covers features of a manufactured article judged by appearance, and taken into account when people buy or use the article.

❑ *Topography rights*. This applies specifically to the layout and pattern of integrated circuits and masks used in the fabrication of such circuits.

Articles that cannot be protected by design rights are: (i) surface decoration; (ii) method of construction; (iii) features of shape dictated by function; (iv) connections for fitting the object to another (called the 'must fit' exception); (v) replacement parts (called the 'must match' exception); and (vi) a topology which is commonplace.

Filing a registered design

Protection of design rights and topography rights is automatic. To *register a design*, submit a drawing of the design, a completed application and a *statement of novelty* to the Patent Office. Design Registry searches were

Table 27.2 Typical design registration charges

	Registration Fee	Agent's Charge
Application	£60	£70
Search	–	–
Renewal (every 5 years)	£130 to £450	£110
Total	**£190**	**£180**

abolished in June 1999. Initial registration lasts for five years, renewable for up to 25 years. An indicative list of fees is shown in Table 27.2.

Trademarks

Trademarks encourage customers to purchase products and services through recognition. Thus, trademarks, whether words or symbols, should be easily recognized and remembered, and different from any similar marks used by competitors. Trademarks are registered with the Trade Marks Registry (tel 01633 814 000; www.patent.gov.uk; see Figure 27.5), which is part of the Patent Office.

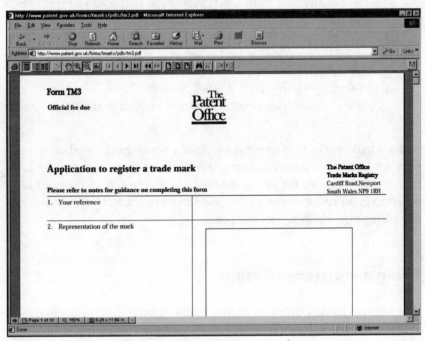

Figure 27.5 Online trademark application form

What makes a good trademark? From the owner's viewpoint it must be distinctive; a good advert. From a legal viewpoint: (i) it must differentiate the products and services from a specific company; (ii) it must not be words 'describing' the products and services on offer, or terms used by the trade in normal business; (iii) it can be a made-up word, or a word taken out of context; (iv) it can be initials; but (v) surnames and place names should be avoided if possible.

Types of trademark

☐ *Symbols*. These are logos made up of one or more pictures and words. A classic example is the 'apple with a bite mark' used by Apple Computers.

☐ *Words invented*. These are specially made-up words not found in the English language, such as 'Sony' for consumer products.

☐ *Words out of context*. These are normal words used in a different context, such as Virgin.

☐ *Initials*. These could be the initials of the company, such as International Business Machines using IBM as its trademark.

☐ *Signatures*. Genuine signatures, like *Kellogg's*, and other scripts can be registered, but the registration is restricted to the actual script rather than the full name.

☐ *Surnames etc.* Surnames and geographical names are problematic, because the law tends to support the right of another person with the same name or a company in the same locality wishing to establish a business. For example, McDonald's tried to stop a Mr McDonald calling his business 'McDonald's Café', and lost the case.

Registering a trademark

Having designed your trademark based on the above guidelines, you next need to decide within which of the 34 different goods classes and eight service classes you wish your trademark to be registered, and for which country or region. Naturally, each additional class and country requires an extra fee.

It will cost you about £600 to register a trademark for a single class for the United Kingdom, using a Trademark Attorney, and not encountering any substantial objections.

Before attempting to register your 'mark', it is wise to employ a search company, like Compu-Mark® (tel 020 7278 4646; www.compu-mark.com), to find out whether the mark is already in use.

Having verified that your 'mark' is not already registered to another company, your next task is to locate a Trademark Attorney to give you advice and prepare your application. Such agents can be found either in *Yellow Pages* or by contacting the Institute of Trade Mark Attornies (tel 0280 686 2052); in Ireland contact the Controller of Patents, Designs and Trade Marks in Dublin.

The application is filed with the Trade Mark Registry, together with the fee (around £200), and is date stamped and given an official number (see Table 27.3). The Registry then examines the submitted mark for suitability, and carries out a search within the classes specified in the application and any related classes for conflicting marks. The Registry then either accepts the trademark, or sets out objections to the registration, which you can challenge. An accepted mark is published in the *Official Journal*, and if no one challenges the mark within three months of publication a Certificate of Registration is issued.

Whether a trademark is registered or not, it is still protected in two areas:

❑ *Get-up*. The visual image of your company, products and services is protected from copying by a competitor. Cover is also provided by copyright and 'passing-off'.

❑ *Passing-off*. This refers to a competitor offering products and services that appear to come from your company owing to the use of a similar get-up. You can stop this by showing that your mark has been copied: the reputation of your trademark has been damaged, customer confusion, and that your business has suffered damage.

Table 27.3 Typical trademark charges

	Application Fee	Attorney's Charge	Renewal Fee (every 10 years)
UK	£200	£400	£200
EU (plus £745 registration fee)	£650	£550	£1,800
US	£150	£1,500	£200

Copyright

Copyright is conferred automatically on a vast range of literary, artistic and technical material without any need to legally register with a statutory body. This covers letters, specifications, drawings, reports, books, plays, music and other types of artistic work, films, television programmes, computer programs and databases, and even the spoken word. However, copyright does not cover an 'idea' until it is conveyed to paper or computer, or something that has been copied. As stated above, copyright is automatic and, in the UK, lasts for the life of the author plus 70 years.

Types of copyright

The range of copyrights is enormous:

☐ *Literary*. Every written document, from a string of works, to a business letter or a classic book, is considered literary copyright, without consideration of literary merit.

☐ *Artistic*. Every drawing, map, chart, picture, photograph, design and plan is covered by artistic copyright, without any consideration of its artistic merit.

☐ *Recordings*. All recordings of sounds, whether music or animal noises, and of images on film are protected by copyright; whatever the recording material.

☐ *Broadcasts*. Radio and television transmissions through the atmosphere are covered by broadcast copyright, but cable services are treated separately.

☐ *Cable services*. These cover the transmission of material over wires and fibre-optic cables, that can potentially support two-way interaction, as with access to online databases, websites and home shopping.

☐ *Computer software*. 'Programs' are considered literary work and covered by literary copyright, with the encoding, whether text or machine code, taken as the written form.

Copyrighting

With many forms of IPR, such as patents and trademarks, you need to engage an agent, prepare an application, apply to the appropriate registry, and pay fees to protect your IPR. Copyright is automatic and all you really need to do to warn-off possible transgressors is place a copyright mark on your material. This mark comprises a copyright symbol (eg ©, *Copyright*, or *Copr.*), the name of the copyright owner and the first year of publication.

In electronic media, such as computer programs, databases and Web pages, a more subtle means of copyright marking is to include redundant code, software bugs or fictitious information which can later be used to prove illegal copying.

Exceptions

Copyright law is not a 'sledgehammer'. There are a number of legal exemptions to copyright that might be classed as 'reasonable use in the public interest'; the term used for this is 'fair dealing'. For example, sections of a copyrighted work can be 'quoted' if part of a review, but the source must be fully identified. Individuals may copy part of a document, journal or book for private study. In addition:

☐ Schools and colleges are, on the whole, 'permitted' to make limited photocopies of copyrighted material for educational purposes, but publishers frown on the copying of substantial parts of one publication without express permission being given in advance. Universities, research establishments and companies can and do make use of licences to copy (see below).

☐ *Public events.* Copyrighted material may be used in a broadcast programme, but ownership should be acknowledged and permission obtained in advance.

If you need to make copies of printed material on a regular basis, you should contact the Copyright Licensing Agency (tel 020 7436 5931; www.cla.co.uk) or (for music and films) the Performing Rights Society (tel 020 7580 5544; www.prs.co.uk). Both these organizations can authorize copying, collect royalty payments, and distribute fees to the owners of intellectual property.

Confidential information

If you want to keep a secret, don't tell anyone! Confidentiality can apply to business ideas, product specifications, test data, customer names and addresses, or sales forecasts; whether on paper, in a computer database or even in an employee's head. Equally, confidential information disclosed in public is lost forever.

Confidential disclosure

Directors, partners and employees have a legal obligation to protect confidential information. However, to protect yourself in negotiations with others you need to get them to sign a confidentiality agreement setting out how the information they receive may be used and not used. Frequently, you will be asked by a company to sign such an undertaking before negotiations commence. Both parties should sign an agreement and both should as a matter of course keep a copy.

These confidentiality agreements can range in size from a single paragraph to an extensive document of tens of pages, all depending on the extent of information to be exchanged, and the strength of the message about confidential disclosure. As a general rule US companies take confidentiality agreements more seriously than UK and Irish companies, perhaps owing to the higher levels of damages awarded in the US.

Even without a formal confidentiality agreement, the law recognizes 'implied confidence'. For instance, if you own the rights to a computer program and pass a copy to a company to fulfil a contract for you, they would be open to litigation if they attempted to use the software for a third party, without your permission.

One of the frequent sources of difficulty with confidential information is when an employee leaves the company to work for a competitor, or sets up in competition. The courts vigorously defend the right of an individual to pursue a career in the same business sector, and will even set aside restrictive clauses in an employment contract deemed unreasonable. In simple terms, an ex-employee can use the knowledge in his or her head, but is not allowed to supplement this information by creating notes. Carrying away documents, drawings and computer disks that are the ex-employer's property is both theft and breach of copyright.

Confidentiality agreements

There are two common ways of protecting confidential information:

☐ *Commercial in confidence.* Documents and letters to be treated as confidential can be marked with a 'commercial in confidence' banner or footnote.

☐ *Non-disclosure agreement.* This is a simple legal document that is signed prior to negotiations, emphasizing the confidential nature of the information to be exchanged.

As always, you have to make a decision about the amount of detailed information you are prepared to divulge before the other party signs a legally binding contract.

Sources of help

Barber, H (1994) *Copyrights, Patents and Trade Marks, protecting your rights worldwide,* McGraw Hill, New York

Chartered Institute of Patent Agents, The. Staple Inn Buildings, High Holborn, London, WC1V 7PZ, tel: 020 7405 9450, fax: 020 7430 0471, email *mail@cipa.org.uk, www.cipa.org.uk*

Copyright Licensing Agency. 90 Tottenham Court Road, London, W1P 0LP, tel: 020 7436 5931, fax: 020 7631 5500, *www.cla.co.uk*

European Patent Office. Erhardtstrasse 27, D-80331 Munich, Germany, tel: +49 89 23 99–0, fax: 49 89 23 99–44 65, *www.european-patent-office.org*

Institute of Trade Mark Agents. 4th Floor, Canterbury House, 2–6 Sydenham Road, Croydon, Surrey, CR0 9XE, tel: 020 8686 2052, fax: 020 8680 5723, *www.itma.org.uk*

Irish, V (1994) *Intellectual Property Rights for Engineers – The legal protection of innovation,* Institution of Electrical Engineers, London

Patent Office. (London Search Office – Personal Callers) 25 Southampton Buildings, Chancery Lane, London WC2A 1AY, tel: 020 7438 4718, *www.patent.gov.uk.*

Patent Office. Cardiff Road, Newport, Gwent, NP10 8QQ, tel: 01633 814000, fax: 01633 814444 email: enquiries@patent.gov.uk, *www.patent. gov.uk*

Stationers Hall. Ave Maria Lane, London, EC4M 7DD, tel: 020 7248 2934, pitcairn.lib.uci.edu/largo/sh/shx.html

28 High-tech Law

High-tech law is the cutting edge of legislation. A good example of this is the growing significance of communications and the Internet on issues such as intellectual property, contracts, and even defamation. Today, this encompasses the World Wide Web, electronic mail, bulletin boards, online services and electronic commerce; tomorrow, digital interactive television, digital cash, electronic contracts and digital signatures. This in turn has produced *tech*-law firms like the legendary Wilson Sonsini (www.wsgr.com) and Venture Law (www.venturelaw.com) in Silicon Valley.

In this chapter we look at:

❏ areas of 'high-tech', namely electronic trading, software, hardware and biotech;
❏ important high-tech legal issues such as ease of reproduction and security;
❏ the Data Protection Act;
❏ software and hardware contracts;
❏ licensing agreements.

What we mean by 'high-tech' is, broadly, the 'hot' technologies: *software*, *hardware* and what might be jokingly called *wetware* – biotechnology, etc.

Software covers information, multimedia, entertainment (eg music, films and television) and computing (eg programs, databases and the Internet), whether stored in digital or analogue form.

Hardware covers physical devices, including consumer electronics, computers, telecommunications and semiconductor silicon chips.

Wetware covers biological and molecular systems, including biotechnology, pharmaceuticals, medicine and biomedical informatics.

High-tech legal issues

This chapter focuses on electronic commerce, software contracts and licensing. To use the *e* centre definition(www.e-centre.org.uk; see Figure 28.1):

> *electronic commerce covers any form of business or administrative transaction or information exchange that is executed using any information and communications technology.*

It therefore spans:

- ☐ telecommunications – telephones, faxes, telex and pagers;
- ☐ the Internet – electronic mail, the Web and bulletin boards;
- ☐ interactive television – digital interactive TV shopping and games shows;
- ☐ electronic data interchange (EDI) – automated electronic ordering;
- ☐ systems – the order–delivery–payment systems common in retail;

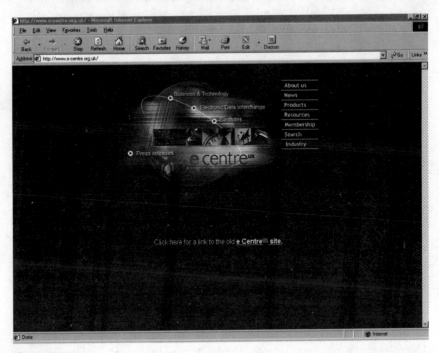

Figure 28.1

❏ payment systems – EDI cheque clearing and payments.

Electronic trading in its simplest form is where one computer is linked to another for exchanging information. Where electronic trading becomes legally interesting is where messages are processed (and contracts made) automatically. From a legal standpoint, this is sometimes called 'paperless trading'. The principal legal concerns relate to:

❏ *Multimedia issues.* The media is characterized by: (i) the ease of reproducibility; (ii) the difficulty of detecting alterations; (iii) the absence of proof of originality; and (iv) the anonymity of the source who created the media.

❏ *Security issues.* The media has a number of security related issues: (i) *technical* – the content must be protected from modification; (ii) *commercial* – the contents' secrecy must be protected; (iii) *legal* – the legal status of the content must be admissible in evidence; and (iv) *national* – the government security services must have access to the information to uphold the law.

❏ *Authentication issues.* How the integrity of the information can be protected: (i) *authentication* – the message did originate from the person who purportedly sent it; (ii) *integrity* – the message has not been altered in any way; (iii) *trusted third parties* – the organizations that validate the integrity of messages and the identity of the sender; and (iv) *encryption* – protects a message by encrypting it, via a key, which is used at the destination to decrypt the message. PGP (pretty good privacy) is a popular encryption scheme.

Data protection

If you hold information in an electronic form about living people in the UK (information that is 'automatically processed'), then you are governed by the Data Protection Act 1998 and need to register with the Data Protection Registrar (see Chapter 25). The purpose of the Act is to 'regulate the use of automatically processed information relating to individuals and the provision of services in respect of such information'.

The information need not be particularly sensitive, and it can be little more than names and addresses. The Act requires those who record and use personal information (on computers, smart cards, optical image processors etc) to be open about its use, to follow sound and proper practices, to give individuals certain rights of access to the information, and allow them, where appropriate, to have the data corrected or deleted.

Main provisions

The provisions of the Act are very wide, and cover not just computers but also data stored on any magnetic device, tape, disk or card, and even volatile computer memory:

- ☐ *Data* covers all 'information recorded in a form in which it can be processed by equipment operating automatically in response to instructions given for that purpose...'.
- ☐ *Personal data* covers 'data consisting of information which relates to a living individual who can be identified from that information (or from that and other information in the possession of the data user), including any expression of opinion about the individual but not any indication of the intention of the data user in respect of that individual...'.
- ☐ *Processing* – in relation to data – means 'amending, augmenting, deleting or re-arranging the data or extracting information constituting the data and, in the case of personal data ... performing any of those operations by reference to the data subject'.
- ☐ *Data user* is the person who 'holds' a collection of personal data in a form capable of processing, and controls the processing of the data.

However, certain information is excluded from the provisions of the Act:

- ☐ information necessary for maintaining national security;
- ☐ paper-based information on individuals;
- ☐ information used within a company to pay staff;
- ☐ mailing lists – names and addresses used only for distribution of information.

Forms for registration are available from the Data Protection Registrar (see Chapter 25), and it is possible to register online (www.dpr.gov.uk; see Figure 28.2) and search the public register of data users.

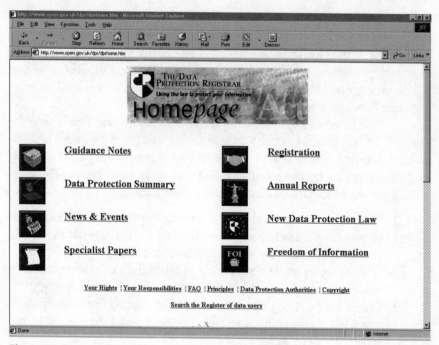

Figure 28.2

Access to personal data

The Act allows individuals to have access to information held about them on computer-based systems, and where appropriate have this personal data amended. To access your personal data, you should send a written request (preferably by recorded delivery) to the data user, who must respond to you within 40 days but may charge you a fee of up to £10 for each entry requested. You are also entitled to see your credit reference data that is covered separately by the Consumer Credit Act 1974.

The Registrar's website provides a range of useful documents, including an introduction to the Data Protection Act 1998, and contact details for the Registrar (tel 01625 545 745), Office of Fair Trading (tel 020 7211 8000; www.oft.gov.uk), and the two main credit reference agencies Experian (www.experian.com) and Equifax Europe (www. equifax. co.uk).

The Internet

'Cyber law' – the law of the Internet – is one of the most rapidly developing areas of high-tech law. An introduction to the legal aspects of setting up an online business, including sample legal forms, is provided in *Internet Legal Forms for Business* by Brinson and Radcliffe.

The Internet's whole *raison d'être* is to allow and encourage the conduct of commercial activity by electronic means. With cyber law the main concerns relate to letters, contracts and licences being held digitally and signed online by means of so-called *click–wrap* agreements. The principal legal issues specific to electronic commerce involve:

☐ *Electronic contracts.* Even an electronic contract must contain the elements of an offer, an acceptance and a consideration, and in certain special cases must be *evidenced-in-writing*.

☐ *Multimedia copyright.* Everything published on the Internet is a literary work and so is covered by the normal laws of copyright.

☐ *Online licence.* The popular way to meet electronically the criteria of *evidenced-in-writing* is to click on the 'I agree' button in an on-screen licensing agreement.

☐ *Digital signatures.* Fortunately, typing your name is an effective legal signature, although new legislation is presently planned to confirm this.

☐ *Legal contract.* Did the offer and acceptance submitted electronically create a binding contract?

☐ *Time of contract.* If the contract is valid, when was it made?

☐ *Governing law.* Is the contract subject to English, Irish or possibly American law?

☐ *Evidence.* Can a printout of a computer record be used to prove that the transaction occurred?

European directives

The legal framework for electronic commerce in the UK and Ireland is being laid down by directives from the European Commission. Over recent years the Commission has produced five significant directives:

☐ *Data protection.* This deals with the holding of personal data on living individuals, and is covered in the UK by the Data Protection Act 1998.

❏ *Distance selling.* This provides European-wide protection for consumers of direct selling. Specifically, it provides consumers with a 14-day cooling-off period within which they can cancel the contract without liability.

❏ *Distance selling of financial services.* This is broadly similar to the provisions of the directive mentioned above.

❏ *Digital signature.* This recommends a 'voluntary licensing' scheme for certification authorities of electronic signatures.

❏ *Electronic commerce.* This draft directive relates to the modification of European laws that are seen as barriers to electronic commerce, such as the admissibility of computer-based evidence in law.

Electronic data interchange (EDI)

At a simple level, EDI is the automatic exchange and processing of business information between computers. There are two common uses. The first is supply chain management, whereby one computer automatically replenishes its stock by sending an electronic request to another computer, possibly in a different country. The second use is in payment systems such as BACS, CHAPS and SWIFT, and online Internet banking. EDI's principal benefits are:

❏ *automated ordering* – automation of supply chain management; ordering, delivery and payment;

❏ *paperless operation* – the abolition of paper-based documents previously used in the ordering–delivery–payment cycle;

❏ *cost reduction* – reducing the cost of processing orders by up to 10 per cent of the value of the goods.

❏ *stock reduction* – reduction of stock levels because of the availability of what is called 'just-in-time' ordering.

Legal issues

The legal implications of EDI fall into four areas:

❏ *Business-to-business users.* This covers the relationship between two business users working through EDI and involves the *interchange agreement*, *contract formation*, and *evidential* issues.

❑ *Business user–network provider.* This covers the relationship between the business user and their network provider, which is largely contractual and involves *message conveyance, security* and *confidentiality.*

❑ *Business-to-consumer.* This describes the present fast-growing electronic shopping via the Internet.

❑ *Government-to-citizen.* This describes the developing use by government of electronic means to communicate with public and business users.

Business-to-business EDI is governed by an interchange agreement setting out the terms by which two parties will use EDI to conduct their business. Legally, it is important to separate the *interchange agreement* which governs the communication process, and the *contract* which governs the actual trading process.

Finally, recall that a contract must contain an offer, an acceptance and a consideration. This applies equally to electronic contracts, such as goods being ordered through EDI.

Hardware contracts

Hardware contracts cover physical systems and devices, notably computers, but also electrical plant, consumer electronics products, telecommunications and even individual semiconductor chips. When considering hardware contracts, there are four 'dimensions' to consider:

❑ *Type of product.* Unique, expensive supercomputers and electrical plant often justify special hardware contracts signed by the supplier and purchaser. Personal computers or consumer electronics products are commodity items for which the supplier expects the buyer to accept their standard terms and conditions.

❑ *Type of contract.* In a similar vein, whereas most hardware results in outright sales with ownership passing to the buyer, an alternative is to lease the hardware with ownership remaining with the supplier.

❑ *Negotiation medium.* Contracts can be in writing and signed by both parties, or in writing and signed by the buyer. They can be interactive via the Internet or digital television, or concluded over the telephone.

❏ *Consumer protection.* Whether a contract be written, oral or electronic, the contract must still conform to the law. Legislation includes the Unfair Contract Terms Act 1977 and the Sale of Goods Act 1979.

Legal issues

Whether a hardware contract be a special legal agreement, the terms and conditions on an invoice, or a 'click–wrap' agreement, it is likely to contain the terms set out in Figure 28.3.

Software contracts

Software contracts are of particular interest to high-tech companies, because most companies deal with software either as a purchaser, supplier or both. Legally, the supply of software, which spans computer programs,

---

HARDWARE CONTRACT

THIS AGREEMENT IS MADE the ....day of ....20....

BETWEEN (1) .... **of** ....(the "Supplier")

and (2) .... **of** .... (the "Purchaser")

This document sets out the terms and conditions ...

1. DEFINITIONS	- terms used in the contract
2. FORM OF AGREEMENT	- nature of the contract
3. SYSTEM SPECIFICATION	- specification of the hardware
4. VARIATION OF THE SPECIFICATION	
5. INTELLECTUAL PROPERTY RIGHTS	
6. THE PRICE	- the price to be paid for the hardware and maintenance etc
7. DELIVERY DATES	- completion and delivery times for the goods
8. ACCEPTANCE TESTING	- criteria for accepting the goods
9. MAINTENANCE	- duties of the supplier to rectify errors and faults
10. TRAINING	- responsibilities for training
11. WARRANTY	
12. EXCLUSION CLAUSES	
13. WAIVER AND VARIATION CLAUSES	
14. RETENTION OF TITLE	
15. CONFIDENTIALITY	- duty of purchaser to protect supplier information
16. ENTIRE AGREEMENT	
17. GOVERNING LAW	- that the contract is governed by English law

IN WITNESS OF WHICH ....

Supplier .... Signature .... Date

Purchaser .... Signature .... Date

Figure 28.3 Typical terms for a hardware contract

music and films, has to be dealt with in the same way as the supply of a literary work, such as a book. Ownership of the paper or magnetic medium is transferred, but the intellectual property remains with the author, unless IPR is explicitly transferred to the purchaser.

Conceptually, the purchaser has the right to use the book or software, but not necessarily to reproduce it. However, given the nature of software, the purchaser must be granted rights so that it can be copied to be executed and for backups to be taken in case of system failure. Therefore, a purchaser needs a *licence* which allows use of a software product, but which precludes the making of illegal copies.

The main types of software contract are:

- ❏ *Consultancy*. The contract covers the supply of expert advice, and terms for liability should the advice prove negligent.
- ❏ *Writing bespoke software*. This written agreement precisely defines what the supplier will deliver to the client in return for payment, as well as the timetable, ownership and protection of IPR, and legal redress for failure to deliver. It is a minefield!
- ❏ *Off-the-shelf software*. The customer needs to read and accept the vendor's terms and conditions prior to installing the product. The three popular ways, discussed below, of obtaining agreement are called *click-wrapped*, *shrink-wrapped* and *seal-wrapped* licences.
- ❏ *Software author–publisher*. The software author grants a licence to a publishing company permitting them to market the product on the basis of an agreed royalty payment. The licence may be exclusive or non-exclusive.

Legal issues

The pitfalls associated with software and software writing are legion: software bugs, programming overruns, obsolescence, the year 2000 bug, computers crashing, magnetic storage corruption, and temperamental programmers! So software contracts should be approached with extreme caution.

Figure 28.4 shows the elements of a software contract. The terms and conditions for the software being supplied need to be set out precisely. This covers their performance and criteria for acceptance. In addition, usage by the client, together with future enhancements and upgrades

---

SOFTWARE CONTRACT

THIS AGREEMENT IS MADE the ....day of ....20....

BETWEEN (1) .... of ....(the "Supplier")

and   (2) .... of .... (the "Purchaser')

This document sets out the terms and conditions ...

1. DEFINITIONS	- terms used in the contract
2. FORM OF AGREEMENT	- nature of the contract
3. ASSIGNMENT	- whether the goods can be transferred to a third party
4. DETAILS OF ITEMS	- a list of the items to be delivered by the contract
5. PRICE	- price, licence and/or royalty fees to be paid for the software
6. SPECIFICATION	- details of the specification of the goods to be delivered
7. DELIVERY	- completion and delivery times of the goods
8. LIQUIDATION DAMAGES	- penalties for late delivery
9. ACCEPTANCE	- criteria for accepting the goods
10. USAGE	- scope of use the client may make of the goods
11. MAINTENANCE	- duties of the supplier to rectify errors and faults
12. ENHANCEMENTS/MODIFICATIONS	- upgrades to be supplied or modifications allowed
13. TRAINING	- responsibilities for training
14. INTELLECTUAL PROPERTY	- duty of client to prevent unauthorised copying
15. ESCROW	- safeguards to protect the source code, should the supplier cease trading
16. CONFIDENTIALITY	- duty of supplier to protect client information
17. LIABILITY/INDEMNITY	- to protect the supplier and the client in the event of legal action
18. TERMINATION	- provisions for terminating the contract
19. GOVERNING LAW	- that the contract is governed by English law

IN WITNESS OF WHICH....

Supplier   .... Signature .... Date

Purchaser .... Signature .... Date

Figure 28.4 Typical terms for a software contract

from the supplier, and allowed enhancements by the client, need to be specified; as do agreed levels of training and maintenance.

Other issues include: (i) an *escrow agreement* to deposit the source code and documentation with a trusted third party should the supplier cease trading; (ii) terms of confidentially placed on the supplier and client; and (iii) terms and conditions of legal redress, should everything (as they say) go pear-shaped!

Licensing

'Copying' is at the heart of executing any computer program, whether it be copying the program from floppy disk or CD ROM to the hard disk for storage, or copying the program from disk to main memory for execution. Therefore, the owner of a program needs to explicitly license permission for the program to be copied, but with restrictions: (i) only a single copy for a specific machine; (ii) not accessible across a network; and (iii) not accessible via the Web.

There are three typical forms of software licensing:

- ❑ *Written licences.* The purchaser signs a written software licensing agreement similar to traditional contracts (see Figure 28.5). This is typical with bespoke software systems.
- ❑ *Click-wrapped licences.* The purchaser is asked to read a licence agreement displayed by the installation program or on a Web page, and click a button to acknowledge agreement (see Figure 28.6). This is normal for mass-market applications.
- ❑ *Shrink-wrapped licences.* The software is delivered in a box with a plastic wrapper, through which the purchaser can read the licence agreement printed on the packet. The purchaser is informed that breaking the seal and opening the wrapper acknowledges acceptance of the agreement.

Software packages are increasingly being downloaded from the Internet or delivered on CD ROM. Click–wrap licensing agreements are becoming the accepted paradigm for the client actively manifesting 'assent' after having had an opportunity to review the terms of the agreement.

SOFTWARE LICENCE AGREEMENT

THIS AGREEMENT IS MADE the ....day of ....20....
BETWEEN (1) .... of ....(the "Owner")
and   (2) .... of .... (the "Licensee")
WHEREAS   - a statement explaining the agreement

1. DEFINITIONS   - terms used in the agreement
2. LICENCE GRANT   - the Owner grants a specified licence to the Licensee
3. TERMS AND CONDITIONS   - start and termination of terms and conditions
4. INTELLECTUAL PROPERTY RIGHTS
   AND CONFIDENTIALITY
5. PAYMENT   - the consideration to be paid
6. LIMITATION OF LIABILITY   - statement of limit of liability
7. WARRANTIES   - scope of warranties
8. WAIVER   - scope and procedure for any waivers
9. ENTIRE AGREEMENT
10. MUTUAL CONSULTATION
11. GOVERNING LAW   - governed by English law

IN WITNESS OF WHICH ....
Owner .... Signature .... Date .... Name .... Title
Licensee .... Signature .... Date .... Name .... Title

---

Figure 28.5 Software licence agreement

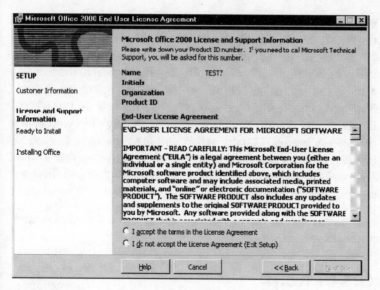

Figure 28.6

For ready-made (off-the-shelf) software packages, manufacturers have tried various methods to give their licence agreements the force of law. The big problem is that under English contract law a customer must *see* the terms before the contract is made, so printing the terms on the back of an invoice or putting the terms inside the box voids the terms. With shrink-wrapping the licence is printed on the *outside* of the box and covered in plastic, so the licence can be read before the product is purchased. With a seal-wrapped licence the terms are printed on the outside of the sealed package, with a statement saying that breaking the seal signifies acceptance of the agreement.

Special licences

There are a number of other types of software licence terms that you may come across. These include:

- [ ] *Trial licences.* As an encouragement for a user to try a software package, the manufacturer will often allow the downloading of a trial version from the Internet and free use for typically 30 days, after which the potential customer is supposed to purchase it.
- [ ] *Academic licences.* Software packages are sold at a discount to

educational institutions (to encourage take-up) and the licence forbids commercial usage of the software.

❏ *Site licences*. If an organization needs to install multiple copies of a piece of software, manufacturers usually will sell them a 'site licence' so they make multiple copies for the organization.

❏ *Shareware*. This is software you can copy for private use without payment, but if you plan to use it commercially then you have to purchase a licence. Usually, when you load the software you are presented with an agreement you need to click to start the system.

❏ *Freeware*. This is software that can be freely copied and used, but not in commercial products.

(*Note*: The contributions of David Warsh of Needham & Grant (Solicitors) are gratefully acknowledged.)

Sources of help

Bainbridge, D (1996) *Introduction to Computer Law*, Pitman Publishing, London
Brinson, D and Radclife, M (1997) *Internet Legal Forms for Business*, Ladera Press, Menlo Park, CA
CyberLaw Organisation. *www.cyberlaw.com*
Data Protection Registrar. Wycliffe House, Water Lane, Wilmslow, Cheshire, SK9 5AX, tel: 01625 545 745, *www.data-protection.gov.uk*.
Federation Against Software Theft. (FAST) 1 Kingfisher Court, Farnham Road, Slough, Berkshire, SL2 1JF, tel: 01753 527999, fax: 01753 532100, email: *fast@fast.org.uk, www.fast.org.uk*
Irish, V (1994) *Intellectual Property Rights for Engineers – The legal protection of innovation*, Institution of Electrical Engineers, London
Reed, C (1996) (ed.) *Computer Law*, Blackstone Press Ltd., London
Rosenoer, J (1997) *CyberLaw: The law of the Internet*, Springer, New York

29 High-tech Intellectual Property Rights

'Knowledge' is the life-blood of most high-tech start-ups, so intellectual property rights (IPR) are of fundamental importance. A good starting point for information is Vivien Irish's *Intellectual Property Rights for Engineers: The Legal Protection of Innovation*.

In this chapter we focus briefly on IPR related to high-tech, specifically software, hardware, the Internet and multimedia:

❑ the protection, ownership and licensing of high-tech intellectual property;
❑ patenting of hardware and biotech;
❑ design rights protection for semiconductors;
❑ trademarking domain names;
❑ software copyright protection of programs and Web pages;
❑ software patenting.

High-tech intellectual property

We start by summarizing the main IP legal issues introduced in Chapter 27: protection, ownership and licensing:

❑ *Protection. Patents* protect new, useful and 'non-obvious' inventions and processes, such as hardware and biotech. *Design rights* protect the appearance of articles or products, including the layout of semiconductors. *Trademarks* protect words, names and symbols used by businesses to identify their goods and services; for example, Internet domain names. *Copyright* protects written,

High-tech IP	Patent	Rights-in-design	Trademark	Copyright	Confidential Information
Computer contracts					✓
Internet domain names			✓		
Web pages				✓	✓
Computer software	✓	✓		✓	✓
Databases	✓			✓	✓
Test method	✓				✓
Hardware device	✓	✓			
Semiconductors	✓	✓			

Figure 29.1 Protection of high-tech IPR

drawn and computer-generated original 'works of authorship'. *Confidential information* protects valuable company information not generally known that has been kept secret by its owner. Figure 29.1 illustrates the protection available for various types of high-tech intellectual property.

☐ *Ownership.* Recall, your ownership of IPR is not as straightforward as it might seem. Ownership depends on whether you created the IP as an 'employee', as a 'contractor' commissioned to do the work, or as an 'instigator' who commissioned the IP. An *employee* is bound by a 'contract of service', typically stating that IPR generated as 'normal duties' is to be the property of the company. A *contractor* commissioned to deliver products and services to a company typically owns the IPR unless the commissioning company specifies ownership in the terms of the contract. An *instigator* (eg you or your company) causes the IPR to be generated and hence owns the IPR.

☐ *Licensing.* You can issue an IP licence for any or all of the IP that you own. This can be for specific regions, and on a non-exclusive, sole or exclusive use basis. *Non-exclusive licences* may be granted to any number of competing companies. A *sole licence* is granted to a single company, but the IPR owner may compete with them. An *exclusive licence* is granted to a single company, and the IPR owner undertakes not to compete with the company.

Patents

Patent law protects inventions and processes (called 'utility' patents) and ornamental designs (called 'design' patents). Three specific high-tech areas of interest are hardware, software and biotech:

❑ *Hardware*. Just like any other tangible device, hardware can be patented if it can be shown that it is a 'new, useful and non-obvious invention'.

❑ *Software*. Although computer programs were specifically excluded from patent protection by the UK Patent Act 1977, patents give much stronger protection than copyright. Therefore, applications are being made (and granted) for patents on the grounds that 'programs make a contribution to the state-of-the-art of the total computer system'. The limitation of the 1977 Act exclusion is becoming more and more eroded by recent case law and registrations of software-based patents with the European Patent Office.

❑ *Biotech*. This receives patent protection by showing a new, useful and 'non-obvious' process and possibly invention.

Design rights

As discussed in Chapter 27, there are three rights-in-designs. For *design rights* the article must be a tangible 3D object. *Registered designs* covers features of manufactured articles judged by their appearance. *Topography rights* apply specifically to the pattern of integrated circuits and masks. Of particular interest in high-tech IP is the protection of integrated circuits.

Semiconductor products

Why give semiconductors special protection? Most of the advances in the past 30 years have been underpinned by integrated circuits composed of devices etched on a wafer of semiconductor material. Given the importance of semiconductor products, the law naturally wishes to protect the intellectual property.

Patent law protects the fabrication process involved in making the integrated circuits, with the most important patent being issued in 1959 to

Robert Noyce who subsequently founded Intel. New integrated circuits are unlikely to have sufficient novelty to be patentable. However, the integrated circuit patterns are protected by the Design Rights (Semiconductor Regulations) 1989. This protects the integrated circuit pattern and also the masks used to create the pattern.

Trademarks

High-tech trademarks follow standard trademark law, with a mark being registered in one or more class (eg class 9 – electric apparatus, or class 38 – telecommunications), for one or more regions. One interesting new area of trademark law is *Internet domain names*.

Internet domain names

When you set up your high-tech start-up, good branding dictates that your company name and Internet domain name should be the same, say NewCo.com. However, if someone else registers the trademark, they could stop you from using the name.

But it does not end there. When you submit NewCo.com to the Trade Mark Registry, they will tell you that for domain names they do not consider the '.com', '.net', '.org' or '.co.uk', only the 'NewCo'. This in itself could obviously affect whether you can register the mark.

So, given the global nature of domain names, and the fact that trademarks are registered by region, you could presumably get a situation where you own the NewCo.com trademark for Europe and a competitor NewCo.net owns the trade mark for the United States. Very interesting!

Software copyright

Copyright law protects 'software' in its broadest sense of digital multimedia and computer programs. *Literary works* covers programs, databases, computer files, printed documents, training manuals, brochures and directories. *Audiovisual works* covers music, sounds, videos, CD ROMs, films and television programmes. *Graphical works* covers images, photographs, cartoons, and paintings. Copyright is obtained 'automatically' when an original work of authorship is recorded in a tangible form, including digital multimedia.

Under UK and Irish law, digital material, whether stored in memory, held in a database, sent over the Internet, or stored on Web servers, is generally protected in the same way as material in other media.

Now for some dangerous myths.

Myths and principles

Many people hold the mistaken belief that software and information placed on the Internet is free to take. This is not the case, whether a copyright notice (eg ©2000 Microsoft) is included or not. Under UK and Irish law, copyright programs and material sent over the Internet, stored on Web servers or placed on bulletin boards are generally protected in exactly the same way as material in other media. So, anyone wishing to put copyright material on the Internet, or further distribute or download such material that others have placed on the Internet, should ensure that they have the permission of the owners of rights in the material.

Multimedia

All digital recordings of sounds, whether music or animal noises, and of images on film, are protected by copyright, whatever the recording material – be it tape, film, disk or magnetic memory, both now and in the future. Broadcast media – radio and television transmissions through the atmosphere – are covered by broadcast copyright, but cable services are treated separately.

Computer programs

Programs and databases are covered by literary copyright, with the encoding – whether text or machine code – taken as the written form. Interestingly, a database is likely to be covered by two copyrights, the first covering the program determining the structure of the database and the second the actual data stored.

The Internet

World Wide Web, e-mail, bulletin boards (BBs) and newsgroups raise a number of interesting legal issues. Clearly, if the person posting the information does not own copyright in the material, then this is an infringement. By implication, anyone subsequently copying the material is also breaching copyright; likewise, theoretically, each service provider on to whose computer the material is posted. Even if the person posting the information owns the copyright and is donating the material, a suitable statement should be included to the effect of: *the owner gives permission for the work to be used for non-commercial purposes* and typing their name, deemed a 'signature'.

Telecommunications services

Copyright also covers the transmission of material over wires and fibre-optic cables, that potentially can support two-way interaction, as with access to online databases, websites and home shopping. However, excluded from this form of copyright are telephone services, home banking and closed-circuit television.

Avoiding infringement

Digital technology makes it straightforward to combine copyright material into a multimedia product. So, start by assuming that most digital material is copyrighted and that to utilize it commercially you need to obtain an assignment or a licence:

- ☐ *Assignment* legally transfers all intellectual property rights to the new owner.
- ☐ *Licence* legally provides the licensee with the specified rights to use the multimedia IP.

When you do not need a licence

In certain circumstances you do not need a licence, but this can be a legal minefield!

- ☐ *Fair use.* This covers the use of a 'small amount' of material for review, news reporting, teaching and research, when no commercial gain is involved.
- ☐ *Public domain.* Material not covered by copyright (such as

Shakespeare's plays, because the author has been dead for longer than the period of copyright) can be freely copied.

❑ *Ideas/facts.* You are free to copy ideas or facts from a copyrighted work.

Software patents

Software patenting is undoubtedly the hottest topic in high-tech IP. The primary benefit of protecting computer software through the patent system is the strength of the protection provided by the patent law (www.bitlaw.com). The owner of a software patent can prevent others from utilizing a certain algorithm or creating software that performs a function in a certain way. In contrast, copyright law can be used only to prevent the total duplication of a computer program, as well as copying portions of the software code.

The costs of software patent infringement can be high. For instance in 1994, Stac Electronics was awarded $120 million against Microsoft for infringement of two of its software patents.

In recent years the United States Patent and Trademark Office (USPTO) has granted over 10,000 applications for software patents.

As to the million dollar question of what constitutes a 'good software patent', you are recommended to look at some of the excellent sites on the Internet (eg www.spi.org).

Broadly, software is *patentable* if the invention uses the computer to manipulate information that represents concrete, real-world values. Then the invention is a process relating to real-world concepts. Software is *unpatentable* if the invention is actually only a mathematical algorithm, such as a sorting routine.

Software patents have a number of advantages and disadvantages, as summarized in Table 29.1 (see also http://cla.org/matsnpubs/memberarticles).

In the United States, the law is seen as a legitimate business weapon to fight competitors, in the same vein as investment, marketing and public relations. Henceforth, any aspiring software entrepreneur needs to ensure that they are not infringing any (US) software patent or they could find themselves being sued for potentially enormous damages. Likewise if you have a novel business concept, you should look seriously at the expense of patenting it in the US to protect the underlying

Table 29.1 Advantages and disadvantages of software patents

Advantages	Disadvantages
• Protection - the breadth of protection allows the owner to establish a de-facto standard in the marketplace.	• High Standard - a patent must demonstrate a significant contribution to a technology.
• Algorithm - a patent can protect the 'algorithm' underlying a 'display' of information.	• Uncertainty - what software can be patented is still a subject for the courts.
• Independent Creation - protects against someone who independently creates, as against copying.	• Databases/Documentation - patents cannot protect documentation, but may protect databases.
• Copying - unnecessary to show copying, as in copyright protection.	• Time Factor - the time from patent application to issue can be 24 months.
• Licensing - a patent makes it easier to license a technology.	• Preliminary Relief - far fewer preliminary injunctions are granted in patent litigation, compared to copyright.
• Commercial Disclosure - a published patent facilitates commercial disclosure.	• High Cost - patent application and litigation are often drawn-out and expensive.
• Long Term - a patent offers protection for a reasonably long period.	

functionality. A software patent, or the possibility of gaining one, can be very helpful in attracting potential investors. Although expensive, is often worthwhile in the long run.

Sources of help

Bainbridge, D (1996) *Introduction to Computer Law,* Pitman Publishing, London

Brinson, D and Radcliffe, M (1996) *Multimedia Law and Business Handbook,* Ladera Press, Menlo Park, CA

Copyright Licensing Agency. 90 Tottenham Court Road, London, W1P 0LP

Design Registry. Patent Office, Concept House, Cardiff Road, Newport, Gwent, NP9 1RH, tel: 01633 814000, *www.patent.gov.uk*

European Patent Office. Erhardtstrasse 27, D-80331 Munich, Germany, tel: +49 89 23 99–0, fax: +49 89 23 99–44 65, *www.european-patent-office.org*

Irish, V (1994) *Intellectual Property Rights for Engineers – The legal protection of innovation,* Institution of Electrical Engineers, London

Patent Office. Cardiff Road, Newport, Gwent, NP10 8QQ, tel: 01633 814000, fax: 01633 814444, email: commercial searches@patent.gov.uk, *www.patent.gov.uk*

Reed, C (1996) (ed.) *Computer Law,* Blackstone Press Ltd., London

Part 6

Marketing
for
Start-ups

---

30 **Marketing**

To the fury of marketing executives, the terms 'marketing', 'public relations', 'advertising' and even 'sales' are often used interchangeably by the rest of the population. So we will start with some definitions. To quote the experts:

- ❑ *Marketing* 'is the management process responsible for identifying, anticipating and satisfying customer requirements profitably.' Hmm!
- ❑ *Public relations* 'is the planned campaign to establish and maintain goodwill and mutual understanding between an organisation and its *publics*.' Hmm!
- ❑ *Advertising* 'is paid-for communications that aim to bring a business and its products to the attention of potential consumers, and persuade then to ultimately buy.' Better!
- ❑ *Sales* is finding out potential customers' needs, showing how your product meets these needs, persuading them to buy, and looking after your customers.

In this chapter we look at:

- ❑ marketing and the marketing mix;
- ❑ marketing and its relationship to the product;
- ❑ marketing and the customer;
- ❑ promotion: branding, public relations, advertising and sales;
- ❑ distribution: wholesale, retail, direct response and electronic marketing;
- ❑ preparing a marketing plan;
- ❑ simple computer aids, such as mail-merge, e-mail lists and customer databases.

Most importantly, high-tech start-ups need to be market-focused, if they

Table 30.1 High-tech start-up marketing

Advantages	Disadvantages
▪ Focus on niche market segment	▪ Need to compete in global marketplace
▪ Use of interactive marketing	▪ Limited financial resources
▪ Flexibility to react to market changes	▪ Limited management capacity
▪ Personal touch with customers	▪ Limited market
▪ Improvization	▪ Compete with established players

are going to become the 800-pound 'gorilla'. High-tech start-ups have a number of distinct marketing advantages, but also disadvantages (see Table 30.1). In Chapter 15 we looked at Internet marketing. Here we look at marketing in general.

Principles of marketing

In simple terms, marketing is the *link* between your business and your customers. You give customers something of value (product or service) and they give you something of value (money, patronage and endorsement); marketing enunciates the value of your products. Customers buy for numerous (often intangible) reasons: *need* (bread); *advertising* (Andrex), *fashion* (Armani), *image* (Prada) and *peer pressure* (Nike); *fear* (insurance), *legislation* (TV licence) and *security* (uzi); *quality* (Sony) and *reputation* (Mercedes Benz); *price* (Hotmail), *value* (Marks & Spencer) and *guarantees* (John Lewis); *standards* (Microsoft) and *specification* (VHS).

What is marketing?

Marketing is a comprehensive set of functions from the inception of the product (design, pricing, promotion, distribution, selling) until it reaches the customer, as well as the after-sales service (instruction booklets, servicing, repairs, replacements). Marketing is designed to bridge gaps between you and your customers (see Table 30.2).

The marketing mix

The main concept of marketing comprises the so-called four Ps: *product, price, place* and *promotion*. And the so-called marketing mix – the 'Holy

Table 30.2 Linking products and customers (adapted from R Machado, *Marketing for Small Business*)

Marketing link	Your business ...	Your customers ...
Geographic gap	is sited at a single location	are dispersed possibly worldwide
Time gap	releases products at one time	want the products at another time
Information gap	doesn't know what customers want	don't know what is available
Value gap	values products by cost and price	value products by want and need
Quantity gap	prefers to sell in large quantities	prefer to buy in small quantities
Product range gap	specializes in one or more products	want a complete range of products
Service gap	wishes to minimize overheads	expect a full after-sales service

Grail' of marketing – is the mix of product, price, place and promotion that best satisfies the needs of the target market:

❑ *Product.* The success of a product depends on many factors: quality, design, construction, packaging, functionality, ease of use and, most importantly, its ability to satisfy customers' wants and needs.

❑ *Price.* The price at which a product may be sold also depends on numerous factors: the production cost, the distribution cost, the desired profit margin to achieve an acceptable return on investment, and even the market reaction to the price charged. A lower price reduces the profit margin per item, but might convey 'value-for-money' to the customer. A higher price increases the profit margin and may convey 'quality' to the customer.

❑ *Place.* The choice of distribution channels varies greatly. Channels include via an agent/wholesaler to a retailer, direct to the retailer, or direct to the customer through mail order or the Internet. Frequently, customer convenience and accessibility determine the most appropriate channel.

❑ *Promotion.* This covers the portfolio of methods for promoting a product. These include branding, public relations, advertising, sales promotions, merchandising, exhibitions, in-store displays, Web promotion (banners ads etc), and personal selling.

Customer care

Customers are becoming ever more demanding of products and service:

- ☐ *Customer expectations.* Improved consumer affluence and improved product quality have raised customer expectations of quality of service.
- ☐ *Staff awareness.* Progressive businesses have instigated 'customer-care' policies, from the board of directors down, to raise the workforce's awareness of the importance of customer service.
- ☐ *Customer complaints.* Complaints from customers are one of the most valuable forms of feedback to a business and should be treated accordingly. (One satisfied customer tells five other people; one dissatisfied customer tells thirty!)
- ☐ *Satisfaction checks.* You should also survey your customers regularly to monitor their satisfaction levels. Retailers employ so-called 'mystery customers' to visit stores and report on the attitudes of sales and support staff, and telephone various departments in the company to monitor staff responses.
- ☐ *Business partnership.* Care must also be shown to your external partners and the internal staff forming the business supply chain, where personal relations can have a profound effect on efficiency and productivity. This might be referred to as the *internal marketing mix.*

Having looked at the principles, we now look at marketing from four different aspects: the *product*, the *customer*, the *distribution* and the *promotion*.

Marketing and the product

Most high-tech start-ups launch themselves with an innovative product. Therefore, new product development is one of the key methods that a small business can use to market itself and develop a reputation as an innovator, ensuring it has a future. A good starting point is to look at how phenomenally successful high-tech companies, like Intel, repeatedly innovate.

Product development

Obtaining new product ideas is an ongoing process for a business. The first step is to generate candidate ideas. As illustrated by Figure 30.1, ideas can come from a number of external and internal sources. The process involves:

❏ *Idea generation*. One popular method is *brainstorming*: a method of creating product ideas where a group of people uninhibitedly propose and discuss ideas.

❏ *Idea screening*. Candidate product ideas are screened for viability, including your financial, marketing and manufacturing capabilities.

❏ *Market analysis*. The potential business and market are analysed.

❏ *Prototype development*. Actual prototypes of the product are developed.

❏ *Market testing*. The product is launched in a small area to judge consumer reaction.

❏ *Product launch*. The product is launched as fully as your business resources allow.

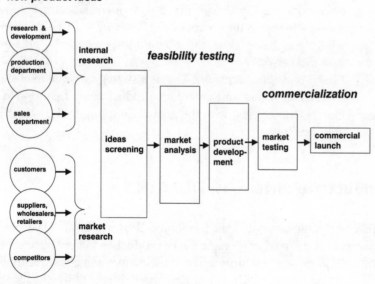

Figure 30.1 New product development process

Product pricing

Price is a major element of the marketing mix. In Chapter 19 we looked at the factors affecting price, and how to calculate the basic price level for your product to achieve your desired profit level. Here we briefly look at pricing from a marketing mix viewpoint. The three basic choices are firstly to *increase profits*, secondly to *increase market share*, or thirdly to *increase sales volume*. Typical pricing strategies include:

- ❏ *Cost-oriented pricing*. With this strategy you set your price high enough to cover your costs and make a profit. Three variants of this strategy are: *cost-plus* a percentage, *rate-of-return* on investment, and *break-even analysis* where sales equal costs.
- ❏ *Customer-oriented pricing*. With this strategy you set your price so that it is perceived by your customers as competitive, or 'value for money'. There are a number of variants: *backward* – what the customer is prepared to pay; *prestige* – to imply quality; *odd numbers* – eg £2.99; *price lines* – a range of economy, medium and quality product prices; and *bundled* – the price combines two or more products.
- ❏ *Competition-oriented pricing*. With this strategy you set your price depending on your competitors. Variants include: *above market* – to emphasize quality; *below market* – to increase sales volume; *at market* – to match the competition; *skimming* – to maximize profits where you have few competitors; and *penetration* – price set to gain market share.
- ❏ *Market capitalization pricing*. This is a strategy unique to electronic commerce, where you give your product away free to gain customers (subscribers) with the goal of ramping up the valuation of your business.

Product life cycle

With a new company, one of the fundamental laws of business you need to be aware of is the *product life cycle*. Every product and every business has a birth, a rapid growth, maturity and a subsequent decline (see Figure 30.2).

To quote Andy Grove, chairman of Intel: 'Only the paranoid survive'. A company who can innovate and bring new products to the

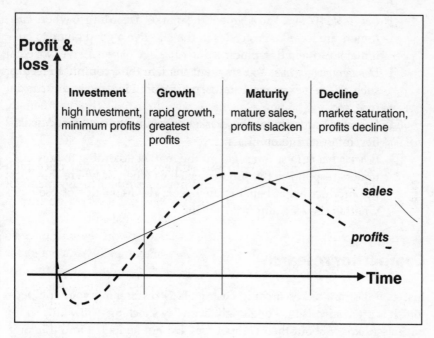

Figure 30.2 Product life cycle

market will survive (this includes modifications to existing products to stop them rolling over the 'peak' into decline).

Marketing and the customer

Identifying the needs and aspirations of your customers is a continuous process. Fortunately, for a high-tech start-up, mass consumption and the US domination of the global media have brought about a standardization in habits and tastes of the vast majority of consumers. It is therefore possible to analyse the purchasing habits of a whole market by conducting tests on a small sample of potential customers. This is popularly called consumer or market research, and is covered in Chapter 6.

Consumer research

To help analyse customer profiles and purchasing behaviour, markets are *segmented*. Four factors are used typically for market segmentation:

❑ *Geographic factors*. You segment the market according to where customers are located. Postcodes in the UK give a good guide to customer socio-demographics.

❑ *Demographic factors*. You segment the market according to factors such as age, sex, marital status, occupation, income and expenditure, etc.

❑ *Lifestyle*. You segment the market according to customers' activities, interests and opinions.

❑ *Behavioural factors*. You segment the market according to how customers respond to the product, such as when or where they buy the product, what benefits they seek, the frequency of use, and whether they are 'impulse' buyers.

Competitor research

Just as important as researching customers is researching your competitors. It is often surprising – one might even say shocking – how little some businesses know about their competitors. Do not be fooled into thinking that because you have an innovative technological product that you do not have any competitors. The type of questions you should be able to answer are:

❑ *Competitors*. Who are your strongest competitors and is their business growing or contracting? As a starting point you can get hold of their annual accounts from Companies House.

❑ *Products*. How does their product range compare with yours in terms of price and quality? Buy their products and reverse-engineer them.

❑ *Management*. Are they well managed? Ask ex-staff and customers for their opinions.

❑ *Marketing strategy*. What is their marketing strategy and which sectors are they targeting?

❑ *Customer service*. Do they provide good customer care and what is their reputation in the marketplace?

❑ *Strengths and weaknesses*. Do a SWOT analysis on your competitors and then one on your own business.

Marketing and distribution

Distribution is the 'place' part of the marketing mix; the system that gets your product to the place where the customer wants to buy it. Two important aspects are firstly the *distribution channel* and secondly (physical) *movement* of the product. Issues to be considered when selecting your distribution system are:

- ❑ *Intensity of distribution*. The properties of the product will instruct this decision: *intensive* – all possible outlets including the Internet; *selective* – suitable for selected outlets; *exclusive* – expensive and appropriate for special outlets.
- ❑ *Product characteristics*. The level of exclusivity and technical complexity of the product will influence where it can be sold successfully. For instance, expensive, technically complex products require special sales and servicing requirements.
- ❑ *Types of intermediaries*. These are middlemen handling distribution between the producer and the consumer: *brokers* – who bring buyers and sellers together, such as eBay (www.ebay.com), E-Trade (www.e-trade.com) and LastMinute.com (www.lastminute.com); *agents* – who help a producer sell to wholesalers, charging a commission; *wholesalers* ('resellers' in the US) – who buy in bulk and distribute to retailers; and *retailers* – who sell directly to consumers.

Sophisticated communications, such as the Internet, and reliable courier services, like DHL, allow small firms and high-tech start-ups to market directly to consumers, even on a global basis. The area is called *direct-response marketing*. Mail order is the principal sector, with 90 per cent of the market being dominated by the major catalogue companies, GUS, Littlewoods, Freeman's etc. However, in the past few years many leading retailers have introduced mail order catalogues and home delivery, seen as an obvious prelude to Internet and interactive television shopping.

There are a number of direct marketing channels available:

- ❑ *The Internet*. This supports global direct marketing, through electronic catalogues and electronic mail.
- ❑ *Mail order*. This is the major fulfilment mechanism whether customers are shopping by catalogue, over the telephone or the Internet.

❑ *Direct mail.* This is an increasingly popular form of directed advertising. However, it is important to target your market effectively to
avoid impersonal and in some cases puerile communications.

❑ *Telephone sales.* We tend to think of telephone sales as someone
phoning to sell you double glazing when you are just sitting down
to dinner. However, if you are calling the MD of a prospect
company it is also telephone sales. Customers calling you to make
a purchase after reading your mailing piece are also phone sales.

❑ *Door-to-door.* Selling door-to-door is an alternative to direct mail
and selling, but may be inappropriate for a high-tech company.

❑ *Networks.* There are a number of direct marketing 'schemes' for
developing a personal relationship with your customers, such as
clubs, party plans and multi-level marketing.

Marketing and promotion

The final 'P' is *promotion* – the area of the marketing mix dealing with how
you are going to make your target market aware of your product. There
are many ways of doing this, each covered in this part of the book by a separate chapter: branding, public relations (PR), advertising, and selling.

There is also *merchandising* – a term used in marketing to cover all
those sales promotion activities used to rouse a customer's interest in your
product, excluding conventional press and television advertising, and
public relations.

Marketing plan

To be successful you need a marketing plan to set out what the business
wants to achieve through its marketing, how it will achieve this, and how
much investment it will need. The main components of a marketing plan
are:

❑ *An executive summary.* A run-down of the main goals, market analysis, decisions and recommendations that are in the marketing
plan.

❑ *Current marketing situation.* This section covers the current market:
the market description, product review, competition review,
distribution review, and a business environment analysis.

❏ *Market analysis.* This must be a realistic analysis of your business compared with your competitors in the marketplace. A common way of doing this is by means of a SWOT analysis.

❏ *Objectives of campaign.* This sets out the objectives for the campaign. These should be quantifiable, ranked in order of importance, given a time deadline, and be achievable.

❏ *Marketing strategy.* This identifies your target market, your positioning and your marketing mix for the target market.

❏ *Action programme.* This is the specific programme of work to achieve the objectives of the campaign. It answers the questions: what?, when?, who? and how (much it will cost)?

❏ *Budget.* This sets out the budget for the campaign, including a projected profit/loss statement and projected sales forecast.

❏ *Controls.* This monitors the performance of the plan, measuring and evaluating the results and taking any remedial actions to ensure that the objectives are achieved. This includes: sales analysis, profitability, and market research.

Simple computer-based marketing aids

Mail merge and mail shots

Central to your marketing campaign is building an increasingly sophisticated customer address list. Mail merge can be achieved using a word processing package, such as Microsoft's Word, to prepare name and address tables and then generate letters for mail shots.

Create an MS Word table of names and addresses, prepare a form letter, then use *Mail Merge* (in the *Tools* menu) to generate a personalized letter for each entry.

Fax and e-mail lists

Most people assume that faxes are urgent or important and therefore read them. So companies, especially it seems those selling personal computers and office supplies, have resorted increasingly to 'fax mailshots'. Fax mailshots can be a highly efficient, automated and cheap way of communicating with customers, but should be used carefully to avoid antagonising them. More importantly, new laws are being introduced to outlaw unsolicited fax (and e-mail) mail shots.

Most PC fax and e-mail packages support mailing lists and the more advanced ones interface with database packages. With fax packages look for the *Phonebook* entry in the menu bar to create groups of recipients, and with e-mail packages look for the *Address Book* entry.

Slide presentations

Having made contact with a potential customer, you need to present your company and products in a professional way. Here, a presentation tool such as Microsoft's PowerPoint can be used to create a professional offering. PowerPoint is a powerful tool for preparing slides for presentations. Once prepared, the slides can be printed in black and white or colour for overhead projector (OHP) transparencies, for notes or output from your PC to an online video projector.

Sources of help

Chartered Institute of Marketing. Moor Hall, Cookham, Maidenhead, Berks., SL6 9QH, tel: 01628 427500, fax: 01628 427499, *www.cim.co.uk*

Direct Marketing Association (UK) Ltd, The. Haymarket House, 1 Oxendon Street, London, SW1Y 4EE, tel: 020 7321 2525, fax: 020 7321 0191, email: dma@dma.org.uk, www.dma.org.uk

Elvy, H (1997) *Marketing Made Simple*, Made Simple Books, Oxford

Machado, R (1996) *Marketing for a Small Business*, JUTA, Kenwyn, South Africa

Marketing Society, The. St Georges House, 3–5 Pepys Road, London, SW20 8NJ, tel: 020 8879 3464, fax: 020 8879 0362

Pattern, D (1998) *Successful Marketing for the Small Business*, Kogan Page, London

Peterson, R (1997) (ed.) *Electronic Marketing and the Consumer*, Sage, London

Rohner, K (1996) *Marketing in the Cyber Age*, John Wiley & Sons, New York

31 **Branding**

Successful high-tech start-ups are by definition good at branding. A *brand* is the all-pervasive 'image' of your product or company. It conveys the qualities of your product and company. It is the lifeblood of the organization, starting with a meaningful or memorable company name, then dovetailing in the names of its innovative products and services. Not all brands travel well. My favourites are *Super Piss* (a Finnish product for unfreezing car locks) and *Pocari Sweat* (a Japanese sports drink)! An excellent introduction to branding in general is *Brands: The New Wealth Creators* by Susannah Hart and John Murphy.

In this chapter we look at:

- [ ] the principles behind brand names;
- [ ] global branding for high-tech companies;
- [ ] the processes of creating and evaluating your brand;
- [ ] brand exploitation through licensing, franchising and sales.

We normally associate branding with products: *Coca-Cola* drink, *Heinz* baked beans or *Kellogg's* cornflakes. However, in the marketing-driven world of high-tech start-ups it increasingly means international company branding, which is the focus of this chapter.

The function of a brand is to distinguish a company, product or service from its competitors. Branding is a marketing 'jigsaw puzzle'. In terms of a high-tech company, it develops a name with a coherent set of attributes and values that are focused, distinctive and appealing to potential customers, employees, partners, investors and the media. International branding provides companies with a mission statement (and coherence) for their international activities.

Trademarks, design rights and copyrights allow you to protect your 'brand' and exploit its financial value. A high-tech start-up typically starts out by focusing on a niche market. Having established its brand reputation it can then extend, or *leverage*, the brand into other markets. Brand extension reduces the risk and the cost of developing new products and services, increases the visibility of the brand, and – through being the market leader – gives reassurance to customers. A good example is People-Soft (www.peoplesoft.com), who established themselves as a client/server software company initially through the market niche of human resources. Having 'built their brand' in human resources, PeopleSoft were able to catapult themselves into the more mainstream and lucrative markets of financial, order processing and manufacturing systems.

Principles of branding

We start by looking at the main issues of branding, namely brand name creation and brand name evaluation.

Brand names

Brand names typically fall into a small number of categories (examples are shown in Figure 31.1):

- ☐ *Founder's name.* The name is associated with the person who established the business, product or service: the *creator*, Walt Disney; the *entrepreneur*, Michael Dell; the *shopkeepers*, Marks & Spencer; the *inventor*, Dyson.
- ☐ *Place name.* The name is associated with the place where the

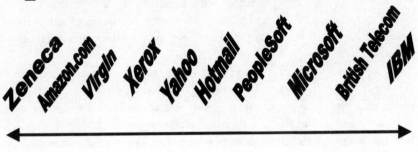

Free-standing   Associative   Descriptive

Figure 31.1 Brand name spectrum (adapted from S Hart, *Brands: The New Wealth Creators*)

company was established: British Telecom and Kawasaki motor bikes.

❏ *Scientific name.* The name is an 'invented' scientific name often based on Latin or Greek. This is popular with pharmaceutical products; for example, Xerox is associated with the Greek word for 'dry'.

❏ *Quality name.* The name has an association with 'quality', for instance Excel and Pioneer.

❏ *Artificial name.* The name is made-up to be simple, memorable and 'trademark*able*' internationally. Classic examples include Kodak, Sony and Zeneca.

❏ *Descriptive name.* The name loosely describes the products or services of the company. For example, Coca-Cola is based on the product's two principal ingredients, *coca* leaves and *cola* nuts; and Microsoft is based on *micro*(computer) *soft*(ware).

❏ *Provocative name.* The name is chosen to grab the attention of potential customers. Examples are Virgin, French Connection's FCUK, Hotmail and Demon.

❏ *Abbreviated name.* The name is an abbreviation, typically the initials, of the company. Classics include IBM (International Business Machines), NCR (National Cash Registers) and BT (British Telecommunications).

Brand name creation

The key to success of a high-tech start-up is not only identifying the market opportunity, but also developing a product or service that is different, relevant and appealing to potential customers and investors. Branding is the 'packaging' that brings this all together. In most start-ups the company and its launch product or service are one and the same thing. So a brand name needs to be chosen carefully to convey the correct message, and so that it can be used (and protected) internationally.

The role of the brand name is to:

❏ *identify* the company, its product(s) and service(s) uniquely;
❏ *communicate* the company vision and focus to all 'stakeholders', customers, employees, partners, and investors (this is the association of your 'message' with your brand);
❏ *protect* the company's intellectual property;

❏ *allow expansion* of the company into foreign markets, and into new products and services.

Amazingly, some start-ups select names with profound marketing, organizational and legal defects. The most elementary is not being able to use the same brand name for your company and your Internet domain.

International branding

High-tech start-ups, especially those in computing and media, are by definition global with an 'export or die' attitude. Fortunately, customers and investors are also becoming increasingly international. This leads to global markets with consumers craving similar products, services and wealth-creating opportunities.

Globalization is most evident in the 20–30 age group in Europe and also Asia, where English has become the *lingua franca* for an entire generation who watch MTV, CNN, SkyNews and BBC News 24, or read *TIME, Newsweek, Business Week* and the *Financial Times*. Well over 50 per cent of all people under 35 in Western Europe speak English (or, more accurately, American). For international brands there is significant marketing overlap between countries. One company, one product, one service, and one message is the nirvana.

But as graphically illustrated by the European Union, there is as yet 'no single market in branding'. Consumer preferences vary considerably from Germany to Greece. The differences between Europe, America and Asia are even more pronounced:

❏ *Taste*. National tastes differ, most notably in foods, primarily influenced by differences in climate and agriculture.
❏ *Attitude*. National attitudes differ, for instance in respect to the law (with implications for the safe delivery of international mail order products), and to religion.
❏ *Lifestyle*. Attitudes to high-tech products and services, international purchasing, family structures, even eating out, vary markedly even within a single country. One only needs to note the difference between central London and the regions.
❏ *Language*. Different languages and comprehension dictate the perception of a brand, its advertising and packaging. Certain brands do not travel, like *Pocari Sweat*. Concepts associated with a brand

have different psychological and physiological impacts in different countries. And global products and services may require multilingual packaging and instructions, even though consumers dislike these.

❏ *Income*. Levels of income shape the market segments, determine the level of investment in new technology by business and the disposable income of consumers.

❏ *Competitors*. Yes, even the competitors in a local market will shape the brand. What may be seen as a luxury in one market needs to be re-branded as a necessity in another.

Fortunately, in the high-tech arena, American culture is all-pervasive, even to the extent that many Israeli and British companies relocate to Silicon Valley, so they can pass themselves off as US companies.

Brand name evaluation

Interbrand (www.interbrand.com), the leading branding consultancy, has a proprietary technique called *Nometrics*, which can be used both qualitatively and quantitatively:

❏ *Memorability* – how easily will customers in the key international markets be able to remember the name?

❏ *Pronounceability* – how easy will the name be to pronounce in key markets?

❏ *Scriptability* – how easy is the name to write, particularly relevant to prescription pharmaceuticals.

❏ *Imagery* – the mental image conjured up by the product.

❏ *Association* – does the name attract any negative associations (eg Burroughs sounds like 'donkeys' in Spanish).

❏ *Similarities* – positive and negative similarities to existing companies, products and services (eg Polo clothes, Polo cars, Polo sweets).

❏ *Coherence* – fit to brand concept (eg Microsoft).

❏ *Focus* – likely company, product and service areas suggested by the name (for example, e-trade).

So, how do you go about creating a brand name?

Creating your brand

High-tech start-ups (eg Yahoo!) and the most well-managed brands (eg Virgin, The Body Shop, Microsoft) share two major attributes: they are highly focused and inextricably linked with the personality and vision of their founders.

The process

In designing your brand name, remember that ideally you want to use the same name globally, use a common packaging, target a broadly similar customer segment in each market, and use the same marketing mix. Hence, your branding strategy is a 'jigsaw puzzle' of tangible and intangible components.

The 'tangibles'

You need coherent branding of:

- ❑ the corporate name both as a registered company name and as a trademark;
- ❑ the registered Internet domain name, including website and e-mail;
- ❑ potential product trademarks, giving an integrated set of product and service names (a good example is Microsoft's office products, MS Word, MS Excel, MS Access, etc);
- ❑ possibly even the building name and address.

The 'intangibles'

You must bear in mind the brand name's multiple roles:

- ❑ it identifies and advertises your product and service to your customers;
- ❑ it communicates your vision, mission or message to customers, employees, partners and investors, as well as your competitors;
- ❑ it protects your valuable intellectual property.

Attributes and objectives

Thirdly, when designing your brand name you need to quantify its attributes and objectives with respect to the target market:

- ❑ the opportunity you are addressing;
- ❑ the potential of your product or service to be leveraged;
- ❑ the attitudes of your customers;
- ❑ the dynamics of the marketplace;
- ❑ the response of your competitors.

Interbrand summarizes these 'intangibles' as shown in Table 31.1.

Specialist brand name companies are increasingly being used to develop national and international brand names. However, as a start-up, high on enthusiasm and low on cash, you will probably get together the founders and 'brainstorm' it.

Firstly, list the objectives of the name. Secondly, make a list of 20–30 names. Thirdly, use the objectives to cull the candidate names. Fourthly, you need to do 'due diligence' on the candidate names for 'registrability': company name, domain name, international trademark, etc.

Exploiting your brand

The commercial value of brands is increasingly being upgraded – not merely the customer value, where the brand acts as a guarantee, but more importantly the financial value, measuring its dollar worth. For a high-tech company this might be its *valuation* or *market capitalization*. For a product or

Table 31.1 Brand creation (adapted from S Hart, *Brands: The New Wealth Creators*)

	Consumer Values	Brand Values
Central Values	What kind of *life* do I want to lead? (eg success, fulfilment, stability)	What the brand and the consumer *share* (eg The Body Shop, Virgin, Nike)
Expressive Values	What kind of *person* do I want to be? (eg active, socially responsible)	What the brand *says* about the consumer (eg Porsche, Apple)
Functional Values	What kind of *products/services* do I want to have? (eg convenient, money-saving)	What the brand *does* for the consumer (eg Amazon.com, Yahoo!)

service the two approaches are *economic use* (based on the discounted value of future brand earnings), or *royalties* (the royalties the company would notionally have had to pay if the brand were owned by another company).

So what does 'exploiting your brand' mean to an average high-tech start-up? It might mean a number of things:

- ❏ *Trade sale.* Sell the 'branded' company (and its associated products and/or services) to another company (eg Hotmail sold to Microsoft for $400 million).
- ❏ *Flotation.* Float the company on a stock market such as NASDAQ (eg Yahoo! worth $35 billion).
- ❏ *Globalization.* Take the brand from a niche national market to a number of other foreign markets (eg e-trade) or alternatively from a global market (Yahoo.com) to niche national markets (Yahoo.co.uk).
- ❏ *Brand expansion.* Use an established brand to move into a new adjacent market (eg Amazon.com's move into music).
- ❏ *Brand franchising.* Form a partnership between the owner of a branded business system and a network of individuals each selling the branded product or service through branded operating units which they own and run (McDonald's being the classic).
- ❏ *Brand licensing.* Allow the licensor to make use of your intellectual property. For instance, Japan's JVC licensed (without charge) its VHS video recorder technology to establish an international standard.

Sources of help

DTI, *Business Names and Business Ownership – and five other leaflets,* Companies House, tel: 0 388 588, *www.companies-house.gov.uk*

Hart, S and Murphy, J (1998) *Brands – The New Wealth Creators,* Macmillan Business, London

Kochan, N (1996) (ed.) *The World's Greatest Brands,* Macmillan, Neq York

MacCrae, C (1995) *World Class Brands,* Addison-Wesley, New York

Pringle, H and Thompson, M (1999) Brand Spirit. John Wiley & Sons, Chichester, UK

32 Public Relations

Getting one's face on the cover of *TIME*, *Newsweek* or *Business Week* is the PR goal of every aspiring high-tech entrepreneur. It is the ultimate accolade. Achieve this and your company's market capitalization will go into orbit. Public relations is about promoting your company and yourself in the media: creating goodwill and understanding, and improving the reputation of your business. Major companies spend large sums on both in-house PR and using specialist PR companies. However, as Richard Branson regularly shows, if you have an interesting story (with a *spin*) the media are happy to promote you for free. Fortunately, high-tech and entrepreneurship are popular topics with the media.

In this chapter we look at:

❑ the principles of public relations and its 'publics';
❑ dealing with the broadcast media and the press;
❑ campaign planning, measurement and evaluation;
❑ selecting your *channel* from the press, television, and the Internet;
❑ communicating effectively through press releases and interviews.

Public relations attracts customers and venture capital, and ultimately drives up the valuation of the business. Good PR ensures that your branding, advertising and sales are effective.

Principles of PR

The Institute of Public Relations defines PR practice as: 'the planned and sustained effort to establish and maintain goodwill and mutual understanding between an organization and its publics'. So now you know!

Publics

In the PR world, a company's 'publics' are the various target groups with which to communicate. Table 32.1 shows what these might include.

Each of these 'publics' has different interests and roles in the business. They hence require a different form of communication, delivered through the appropriate medium. The one deliberately missing group is *the media*. They are the 'channels' for communicating with the 'publics'.

There are a number of excellent media guides, listing all the UK media companies by category and by area covered (see Table 32.2). These guides are available in the larger public libraries.

Table 32.1 Public relations 'publics' and 'channels'

Publics	Examples	Channels	Examples
Consumers	Retail customers	Consumer magazines	*Vogue*
Staff	Employees, their families	Staff newspaper, intranet	
Business customers	Suppliers, wholesalers, distributors	Trade press, Internet	*Computing*
Opinion formers	Politicians, journalists, academics	National newspapers and television	*The Guardian* BBC news
Investors	Financial institutions, shareholders	National newspapers	*Financial Times*

Table 32.2 Press and media guides

Benn's Media	Comprehensive three-volume media directory
Hollis Press and PR Annual	PR contacts in private and public organizations, PR consultancies, plus reference information
PACT	Listing of television production companies
PIMS directories	Range of media directories
PR Planner (UK and Europe)	Addresses for press, radio and television; also on disk
The Media Guide	*The Guardian*'s comprehensive media guide
Two-Ten Communications	Media directory plus investment research analysis

Broadcast media and the press

It is likely that you already know the types of publications and television programmes that cover your area of business. Now, given the rise of interest in high-tech and the global nature of the business, there is increasing opportunity to get national and even international coverage (see Table 32.3).

Clearly, you need to target the media carefully. You need to interest a TV channel or publication in a story, where the maximum number of your target 'publics' will see it – perhaps a stock market flotation or innovative business product announcement to the *Financial Times, Business Week* or the Money Programme; or a technology breakthrough to Discovery, Horizon or Tomorrow's World; or the opening of a new office to the local newspaper.

Campaign planning

Public relations need to be planned on a long-term basis, not just when a journalist knocks at your door or something goes wrong with your company's products or service. PR, just like an advertising or sales campaign, needs clearly defined objectives and target publics, and quantifiable measurements of success.

PR campaign planning involves a series of questions:

❑ *The message.* What information do you wish to convey? What are the strengths and opportunities for the business, and its products and services that will shape the campaign? From where will the information for the campaign come? What is the key message?

Table 32.3 The range of media channels

	International	National	Local	Specialist
The press	TIME, Newsweek, Business Week, Forbes	Financial Times, Times, etc; consumer magazines	Local papers	Trade press, consumer magazines
Television	CNN, Discovery	BBC, ITV, Sky	Regional stations	FT Television, Money Programme
Radio	BBC World Service	BBC	Local stations	
Internet	Yahoo!, TradeUK	Yahoo.co.uk		

❏ *Publics*. To which groups will the message be directed? What are the characteristics of the publics? What are their interests and needs?

❏ *Channels*. What channels will you use? What are the channels' individual characteristics? What is the strategy for customizing the message for each channel?

❏ *Analysis*. What is the cost/benefits analysis? What will the campaign cost? How will the impact of the campaign be assessed?

Measurement and evaluation

As far as possible, PR objectives should be quantifiable and measurable. The following are three common industry coverage measurements:

❏ *Opportunities to see* (OTS) – the cumulative readership, viewing or listening figures. This spans the numbers of articles, position on the page, relevance of the publication, circulation, and whether the coverage was favourable or not.

❏ *Advertising value equivalent* (AVE) – the advertising cost for equivalent editorial space and broadcast media time. This includes, for instance, the column inches of coverage in a newspaper, but does not take account of greater customer impact of an editorial over an advert.

❏ *Market shift*. Market research is used at the start of a campaign to establish an 'opinion benchmark' and then later to measure the 'opinion shift'.

Unsurprisingly, the PR industry are less than enthusiastic about the application of such quantitative measures by their own clients.

PR agencies

To retain a PR agency, you can expect to pay £1,000 a month at the very minimum, and on a continuing basis. For most start-ups, the best option is to handle the PR yourself at the beginning. You have the motivation, and the knowledge of your product or service and the publics you wish to reach, plus the best channels to reach them.

However, there are situations when employing professionals is highly cost-effective. Examples are the launch of a major new product or service which proves to be flawed, and the public need to be informed. Recall the obscure design fault in the original Pentium processor that became a PR nightmare for Intel.

Channel selection

Traditionally, 'channels' cover the press, television and radio, but should now include the Internet.

The press

National newspapers and magazines are interested in stories with a 'spin': human interest, unusual angle and visual appeal. Regional and local media are interested in 'good news' stories in their area.

Then there are consumer magazines, company magazines and the trade press. Consumer magazines are publications bought by the public, spanning the whole range from *Hello* to special interests, such as *Investors Chronicle*. In addition, airlines, such as British Airways, and credit card companies, such as Barclaycard, produce free magazines which often feature interesting business stories.

Lastly, trade publications are particularly important because research shows that 40 per cent of company buying decisions are based on technical articles in such publications.

Television and radio

Television has international (eg CNN), national (BBC, ITV, Sky) and regional (Granada, Carlton) dimensions, each covering everything from the news and current affairs to specialist programmes. Once you have selected your story, ring the television station, ask to speak to a researcher on the target programme, tell them your theme and get advice as to whom you should send the press release. Usually this will be the editor or a named journalist.

Many television programmes are produced by independent production companies, so you can either approach the television station directly or a production company. A list of production companies and the programmes they make is given in the *PACT Directory* (tel 020 7331 6000, www.pact.co.uk); in the Republic of Ireland see www.iftn.ie, which gives news and info about Irish production companies.

But a word of caution is in order. However good your idea, TV companies are unlikely to devote a whole programme to you; but they may well build a programme around you *and your competitors*.

Radio stations are proliferating, and are often keen to cover items on local business.

The Internet

Lastly we need to acknowledge the increasingly important role the Internet and company Intranets will play in PR. One popular way of promoting your company is to write a so-called 'white paper' surveying your product area, and post it on the Internet. Banners and search engines are of course the obvious ways of gaining an Internet presence by means other than your own website.

Communications

Most of the PR and free publicity for a small business will start with a good press release. But you need a good story with a 'spin' that will interest journalists. Launching a new product or service, winning a major order, or a multi-million pound trade sale, provide you with opportunities.

Press releases

A press release is *not* an advert. You want it to appear as a story in the editorial pages of newspapers (or be read on television or radio), and appear like an unbiased endorsement. So you should imitate the style used in your target publication. Prepare an 'interesting' press release that grabs the reader's attention, and is easy to digest:

- ☐ The document should be entitled 'PRESS RELEASE', be on a single sheet of A4 paper, and typed double spaced for easy editing.
- ☐ The headline must grab the editor's attention, but also explain what the story is about.

❑ The introductory paragraph must be interesting, succinct and topical.

❑ End the press release with a contact name and telephone number for further information.

❑ Any photographs should be in black and white, of a reasonable size and with a caption on the back.

The aim of the press release is to answer the five W's – *who, what, when, where* and *why* – as succinctly as possible. Don't forget the contact name and telephone number where journalists requiring additional information can contact you; they may wish to interview you.

Interview techniques

In an interview, think what message you wish to get across and do not allow the interviewer to distract you. There are three basic interview situations:

❑ *Press interview.* A journalist talks to you and then writes up the story for their newspaper or magazine.

❑ *Television and radio.* You are interviewed for either a pre-recorded or live broadcast.

❑ *Telephone interview.* For the radio, and occasionally television, it is increasingly popular to record you over the telephone.

The first time you are interviewed on television or radio can be a traumatic experience. Be prepared. Prior to the interview, ask the programme researcher what 'angle' or theme the interview will take and what sorts of comments or answers the interviewer is seeking. Since you are the 'expert' you can also make suggestions for 'angles' and questions that will improve the story line.

Most importantly, before the interview, decide on one or two key points that you wish to get across.

If you are being interviewed at a studio, on the day of the interview arrive in good time. Compose yourself, have a drink of water and make sure you have been to the toilet. For television interviews, dress in sober and plain colours, because checks and stripes can distort the picture. During the interview sit forward in your chair, and speak clearly, distinctly and at a measured pace. Keep to your theme, and try not to make any off-the-cuff remarks. And if you want to come across as sincere and enthusiastic, try to appear relaxed and friendly, and smile – even on radio!

Most interviewers will work with you to get the best from the story. They may even coach you. Occasionally you will come up against an abrasive interviewer, when being well prepared pays dividends. If the interviewer misinterprets what you are saying, correct them immediately, and, most importantly, remain calm and polite, even when being attacked. This will generate audience sympathy.

Press conferences

If you have such a 'big news' story to tell the media, you may need to hold a press conference to really do it justice. The general advice from all public relations experts is that a press conference is 'high-risk activity' because you will be in the full glare of the media! The key rules are:

- ❑ *Important story*. Hold a press conference only when you have something really newsworthy, otherwise the press will savage you for wasting their time.
- ❑ *Good venue*. Choose a well-located venue, possibly with some novelty value. And if you want to attract the national media, then it has to be in central London or central Dublin.
- ❑ *Good timing*. The day and time are also important. Choose 'quiet news days', which means avoiding major events and similar press conferences. Choose a good time – mid-morning 10.00 to 11.00am – and provide coffee and light refreshments.
- ❑ *Personal invitations*. A few days before the press conference, send out personal invitations and a press release to named journalists. Just before the event, telephone the invited journalists to encourage them to attend.
- ❑ *Managed presentation*. You need to ensure that all the presentations at the press conference are co-ordinated and give the same message, and that all staff are well briefed and counselled against making any off-the-cuff remarks.
- ❑ *Press pack*. It is also good practice to prepare a press pack for distribution to the journalists. This can contain the press release, background information on your company, products and services, and black and white photographs of the people speaking at the press conference.

Finally, remember to keep the press conference brief and to the point. Journalists are busy people.

Public speaking, sponsorship, stunts...

There must be thousands of different PR methods for generating goodwill and publicity, so we will finish this chapter with a brief tour of other popular PR methods.

Public speaking

Offer to speak on your area of expertise at any venue from professional organizations to the local Rotary Club. Basically, go to any venue where you can meet potential customers and business partners, but remember not to appear to be 'selling' to the audience.

Conferences and exhibitions

Business conferences and seminars are another good source of free publicity, but you need to ensure that the audience are predominantly potential customers rather than, as usually happens, your fiercest competitors. Depending on your product or service, an exhibition or trade show is a good way to meet customers who share a common interest with you.

Sponsorship and charities

There are many ways a business can support good causes and receive public recognition. They range from financial and equipment donations to encouraging employees to volunteer their time.

Noticeboards and newsletters

One 'public' often overlooked by companies is their own staff. It is good for staff morale to keep them informed of developments in the company. Noticeboards are OK, but a company newsletter is even better, and can also be sent to business partners to build the relationship.

Publicity stunts

As Richard Branson has repeatedly shown, if you can carry it off, 'stunts' are an excellent way to get masses of good publicity and free advertising, both for the entrepreneur and their latest venture.

Networking

Perhaps the most enjoyable form of PR is 'wining and dining' your most important customers and business partners. This is referred to as 'networking'.

Sources of help

Benn's Media – now known as Miller Freeman Information Services. Sovereign Way, Tonbridge, Kent, tel: 01732 362666, fax: 01732 770482
Conferation Europeene des Relations Publiques (CERP). 1 Rue Bleue, 75009 Suresnes, France, *www.sbg.ac.at/cerp*
Hollis Press and PR Annual. tel: 020 8977 7711
Institute of Public Relations (IPR), The. The Old Trading House, 15 Northburgh Street, London, EC1V 0PR, tel: 020 7253 5151, *www.ipr.org.uk*
International Public Relations Association (IPRA). Cardinal House, Wolsey Road, Hampton Court, Surrey, KT8 9EL, *www.ipranet.org*
Nally, M (1994) (ed.) *International Public Relations in Practice*, Kogan Page, London
PACT. 45 Mortimer Street, London, W1N 7TD, tel: 020 7331 6000, fax: 020 7331 6700, email: enquiries@pact.co.uk, *www.pact.co.uk*
Peak, S and Fisher, P (1999) (eds.) *The Media Guide 1999*, Fourth Estate, London
PIMS Directories. Mildmay Avenue, London, N14RS, tel: 020 7226 1000, fax: 020 7354 7053
PR Planner (UK and Europe). Hale House, 290–296 Green Lanes, London, N13 5TP, tel: 020 8882 0155, fax: 020 8886 0703
Public Relations Consultants Association (PRCA). Willow House, Willow Place, London, SW1P 1JH, tel: 020 7223 6026, *www.martex.co.uk/prca*
Smith, H (1997) *Teach Yourself Public Relations*, Hodder & Stoughton, London
Two-Ten Communications. Communications House, 210 Old Street, London, EC1V 9UN, tel: 020 7490 8111, fax: 020 7490 1255

33 Advertising

As an American advertising executive once said: 'Advertising is what you do when you can't go to see somebody.'

Advertising is paid-for communication that aims to bring your business and its products to the attention of potential consumers and persuade them to buy. Adverts range from sophisticated TV commercials, to display ads in national newspapers and banner ads on the Internet, to simple classified ads in the local paper or leaflets.

The total advertising spend for the UK is around £10 billion a year. However, as a small business you can keep down the cost by preparing your own advertising campaign and copy. And remember, the best advert is a personal, word-of-mouth recommendation from a satisfied customer.

In this chapter we look at:

❑ the principles of advertising – AIDA (attention, interest, desire, action);
❑ the unique selling proposition or USP of your product or service;
❑ different types of *above-the-line* and *below-the-line* advertising;
❑ selecting the appropriate channel: television, display, direct response, Internet;
❑ how to go about creating imaginative and successful adverts.

Principles of advertising

As a starting point you must ask yourself why you want or need to advertise, who you are trying to reach, what media you plan to use to reach them, what measurable goals you expect to achieve, and how much you are prepared to pay. A good text is *Advertising for the Small Business* by Nick Daws.

Having decided to advertise, you next need to create your advertisement. The philosophy behind much advertising is A–I–D–A:

❑ *Attention* – attract the customers' undivided attention to the advert.

❑ *Interest* – arouse their interest in the benefits of the product or service.

❑ *Desire* – stimulate their desire to purchase.

❑ *Action* – prompt the customers to take some action to respond.

Why people buy

For most consumer products, *price* and *convenience* and *benefits* sought are the key drivers:

❑ *Price.* You have the cheapest or most competitive price (*we are never knowingly undersold!*).

❑ *Convenience.* The product, such as food or petrol, is the most convenient to obtain.

However, for the products and services of a high-tech start-up, being the market leader (the 'gorilla') may be a key decision:

❑ *Market leader.* Customers buy for future compatibility, as for instance with VHS versus BetaMax, or Microsoft versus Apple. The biggest gorilla, Microsoft, has 98 per cent of the operating systems marketplace, so people naturally buy Word, Excel, Access etc. for compatibility.

Beyond this, customers have a wide range of reasons for buying:

❑ *Friendship.* They know and like you; or the chairman likes you.

❑ *Reputation.* Your company has a good reputation in the marketplace, and is recommended by existing customers.

❑ *Quality.* Your products and services are known for reliability and performance.

❑ *Well organized.* You offer delivery and good after-sales service.

❑ *Marketing mix.* They like your adverts, PR and the appearance of the packaging.

❑ *Image.* They want to appear stylish and trendy, or perhaps safe and conformist.

❏ *Bribery*. Well, not seriously, but there are many more intangible reasons for buying other than price and convenience.

Having completely failed to understand why your customers buy from you, you next need to decide the so-called unique selling proposition (USP) of your product or service.

Features, benefits and USPs

The aim of your advert is to 'enlighten' potential customers about your product or service, and stimulate them to buy. To do this you need first to understand your offering, and why anyone should wish to purchase. In particular it is important to distinguish between the features, benefits and USP of your product or service:

❏ *Features* are the things you incorporate in your product or service to make it attractive to your customers.
❏ *Benefits* are the advantages obtained by a customer when purchasing your product or service.
❏ *Unique selling propositions* (USPs) are features that no other competitor offers.

Put simplistically, *features* are important to you, *benefits* to your customers and *USPs* to the competition.

USP is ad-man jargon for the unique features offered by your company, product or service. Based on the USP, an effective advert focuses on the customer-oriented 'benefits' of owning a product or using a service, rather than the company-oriented 'features'. Whatever you as a company think, it is the benefits rather than the features that are foremost in a customer's mind at the time of purchase.

Obviously, you need to identify your USP so that you can craft your advert to target your customers, and also select the medium – television, the press or Internet – to convey your message.

Above- and below-the-line advertising

There is an enormous choice of advertising media or channels. By tradition, advertising agencies are paid a commission when they place an advert in the press and TV. This has led to media being subdivided, again in ad-man's jargon, into 'above-the-line' and 'below-the-line':

❏ *Above-the-line advertising* means press, TV, cinema and outdoor advertising, which traditionally pay a commission to ad agencies when they purchase the media.

❏ *Below-the-line advertising* means everything else – Internet, direct mail, point-of-sale, leaflets, brochures etc.

Market segmentation

To really understand why your customers buy, and hence be able to target them, you need to segment your marketplace (as discussed in Chapter 30). The aim of segmenting is to obtain a profitable group of customers who are broadly homogeneous in their attitudes. Below we list some of the common ways of market segmentation. Clearly this will depend to a large extent on whether your market is business-to-business (trade customers) or business-to-consumer (general public):

❏ *Socioeconomic positioning.* This subdivides the population and consumers into six broad groupings, as shown in Figure 33.1.

❏ *Geographic positioning.* Your trade or public customers are subdivided by their location, and the distance from your company. For an Internet-based company this might be country or region. Postcodes in the UK are a surprisingly good way of segmenting markets.

❏ *Sex, age, etc.* Customers are divided into sex (female, male) and age groups (retired, middle-aged, young adults, teenagers, children).

❏ *Geo-demographic positioning.* Customers are divided both by geographical and social grouping.

❏ *Business sectors.* For business-to-business trade, customers are divided by sector: financial services, retail, leisure, transportation and distribution, public sector, health, etc.

A	Upper middle class (eg higher professionals, administrative, managerial, aristocrats)
B	Middle class (eg intermediate professionals, administrative, managerial)
C1	Lower middle class (eg junior administrative, managerial, supervisory, clerical)
C2	Skilled working class (eg skilled manual workers)
D	Working class (eg semi-skilled, unskilled workers)
E	Under class (eg unemployed, basic state pensioners, casual workers)

Figure 33.1 Classes

Measurements and evaluations

The most important aspect is accurately to estimate the size, potential profitability and level of competition of a particular sector.

A direct link between spending money on advertising and generating more sales is frequently difficult to quantify. When choosing your advertising medium, the three important measures are:

❏ *Impact* – measuring the number of potential customers who may see the advertisement. This includes: *circulation* – the number of copies of a publication either printed or distributed; *readership* – how many people actually read the publication (varies significantly from the circulation figure); *footfalls* – how many people pass an outdoor advertisement; *viewers* – how many television or cinema viewers will see the advertisement; *click-thru* – how many Internet users will see the advert and actually 'click' on it.

❏ *Coverage* – the extent to which a publication or broadcast will reach your target market segment. This is also known as *penetration*.

❏ *Response* – the percentage rate of response of customers to your advertisement. Response rate is most typically used with direct mail advertising.

When measuring the impact of advertising, a crude but useful way of expressing it is as the cost per thousand (CPT) of the known circulation of the medium. However, this does not truly take into account the number of people who actually read the publication, or their socioeconomic grouping. For instance, a technical or trade journal may have a small circulation but a large readership, whereas a free newspaper can have a huge circulation but may be 'binned' by the vast majority of recipients.

Most publications are 'audited' independently by the Audit Bureau of Circulation (ABC), and these circulation figures are published in BRAD, the advertisers' bible (tel 020 8242 3000; www.brad.co.uk).

Finally, obviously it is important to monitor the response rate to your advertisement. For Internet and interactive television advertisements, monitoring is relatively automatic since you know which customer is accessing your site. (This information is recorded in the log file – see Chapter 15.) For press and broadcast media where the customer is responding by mail, the usual method of monitoring is by including a department number, such as Dept DT1, in the address. For customers responding by telephone, the call centre personnel need to ask the callers where they saw your advert.

Channel selection

As we saw in the chapter on public relations, there is a huge range of media in which to advertise. Most companies will choose a mixture of media.

Television, radio and cinema

Television advertising is the most expensive and is probably best approached via an advertising agency. In the last few years the television market has expanded enormously. You now have the choice of terrestrial (BBC, ITV, Channels 4 and 5), satellite (Sky), cable (Live TV), and the new digital channels (SkyDigital, BBC Digital, OnDigital). Owing to competition, these channels are able to offer national, regional and local advertising at increasingly competitive rates. It is not quite *Wayne's World*, but it is becoming viable for a start-up both to advertise on television and to consider own direct sales on cable.

Commercial radio is able to offer regional coverage at very competitive rates, and is becoming increasingly popular for advertising a diverse range of goods, including insurance, mobile phones, restaurants, garages, books and music CDs. Virgin Radio and Classical FM provide national services. Others, like Capital Radio (London), BRMD (Birmingham) and Piccadilly Radio (Manchester), cover major cities and regions.

Cinemas provide a means of targeting individual towns. Rank Screen Advertising (tel 020 7706 1111) and Pearl & Dean are the leading agencies for cinema advertising. The main considerations are that different films will attract different audiences, and the typical customer age range is 15–24 year-olds.

Broadcast media adverts are usually sold in 'slots' of 20, 30 or 40 seconds, with the charge tied to the size of the viewing audience.

Display advertisements

As they say, 'a picture is worth a thousand words'. A display advertisement typically incorporates a caption or heading, a text body, illustrations and possibly an order form, and is designed to be eye-catching.

A good starting point, if creating your own display advertisements, is to look at current campaigns in the newspapers and magazines. Choose those that are run repeatedly, on the assumption they must be successful to be repeated. Build up a library and note the best features of each. The Japanese call this 'reverse engineering'.

Classified advertisements

Classified advertisements normally comprise a heading and a few lines of text. They have the advantage of being simple and cheap, but lack the 'attention-grabbing' properties of display ads.

You need to choose your words carefully, and the target publication. Tell the reader in as few words as possible about your product or service, and the benefits of buying it. Enthuse about it. And tell the reader what to do to buy the product or service.

Direct advertising

Two areas of 'direct advertising' are direct response and direct mail:

- ❏ With *direct response*, a company advertises and sells directly to the customer, either by letter, telephone, fax or e-mail.
- ❏ With *direct mail*, adverts are sent to individual customers using a 'mail shot' of personalized letters.

Direct response is the fastest growing form of advertising in the UK, and is used for a wide range of products: financial services, books, health food and much more.

Internet advertising

Electronic advertising on the Internet and interactive television are becoming increasingly popular. They combine the impact of broadcast advertising, the fulfilment of direct response and the low cost of display advertising. Briefly, the principal forms are Web pages, banners ads, electronic mail, screen savers and Web casting (see Chapter 15).

Creating advertisements

To design a great advertisement you need to know what motivates people to buy. In fact, there is a famous advertising quote:

> *Every man is really two men – the man he is and the man he wants to be.*

Creating your own display advertisements and sales letters is a good way to learn about the advertising business.

Advertisements and sales letters needs to meet the A–I–D–A specification: attract **a**ttention, arouse **i**nterest, stimulate **d**esire and prompt **a**ction:

- ☐ *Role models.* Look for good examples of advertisements and sales letters and work out why they are effective. This includes layout, heading, illustrations and action details. Learn from the professionals.
- ☐ *User benefits/USPs.* For your product, list all its user benefits and unique selling points.
- ☐ *Layout.* Make the advertisement or letter visually appealing, with an attention-grabbing heading and illustration. Also, make the text crisp, clear and concise.
- ☐ *Text.* Write from the customer's point of view and clearly state the user benefits and USPs. The writing style should be friendly, informal, interesting and, above all, honest.
- ☐ *Polish.* Do not be in a hurry to send off your advert. Re-read your copy putting yourself in a potential customer's position. Ask yourself: 'Would I buy this?'

Brochures, exhibitions, etc

This last section looks at some of the many 'other' forms of advertising.

- ☐ *Brochures.* These are small glossy booklets, normally a folded A3 sheet or a few pages stapled down the middle that provide details of your company, and its products and services. (See Chapter 9.)

☐ *Exhibitions.* A stand at a trade show or exhibition is a good place to advertise and also meet customers. The main consideration is to choose your venue carefully and ensure when negotiating with the organizers of the event that your stand is in a prominent position.

☐ *Directories.* These range from the general, such as *Yellow Pages* (www.yell.co.uk; in Ireland, www.goldenpages.ie) and Thomson (www.thomson.co.uk), to specialized publications covering specific business sectors.

☐ *Tee shirts.* Yes, you can even get your message across by printing it on tee shirts.

☐ *Cards.* Most high-tech businesses should wince at the thought of placing a card in a shop window. However, printing an advertising message on a business card is both cheap and highly effective.

☐ *Leaflets.* Leaflets or handbills typically are single sheets of paper that are cheap to produce and therefore can be handed out at exhibitions or inserted in mail-shots. However, it is important that the quality of the leaflets does not detract from your company's image.

☐ *Poster sites.* There are over 140,000 poster sites across the UK, as well as smaller sites at railway stations, bus terminals and airports.

Finally, do not forget transport advertising. You can advertise in/on public service vehicles, buses, trains and taxis. Your own company vehicles are another possibility.

Sources of help

Advertising Association, The. Abford House, 15 Wilton Road, London, SW1V NJ, tel: 020 7828 2771, *www.aa.org.uk*

Advertising Standards Authority. 2/16 Torrington Place, London, WC1E 7HN, tel: 020 7580 5555, *www.asa.org.uk*

BRAD (British Rate and Data). Maclean Hunter House, Chalk Lane, Cockfosters Road, Barnet, Herts, EN4 0BU, tel: 020 8242 3000, fax: 0282 242 3134, *www.brad.co.uk*

Campaign. *www.campaign.co.uk*

Daws, N (19960 *Advertising for the Small Business,* Otter, Chichester, UK

Institute of Practitioners in Advertising (IPA). 44 Belgrave Square, London, SW1X 8QS, tel: 020 7245 7020, fax: 020 7245 9904, *www.ipa.co.uk*

34 Sales

Being an entrepreneur is all about selling. You can be the nicest person in the world but if you don't 'do the deal' your company will not be in business long. Equally, if you treat your customers badly, you will not do any repeat business. But selling is fun – selling your business idea to investors and the media; selling your company's vision or mission to partners and staff; selling your products and services to customers. Successful entrepreneurs like Bill Gates and Steve Jobs are obviously charismatic and good at selling.

    In this chapter we look at:

- [ ] the psychology of buying and selling;
- [ ] classical sales methods, organising yourself to sell and developing customers;
- [ ] selecting the appropriate channel: face-to-face, telephone, interactive, sales letters and brochures;
- [ ] planning a sales campaign, making the appointment, identifying needs and asking for the order.

The two principal tasks are to make a sale and then to care for your customer.

Principles of selling

In order to sell effectively you need to 'believe' in your products and services, create a good first impression with customers, have the right positive mental attitude to sell, be resilient when customers say no, and be well organized in targeting the most profitable prospects. Let us start with some pseudo-psychology of buying and selling.

Psychology of buying and selling

Customers buy for a number of subtle reasons:

❑ *Prestige*. Customers like to be associated with 'prestige' attributes like strong *branding* (eg Sony), *quality* (Intel Pentium), *success* (Porsche), *innovation* (USRobotics PalmPilot) and market *leadership* (MS Office 2000).

❑ *Profit*. Customers want to save or make money through the purchase (eg E-bay, E-Trade).

❑ *Safety*. Customers purchase for health, safety and security reasons (eg CheckPoint Firewall software).

❑ *Legal requirement*. Customers purchase a product or service because of a statutory legal requirement (eg TV licence).

❑ *Comfort*. Customers like the 'peace of mind' feeling they get from purchasing food, books and clothing (eg Amazon.com).

❑ *Appeal*. Customers want something badly enough that they 'must have it', be it a car, a boat or clothes (eg Armani).

To help understand the psychology of buying and selling, writers such as Jean Atkinson in *Teach Yourself Selling* have grouped salespeople and customers into various amusing stereotypes. Salespeople fall into:

❑ *All-rounders*. These salespeople are well organized, have a good rapport with customers, make the sales, and nurture the customer base.

❑ *Bulldozers*. In contrast, these are interested only in making the sale and getting their bonus, and not in the long-term 'care' of customers and repeat business.

❑ *World's friends*. These are reluctant to offend the customer by asking for an order. Everybody likes them, but they just don't meet their sales targets.

❑ *Order-takers*. These have lost all interest and motivation to sell. They will take an order if one is offered but won't push customers to close a sale.

Now for *customers*:

❑ *Salesperson's delight*. These customers evaluate your product or service, place an order and give repeat business over time. The 'all-rounder' salesperson focuses on this group.

❏ *Steamrollers*. These want you to believe they know more about your products or services than you do, and continually beat you down on price and delivery. What is needed is not the 'bulldozer' who would antagonize the 'steamroller', but a persistent 'all-rounder'.

❏ *Ditherers*. These seem unable to make up their minds. This is where a *small* 'bulldozer' is useful.

❏ *Remorse specialists*. These customers agree to a sale, because deep down they want to be loved. Unfortunately they always seem to cancel the order. Be a 'world's friend' and shame them into sticking to the agreed sale.

Classic sales methods

In order to sell, and sell more, you need to stick to reliable sales methods. The classic sales structure involves:

❏ *Planning*. To be effective you need to organize yourself. You need all the facts of your business' products/services, customers, delivery and finances at your finder-tips. When customers contact you, you need to record their names and addresses, and the action taken or required. And you need to plan your time.

❏ *Appointment*. For most sales you need to make an appointment with the customer or buyer. This involves navigating a series of hurdles: talking to the receptionist to identify the customer's name and position; talking to the customer's secretary; sending a letter or sales brochure; following up with a telephone call to talk to the customer; and arranging a face-to-face meeting.

❏ *Questioning*. You need to identify the needs of the customer and organization, but at the same time advance the sales process. Make a list of questions: What is the current situation in the organization? Why does this exist? What if they do not buy your product or service? Summarize your understanding to the customer to check it is correct.

❏ *Presenting*. Customize your presentation to address and focus on the customer's needs and motivations. Remember the buying motivations: *prestige, profit, safety, legal requirement, conformity* and *appeal* – and address them in your presentation.

❑ *Responding*. Answer any questions and objections raised by the customer.

❑ *Closing*. 'Closing' is the term for clinching the sale.

Organizing yourself to sell

The better you are organized, the more confident you will approach a sales opportunity. Most of the things you should do are obvious business procedure:

❑ *Accessibility*. Make it easy for customers to contact you and place an order – by phone, answering service, fax, e-mail and Website.

❑ *Diary*. Keep an up-to-date computer-based record of your movements.

❑ *Business facts*. Assemble a detailed 'facts list' of your company, and its products and services.

❑ *Contacts list*. When customers contact your office, make a list of their name, address, telephone number etc, their request, the action taken and when to contact them.

❑ *Customer database*. Start building a customer address file that can be used for mail-merge letters. Quickly move to a full-blown customer sales database holding contact details, and a record of all contacts, actions and sales.

❑ *Sales plan*. Prepare a detailed sales plan using a spreadsheet, so that you can perform 'what if. . .?' forecasts on the data. List target customers, estimate sales and estimate costs. Err on the conservative side.

❑ *Schedule your time*. The old saying goes, 'time is money'. So you need to schedule yourself.

Developing customers

The famous 80:20 rule says 80 per cent of your sales come from 20 per cent of your customers. This has three implications for selling. Firstly, some customers are more valuable than others. Secondly, focus your sales effort in relation to customer value. Thirdly, concentrate on your current customers who already know you, and your products and services.

Here are a number of considerations:

☐ *Developing an account*. For an existing account the three basic ways of increasing sales are: sell more of the product or service to the customer, sell related products or services to the customer, or sell to other departments in the same organization.

☐ *Customer factors*. You need to identify two important groups in an organization. There are the *influencers*, who must be convinced to promote you within the organization, and then there are the *decision-makers*, who make actual purchasing decisions.

☐ *Competitor factors*. A potential customer already using a competitor's products is a sales opportunity, because the customer already understands the types of products and services you are offering. However, be very careful when criticizing a competitor. By implication you are also criticizing the customer's judgement in purchasing from the competitor.

Channel selection

Having looked at the broad principles of selling, we now look at the sales techniques for specific channels.

Face-to-face selling

Face-to-face selling is possibly the ultimate commercial art. When two people meet for the first time, 'human chemistry' says anything can happen. Customers respond firstly to you the salesperson, and only secondly to your company and its products. You basically have one five-second chance to make the body language work and create a good impression. Americans call this the *elevator pitch*. Here are some dos and don'ts:

☐ *Punctuality*. Arrive five minutes early, giving time to compose yourself and the receptionist time to locate your host and announce you, so the meeting starts on time.

☐ *Dress*. Be well groomed, dressed neutrally and to suit the occasion. Body piercing may be 'cool' at college, but might not elicit the same warm admiration from your bank manager.

❏ *Entrance*. Make a confident and orderly entrance to the customer's office. Introduce yourself professionally and ask where the customer would like you to sit. If you have brochures, samples or a presentation, make sure it is packaged professionally. Do not waddle in like the bear in the beer advert, with your brochures in a supermarket carrier bag.

❏ *Body language*. Exude confidence; stand up straight, move confidently, smile and maintain eye contact. When you arrive, greet the customer with a 'positive' handshake.

❏ *Speech*. You need to sound enthusiastic, friendly and confident. Speak slowly and slightly louder to emphasize the importance of what you are saying.

❏ *Building rapport*. Customers come in all shapes and sizes: arrogant, insecure, friendly, professional. You need to build a rapport with all of them. Stroke the egos of the arrogant, build up the insecure, and entertain the friendly.

❏ *Sales aids*. A visual presentation (ideally with Microsoft's Power-Point or the Internet) has 'instant' impact; but, for reference, leave copies of the slides and brochures with the customer.

Telephone selling

Telephone selling is important to you and your customers. Customers get instant answers to their sales enquiries, and you can speak directly to the person in charge – the buyer.

General principles

❏ *Organization*. Keep key information by the telephone – key financial and technical facts, your diary, and customer-enquiry forms.

❏ *Telephone enquiries*. When a customer telephones, first ask them for their details. Make a list of their name, contact details, address, purpose of call, action taken or required, and if possible where they heard of your company. Try to get the customer to act: to close the sale or to meet.

❏ *Customer complaints*. These need extra care in handling. Thank the customers for bringing the problems to your attention. Get them to explain their dissatisfaction and repeat what they have told you to verify you understand the problems. Then state what actions you propose to take.

Telephoning potential customers

The name of the game is to identify the decision-maker, breach the defences (receptionist, secretary, and personal assistant), speak directly to the customer, and arrange a face-to-face meeting:

- ❏ *Introduction.* Before approaching a company, find out whether a friend or acquaintance can give you an introduction to a decision-maker.
- ❏ *Organization.* In preparation for telephoning a customer, gather a sales script, brochures, your diary and, most importantly, the name of the decision-maker.
- ❏ *Receptionist.* Say you wish to write to the person responsible for 'X' in the company, so can you please be given the full name and job title of the relevant person. Later, telephone and ask to speak to the decision-maker. By giving the full name the receptionist will assume you know each other, and put you through at least to the secretary.
- ❏ *Secretary.* Most secretaries are highly skilled at screening their boss. My advice is to be polite and honest. Tell them your name and reason for calling, that you are planning to write to the boss and wish to speak to him or her briefly to see if they are interested.
- ❏ *Customer.* If you get through to the decision-maker, again be honest and brief. Explain your business, that you propose to write to him or her, and (if interested) to arrange a meeting. Then fax the letter while it is still fresh in their mind, and also post it. The next day, telephone the secretary to try to arrange the meeting.
- ❏ *Follow-ups.* Once you have built up a rapport with the customer and, just as important, are known to the secretary, the secretary will probably schedule an appointment without even consulting her boss.

Interactive selling

If telephone selling was the sales phenomenon of the late 1990s, then inter-active selling via the Internet, electronic kiosks and interactive television will be the 2000 phenomenon.

The Internet offers online interaction using the Web and e-mail. Electronic kiosks embrace shopping kiosks in stores, ticketing kiosks in stations, information kiosks and even bank teller machines (ATMs). Probably the most exciting prospect is interactive digital television – two-way inter-action using a TV, either two-way via cable, or receiving via broadcast TV with the response via a telephone line.

Sales promotions

The term 'sales promotion' covers a range of short-term activities designed to increase sales. Sales promotions are typically undertaken to reduce stock levels, gain market penetration for a new product, to raise awareness of a product with customers and suppliers, and to gain publicity. Some of the many types of sales promotion include:

❏ *Price cutting*. Reducing the price of a product in conjunction with an advertising campaign is arguably the most common form of sales promotion.
❏ *Annual sale*. The aim of a 'sale' is to increase your normal (non-sale) trading by temporarily lowering the price of some of the busi-nesses' products or services. The Trades Description Act (1968) states that the sales goods must have been advertised at the higher price for a continuous period of 28 days in the previous six months.
❏ *Vouchers*. Companies frequently provide 'money-off' vouchers or coupons with their products, both to attract customer attention and to encourage follow-on sales.
❏ *Competitions*. Consumer competitions typically consist of answer-ing one or more trivial questions related to the product, and com-pleting a so-called tie-breaker slogan 'I love X because...' However, the law governing competitions is strict, so you are advised to contact the Institute of Sales Promotion (tel 020 7837 5340; www.isp.org.uk), who can supply you with the *British Code of Sales*

Promotion Practice; in the Republic of Ireland contact the Advertising Standard Authority for Ireland, and consult the *Code of Advertising Standards for Ireland* (www.asai.ie).

☐ *Discounts.* These are price reductions either for 'loyal customers' or for bulk purchases.

☐ *Free gifts/samples.* A gift can be given with a purchase. Popular with the cosmetics industry is the giving of small free samples.

☐ *Banded offers and multi-packs.* Banded offers are two or more products sold together at a discount price. Multi-packs consist of the same product.

☐ *Loyalty schemes.* Schemes for customer retention became the marketing phenomenon of the late 1990s. The most prominent are customer loyalty cards and Air Miles.

A sales campaign

Planning and preparing

The planning and preparation of a sales campaign falls into five broad areas: customer prospecting, customer classification, sales planning, sales scripts and sales aids.

Finding potential customers

For certain specialized high-tech businesses there may be only a few large customers, such as the clearing banks or major retailers. For electronic commerce businesses selling to the general public, every family or business with an Internet-connected PC is a potential customer. So, potential sources for customers include:

☐ *The Internet.* Online sources of business information (see Chapter 6) comprise: *online services* (eg Reuters), *search engines* (eg Yahoo!), *directories* (eg *Yellow Pages*) and *hotlists* of links to related Web pages.

☐ *Directories.* The traditional sources of information on local businesses are *Yellow Pages* and Thomson's local directories. Kompass and similar directories (see Chapter 6) give extensive lists of companies classified and cross-referenced by the business sector, etc.

❑ *Trade press.* Look for advertisements, articles, reports and trade lists of businesses.

❑ *National press.* Look for articles and reports on companies in the broadsheets and Sunday papers, especially special supplements to the *Financial Times.*

❑ *GOYA.* The so-called GOYA approach stands for 'Get off your arm-chair' (or 'ass') and tour the area looking for potential clients.

Grouping customers

You need to group customers (both current and potential) by their likelihood to buy:

❑ *First class.* This is your primary customer base. Their business is booming, you are their main supplier and they pay invoices on time. While giving them excellent service, you need to allocate some time to nurture new business.

❑ *Second class.* This is your secondary customer base. They buy small amounts from you, but you are not their main supplier. Your goal is to give them just enough attention to convert them to 'first class' customers, without neglecting the latter.

❑ *Third class.* They buy large amounts from your competitors. Visit them occasionally to demonstrate interest and follow this up with mail shots.

❑ *Fourth class.* These are companies in decline. They may have been important customers once, but now are buying less and less and, even worse, taking longer to settle their invoices. Contact them by phone and mail shot.

Making a plan

Just like a general about to conduct a military campaign, you need to make a plan:

❑ *Plan your time.* Your *premium* time is when you are actually selling face-to-face or on the phone to a customer. Everything else is preparation or time squandered sitting in traffic jams. You need good time management. As a friend once told me, 'Don't confuse effort with achievement.'

❑ *Plan your income.* If your sales force is paid on a commission structure, make them plan their income. This will really focus their sales options.

❏ *Plan your sales.* Take a spreadsheet, across the top list the months and down the left the company's products. List the average net sales price to a customer, the number of each product you are likely to sell, and the estimated sales revenue. This will give your estimated monthly sales.

A sales script

You need a 'sales script' setting down your sales message to potential customers:

❏ *Sales message.* Prepare a bullet-point list of the key features (USPs) of your product. These are the important points you need to get across clearly to the customer in the first five seconds (the *elevator pitch*).
❏ *Enthusiasm.* Sound enthusiastic about your product; at the beginning of the day, at the end, and after several rejections.
❏ *Customer response.* Whether selling face-to-face or over the telephone, give customers time to respond and ask questions about your product.

Sales aids

Sales aids make you look professional and help with your sales campaign:

❏ *Pen, paper and diary.* Make sure you always have a pen and pad for making notes during the meeting, and your diary for scheduling follow-up meetings.
❏ *Business cards and brochures.* Have a good supply of business cards and brochures to leave with customers. This is particularly important with Asian business people, where exchanging business cards has the same status as shaking hands in the West.
❏ *Product and price lists.* You need all your product details close at hand: product lists, price lists and delivery schedules.
❏ *Slide presentation.* If you are going to make a presentation to prospective customers, you will need colour overhead transparencies or PowerPoint slides as well as printed copies.

Making the appointment/contact

Identify the decision-maker, and if possible get a personal introduction. Other tips for making contact were discussed above under telephone selling.

Presenting your product or service

Having identified the customer's requirements, raised questions about their future business strategy and got them thinking about your product, we next need to consider the presentation. A presentation of your high-tech product to potential customers (or investors) typically consists of yourself plus one or two colleagues making a slide presentation to 3–5 customer representatives:

❑ *Setting up.* Plan to arrive 5–10 minutes early and ask the receptionist if you can 'set up' your presentation. Make sure the overhead projector or video projector and laptop PC are working. Also, rearrange the furniture so that everyone can see both the presentation and each other.

❑ *Introductions.* Introduce yourself and your colleagues and exchange business cards.

❑ *Agenda.* Set out how you propose to structure the presentation, and confirm what time is available.

❑ *Company/product overview.* Outline the background to your company and the product to be presented.

❑ *Handouts.* Distribute brochures and copies of the slides to be used in the presentation.

❑ *Customer needs.* Outline the perceived customer's needs to confirm your understanding.

❑ *Presentation.* Present the key features and benefits of your product.

❑ *Demonstration.* If you have a software product or service, give a short demonstration.

❑ *Questions.* Deal with any questions raised, and, if you are unable to answer a question, do not be afraid to say you will follow up with the details.

☐ *Actions*. State your recommendations and agree a set of follow-up actions with the customer representatives.

Closing the sale

The six main approaches to closing are:

☐ *Direct close*. The customer is asked directly for the sale. This is appropriate for the customer who makes quick decisions.

☐ *Alternative close*. The customer is invited to choose from a range of products. This close makes it easy for the customer to agree to buy.

☐ *Assumptive close*. You simply assume that the customer will buy and ask, 'When would you like it delivered?' This is appropriate for the indecisive buyer.

☐ *Incentive close*. The customer is offered a motivation to sign, such as a discount for a deal on the spot. Again, this is appropriate for the indecisive buyer.

☐ *Exasperated close*. This is the fall-back situation: 'What more can I do to get you to sign?'

☐ *Silence*. After you have asked, 'Will you buy?', simply sit in silence waiting for the reply; no matter how long or uncomfortable the silence, you must wait. The rule in this game is that the first one to speak loses!

A good sales person will identify the best way to ask for an order from the above options.

Sources of help

Atkinson, J (1998) *Teach Yourself Selling*, Hodder & Stoughton, London

Direct Selling Association. 29 Floral Street, London, WC2E 9DP, tel 020 7497 1234, fax: 020 74971344, *www.dsa.org.uk*

Institute of Sales and Marketing Management. 31 Upper George Street, Luton, Beds, LU1 2RD, tel: 0172 7812500, email: *ismuknet@nildram.co.uk*

Institute of Sales Promotion. Arena House, 66–68 Pentonville Road, Islington, London, N1 9HS, tel: 020 7837 5340, fax: 020 7837 5326, *wwwisp.org.uk*

Johnson, N (1997) *How to Sell More – a guide for small business*, Kogan Page, London

35 Global Marketing and Exporting

Think of 'exporting', and the image conjured up is one of massive containers being loaded on to ships. However, when someone in the UK or Ireland buys a book from Amazon.com, music from CDNow, or downloads software from Microsoft or Netscape, these companies are 'exporting'. High-tech start-ups, by definition, trade globally.

In this chapter we look at:

- ❑ how high-tech start-ups launch into global marketing and trading;
- ❑ how to establish a traditional organization for exporting goods;
- ❑ how to research a new export market;
- ❑ handling prices, terms and payments;
- ❑ organizations and information sources to help you set up an export business.

Global marketing

Even a small high-tech start-up needs to recognize the implications of operating in a global marketplace. Competitors from the United States, Europe and even Asia will easily be able to compete with you. For instance, Amazon.com and Borders (www.borders.com) started off serving their British customers from America, but are now establishing a local UK presence to challenge the Internet Bookshop (www.bookshop.co.uk), Blackwells (www.blackwells.co.uk) and Waterstones (www.waterstones.co.uk). With high-tech start-up, it is certainly the case of 'do unto others before they do unto you'.

Once you have established your presence in the UK or Irish market, you will look to expand abroad. Traditional exporters naturally start with the European Union owing to the harmonized trade procedures. For high-tech start-ups the paradox is that it is frequently easier to export to Europe from the US than it is from the UK or Ireland. This has led to numerous British, Irish and Israeli companies moving their headquarters to Silicon Valley to masquerade as an American company while retaining their technical development at home.

As discussed in Chapter 4, a classic UK or Irish software start-up scenario is:

❑ *Local launch*. Use the low-risk start-up model to demonstrate your business idea. Focus on an entry-level product that is a 100 per cent complete offering.
❑ *Venture capital*. As soon as your idea is proved, use venture capital to accelerate growth.
❑ *US launch*. If you want to be a global player you need a US presence. If you are a specialist company, this might be a US marketing and sales support office. For an electronic commerce company with pretensions to dominate the global market, you need to become a US company. You need US venture capital money, US tech-lawyers and the associated kudos, and all of this is much easier if you are located in the United States.

Dealers and distributors

Many high-tech companies can simply do business globally online through the Internet. Others provide customer support through telephone call centres, in Scotland and Ireland. However, many products and services require real people to sell and support them. For instance, if you plan to sell software in Japan you will undoubtedly need local dealers and distributors.

In choosing a dealer or distributor you need to ensure they are technically competent, are financially stable, and have the resources and incentive to sell. Locating and choosing a partner is enormously difficult for a start-up, especially when the dealer or distributor is located in a foreign country.

Below, we look at how to establish a more traditional export business.

Researching the market

What to export will be dictated largely by whether your business is product, service or consulting based, and whether it is strategic or mass market.

What to export

Start your export planning with some market research, obtaining as much information as you can for free, and minimize costs, because you are unlikely to generate any immediate business. The primary questions are: firstly, the local business environment of your target export area; secondly, whether your product, service or consulting is suitable for the target customers; thirdly, how your offering can be made available to the customers; fourthly, the appropriate physical distribution method; and fifthly, the prices, terms and payments, and more importantly, if the trade will be profitable.

Where to export

Where should you start? The best choice is probably with a market whose customers are much like your domestic customer base market – for instance the United States, Canada or Australia. Alternatively it could be a market where you have personal contacts, a spouse, a family member, or a friend from college. In practice, every market has its individual peculiarities.

You could start with the European Union. It already takes 70 per cent of British exports, 11 of the 15 countries are standardizing on the euro currency, and there are no customs duties on EU goods. Europe also has groupings of compatible customers, such as Holland, northern Belgium and north-west Germany, who understand German and Dutch; or southern Belgium, France and western Switzerland, speaking French.

Many countries, including China, Burma and Iraq, will exclude themselves because of restrictions or lack of foreign currency, or unreliable delivery.

How to export

Before exporting a product, service or consultancy (know-how), you need to decide whether it needs modification for the local market (called *localization*). Trademarks, labels or manuals may need translation. The user interface of software or the 'look-and-feel' of a product may need re-implementation to suit local tastes. (Coca-Cola employ anthropologists to make sure they get their international marketing right.) In addition, for physical goods most countries impose regulations on the exact specifications of the goods, and you, as the exporter, will need to meet these.

Your overriding goals are to sell:

❑ where you can make the largest profit;
❑ where you have to make the fewest number of changes to your product or service;
❑ where the prices, terms and payments are attractive;
❑ where there is the easiest distribution.

Distribution channels

❑ *Electronic distribution.* If your product or service is 'digital', then it can be distributed globally over the Internet and through interactive television. Currently, the preferred method of payment is the credit card. Soon, so-called micro-payment mechanisms will be in place whereby customers can be billed for minor amounts of money, as with telephone calls. This will open up a whole New World of global information services and allow online consultancy charged by the second or minute.

❑ *Physical distribution.* If your products need physical distribution then you need to arrange transport and the necessary documentation. Much of this can be subcontracted. *Freight forwarders* specialize in overseas distribution, recommending and organizing the most appropriate transportation, by air, sea, rail or road, or even post or courier. They will advise on suitable packaging to ensure the product gets to its destination in one piece. They will also handle the documentation for customs declarations and clearance.

❑ *Your own sales force.* Most high-tech start-ups are selling sophisticated products, services and know-how. Therefore, a company person, with detailed knowledge of the products and services, is the most expert and the most motivated to sell. Hence, if you wish to export high-tech products and services, and support them locally, usually your own staff are the best equipped.

❑ *Licensing and joint ventures.* An alternative to exporting is to license your product. You 'license' a foreign company to sell your products and services in their local market and to pay you a royalty. This allows you to service a foreign market which demands a local presence, like Japan, or which may be of limited market value, like parts of eastern Europe and Central America. Equally important, you do not have to worry about shipping goods overseas, handling the documentation, or how you will get paid.

❑ *Agents.* To develop business in a country or region, you can consider appointing an agent who will liaise between you and your customers. *Export agents* buy your products and resell them to their customers overseas, relieving you of all the distribution problems. *Commission agents* sell for a commission, leaving you to arrange delivery to the customer. Commissions vary from 2.5 per cent to 15 per cent depending on the difficulty of selling.

Prices, terms and payments

At the top of your agenda will be calculating the additional export price of your product or service, and ensuring prompt payment. Considerations include:

❑ *Pricing.* For *products and services*, initially you must allocate some proportion of your overheads to the increased cost of your product, and subsequently ensure that the price reflects the full cost so as to get a reasonable margin of return. For *licences*, prices are in two parts: firstly a one-off payment for the licence, and secondly an annual royalty at so much per unit sold, with a minimum annual sales royalty.

❑ Terms and quotations. There are a number of internationally accepted *terms of delivery*. These are known as *Incoterms* and are available from the International Chamber of Commerce (tel 001 303 691 0404; www.icc.org). Example terms include 'free on board' (fob) and 'delivered duty paid' (ddp). Quotes can be in the local currency, euros or dollars, depending on the market, but beware of potential currency fluctuations.

❑ *Payments*. The generally accepted ways of being paid from overseas are: (i) by credit card – typically in international mail order; (ii) by letter of credit drawn on a UK or Irish bank; (iii) by a draft or bill of exchange arranged between your bank and a bank overseas; and (iv) dealing through a *factor*, who for a fee will handle all payments.

❑ *Insurance*. Where physical goods are concerned, an exporter can guard against non-payment by taking out *credit insurance*. Companies such as NCM Credit Insurance Ltd and Trade Indemnity Plc pay 85 per cent of the value if the buyer fails to pay.

Export services

A number of government organizations and business associations, and information sources, are available to help you export.

Export organizations

The DTI (www.dti.gov.uk) supports a number of export organizations:

❑ The British Overseas Board provides a wide range of services and expertise for first-time exporters, including its Market Entry Guarantee Scheme.

❑ The Export Market Information Centre (EMIC) provides exporters with a valuable market research base for assessing overseas markets (tel 020 7215 5444; dtiinfo1.dti.gov.uk/ots/emic).

❑ Business in Europe provides a range of useful booklets on exporting and export markets in Europe (tel (33) 14546 1818; fax. (33) 14546 2835; www.business-in-europe.com).

❑ Local Business Links provide access to a range of DTI services, funding and information sources (tel 0345 567 765; www.businesslink.gov.uk).

❑ The Overseas Trade Service provides support for exporters (tel 020 7215 584; www2.dti.gov.uk/ots).

Other organisations include:

❑ The Institute of Export, the professional export body providing a forum for exporters to exchange experience and information (tel 020 7247 9812; www.export.org.uk).

❏ European Community Business and Innovation Centres (EC-BIC). This is a network of CEC-funded agencies providing comprehensive help, including funding, to new businesses. Since there are over 100 EC-BICs across Europe, they also provide a valuable resource for small companies seeking to start up a subsidiary in another country. Visit www.eurm.or.at/foerderungen/EC-BIC.htm.

Information sources

Besides the extensive range of publications produced by the DTI, there are numerous commercial services and publications listed below.

A comprehensive list of organizations and sources is given in Part 7.

Sources of help

British Food Export Council. 301–344 Market Towers, 1 Nine Elms Lane, London, SW8 5NQ, tel: 020 7622 0188, fax: 020 76270616

Croner's *Reference Book for Exporters*, Croner House, London Road, Kingston-upon-Thames, Surrey, KT2 6SR, tel: 020 8547 3333, fax: 020 8547 2637, *www.croner.co.uk*

Croner's *Reference Book for Importers*, Croner House, London Road, Kingston-upon-Thames, Surrey, KT2 6SR, tel: 020 8547 3333, fax: 020 8547 2637, *www.croner.co.uk*

DTI Business in Europe, The. Kingsgate House, 66 Victoria Street, London, SW1E 6SW, tel: 020 7215 5000, fax: 020 7215 6140, *www.dti.gov.uk*

Institute of Export, The. 64 Clifton Street, London, EC2A 4HB, tel: 020 7247 9812, fax: 020 7377 5343, email: institute@export.org.uk, *www.export.org.uk*

London Chamber of Commerce, The. 33 Queen Street, London, EC4R 1AP, tel: 020 7248 4444, fax: 020 7489 0391

The Daily Telegraph (1998) *How to Set up and Run Your Own Business*, Kogan Page, London

Twells, H (1998) (ed) *The Export Handbook: in Association with the British camber of Commerce*, Kogan Page, London

Part 7

Information
Sources
and
Glossary

Information Sources

United Kingdom

Business organizations

Association of British Chambers of Commerce. Manning House, 22 Carlisle Place, SW1P 3QB, tel: 020 7565 2000, e-mail: administrator @britishchambers.org.uk, www.britishchambers.org.uk

Association of Scottish Chambers of Commerce. Conference House, The Exchange, 152 Morrison St, Edinburgh, EH3 8EB, tel: 0131 477–7001, fax: 020 7477–7002

British Association of Women Entrepreneurs. Suite F, 123–1251 Gloucester Place, London W1H 3PN, tel: 020 7935 0085, fax: 020 7224 0582, e-mail: Woutersz@msn.com, www.wgozdz.com/bawe

British Chamber of Commerce (BCC). 4 Westwood House, Westwood Business Park, Coventry, CV4 8HS, tel: 024 7669 4492, fax: 024 7669 5844, e-mail: enquiry@britishchambers.org.uk, www.britishchambers. org.uk

British Exporters Association. Broadway House, Tothill Street, London SW1H 9NQ, tel: 020 7222 5419, fax: 020 7799 2468

British Franchise Association. Thames View, Newtown Road, Henley-on-Thames, Oxfordshire, RG9 1HG, tel: 01491 578 050, fax: 01491 573517, e-mail: mailroom@british-franchise.org.uk, www.british-franchise. org.uk

British International Freight Association. Redfern House, Browells Lane, Feltham, Middlesex TW13 7EP, tel: 020 8844 2266, fax: 020 8890 5546, e-mail: bifasec@msn.com, www.bifa.org

British Technology Group (BTG). 10 Fleet Place, London EC4M 7SB, tel: 020 7575 0000, fax: 020 7575 0010, e-mail: info@btgplc.com, www.btgplc.com

Building Centre. 26 Store Street, London, WC1E 7BT, tel: 020 7692 4000, fax: 020 7580 9641, e-mail: manu@buildingcentre.co.uk, www.buildingcentre.co.uk

Business Angels – Now known as 'Lenta Ventures'. National Business Angels Network, 4 Snow Hill, London EC1A 2BS, tel: 020 7236 3000, fax: 020 7329 0226, e-mail: sbds@lenta.demon.co.uk

Business Exchange, 21 John Adam Street, London WC2N 6JG, tel: 020 7930 8965, fax: 020 7930 8437, e-mail: info@business-exchange-plc.co.uk, www.business-exchange-plc.co.uk

Business in the Community. 44 Baker Street, London W1M 1DH, tel: 020 7224 1600, fax: 020 7486 1700, e-mail: information@bitc.org.uk, www.bitc.org.uk

Business LINK. Freepost LON13319, London BC4 4HF, tel: 08457 567765, fax: 020 7557 7301, e-mail: info@london.businesslink.co.uk, www.businesslink.co.uk

Chamber of Commerce and Industry, London (LCCI). 33 Queen St, London EC4R 1AP, tel: 020 7248 4444, fax: 020 7489 0391

College Business Partnerships (CBP). TCD, Hillside House, 79 London Street, Faringdon, Oxon SN7 8AA, tel: 01367 242822, fax: 01367 242831, e-mail: office@tcd.co.uk, www.tcd.co.uk

Confederation of British Industry (CBI). Centre Point, 103 New Oxford Street, London WC1A 1DU, tel: 020 7379 7400, fax: 020 7836 5856, www.cbi.org.uk

English Estates. 120 Main Street, Burley In Wharfedale, Ilkley, West Yorkshire, tel: 01943 864585, www.english-estates.com

European Business Centre Network. Rue D'Arlon 80, 1040 Brussels, Belgium, tel: 00 322 2959421, fax: 00 322 2962572

European Franchise Federation (EFF). Rue la Boetie 60, 75008 Paris, France, tel: (33 1) 5375 2224, fax: (33 1) 5375 2220

European Venture Capital Association. Minervastraat 6, B-1930 Zaventem, Brussels, Belgium, tel: +32 2 715 0020, fax: +32 2 725 07 04, e-mail: evca@evca.com, www.evca.com

Factors and Discounters Association Ltd. Administration office, 2nd floor, Boston House, The Little Green, Richmond, TW9 1QE, tel: 020 8332–9955, fax: 020 8332–2585, e-mail: christine.tout@factors.org.uk

Federation of Recruitment and Employment Services Ltd. 36–38 Mortimer Street, London W1N 7RB, tel: 020 7323 4300, fax: 020 7255 2878, e-mail: info@fres.co.uk, www.fres.co.uk

Federation of Small Businesses Ltd. Whittle Way, Blackpool Business Park, Blackpool, Lancs FY4 2FE, tel: 01253 336000, fax: 01253 348046, www.fsb.org.uk

Forum of Private Business. Ruskin Chambers, Drury Lane, Knutsford, Cheshire WA16 6HA, tel: 01565 634467, fax: 01565 650059, e-mail: spbltd@spb.co.uk

Industrial Common Ownership Movement (ICOM). Vassalli House, 20 Central Road, Leeds LS1 6DE, tel: 0113 246 1737, fax: 0113 244 0002, e-mail: icom@icom.org.uk

Industrial Society. 48 Bryanston Square, London W1H 7LN, tel: 020 7262 2401, fax: 020 7706 1096, www.indsoc.co.uk

Institute of Directors (IoD). 116 Pall Mall, London SW1Y 5ED, tel: 020 7839 1233, fax: 020 7930 1949, www.iod.co.uk

Institute of Small Business Affairs. Leeds Business School, Leeds Metropolitan University, Bronte Hall, Beckitt Park Campus, Leeds LS6 3QS, tel: 0113 283 1742, fax: 0113 283 7542, e-mail: l.j.hunter-smith@lmu.ac.uk, www.isba.co.uk

International Chamber of Commerce. 14–15 Belgrave Square, London SW1X 8PS, tel: 020 7823 2811, fax: 020 7235 5447, e-mail: katherinehedger@iccorg.co.uk www.iccwbo.org

LENTA. 4 Snow Hill, London EC1A 2BS, tel: 020 7236 3000, fax: 020 739 0226, www.lenta.co.uk

London Chamber of Commerce. Manning House, 22 Carlisle Place, London SW1P 1JA, tel: 020 7248 4444, fax: 020 7565 2049

PA Technology. Cambridge Technology Centre, Back Lane, Melbourn, Nr Royston, Herts SG8 6DP, tel: 01763 261222, fax: 01763 260023, www.pa-consulting.com

Regus. www.regus.com

Reuters. Corporate Headquarters, 85 Fleet Street, London EC4P 4AJ, tel: 020 7250 1122, fax: 020 7542 5411, www.reuters.com

Smaller Firms Council. Centre Point, 103 New Oxford Street, London WC1A 1DU, tel: 020 7379 7400, www.cbi.org.uk

Telecottage Association. Freepost CV2312, Kenilworth, Warwickshire CV8 2RR, tel: 0800 616008, fax: 01453 836174, e-mail: tca@ruralnet.org.uk, www.tca.org.uk

UK Business Incubation Ltd. Aston Science Park, Love Lane, Birmingham B7 4BJ, tel: 0121 250 3538, fax: 0121 250 3542, e-mail: info@ukbi.co.uk, www.ukbi.co.uk

UK Federation of Business and Professional Women. 23 Ansdell Street, London W8 5BN, tel: 020 7938 1729, fax: 020 7938 2037

Urban and Economic Development Ltd (URBED). 19 Store Street, London WC1E 7DH, tel: 020 7436 8070, fax: 020 7436 8083, e-mail: urbed@urbed.co.uk, www.urbed.co.uk

Finance

3i Ventures. 91 Waterloo Road, London SE1 8XP, tel: 020 7928 3131, fax: 020 7928 0058, e-mail: Technology@3i.com, www.3i.com

Allied Irish Bank. 12 Old Jewry, London EC2R 8DP, tel: 020 7606 4900, fax: 020 7606 4966, e-mail: aibtoday@aib.ie, www.aib.ie/global

Bank of England. Threadneedle Street, London EC2R 8AH, tel: 020 7601 4878, fax: 020 7601 4771, e-mail: enquiries@bankofengland.co.uk, www.bankofeng-land.co.uk

Bank of Scotland. PO Box 12, Uberior House, 61 Grassmarket, Edinburgh EH1 2JF, tel: 0131 442 7777, fax: 0131 243 5948, www.bankofscotland.co.uk

Bank of Ulster. 35–39 Waring Street, Belfast BT1 2ER, tel: 02890 235232, www.ulsterbank.com

Barclays Bank. Business Sector Marketing Department, PO Box 120, Longwood Close, Westwood Business Park, Coventry CV4 8JN, tel: 024 7669 4242, www.barclays.com

Co-operative Bank. 1 Balloon Street, Manchester M60 4EP, tel: 08457 212 212, www.coopbank.co.uk

Credit Protection Association Ltd. 350 King Street, London W6 0RX, tel: 020 8846 0000

Credit Rating Company Appraisal. ICC Information Group Ltd, Crwys House, 33 Crwys Road, Cardiff CF2 4YF, fax: 029 206 8954

EASDAQ UK. Warwick House, 65–66 Queen Street, London EC4R 1EB, tel: 020 7489 9990, fax: 020 7489 88 80, e-mail: info@easdaq.be, www.easdaq.be

Enterprise Investment and Business Expansion Schemes Association. Tylers Croft, Hitchen Hatch Lane, Sevenoaks, Kent TN13 3AY, tel: 020 7613 0032, e-mail: woody.tylers@lineone.net

Enterprise Zones. DETR, Eland House, Bressenden Place, London SW1E 5DU, tel: 020 7890 3000, www.open.gov.uk

Equifax: Europe UK Ltd. Credit Reference Agency, Capital House, 25 Chapel Street, London NW1 5DS, tel: 020 7298 3000, fax: 020 7723 1999, e-mail: enquiries@equifax.co.uk, www.equifax.co.uk

Euler Trade Indemnity. 1 Canada Square, London E14 5DX, tel: 020 7739 4311, fax: 020 7512 9186, www.trade-indemnity.co.uk.

European Investment Bank. 68 Pall Mall, London SW1Y 5EF, tel: 020 7343 1200, fax: 020 7930 9929, www.eib.org

Experian. Credit Reference Agency, Consumer Affairs Department, PO Box 40, Nottingham NG7 2SS, www.experian.com

Garage.com. www.garage.com

Girobank. 101 Pentonville Road, London N1 9XR, tel: 020 7843 3000

Industrial Common Ownership Finance Ltd (ICOF). 115 Hamstead Road, Handsworth, Birmingham B20 2BT, tel: 0121 523 6886, fax: 0121 554 7117, e-mail: icof@icof.co.uk, www.icof.co.uk

Insurance Brokers Registration Council (IBRC). Higham Business Centre, Midland Road, Higham Ferrers, Northamptonshire NN10 8DW, tel: 01933 359083, fax: 01933 359077, www.hoe.businesslink.co.uk/DIRECT/el/ inbroker. htm

Insurance Industry Training Council – now known as Insurance and Related Financial Services, National Training Organisation (IRFSNTO). 20 Alderman-bury, London EC2V 7HY, tel: 020 7417 4793

Insurance Ombudsman Bureau. City Gate One, 135 Park Street, London SE1 9EA, tel: 08456 006 666, fax: 020 7902 8197, www.theiob.org.uk

Inter-Credit International Ltd. Newby House, 309 Chase Rd, Southgate, London N14 6JS, tel: 020 8482 4444

Lloyds Bank. Retail Banking UKRB, PO Box 112, Canon's House, Canon's Way, Bristol BS99 7LB, tel: 0117 9433138, www.lloydstsb.co.uk

London Stock Exchange. Old Broad Street, London EC2N 1HP, tel: 020 7797 1939, www.londonstockex.co.uk

Midland Bank. Midland Enterprise, Ground Floor, Courtwood House, Silver Street, Gead, Sheffield S1 1RG, tel: 0114 2529037, www.MidlandBank.Co.Uk

NASDAQ. Durrant House, 8–13 Chiswell Street, London EC1Y 4UQ, tel: 020 7374 6969, www.nasdaq.com

National Association of Pension Funds. 12/18 Grosvenor Gardens, London SW1W 6DH, tel: 020 7730 0585, www.napf.co.uk

NatWest. Franchise Section, Small Business Services, Level 10 Drapers Gardens, 12 Throgmorton Ave, London EC2 N2DL, tel: 020 7920 5966, www.natwest.com

Office of the Banking Ombudsman. 70 Grays Inn Road, London WC1X 8NB, tel: 020 7404 9944

Office of the Building Societies Ombudsman. Millbank Tower, Millbank, London SW1P 4XS, tel: 020 7931 0044

Royal Bank of Scotland. 42 St Andrew Square, Edinburgh EH2 2YE, tel: 0131 556 8555, www.rbs.co.uk

Singer & Friedlander Ltd. 21 New Street, Bishopsgate, London EC2M 4HR, tel: 020 7623 3000, fax: 020 7623 2122, www.singer-friedlander.com

Small Firms Loan Guarantee Scheme (SFLGS). Small Firms Loan Guarantee Section, DTI, Level 2, St Mary's House, Moorfoot, Sheffield, S1 4PQ, tel: 0114 259 7308/9, fax: 0114 259 7316, e-mail: David.Moore@SFSH-Sheffield. dti.gov.uk, www.dti.gov.uk/support/sflgs.htm

Small Firms Training Loans. tel: 0800 132–660, www.lifelonglearning.co.uk/sftl/ index.htm

Yorkshire Bank. 20 Merrion Way, Leeds LS2 8NZ, tel: 0113 2441244

Government agencies

Advisory, Conciliation and Arbitration Service (ACAS). Brandon House, 180 Borough High St, London. SE1 1LW, tel: 020 7396 5100, www.acas.org.uk

Board of the Inland Revenue. Press Office, Somerset House, Strand, London WC2R 1LB, tel: 020 7438 6420, www.inlandrevenue.gov.uk

British Copyright Council. Copyright House, 29–33 Berners Street, London W1P 4AA, e-mail: janet@bcc2.demon.co.uk, www.britishcopyright.org.uk

British Safety Council. 70 Chancellor's Road, London W6 9RS, tel: 020 8741 1231, fax: 020 8741 4555, e-mail: bsc1

British Standards Institution (BSI). 389 Chiswick High Road, London. W4 4AL, tel: 020 8996 9000, fax: 020 8996 7400, e-mail: info@bsi.org.uk, www.bsi.org.uk

Business LINK. Freepost LON13319, London BC4 4HF, tel: 08457 567765, fax: 020 7557 7301, e-mail: info@london.businesslink.co.uk, www.businesslink.co.uk

Capital Taxes Office (England and Wales). Ferrers House, PO Box 38, Castle Meadow Road, Nottingham NG2 1BB, tel: 0115 974 2400, www.inlandrevenue.gov.uk

Capital Taxes Office (Northern Ireland). Level 3 Dorchester House, 52–58 Great Victoria Street, Belfast BT2 7QL, tel: 02890505 353, fax: 02890 505305, www.inlandrevenue.gov.uk

Capital Taxes Office (Scotland). 16 Picardy Place, Edinburgh EH1 3NB, tel: 0131 524 3000, www.inlandrevenue.gov.uk

Career Development Loans. tel: 0800 585505, www.open.gov.uk

Central Office of Information. Hercules Road, London SE1 7DU, tel: 020 7928 2345, e-mail: dgodfrey@coi.gov.uk, www.coi.gov.uk/coi

Central Statistical Office Library – now known as the Office for National Statistics (ONS). Government Buildings, Cardiff Road, Newport, Gwent NP10 8XG, tel: 01633 812973, fax: 01633 812599, www.ons.gov.uk

Centre for Business Incubation Policy. Aston Science Park, Love Lane, Birmingham B7 4BJ, tel: 0121 250 3538, fax: 0121 250 3542, e-mail: info@ukbi.co.uk, www.ukbi.co.uk

Charity Commissioners. Harmsworth House, 13–15 Bouverie Street, London EC4Y 8DP, tel: 0870 3330123, www.charity-commission.gov.uk

Commission for Racial Equality. Elliot House, 10–12 Allington Street, London SW1A 5EH, tel: 020 7828 7022, fax: 020 7630 7605, www.cre.gov.uk

Commission of the European Communities (CEC London). Jean Monet House, 8 Storey's Gate, London SW1P 3AT, tel: 020 7973 1992, www.europa.eu.int

Companies House (Companies Registration). 21 Bloomsbury Street, London WC1B 3XD, tel: 029 2038 0801, www.companies-house.gov.uk

Companies House (England and Wales). Crown Way, Maindy, Cardiff CF4 3UZ, tel: 029 2038 8588, www.companies-house.gov.uk

Companies House (Scotland). 37 Castle Terrace, Edinburgh EH1 2EB, tel: 0131 535 5800, www.companies-house.gov.uk

Customs and Excise, HM. King's Beam House, 39–41 Mark Lane, London EC3R 7HE, tel: 020 7620 1313, www.hmce.gov.uk

Data Protection Registrar. Wycliffe House, Water Lane, Wilmslow, Cheshire, SK9 5AX, tel: 01625 545 745, www.dpr.gov.uk

Department of Economic Development. Local Trading Standards Department, Trading Standards Branch, 176 Newtownbreda Road, Belfast BT8 4QS

Department of Education and Employment. Sanctuary Buildings, Great Smith Street, London SW1P 3BT, tel: 020 7273 3000, www.open.gov.uk

Department of Trade and Industry (Small Firms and Business LINK Division).

Level 2, St Mary's house, Moorfoot, Sheffield S1 4PQ, tel: 08700 010172, www.dti.gov.uk

Design Registry. Patent Office, Concept House, Cardiff Road, Newport, Gwent NP9 1RH, tel: 01633 814000, www.patent.gov.uk

Development Agencies and Boards. Welsh Development Agency: Principality House, The Friary, Cardiff, CF10 3FE, tel: 01686 626 965, www.wda.co.uk; Scottish Enterprise: 120 Bothwell Street, Glasgow, G2 7JP, tel: 0141 248 2700, fax: 0141 221 3217, www.scotent.co.uk; Northern Ireland Local Enterprise Development Unit: LEDU House, Upper Galwally, Belfast, Northern Ireland, BT8 6TB, tel: 02890 491 031 www.ednet.ledu-ni.gov.uk

Development Board for Rural Wales – now known as Mid Division Welsh Development Agency. Ladywell House, Newton Powys SY16 1JB, tel: 01686 626965, fax: 01686 622499, www.wda.co.uk

English Partnership (EP). 16–18 Old Queens Street, London SW1H 9HP or St. George's House, Kingsway, Team Valley, Gateshead, Tyne and Wear, NE11 0NA, tel: 020 7976 7070, fax: 020 7976 7740, www.englishpartnerships.co.uk

English Tourist Board – now known as the British Tourist Authority. Development Advisory Service Unit, Thames Tower, Blacks Road, Hammersmith, London W6 9EL, tel: 020 8846 9000, fax: 563 0302, www.visitbritain.com

Equal Opportunities Commission. Overseas House, Quay Street, Manchester M3 3HN, tel: 0161 833 9244

European Commission (CEC). CEC funding programmes, www.europa.eu.int or www.cordis.lu

European Patent Office. Erhardtstrasse 27, D-80331 Munich, Germany, tel: +49 89 23 99 0, fax: +49 89 23 99 44 65, www.european-patent-office.org

Government Office for London. Riverwalk House, 157–161 Millbank, London SW1P 4RT, tel: 020 7217 3456

Health and Safety Executive. Rose Court, 2 Southwark Bridge, London SE1 9HB, tel: 08701 545500, www.open.gov.uk/hse/hsehome.htm

Her Majesty's Stationery Office (HMSO). 49 High Holborn, London WC1V 6HB, tel: 020 7873 0011, www.hmso.gov.uk

Industrial Development Board for Northern Ireland. IDB House, 64 Chichester Street, Belfast BT1 4JX, tel: 02890 233 233, www.idbni.co.uk

Inland Revenue (Public Enquiry Room). West Wing, Somerset House, London WC2R 1LB, tel: 020 7438 6420, www.inlandrevenue.gov.uk

Land Charges Registry. Land Charges Department, Drake's Hill Court, Burrington Way, Plymouth PL5 3LT, tel: 01752 635 600, www.landreg.gov.uk

Local Enterprise Companies. Small Firms and Business LINK Division, Level 2, St Mary's House, Moorfoot, Sheffield S1 4PQ, tel: 08700 010172

Local Enterprise Development Unit (LEDU). LEDU House, Upper Galwally, Belfast BT8 6TB, tel: 02890 491031, www.ednet.ledu-ni.gov.uk

Monopolies and Mergers Commission – now known as Competition Commission. New Court, 48 Carey Street, London WC2A 2JT, tel: 020 72710100, fax: 020 72710367, e-mail: competitiondeskcommission@gtnet.gov.uk, www.open.gov.uk

Northern Ireland Office. Netherleigh, Massey Avenue, Belfast BT4 2JP, tel: 02890 520 700, www.nio.gov.uk

Northern Ireland Tourist Board. St Annes Court, 59 North St, Belfast BT1 1NB, tel: 02890 231 221, www.ni-tourism.com

Northern Ireland Local Enterprise Development Unit (LEDU). LEDU House, Upper Galwally, Belfast BT8 6TB, tel: 01232 491031, www.ednet.ledu-ni.gov.uk

Office for National Statistics. Government Buildings, Cardiff Road, Newport, Gwent NP9 1XG, tel: 01633 815696, www.ons.gov.uk

Office of Fair Trading. Field House, 15–25 Bream Buildings, London EC4A 1PR, tel: 020 7211 8000, www.oft.gov.uk

Office of Water Services. Centre City Tower, 7 Hill Street, Birmingham B5 4UA, tel: 0121 625 1300, www.open.gov.uk/ofwat

OFGAS. 130 Wilton Road, London SW1V 1LQ, tel: 020 7828 0898, www.ofgas.gov.uk

OFTEL. 50 Ludgate Hill, London EC4M 7JJ, tel: 020 7634 8888, www.oftel.gov.uk

Overseas Trade Service (OTS) – now known as British Trade International. tel: 020 7215 5000, www2.dti.gov.uk/ots

Patent Office. Cardiff Road, Newport, Gwent NP10 8QQ, tel: 01633 814000, fax: 01633 814444, e-mail: commercialsearches@patent.gov.uk, www.patent.gov.uk

Prince's Trust. 18 Park Square East, London NW1 4LH, tel: 020 7543 1234, fax: 020 7543 1200, www.princes-trust.org.uk

Race Relations Employment Advisory Service (RREAS). Head Office, 14th Floor, Cumberland House, 200 Broad Street, Birmingham B15 1TA, tel: 0121–244 8142

Regional Enterprise Boards. Centre for Local Economic Strategies, Ground Floor, Barclay House, Whitworth Street West, Manchester M1 5NG, tel: 0161 236 7036, fax: 0161 236 1891, www.cles.org.uk

Regional Selective Assistance (RSA). Will move from following address on 25th June 1999; check for new address after this date. c/o Business Link Heart of England Ltd., 69 Milton Park, Abingdon, OX14 4RX, tel: 01235 442400, fax: 01235 862211, www.hoe.businesslink.co.uk/DIRECT/ps/regrant.htm

Registry of Credit Unions and Industrial and Provident Societies. IDB House, 64 Chichester Street, Belfast BT1 4JX, tel: 02890 234488, fax: 02890 5448888, www.dedni.gov.uk/registry

Research Council (EPSRC) – the Engineering and Physical Sciences Research Council, Polaris House, North Star Avenue, Swindon SN2 1ET, tel: 01793 444 000, fax: 01793 444010, e-mail: infoline@epsrc.ac.uk, www.epsrc.ac.uk

Rural Development Commission – now known as Countryside Agency. Dacre

House, 19 Dacre Street, London SW1H 0DH, tel: 020 7340 2900, fax: 020 7340 2911, www.argonet.co.uk/rdc

Scottish Enterprise. 120 Bothwell Street, Glasgow G2 7JP, tel: 0141 248 2700, www.scotent.co.uk

Scottish Office. Meridian Court, 5 Cadogan Street, Glasgow G2 6AT, tel: 0141 248 2855, www.scotland.gov.uk.

Scottish Tourist Board. 23 Ravelston Terrace, Edinburgh EH4 3EU, tel: 0131 332 2433, www.holiday.scotland.net

Simpler Trade Procedures Board (SITPRO). 151 Buckingham Palace Road, London SW1W 9SS, tel: 020 7215 0825, fax: 020 7215 0824, e-mail: info@sitpro.org.uk, www.sitpro.org.uk

Stationers Hall. Ave Maria Lane, London EC4M 7DD, tel: 020 7248 2934, fax: 020 7489 1975, pitcairn.lib.uci.edu/largo/sh/shx.html

Teaching Company Directorate. Hillside House, 79 Linden Street, Faringdon, Oxon SN7 8AA, tel: 01367 245200, fax: 01367 242831, e-mail: office@tcd.co.uk, www.tcd.co.uk

Tourist Board (London). Thames Tower, Blacks Road, Hammersmith, London W6 9E1, tel: 020 7932 2000, www.londontown.com

Training and Enterprise Councils (TECs). Small Firms and Business LINK Division, Level 2, St. Mary's house, Moorfoot, Sheffield S1 4PQ, tel: 08700 010172

UK Science Parks Association. Aston Science Park, Love Lane, Aston Triangle, Birmingham B7 4BJ, tel: 0121 359 0981, fax: 0121 333 5852, www.ukspa.org.uk

Welsh Development Agency (WDA). Principality House, Friary, Cardiff, South Glamorgan CF10 4AE, tel: 08457 775577, fax: 01443 845589, e-mail: enquiries@wda.co.uk, www.wda.co.uk

Welsh Office. Crown Building, Cathays Park, Cardiff CF10 3NQ, tel: 029 2082 5111, e-mail: webmaster@wales.gov.uk, www.wales.gov.uk

Welsh Tourist Board. Brunel House, 2 Fitzalan Road, Cardiff CF24 4UY, tel: 029 2049 9909, e-mail: info@tourism.wales.gov.uk, www.tourism.wales.gov.uk

Internet and computing

Association for Standards and Practices in Electronic Trade (E-Centre UK). 10 Maltravers Street, London WC2R 3BX, tel: 020 7655 9000, fax: 020 7681 2290, e-mail: info@e-centre.org.uk, www.eca.org.uk

Association of Independent Computer Specialists. tel: 0701 0701 118, e-mail: admin@aics.org.uk, www.aics.org.uk

Association of Professional Computer Consultants. 56 Exeter Road, Harrow, Middlesex HA2 9DP, tel: 020 8422 6460, fax: 020 8208 5151, e-mail: richard.daly @virgin.net

British Computer Society. 11 Mansfield Street, London W1M OBP, tel: 020 7631 1495, fax: 020 7631 1049, e-mail: bcshq@hq.bcs.org.uk, www.bcs.org.uk

Compu-Mark UK. New Premier House, 150 Southampton Row, London WC1B 5AL, tel: 020 7278 4646, fax: 020 7278 5934, www.compu-mark.com

Computing Services and Software Association (CSSA). 20 Red Lion Street, London WC1R 4QN, tel: 020 7395 6700, fax: 020 7404 4119, e-mail: cssa@cssa.co.uk, www.cssa.co.uk

CyberLaw Organisation. www.cyberlaw.com

E-Centre. 10 Maltravers Street, London WC2R 3BX, tel: 020 7655 9000, fax: 020 7681 2290, e-mail: info@e-centre.org.uk, www.e-centre.org.uk

Federation Against Software Theft (FAST). 1 Kingfisher Court, Farnham Road, Slough, Berkshire SL2 1JF, tel: 01753 527999, fax: 01753 532100, e-mail: fast@fast.org, www.fast.org.uk

Information Technology Centres. NAITEC, Suffolk Enterprise Centre, Russel Road, Ipswich, IP1 2DE, tel: 01473 233758, fax: 01473 2524889, www.naitec.co.uk

National Computing Centre. Oxford House, Oxford Road, Manchester M1 7ED, tel: 0161 228 6333, fax: 0161 242 2400/2171, e-mail: webster@ncc.co.uk, www.ncc.co.uk

Legal

Advertising Standards Authority. 2 Torrington Place, London WC1E 7HW, tel: 020 7580 5555, fax: 020 7631 3051, www.asa.org.uk

Association of Company Registration Agents. 20 Holywell Row, London EC2A 4JB, tel: 020 7377 0381, fax: 020 7377 6646

Centre for Dispute Resolution. 95 Gresham Street, London EC2V 7NA, tel: 020 7600 0500, www.cedr.co.uk

Chartered Institute of Patent Agents. Staple Inn Buildings, High Holborn, London WC1V 7PZ, tel: 020 7405 9450, fax: 020 7430 0471, e-mail: mail@cipa.org.uk, www.cipa.org.uk

Commission for Racial Equality. Elliot House, 10–12 Allington Street, London SW1A 5EH, tel: 020 7828 7022, fax: 020 7630 7605, www.cre.gov.uk

Copyright Licensing Agency. 90 Tottenham Court Road, London W1P 0LP, tel: 020 7436 5931, fax: 020 7631 5500, www.cla.co.uk

Equal Opportunities Commission. Overseas House, Quay Street, Manchester M3 3HN, tel: 0161 833 9244, fax: 0161 835 1657, www.eoc.org.uk

Institute of Trademark Agents. 4th Floor, Canterbury House, 2–6 Sydenham Road, Croydon, Surrey CR0 9XE, tel: 020 8686 2052, fax: 020 8680 5723, www.itma.org.uk

Law Society. 113 Chancery Lane, London WC2A 1PL, tel: 020 7242 1222, fax: 020 7831 0344, www.lawsoc.co.uk

Lawyers for your business. PO Box 61, London NW1 7QS, tel: 020 7405 9075, fax: 020 7692 9998, www.lfyb.lawsociety.org.uk

Mail Order Protection Scheme.(national newspapers). 16 Took's Court, London EC4A 1LB, tel: 020 7269 0520, fax: 020 7404 0106, www.mops.org.uk

Performing Right Society. 21–33 Berners Street, London W1P 4AA, tel: 020 7580 5544, www.prs.co.uk

Race Relations Employment Advisory Service (RREAS). Head Office, 14th Floor, Cumberland House, 200 Broad Street, Birmingham B15 1TA, tel: 0121 244 8142

Registry of County Court Judgements. Registry Trust Ltd, 173–175 Cleveland Street, London W1P 5PE, tel: 020 7380 0133

Trademark Registry (London filing facility). 25 Southampton Buildings, Chancery Lane, London WC2A 1AR, tel: 020 7438 4747, e-mail: patents@patent.gov.uk, www.patent.gov.uk

Trademark, Patents and Design Registry. Patent Office, Cardiff Road, Newport, Gwent NP10 8QQ, tel: 01633 814 000, fax: 01633 813 600, e-mail: enquiries@patent.gov.uk, www.patent.gov.uk

Marketing, advertising etc

Advertising Association. Abford House, 15 Wilton Road, London. SW1V 1NJ, tel: 020 7828 2771, fax: 020 7931 0376, e-mail: arabella.price@adassoc.org.uk, www.adassoc.org.uk

British Import Association. 25 Castlereagh Street, London W1H 5YR, tel: 020 7258 3999

British Promotional Merchandise Association. Bank Chambers, 15 High Road, Byfleet, Surrey KT14 7QH, tel: 01932 355660/1, fax: 01932 355662, e-mail: bpma@martex.co.uk, www.martex.co.uk/bpma

Chartered Institute of Marketing. Moor Hall, Cookham, Maidenhead, Berks SL6 9QH, tel: 01628 427500, fax: 01628 427499, www.cim.co.uk

Direct Marketing Association (DMA) UK Ltd. Haymarket House, 1 Oxendon Street, London SW1Y 4EE, tel: 020 7321 2525, fax: 020 7321 0191, e-mail: dma@dma.org.uk, www.dma.org.uk

Direct Selling Association. 29 Floral Street, London WC2E 9DP, tel: 020 7497 1234, fax: 020 7497 1344, www.dsa.org.uk

DTI Business in Europe. Kingsgate House, 66 Victoria Street, London SW1E 6SW, tel: 020 7215 5000, fax: 020 7215 6140, www.dti.gov.uk

Institute of Direct Marketing. 1 Park Road, Teddington, Middlesex TW11 0AR, tel: 020 8977 5705, fax: 020 8943 2535, www.theidm.co.uk

Institute of Export. 64 Clifton Street, London EC2A 4HB, tel: 020 7247 9812, fax: 020 7377 5343, e-mail: institute@export.org.uk, www.export.org.uk

Institute of Practitioners in Advertising (IPA). 44 Belgrave Square, London SW1X 8QS, tel: 020 7235 7020, fax: 020 7245 9904, www.ipa.co.uk

Institute of Public Relations. The Old Trading House, 15 Northburgh Street, London EC1V 0PR, tel: 020 7253 5151

Institute of Sales and Marketing Management. Romeland House, Romeland Hill, St Albans, AL3 4ET, tel: 0172 7812500, e-mail: ismuknet@nildram.co.uk

Institute of Sales Promotion. Arena House, 66–68 Pentonville Road, Islington, London N1 9HS, tel: 020 7837 5340, fax: 020 7837 5326, www.isp.org.uk

Mail Order Traders Association. 40 Waterloo Road, Birkdale, Southport, PR8 2NG, tel: 01704 563 787, fax: 01704 551 247, www.adassoc.org.uk

Manufacturers' Agents Association (MAA). Somers House, 1 Somers Road, Reigate, RH2 9DU, tel: 01737 241025, fax: 01737 224537

Market Research Society. 15 Northburgh Street, London EC1V 0JR, tel: 020 7490 4911, fax: 020 7490 0608, www.marketresearch.org.uk

Marketing Society. St George's House, 3–5 Pepys Road, London SW20 8NJ, tel: 020 8879 3464, fax: 020 8879 0362, www.marketing-society.org.uk

Newspaper Society. Marketing Dept, Bloomsbury House, 74–77 Great Russell Street, London WC1 BDA, tel: 020 7636 7014, fax: 020 7631 5119, www.news-papersoc.org.uk

Public Relations Consultants Association. e-mail: chris@prca.org.uk, www.martex.co.uk/prca

Small Business Bureau. Curzon House, Church Road, Windlesham, Surrey GU20 6BH, tel: 01276 452010, fax: 01276 451602

Technical Help for Exporters. British Standards Institution, 389 Chiswick High Road, London W4 4AL, tel: 020 8996 9000, fax: 020 8996 7048, e-mail: info@bsi.org.uk, www.bsi.org.uk

Women in Direct Marketing. Royal Mail House, 148–166 Old Street, London EC1V 9HQ, tel: 020 72502365, fax: 020 72502021, e-mail: lopa.patel@dms-direct.co.uk

Market research sources

Analyst's Service. Skandia HS, 23 College Hill, London EC4R 2RA, tel: 020 7398 7771, fax: 020 7398 1005, e-mail: steveK@datastreamicv.co.uk, www.info.ft.com

ASLIB Directory of Information Sources in the UK. Staple Hall, Stone House Court, London EC3A 7PB, tel: 020 7903 0000, fax: 020 7903 0011, www.aslib.co.uk

A-Z of Business Information Sources. Croner House, London Road, Kingston-upon-Thames, Surrey KT2 6SR, tel: 020 8547 3333, fax: 020 85472638, e-mail: info@croner.co.uk, www.croner.co.uk

Benn's Media Directory. Now known as Miller Freeman Information Services, Sovereign Way, Tonbridge, Kent TN9 1RW, tel: 01732 362666, fax: 01732 770482

(British) Institute of Management (library and management information). Management House, Cottingham Road, Corby, Northants NN17 1TT, tel: 01536 204222, fax: 01536 201651

British Library Business Information Service. 96 Euston Rd, London NW1 2DB; tel: 020 7412 7454/7977

British Library (science, technology and business information service). 96 Euston Rd, London NW1 2DB, tel: 020 7412 7919, fax: 020 7412 7495, e-mail: patents-information@bl.uk, www.bl.uk

British Rate and Data (BRAD). Maclean Hunter House, Chalk Lane, Cockfoster Road, Barnet, Herts EN4 0BU, tel: 020 7505 8000

Business and Trade Statistics Ltd. Lancaster House, 45 More Lane, Esher, Surrey KT10 8AP, tel: 01372 463121, fax: 01372 469847, e-mail: bts@dial.pipex.com

Business Monitors (*Demographic Yearbook*). Stationery Office. 51 Nine Elms Lane, London SW8 5DR, tel: 0870 600 5522, www.the-stationery-office.co.uk

City Business Library. 1 Brewers Hill Garden, London EC2V 5BX, tel: 020 7638 8215, fax: 020 7600 1185

Croner's Publications Ltd. Croner House, London Road, Kingston-upon-Thames, Surrey KT2 6SR, tel: 020 8547 3333, fax: 020 8547 2637, www.croner.co.uk

Direct Mail Information Services. 5 Carlisle Street, London W1V 6JX, tel: 020 7494 0483, fax: 020 7494 0455, www.dmis.co.uk

Directory of British Associations. CBD Research Ltd, Chancery House, 15 Wickham Road, Beckenham, Kent BR3 2JS

Dun and Bradsheet. Holmers Farm Way, High Wycombe, Bucks HP12 4UL, tel: 01494 422000, fax: 01494 422260, www.dunandbrad.co.uk

Economist Intelligence Unit. 15 Regents Street, London W1A 1LR, tel: 020 7930 8763, fax: 020 7499 9767, www.eiu.com

Euromonitor. 60–61 Britton Street, London EC1M 5UX, tel: 020 7251 8024, fax: 020 7608 3149, www.euromonitor.com

Extel: European Companies Service. Extel: Financial Ltd, Fitzroy House, 13–17 Epworth Street, London EC2A 4DL, tel: 020 7251 3333, fax: 020 7251 2725, www.info.ft.com

Extel's Handbook of Market Leaders. Extel: Financial Ltd, Fitzroy House, 13–17 Epworth Street, London EC2A 4DL, tel: 020 7251 3333, fax: 020 7251 2725, www.info.ft.com

Guide to Official Statistics. Central Statistics Office, Cabinet Office, Information Department, House Guards Road, London SW1P 3AL, tel: 020 7270 6363

ICC Information Ltd (company information service – American, European). Victoria House, 64 Paul Street, London EC2A 4NA, tel: 020 7426 8510, www.icc.co.uk

ICC Financial Surveys. Field House, 72 Oldfield Road, Hamton, Middlesex TW12 2HQ, tel: 020 8783 1122, fax: 020 8783 0049

Industrial Market Research Reports. Frost & Sullivan Ltd, Sullivan House, 4 Grosvenor Gardens, London SW1 0DH, tel: 020 7730 3438, fax: 020 7730 3343, www.frost.com

Inland Revenue Library. Room 28, New Wing, Somerset House, Strand, London WC2R 1LB, tel: 020 7438 6325

Interactive Market Systems. Grosvenor Gardens House, 35 Grosvenor Gardens, London SW1W 0BS, tel: 020 7630 5033, fax: 020 7828 3642, e-mail: imsukltd @compuserve.com

Jordan's Business Information Service. Jordan House, 21 St Thomas Street, Bristol, tel: 0117 9230600, fax: 0117 9230063

Kelly's Business Directories. Windsor Court, East Grinstead House, East Grinstead, West Sussex, RH19 1XA, tel: 01342 326972

Key British Enterprises. Dun & Bradstreet Ltd, Holmers Farm Way, High Wycombe, Bucks HP12 4UL, tel: 01494 424295, fax: 01494 422260

Kompass Publishers. Windsor Court, East Grinstead House, East Grinstead, West Sussex RH19 1XA, tel: 01342 326 972

London Gazette. Parliamentary Press, Mandela Way, London SE1 5SS, tel: 020 7394 4585, fax: 020 7394 4581

Market Forecasts. The BLA Group, 2 Duncan Terrace, London N1 8BZ, tel: 020 7278 9517, fax: 020 7278 6246

Market Information Manual. Neilsen House, London Road, Headington, Oxford, Oxen OX3 9RX, tel: 01865 742742, fax: 01865 742222

Market Intelligence. Intel: International Group, 18–19 Long Lane, London EC1A 9HE, tel: 020 7606 6000, fax: 020 7606 3327

Registry of Friendly Societies. Victory House, 30–34 Kingsway, London WC2B 6ES, tel: 020 7676 1000

Reports Index. Business Survey Ltd, Broadmayne House Farm, Osmington Drive, Broadmayne, Dorset DT2 8EP, tel: 01305 853704, fax: 01305 854162

Retail Directory. Newman Books Ltd, 32 Vauxhall Bridge Road, London SW1V 2SS, tel: 020 7973 6402, fax: 020 7233 5056

Sell's Product and Service Directory. Miller Freeman Information Services Ltd, Riverbank House, Angel Lane, Tonbridge, Kent TN9 1SE, tel: 01732 362666, fax: 01732 770483

Standard and Poor's Register of Corporations, Directors and Executives. Wimbledon Bridge House, Hartfield Road, London SW19, tel: 020 8545 6279

Statistics – Africa, America, Asia and Australasia, Europe. CBD Research Ltd, Chancery House, 15 Wickham Road, Beckenham, Kent BR3 2JS, tel: 020 8650 7745, fax: 020 8650 0768

Store Buyers Guide. Manor House Press Ltd, 3rd Floor, Hill House, McDonald Road, off Highgate Hill, London N19 5NA, tel: 020 7281 6767, fax: 020 7281 8087

Venture Capital Report Ltd. Magdalen Centre, Oxford Science Park, Oxford, Oxen

OX4 4GA, tel: 01865 784411, fax: 01865 784412, e-mail: vcr@vcr1978.com, ww.vcr1978.com

Who Owns Whom. Dun & Bradstreet Ltd, Holmers Farm Way, High Wycombe, Bucks HP12 4UL, tel: 01494 424295, fax: 01494 422260

Professional bodies

Association of Authorised Public Accountants. 10 Lincoln's Inn Fields, London WC2A 3ES, tel: 020 7396 5954, fax: 020 7396 5916, e-mail: aapa.enquiries@ acca.org.uk

Association of British Correspondence Colleges. PO Box 17926, London SW19 3WB, tel: 020 8544 9559, e-mail: abcc@msn.com, www.nationline.co.uk/abcc

Association of British Credit Unions. Hollyoak House, Hanover Street, Manchester M60 0AS, tel: 0161 832 3694, fax: 0161 832 3706, www.abcul.org

Association of British Insurers. 51 Gresham Street, London EC2V 7HQ, tel: 020 7600 3333, fax: 696 8999, e-mail: phil.ward@abi.co.uk, www.abi.org.uk

Association of Consulting Actuaries. 1 Wardrobe Place, London EC4V 5AH, tel: 020 7248 3163, fax: 020 7236 1889, e-mail: acahelp@aca.org.uk, www.aca.org.uk

British Factors and Discounters Association. Boston House, The Little Green, Richmond, Surrey TW9 1QE, tel: 020 8332 9955, fax: 020 8332 2585, e-mail: Chris.Molloy@factors.org.uk, www.factors.org.uk

British Insurance and Investment Brokers Association. BIBA House, 14 Bevis Marks, London EC3A 7NT, tel: 020 7623 9043, fax: 020 7626 9676, e-mail: enquiries@biiba.org.uk, www.biiba.org.uk

British Venture Capital Association (BVCA). Essex House, 12–13 Essex Street, London WC2R 3AA, tel: 020 7240 3846, fax: 020 7240 3849, www.bvca.co.uk

Chartered Association of Certified Accountants. 29 Lincoln's Inn Fields, London WC2A 3EE, tel: 020 7236 8761, www.acca.co.uk

Chartered Institute of Arbitrators. 24 Angel Gate, City Road, London EC1V 2RS, tel: 020 7837 4483, fax: 020 7837 4185, e-mail: 71411.2735@compuserve.com, www.arbitrators.org

Chartered Institute of Management Accountants. 63 Portland Place, London W1N 4AB, tel: 020 7637 2311, fax: 020 7631 5309, www.cima.org.uk

Chartered Institute of Public Finance and Accountancy. 3 Robert Street, London WC2N 6BH, tel: 020 7543 5600, www.cipfa.org.uk

Chartered Institute of Taxation. 12 Upper Belgrave Street, London SW1X 8BB, tel: 020 7235 9381, fax: 020 7235 2562, www.tax.org.uk

Chartered Insurance Institute. 20 Aldermanbury, London EC2V 7HY, tel: 020 7606 3835, fax: 020 8530 3052, www.cii.co.uk

Consumer Credit Trade Association. Tennyson House, 159 Great Portland Street, London W1N 5FD, tel: 020 7636 7564, fax: 020 7323 0096

Finance and Leasing Association. 18 Upper Grosvenor Street, London W1X 6PB, tel: 020 7491 2783

Institute of Business Advisors. PO Box 8, Harrogate, North Yorkshire HG2 8XB, tel: 01423 879208, www.iba.org.uk

Institute of Chartered Accountants in England and Wales (ICA). Chartered Accountants Hall, Moorgate Place, London EC2P 2BJ, tel: 020 7920 8100, fax: 020 7920 0547, www.icaew.co.uk

Institute of Chartered Accountants of Scotland. 27 Queen Street, Edinburgh EH2 1LA, tel: 0131 225 5673, www.icas.org.uk

Institute of Chartered Secretaries and Administrators. 16 Park Crescent, London W1N 4AH, tel: 020 7580 4741, e-mail: icas@dial.pipex.com

Institute of Company Accountants. 40 Tyndalls Park Road, Clifton, Bristol BS8 1PL, tel: 0117 973 8261

Institute of Credit Management. The Water Mill, Station Road, South Luffenham, Oakham, Leics LE15 8NB, tel: 01780 722900, www.icm.org.uk

Institute of Inventors. 19/23 Fosse Way, Ealing, London W13 OBZ, tel: 020 8998 3540

Institute of Linguistics. 24a Highbury Grove, London N5 2EA, tel: 020 7359 7445

Institute of Management Consultants. 5th Floor, 32–33 Hatton Garden, London EC1N 8DL, tel: 020 7242 2140, fax: 020 7831 4597, www.imc.co.uk

Institute of Management. Management House, Cottingham Road, Corby, Northants NN17 1TT, tel: 01536 204222, fax: 01536 201651, e-mail: savoy@inst-mgt.org.uk, www.inst-mgt.org.uk

Institute of Patentees and Inventors. Suite 505a, Triumph House, 189 Regent Street, London WR1 7WF, tel: 020 7434 1818, fax: 020 7434 1727, e-mail: paulamb@archer.win-uk.net

Institute of Personnel and Development. IPD House, 35 Camp Road, Wimbledon, London SW19 4UW, tel: 020 8971 9000, fax: 020 8263 3333, e-mail: ipd@ipd.co.uk

London Society of Chartered Accountants. 15 Basinghall, EC2B 5BR, tel: 020 7726 2722

Royal Institution of Chartered Surveyors. 12 Great George Street, Parliament Square, London SW1P 3AD, tel: 020 7222 7000, www.rics.org.uk

Society of Pension Consultants. St Bartholomew House, 92 Fleet Street, London EC4Y 1DG, tel: 020 7353 1688, e-mail: john.mortimer@spc.uk.com, www.spc.uk.com

Irish Republic

Business organizations

Bord Failte. Baggot Street, Dublin 2, tel: 01 6765871, fax: 01 6764768

Business Incubation Centre. Ossory Road, North Strand, Dublin 3, tel: 011 363 994, fax: 011 363 997

Business Innovation Centre (BIC). The Tower, IDA Enterprise Centre, Pearse Street, Dublin 2, tel: 01 671-3111, fax: 011 671-3330; Cork, tel: 021 397711; Galway, tel: 091 567974; Limerick, tel: 061 338177; Waterford, tel: 051 354410; Derry, tel: 0801 504 264 242

Business Innovation Fund. Molyneux House, 67–69 Bride Street, Dublin 8, tel: 01 4753305

CERT. Cert House, Amiens Street, Dublin 2, tel: 01 8742555, fax: 01 8742821

Chambers of Commerce of Ireland. 7 Clare Street, Dublin 2, tel: 011 661 4111, fax: 011 676 6043, e-mail: info@dubchamber.ie, www.dubchamber.ie

Co-operative Development Society. 29 Dame Street, Dublin 2, tel: 011 677 0045

Dublin Business Innovation Centre. Enterprise Centre, Pearse Street, Dublin 2, tel: 01 6775655

Enterprise Ireland. Glasnevin, Dublin 9; Strand Road, Dublin 4; Wilton Place, Dublin 2, tel: 01 857 0000, e-mail: clientservice@irish-trade.ie or infodesk@forbairt.ie, www.enterprise-ireland.com

European Business Information Centre (EBI). Irish Trade Board, Merrion Hall, Strand Road, Sandymount, Dublin 4, tel: 01 2695011

Excellence Ireland. Merrion Hall, Strand Road, Dublin 4, tel: 01 2695255

First Step. Jefferson House, Eglington Road, Donnybrook, Dublin 4, tel: 01 2600988

Forbairt. Wilton Park House, Wilton Place, Dublin 2, tel: 01 660–2244, fax: 01 808–2020

Franchise Unit. Ulster Bank, 33 College Green, Dublin 2, tel: 01 6777623

Guaranteed Irish Ltd. 1 Fitzwilliam Place, Dublin 2, tel: 01 6612607

Guinness Ireland. St James's Gate, Dublin 8, tel: 01 4536700

Inner City Enterprise. 56–57 Lower Gardiner Street, Dublin 1, tel: 01 8364073, fax: 01 8363742

Irish Business & Employers Confederation. Baggot Bridge House, Lr Baggot Street, Dublin 2, tel: 01 6601011

Irish Franchise Association. 13 Frankfield Terrace, Summerhill South, Cork, tel: 021 270059

Irish Small & Medium Enterprises Association. 17 Kildare Street, Dublin 2, tel: 01 6622755

Running Your Business Magazine. 24 Terenure Road East, Rathgar, Dublin 6, tel: 01 4902244

Shannon Development. Town Centre, Shannon, Co. Clare, tel: 0161 361 555, fax: 0161 361 903

Small Business Programme. Wilton Park House, Wilton Place, Dublin 2, tel: 011 668 6633, fax: 011 660 5095

Small Firms Association (SFA). SFA Dublin Office, 84/86 Lower Baggot Street, Dublin 2, tel: 011 660 1011, fax: 011 661 2861, e-mail: sfa@iol.ie, ireland.iol.ie/sfa

Udaras na Gaeltachta Na Forbacha. Galway, tel: 0191 503100, fax: 0191 503101, e-mail: eolas@udaras.ie, www.udaras.ie

Finance

AIB Bank Enterprise Development Bureau. Bankcentre, Ballsbridge, Dublin 4, tel: 011 660 0311, fax: 011 668 2508, www.aib.ie

AIB Finance & Leasing Ltd. Sandyford Business Centre, Blackthorn Road, Sandyford, Dublin 18, tel: 01 6600311, fax: 01 2959898, www.aib.ie

AIB Venture Capital Centre. Jefferson House, Eglinton Road, Dublin 4, tel: 011 260 0966, fax: 011 260 0538, www.aib.ie

Arthur Andersen & Co (chartered accountants). Andersen House, Harbourmaster Place, Dublin 1, tel: 011 670 1000, fax: 011 670 1010, www.arthurandersen.com

Bank of Ireland Enterprise Support Unit. Head Office, Lower Baggot Street, Dublin 2, tel: 011 661 5933, fax: 011 676 3493, www.boi.ie

BES – Seed Capital Relief. Office of the Revenue Commissioners, Dublin Castle, Dublin 2, tel: 01 679 2777

Business Innovation Fund. Karl Schutte, 40 Merrion Square, Dublin 2, tel: 011 473 3305, fax: 011 661 2473

Carey O'Connor (chartered accountants), 1 Drinan Street, Sullivan's Quay, Cork, tel: 0121 961 122

Chartered Association of Certified Accountants. Leeson Park, Dublin 6, tel: 0111 963 260, www.acca.co.uk

Coopers & Lybrand (chartered accountants). Fitzwilton House, Wilton Place, Dublin 2, tel: 011 661 0333, fax: 011 660 1782

Development Capital Corporation. DCC House, Stillorgan, Co. Dublin, tel: 011 283 1011, fax: 011 283 1017, www.dcc.ie

Ernst & Young (chartered accountants). Harcourt Centre, Harcourt Street, Dublin 2, tel: 011 475 0555, fax: 01 475 0599, www.e-y.ie

Institute of Chartered Accountants in Ireland. 87–89 Pembroke Road, Dublin 4, tel: 0001 680 400, www.icai.ie; and 11 Donegal Square South, Belfast, BT1 5JE, tel: 02890 321 600

International Fund for Ireland. PO Box 2000, Dublin 2, tel: 01 478 0655, fax: 01 671 2116

KPMG Stokes Kennedy Crowley (chartered accountants). 1 Stokes Place, St Stephens Green, Dublin 2, tel: 011 708 1000, fax: 011 708 1122, www.kpmg.ie

Liffey Trust. 117–126 Upper Sheriff Street, Dublin 1, tel: 011 364 651, fax: 011 364 818

Smurfit Job Creation Enterprise Fund. Smurfit Venture Investments, Clanwilliam House, Clanwilliam Place, Dublin 2, tel: 01 1662 8600, fax: 01 1662 8700, e-mail: info@smurfit.ie

Government agencies

Area Partnerships. Department of the Taoiseach, Government Buildings, Upper Merrion Street, Dublin 2, tel: 01 668–9333, fax: 01 678–9791

Arts, Culture and the Gaeltacht. tel: 01 667 0788

Bord Bia (Food Board). www.bordbia.ie

Bord Failte (Tourist Board). www.ireland.travel.ie/home/index.asp

Business Expansion Scheme. Secretariat of Taxes, Office of the Revenue Commissioners, 85–93 Lower Mount Street, Dublin 2, tel: 011 679 2777, fax: 011 679 9287, www.revenue.ie

Central Statistics Office. Ardee Road, Dublin 6, tel: 01 4977144; Skehard Road, Cork, tel: 01 -21 359000, fax: 01 -21 359090, www.cso.ie

Companies Registration Office. Lower Castle Yard, Dame Street, Dublin 2, tel: 01 6614222

Crafts Council of Ireland. Castle Yard, Kilkenny, tel: 011 679 7368, fax: 011 679 9197

Department of Agriculture, Food and Forestry. Rural Development Division, Kildare Street, Dublin 2, tel: 01 6072000, fax: 01 662 0198

Department of Enterprise and Employment. Kildare Street, Dublin 2, tel: 011 661 4444, fax: 011 676 2654, www.irlgov.ie

Department of Labour. Davitt House, Mespil Road, Dublin 4, tel: 011 676 5861, fax: 011 660 3210, www.irlgov.ie

Department of Finance. Government Buildings, Merrion Street, Dublin 2, tel: 011 676 7571, fax: 011 678 9936, www.irlgov.ie

Enterprise Ireland. Glasnevin, Dublin 9; Strand Road, Dublin 4; Wilton Place, Dublin 2, tel: 01 857 0000, e-mail: clientservice@irish-trade.ie or infodesk@forbairt.ie, www.enterprise-ireland.com

'Enterprise Link' Help Line. Department of Enterprise & Employment/Forbairt, tel: 01 1850 35 33 33

Environmental Protection Agency. tel: 053 47120

European Business Institute. 11 Ely Place, Dublin 2, tel: 011 676 8804, fax: 011 676 8805

European Commission. 39 Molesworth Street, Dublin 2, tel: 011 671 2244, fax: 011 671 2657

FAS. Co-operative Development Unit, Upper Baggot St, Dublin 4, tel: 01 668 5777, fax: 01 668 2691

Forfas. Promoting Enterprise, Science and Technology for Economic and Social Development in Ireland, www.forfas.ie

Government Information Services. tel: 01 662 4422

Government of Ireland. Government agencies, departments, links to organizations in Ireland, www.irlgov.ie

Health & Safety Authority. 10 Hogan Place, Dublin 2, tel: 01 6620400

Industrial Development Agency (IDA). 57 High Street, Killarney, Co. Kerry, tel: 0164 34133, fax: 0164 34135, www.idaireland.com

Inner City Enterprise. 56–57 Lower Gardiner Street, Dublin 1, tel: 01 836 4073, fax: 01 836 3742

International Fund for Ireland. PO Box 2000, Dublin 2, tel: 01 4780655, fax: 01 6712116

Irish Productivity Centre. Knockmaun House, 43–47 Lower Mount Street, Dublin 4, tel: 011 662 3233, fax: 011 662 3300, e-mail: ipc@indigo.ie

Irish Quality Association. Merrion Hall, Strand Road, Sandymount, Dublin 4, tel: 011 269 5255, fax: 011 269 8053, e-mail: iqa@iol.ie

Irish Republic Business Innovation Centres (BICs). The Tower, ISA Enterprise Centre, Pearse Street, Dublin 2, tel: 011 671 3111, e-mail: info@dbic-ie

Irish Science and Technology Agency (EOLAS). Glasnevin, Dublin 9, tel: 011 370 101, fax: 011 379 620

Irish Trade Union Trust. Liberty Hall, Eden Quay, Dublin 1, tel: 01 878 7272, fax: 01 878 7182

National Food Centre. Dunisea, Castleknock, Dublin 15, tel: 011 383 222, fax: 011 383 684

National Industrial Safety Organisation (NISO). Davitt House, Mespil Road, Dublin 4, tel: 011 676 5861

National Standards Authority of Ireland (NSAI). Glasnevin, Dublin 9, tel: 011 8073800, fax: 011–353–1–8073844, www.nsaicert.com

Office of Consumer Affairs & Fair Trade. Shelbourne House, Shelbourne Road, Dublin 9, tel: 01 6613399

Patents Office. 45 Merrion Square, Dublin 2, tel: 01 6614144

Revenue Commissioners. Castle House, South Great George's Street, Dublin 2, tel: 011 679 2777, fax: 011 671 8653

TEAGASC. 19 Sandymount Ave., Ballsbridge, Dublin 4, tel: 01 6688188

Udaras Na Gaeltachta. Na Forbacha, Gaillimh, tel: 091 503100

Internet and Computing

National Microelectronics Application Centre (MAC). University of Limerick, Plassey, Limerick, tel: 0161 333 644, www.ul.ie

National Microelectronics Research Centre (NMRC). The NMRC, Lee Maltings, University College, Cork, tel: 0121 276871, fax: 0121 270271, www.ucc.ie

National Technological Park. tel: 061 336555

Legal

Patents Office. Kilkenny, tel: 01 56 20111

Registrar of Friendly Societies. Parnell House, 14 Parnell Square, Dublin, tel: 011 804 5499

Registry of Business Names. Parnell House, 14 Parnell Square, Dublin, tel: 011 804 5200

Marketing, advertising etc

An Bord Trachtala. Merrion Hall, Strand Road, Sandymount, Dublin 4, tel: 01 269–5011, fax: 01 269 5820

Bolton Trust. Pigeon House Road, Ringsend, Dublin 4, tel: 011 668 7155, fax: 011 668 7945

Society of St Vincent de Paul. 8 New Cabra Road, Phibsboro, Dublin 7, tel: 01 838 4164, fax: 01 878 7182

Market research sources

Business Information Centre. Central Library, Ilac Centre, Henry Street, Dublin 1, tel: 011 873 3996, fax: 011 872 1451

Centre for Co-operative Studies. University College Cork, Western Road, Cork, tel: 01 21 276 871 www.ucc.ie

National Microelectronics Research Centre (NMRC). The NMRC, Lee Maltings, University College, Cork, tel: 0121 276871, fax: 0121 270271, www.ucc.ie

Small Business Information Centre. Wilton Park House, Wilton Place, Dublin 2, tel: 011 660 2244, fax: 011 660 5095

Professional bodies

Ark Life Assurance Company Ltd. 8 Burlington Road, Dublin 1, tel: 01 6681199

Chartered Association of Certified Accountants. 9 Leeson Park, Dublin 6, tel: 01 4963144

Electricity Supply Board. tel: 01 676 5831

Irish Goods Council. Merrion Hall, Strand Road, Sandymount, Dublin 4, tel: 01 2696011

Irish Management Institute (IMI). Sandyford Road, Dublin 16, tel: 01 2956911

Irish Quality Association. Merrion Hall, Strand Road, Dublin 4, tel: 01 2695255

Irish Trade Board. Merrion Hall, Strand Road, Sandymount, Dublin 4, tel: 01 2695011

Irish Trade Union Trust. Solidarity House, 48 Fleet Street, Dublin 2, tel: 01 6778294

Institute of Certified Public Accountants in Ireland. 9 Ely Place, Dublin 2, tel: 01 6767353

Institute of Chartered Accountants in Ireland. 87–89 Pembroke Road, Ballsbridge, Dublin 4, tel: 6680400

Irish Exporters Association. Holbrook House, Holles Street, Dublin 2, tel: 01 6612182

National Development Corporation. Wilton Park House, Wilton Place, Dublin 2, tel: 01 6600611

Telecom Eireann. Freephone 1800 714444

Business 'Buzzword' Glossary

80:20 rule Industry wisdom that 80 per cent of a company's business comes from 20 per cent of its customers.

above-the-line advertising Term used to cover press, TV, radio, cinema and outdoor advertising, that traditionally pays commission to advertising agencies on media purchases. See *below-the-line advertising*.

ACAS Advisory, Conciliation and Arbitration Service for resolving industrial disputes.

access time The time between asking a computer for information and the information becoming available.

accounting periods The yearly period covered by the accounts.

accounts The annual financial records of a business.

accruals The accounting concept whereby all income and expenses, whether cash or credit, are included for an accounting period.

ACORN A classification of neighbourhoods used by market researchers and advertisers.

acquisition The act of one company acquiring a controlling interest in another business.

ACT Advanced corporation tax.

advertising Paid-for communication that brings a business, product or service to the attention of potential customers, with the aim of persuading them to buy.

advertising agency A company that handles advertising on behalf of other businesses.

advertorial A paid-for advertisement, masquerading as an editorial piece.

agent In computing, a program with some degree of 'intelligence' that performs a task for its user.

aggressive buying Buying shares in small, potentially high-growth companies with the aim of achieving high capital appreciation.

AI   Artificial intelligence or artificial insemination, depending on your business.

AIDA   An acronym defining the goal of every advertisement.

AIM   Alternative Investment Market. The junior stock market of the London Stock Exchange, which raises money for small and medium-size go-ahead businesses.

alias   A simplified electronic mail name for a user or group of users.

alpha   The measurement of market volatility. *See beta volatility.*

analyst   A person in a brokerage firm or investment group who researches companies and industry sectors, and makes buy/sell recommendations.

angel   In venture capital a private investor in a business, but traditionally someone who puts up risk capital for a show or film.

annual meeting   The shareholders' meeting held annually where the company officers report the year's results, elect the board of directors, etc.

annual report   The yearly report of the company's trading position including its operations, balance sheet, and other information of interest to shareholders.

APR   Annual Percentage Rate. The annual rate of interest that all financial institutions must quote in their rates for meaningful comparison.

ARD   Accounting Reference Date. The start date of the company's financial year.

ARP   Accounting Reference Period. The date for the company's financial year; a 12-month period.

Articles of Association   The articles set out the shareholders' rights and obligations for the company. *See Memorandum of Association.*

ASA   Advertising Standards Authority. The regulator for the advertising industry.

ask   The lowest price a broker asks customers to pay for a security.

asset   Something owned by a business that has a measurable value.

attachment   A file appended to an electronic mail message.

auction market   Used to describe Stock Exchanges, such as NYSE, where many buyers and sellers competitively bid for the best price. See *over-the-counter* markets, such as NASDAQ.

audit   A yearly process carried out on the financial records of a company to check their accuracy.

authoring   Writing a document, program or Web page.

authorized capital   The share capital of a company authorized by law.

average down   A strategy of buying additional shares of a security at a lower price to reduce the overall average price.

backbone   A very high-speed communication link used to connect information service providers together across the world.

back-up   Making additional copies of programs or data so they are available if the original is destroyed.

balance sheet   A statement of the assets owned by a business and the way in which they were financed.

banded offer   A sales promotion where two or more related products are offered for sale together at a discount.

bandwidth   The amount of data a computer network can carry during a given time.

bank base rate   The rate of interest set by the Bank of England, which forms the basis for charges for bank loans and overdrafts.

banker's draft   A draft is an order for payment made by the payer's bank, and cannot be cancelled like an ordinary cheque.

banner ad   An advertisement appearing on a Web page, often in the form of an animated GIF.

BANS   Business Angel Networks. Groups of wealthy individuals who invest in start-up companies.

barriers to entry   The difficulties faced by a new company in competing in the market place with existing (large) businesses. Examples include research & development, distribution channels and economies of scale.

BBS   Computer bulletin board service. The electronic noticeboards used by news groups.

bear market   Used to characterize a prolonged period of falling stock prices (cf bears going into hibernation).

bearer cheque   A bearer cheque is negotiated by handing it over and delivering it to another holder.

below-the-line advertising   Term used to cover direct mail, point-of-sale ads, leaflets and brochures, not covered by *above-the-line advertising*.

bespoke software   A computer program written with the unique requirements of a specific customer in mind.

beta   The measure of a specific stock's volatility relative to the market as a whole. *See alpha*.

bid   The highest price a broker is prepared to pay at a given time for a security. *See ask*.

big bang   October 1986, when fixed commissions charged by stockbrokers were abolished, and all financial institutions had free and open access to the capital markets.

bill of exchange   A cheque.

bill of lading   Receipt for goods sent by sea, which is semi-negotiable.

bit   The basic storage unit used in computers.

black economy   Refers to businesses run by the self-employed who illegally avoid paying tax and National Insurance.

blue chip   In business 'blue-chip' refers to high-status companies and their shares.

body   The main part of an electronic mail message, or Web page.

body language   Involuntary gestures a person makes with their body during meetings that reflect their emotional state.

BOGOF Buy One, Get One Free. Acronym for a form of sales promotion.

book value The figures at which an asset appears in a company's accounts, which may be significantly different from the asset's market value.

boutique In venture capital, a specialist company that arranges investment funding, flotations and expansions for (high-tech) start-ups.

bps Bits per second. Number of bits per second transmitted through a channel.

BRAD British Rate and Data. The acronym for the so-called advertisers' bible.

branding The development and maintenance of a set of product attributes and values, which are coherent, appropriate, distinctive, protectable and appealing to consumers.

breakeven point The point in production or sales where revenue matches costs exactly.

bridge A device for interconnecting local area (computer) networks.

brochure A short, typically glossy, publication giving details of a company and its products and services.

browser Computer software used to access and display Web pages. The two main products are Netscape Communicator and Microsoft Internet Explorer.

BSI British Standards Institution. The government organization responsible for standards in the United Kingdom.

bull market Used to characterize a prolonged period of rising stock prices. *See bear market*.

burn rate The rate at which a company requires additional cash to keep going.

business angels Wealthy individuals who invest in start-up companies.

buy on the bad news An investment strategy where an investor buys shares that have plunged in value after bad news, on the assumption they will 'bounce back' over a period of time.

buy-and-hold strategy An investment strategy where an investor buys shares of a company they intend to keep over a long period.

call An option giving the holder the right to buy a specified number of shares of a security at a given price by a fixed date.

camera-ready-copy (CRC) The 'copy' or material given to a printer, from which a document, brochure or advertisement is prepared.

capital It has a number of meanings in business, such as 'all the assets of the business'.

capital gains tax Tax paid on profits from the disposal of assets such as equipment, buildings, land and also goodwill.

capital register The record of all the capital assets owned by a company, such as equipment, vehicles and buildings.

capitalization The value of a company calculated by multiplying the number of shares by the share price. See large-cap, mid-cap, micro-cap and small-cap companies.

cash The 'money' assets of a business, covering cash in hand and cash in the bank.

cash books The record of all the cheques and notes/coins (collectively called *cash*) received or paid by the business.

cash flow The money received by a business, minus the money spent by the company.

cash-in-hand A cash payment for goods or services that are not declared to the tax authorities. *See black economy.*

CD ROM Compact-disk, read-only memory. A CD ROM is an exchangeable, read-only device holding 650 million bytes used to hold software or data for computers.

CGI Common Gateway Interface. An Internet standard defining how a Web page can call programmes, called scripts, on an Internet computer to carry out functions, such as processing Web forms.

CGT Capital Gains Tax. A tax on substantial disposals of assets.

CIF Cost, Insurance, Freight. Insurance covering the cost, insurance and freight handling of goods.

circulation The number of copies of a publication that are either printed, distributed or purchased.

classified advert A heading plus a few lines of text in a publication, representing the cheapest and simplest form of advertising.

click-through A term used in interactive advertising to denote that a customer actively interrogated an advert, for example by 'clicking' on its icon.

client In business, a customer. In computing, a workstation computer that communicates with a server computer.

common stock In a start-up, the stock held by employees and others working for the company.

Companies Acts The Companies Act 1985 and 1989, etc.

company director A person elected by the shareholders of a limited company to handle day-to-day management of the business.

company doctor An experienced manager brought in to turn-round an ailing company.

company secretary A person appointed in a limited company to carry out the legal duties of the company.

competition A form of sales promotion, containing an element of skill, used to generate extra interest in a product or service.

confidential information Information, including trade and technological secrets, commercial records and marketing, professional and managerial processes, that are protected by obtaining undertakings to keep it confidential.

constructive dismissal Putting an employee in an untenable position, thereby compelling them to resign.

copy   The text (but not the illustrations) provided for a printer. *See camera ready copy.*

copyright   Legal protection of intellectual property stopping others from using it.

corporate image   The image a company presents to the 'outside world'; its customers and investors.

corporation tax   Taxation applied to a limited company, combining income tax and capital gains tax.

correction   A downward movement of a security's price to reflect a more realistic value.

cost per thousand   The cost of reaching 1,000 customers through advertising in a particular media, typically a publication.

crash   When the program currently running on the computer stops and all current work is probably lost.

creative accounting   Used to describe a 'cavalier' approach to accounting rules either to make the accounts appear better than they really are or to conceal fraud.

credit note   A note given to a customer for returned goods that can be redeemed against future purchases.

CT   Corporation Tax. Taxation applied to a limited company, combining income tax and capital gains tax.

customer loyalty scheme   A sales promotion technique used by retailers to retain existing, and attract new, customers.

cyclic stock   A stock that is strongly affected by changes in the economy, rising when the economy rises and dropping during downturns.

DAs   Development Areas. A designated area of the country in which a new business attracts special grants and loans for setting up.

Data Protection Act   The UK Act covering the recording of information on individuals on computers.

database   A computer program used to hold information in an organized way so that it can be retrieved and analyzed.

day books   The initial records of every transaction occurring in the business.

day order   An order to buy or sell a specified security at a given price on the day it is placed.

dead cat bounce theory   The tendency of a stock market to have a short-term 'bounce-back', immediately following a sharp fall.

deal flow   The number of new companies seeking venture capital.

dealer   An individual or firm in the securities business who buys and sells shares for their own account to make money, rather than acting as an agent for an investor.

debenture   A long-term loan with specific terms covering interest, capital repayment and security.

defensive stock A security that is more stable that the average, and thus a safer investment in a volatile market.

depreciation A measure of the cost of using a fixed asset such as a building.

derivative An investment that derives its value from the value of another (underlying) asset such as a futures contract or an option.

design rights The automatic protection of the outward shape or decorative appearance of a product or service given to the owners.

dial up A computer connection that uses a standard telephone or ISDN line to connect a personal computer to an internet service provider.

dip A small drop in the price of a security after a prolonged rise in the price.

direct costs Expenses, such as labour and materials, which are 'directly' tied to the amount of work undertaken. Also called Variable costs.

direct mail An advertising method where individual customers are contacted directly by mail.

direct response A marketing method where a company (typically a manufacturer) contacts the customer directly, bypassing traditional distribution channels, such as retailers.

directory A paper or electronic publication listing suppliers of goods and services.

discount broker A brokerage firm that executes buy and sell orders at a lower commission rate than a standard (full-service) broker.

display advert An advertisement containing a heading, body text, illustrations and often an order form.

diversification This term has a number of meanings. For a company it means moving from its core business into new markets. In risk management it means investing in a range of stocks to minimize the impact of any one security on the portfolio.

dividends Money distributed by a company to its shareholders.

DNS Domain Name System. The system translates computer domain names into numerical Internet (IP) addresses.

DNS Domain Name Server. A computer that stores the names and addresses of every other computer on the Internet, and looks up the correct destination address for a Web page or e-mail.

dollar-cost-average An investment strategy involving buying equal 'dollar' amounts of a security at regular intervals, regardless of the price.

domain name The World Wide Web or e-mail address which identifies a computer on the Internet.

Dow Jones industrial average The oldest and most widely quoted of the market indicators. It is based on a price-weighted daily average of blue chip stocks actively traded on the NYSE.

download Retrieving a file from a remote computer and storing it on your local disk.

downside risk In business, the calculation of the likely loss should the business venture fail. In finance, an assessment of the extent that a security could decline in value, taking into account all possible risks.

downtick The next trade at a lower price than the previous trade. *See uptick.*

DSS Department of Social Security. The UK ministry of social security.

DTI Department of Trade & Industry. The ministry of trade and industry.

dual listing A security that is listed on a number of exchanges, which might include NYSE, NASDAQ and possibly a regional exchange.

due diligence A careful investigation by potential investors in a company to ensure that all relevant information has been disclosed and the market implications understood.

earnings The amount of profit produced by a company after all expenditure and tax has been paid.

earnings per share The amount of company earnings per share. Specifically the net income divided by the number of common shares.

EASDAQ European Association of Securities Dealers Automated Quotation System. Europe's NASDAQ.

E-Centre^UK The main professional association in the United Kingdom concerned with electronic commerce.

ECGD Export Credits Guarantee Scheme.

economies of scale The gains achieved by a company in being able to spread its costs over a larger workload, for instance larger volume of output.

editorial Text written by a journalist, which is assumed unbiased.

edutainment Typically used to describe television programmes combining elements of education and entertainment.

EGM Extraordinary General Meeting. Meeting of the shareholders to discuss and vote on an unusual event.

ego trip Undertaking a task, such as a business venture, primarily for self-adulation.

EIF European Investment Fund. The fund established by the European Union to help new businesses.

e-mail The sending and receiving of messages by electronic means, typically associated with the Internet.

embargo A time limit placed on press releases before which the information should not be published.

encryption The encoding of information to stop its access by unauthorized parties.

endorsements Quotes from satisfied customers or celebrities used to promote a product.

EIS Enterprise Investment Scheme. This scheme encourages equity investments in unquoted companies by tax concessions.

entrepreneur   An entrepreneur is a risk-taker who sees an opportunity, raises the investment and establishes the business.

EOLAS   The Irish Republic Science and Technology Agency.

equity   A shareholding in a company. Specifically the owner's claim against the business, encompassing the share capital plus the retained profits of the business.

equity financing   Raising money by selling stock to investors, the money being used either for working capital or capital expenditure.

euro   The new European monetary unit.

exit route   The mechanism for an investor to cash-in their investment in a business.

extranet   A network of computers supporting access to Web pages and electronic mail, but with access restricted to a specific group of companies who do business with each other.

factoring   An arrangement which allows a business to receive up to 80 per cent of the cash due from a customer, with a 'factoring' company taking over pursuit of the debt.

FAQ   Frequently Asked Questions. A list of common questions concerning a product or service, together with corresponding answers, provided for customers.

features   The characteristics of a product or service which customers find attractive.

financial ratio   The relationship between two financial measures, used to assess business results.

financial statement   In investment terms, a record of the financial status of an individual or company, including a balance sheet, income statement, cash flow, etc.

first mover advantage   Being first in the marketplace with a new business, product or service, conveys significant advantage for a high-tech start-up.

fixed assets   Assets such as land, buildings and equipment, etc, acquired for long-term use by the business.

fixed costs   Expenses that do not vary directly to amount of work undertaken. *See variable costs.*

flash reports   Monthly financial reports drawn from the ledgers showing the financial 'health' of the business.

floating charge   The security given to a lender that when a borrower fails to repay a loan, the lender can lay claim to all assets up to the charge.

flotation   Term used to describe the entry of a company to a stock market.

flyer   A single-page leaflet used for advertising.

fob   Free-on-board. An export contract where the seller pays for sending the goods to the port of shipment and loading them on board.

forecast   A statement of what is likely to happen in the future based on analysis of previous trading.

franchising   A marketing technique used to improve and expand the distribution of a product or service, whereby the *franchiser* supplies the products or teaches the service to the *franchisee*, who in turn sells it to the public.

free gifts   A form of sales promotion used to encourage impulse buying.

FTP   File Transfer Protocol. FTP is a system used for copying files from one computer to another on the Internet

FT-SE 100   Financial Times Stock Exchange index. A weighted arithmetic index representing the price of 100 securities.

fulfilment   The retail term for the delivery of the product or service to the customer.

full-service broker   A broker who provides a range of financial services to clients including execution of buy-and-sell orders, and advice on investment decisions, etc. Full-service brokers normally charge higher commissions than discount brokers.

fully valued   The price at which a company's earnings power is accurately reflected in the price of its stock.

fundamental analysis   Using analysis of a company's financial statements, including its balance sheet, to predict future prices of its stock.

funds   Financial resources, including cash, of a company.

futures   Contracts covering the purchase and sale of financial instruments for future delivery on a commodity exchange. *See options and derivatives.*

gateway   An interconnection device which translates and passes data packets from one type of application, computer or network to another.

gearing   The ratio of a business's borrowings to its equity (ie share capital plus retained profits).

GIF   Graphical Interchange Format. GIF is a common format for representing graphical images on the Internet.

going concern   The assumption in accounting that a business will continue trading into the future, unless there is evidence to the contrary.

going long   Buying and holding a stock.

going short   Selling a security that the seller does not yet own, in anticipation that a decline in the price of the security will enable the seller to cover the sale with a purchase at a later date at a lower price.

goodwill   The value associated with a business's name, reputation and other intangible assets.

greenhouse funds   A seed or start-up investment fund used to stimulate the growth of high-tech businesses.

gross   The total (profit) before any deductions.

growth funds   A mutual fund that seeks long-term capital appreciation by selecting companies in which to invest, that should out-perform the market average.

growth stocks A company whose stock is growing far more rapidly than the market average.

gutted How you feel when something very important goes wrong.

handbills Single sheets of paper containing an advert, typically A5 size and printed on one side, handed out as part of an advertising campaign.

HASAWA Health and Safety at Work Act 1974.

heading A short phrase or sentence appearing above a display advertisement.

historical trading range The price range at which a security has traded since going public.

hits The number of accesses to a specific Web page.

home page The principal Internet page of an organization from which all other subsidiary pages are accessible.

home run Used to describe large gains over a short period, obtained by an investor.

HSE Health and Safety Executive.

HTML Hypertext Mark-up Language. The textual notation that describes how a Web page is to be displayed by the browser.

HTTP Hypertext Transfer Protocol. The language used by browsers to communicate requests for Web pages to servers.

hub An important computer that distributes messages to other computers in a network.

hypertext A mechanism where a word or an image is linked to a page of associated information. Hypertext is the basis of the Internet; click on an underlined sentence or graphic and the associated Web page is loaded.

ICOM Industrial Common Ownership Movement.

incubator Special business premises and environment, usually subsidized, established to help start-up companies launch.

index Statistical measurements reflecting the market price of a group of companies.

initial product offering The first complete product offered in the marketplace by a start-up.

insert A separate advertising leaflet inserted in a newspaper or other publication.

institutional investor An organization such as a pension fund or insurance company that trades securities in sufficient volumes that it warrants preferential treatment, such as lower commissions.

intellectual property A intangible asset such as a patent, copyright or trademark.

Internet A worldwide network of interconnected computers used to support public access to the World Wide Web and electronic mail.

intranet A network of computers supporting access to Web pages and electronic mail, but with access restricted to a specific company or organization.

investment bank A financial institution that raises capital for companies.

investment club Individuals who pool their funds and then make joint investments, which are voted on by members.

investor relations department A department within a publicly quoted company responsible for liaising with investors.

IoD Institute of Directors. As the name implies, the principal UK association of company directors.

IP Internet Protocol. A unique number that defines a computer connected to the Internet (cf telephone number). Also, intellectual property.

IPO Initial public offering. The point where a private company, usually a start-up, 'goes public' by selling shares to the public and listing on a stock exchange.

IRR Internal rate of return. The basis by which investors measure their rate of return, being effectively the compounded annual rate of return on their investment, including interest, dividends and realized profits.

ISDN Integrated services digital network. A system allowing digital signals to be transmitted over a telephone line at 64Kbps. One standard telephone line is converted into three digital phone lines.

ISP Internet service provider. A company that connects private users and companies to the Internet, and has high-speed links to other ISPs.

issued capital The amount of cash or asset value, placed in a business at the time of incorporation.

IT Information technology or inheritance tax, depending on your interests.

January effect The period when, historically, stock prices have risen, often sharply.

Java The Internet-oriented programming language developed by Sun Microsystems.

journal A name given to day books or books of original entry, where every transaction is recorded in their order of occurrence.

JPEG Joint Photographic Expert Group. JPEG is a common format for representing video images on the Internet.

keying Entering information into a computer via a keyboard.

KISS Keep It Simple, Stupid. KISS is the philosophy that good designs should be simple.

LAN Local area network. A network for connecting computers in a local site such as a room, floor or building.

large-cap company A company with a total market value of $5 billion or more. *See market capitalization.*

leaflet A single-page advertisement used for distribution via mail shots, inserts and door-to-door distribution.

learning curve A graphic term used to describe the experience gained by a company or individual as the business grows.

ledgers The financial records in a business where transactions of a specified type are entered, such as sales ledger and purchase ledger.

letters of credit Special financial instruments issued by a bank or acceptance house, which guarantee payment when the buyer and seller are unknown to each other.

liabilities All the claims against a business, such as loans and equity.

liability Someone who doesn't pull their weight in a business.

licence The issuing of an agreement for a company to legally exploit the products and services of another business.

limited partners Investors who provide money but do not participate in the management of the company, thereby having limited liability for the company.

LINC Local Investment Networking Company. A nationwide business introduction service which helps small businesses find investment and management help.

liquidity A measure of the ease with which an investment can be converted to cash.

list broker In direct marketing, a company that sells or hires lists of customer names and addresses.

loan capital Money lent to a business for a specific period of time.

log-off Signing off from a multi-user computer system or network.

love money Money invested in a business, typically a start-up, by family, friends or neighbours.

LSE Either the London Stock Exchange or the London School of Economics.

macroeconomics An analysis of the overall economy using information such as inflation, production, unemployment etc. *See microeconomics.*

mail shot Advertising literature sent by post to potential customers.

mailing list A list of names and addresses used in a direct mail campaign.

managing director A company director holding special powers to manage the daily affairs of a company. In small companies the role of MD and chairman may be combined.

marginal cost The (small) extra cost incurred in producing an extra product or service.

margins A calculation of profit based on the selling price, expressed as: (*selling price – cost price*) ÷ *selling price*, multiplied by 100.

mark up A calculation of profit based on the cost price, expressed as: (*selling price – cost price*) ÷ *cost price*, multiplied by 100.

market cap   Market capitalization. The total value of a listed company, calculated by multiplying the number of shares by the share value.

market maker spread   The difference in price between what a market maker is offering to buy a security and the price at which the firm is willing to sell it.

market makers   Security dealers, specifically the NASDAQ, AIM and EASDAQ member firms, who represent specific over-the-counter stocks, buying and selling the stocks as required, even using their own capital.

market share   The ratio of a company's sales of a given product or service in its market, compared to the total sales in that specific market.

market timing   Determining when to buy or sell a security based on fundamental or technical indicators.

marketing   To quote the Institute of Marketing, 'the management process responsible for identifying, anticipating and satisfying customer requirements profitably'.

marketing mix   The combination of techniques used by a business to market its products and services.

marketing strategy   The strategy used by a business to increase its market share.

MBO   Management buy-out. A venture capital strategy where the managers of a company raise investment to buy the business from its owners.

media schedule   The timetable for a media campaign showing the latest dates for delivery or copy and artwork, and the dates when the advertisements will appear in the media.

megabyte   One million bytes.

Memorandum of Association   A legal document drawn up in the UK as part of the process of registering a company. The memorandum states the company name, registered office, its purpose and share capital.

mezzanine financing   A form of financing falling between equity and debt, typically bearing a higher rate of interest than secured loans and an option for the lender to take an equity stake.

micro-cap company   A company with a market value of $100 million or less. *See market capitalization.*

microeconomics   An analysis of specific economy units such as households, companies or industry sectors. *See macroeconomics.*

mid-cap company   A company with a market value of between $1 billion and $3 billion. *See market capitalization.*

MIME   Multipurpose Internet mail extensions. MIME is a standard for encoding attachments to e-mail messages so they can be correctly transmitted over the Internet.

mirroring   The same data are replicated as two or more files on separate computers improve fault tolerance in the network.

mission statement   A short sentence stating a company's purpose for being in business. 'We do anything for money'.

modem Modulator–demodulator. A device that connects computers over the telephone network, allowing them to send and receive information.

MOPS Mail Order Protection Scheme.

moral rights 'Authors' of literary, dramatic, musical and artistic works and film directors have personal rights to their creations that cannot be assigned.

multimedia The combination of a number of media, such as text, graphics, sound, animation and video.

mutual fund A fund operated by an investment company that raises money from shareholders and then invests the funds on their behalf.

NASDAQ National Association of Securities Dealers Automated Quotation System. NASDAQ is the US electronic screen-based stock market specializing in high-tech stocks.

NDA Non-disclosure agreement. A legal agreement in which an individual or company disclosing confidential information to another party is assured that the party will limit the information to certain stated purposes.

NewCo A fictitious name used for a company before its legal formation.

newsgroup An electronic bulletin board devoted to a specific topic of interest where users can read and post messages.

Neuer Markt The German small companies stock market.

NI/NICs National Insurance contributions.

nominal ledger The general company ledger that consolidates all the financial information from all the primary ledgers.

non-executive directors Part-time directors of a company responsible for advice on direction and future plans for the business, without being responsible for its day-to-day running.

NYSE New York Stock Exchange.

odd lot The trading of an 'odd' number of shares; shares normally being traded in multiples of 100 units.

offline Using a computer that is not at that instant connected to a communications network, such as the Internet.

off-the-shelf company A company that has been legally formed (but has never traded) and is used to rapidly establish a limited company.

online Connected to a communications network.

opportunity cost The value of a potential business opportunity that has yet to be taken.

option The right to buy or sell a specified amount of stock at a specified price before a specified deadline.

OTC market Over-the-counter market. A market, such as NASDAQ, for securities that are listed on a 'negotiated' market rather than an 'auction' market like the NYSE.

out-of-favour A stock or industry sector that is currently unpopular with investors.

overdraft A flexible form of bank lending, but with the disadvantage of being payable on demand.

overhead An expense that is incurred but cannot be easily associated with a unit of production or supporting a service.

overtrading Expanding production, sales or a service without adequate financial resources.

overvalued The price of a security which is not considered justified by its current price-earnings-ratio. *See undervalued.*

P&L account Profit and loss account. The profit and loss account monitors income and expenditure over a particular period of time.

P/E ratio Price-to-earnings ratio. The P/E ratio gives an investor an indication of a company's earning power. The P/E is calculated by dividing the company's share price by the earnings per share for a 12-month period.

packet The basic unit of information sent over a computer network during communication.

passing off When a company pretends to be another business by either trading dishonestly or infringing on a trademark.

patent The award of legal protection for a unique article or manufacturing process superior to its predecessors.

payback 'Payback' in a business compares the cash cost of the initial investment with the annual net cash inflows that are generated by the business.

PAYE Pay as you earn. The tax which employers are responsible for deducting from an employee's wages.

PBIT Profit before income and tax.

penetration A measure of the extent that an advertisement or publication reaches a specified target audience.

Perks Any kind of 'benefits' associated with a job or position.

PI Per inquiry. An arrangement in advertising whereby in return for a free ad, the publication is paid a fee for each enquiry that the ad generates.

piggy-backing A term used to describe companies that market other companies' products.

point-of-sale advertising Advertising at the point of sale, typically the checkout in a shop.

PoP Point of presence. A telephone number linking to a modem at an Internet service provider. During dial-up a PC's modem dials this telephone number.

portals Highly popular Internet sites that are gateways to the World Wide Web, and therefore of considerable interest to advertisers. Examples are Yahoo!, Amazon.com, eBay, and E-Trade.

positioning   Where a product or service is targeted at a specific market segment, by careful choice of the price, packaging and the advertising.

post-money valuation   The market capitalization of a company immediately after a financial event, such as an initial public offering.

PR   Public relations. The planned and sustained effort to establish and maintain goodwill and mutual understanding between an organization and its 'publics'.

preference shares/stock   A special class of stock issued to investors (as opposed to employees) in a start-up, giving them certain negotiated privileges (called preferences). They give the holders the rights to a fixed dividend and priority over ordinary shareholders in liquidation, but limit their voting rights.

press pack   This has two meanings: firstly a pack of marketing materials prepared for distribution to the press, and secondly, a collective term for the press who pursue a celebrity.

private ledger   The general company ledger that consolidates all the financial information from all the primary ledgers. Also called the nominal ledger.

product life cycle   The time during which a product can be profitably sold, before being replaced.

professional advisors   The professional bankers, lawyers and accountants retained to advise a company.

profit   The excess of sales revenue over total costs during a given accounting period.

proof   Sheets produced by a printer used to check for mistakes, prior to the print run.

prospectus   The document required to be given to all buyers of a newly registered security.

protocol   Rules defining the format and timing of messages in a network, and used for their translation.

public quotation   The listing of a company on a stock exchange. *See IPO.*

publics   A public relations term describing the target audience(s) that a business's campaign seeks to address.

purchase ledger   A record of all items purchased by the company, each transaction comprising date, description, amount and cost.

push technology   Internet technology downloaded by a user that automatically retrieves and displays selected information. *See Web casting.*

put   A contract that gives the holder the right to sell a specified number of shares of a given stock, at a predetermined price, on or before the option's expiry date.

pyramid selling   A questionable form of selling involving a hierarchy of franchises each paying the manufacturing company a fee.

qualitative analysis   Analysis that studies a company's management experience, staff morale, etc, to predict future financial performance.

quantitative analysis   Analysis of a company's financial data undertaken to predict future performance.

ratchet   An incentive arrangement whereby a number of trigger points for future profits are set such that managers get a bigger share of the equity if the company performs well.

ratios   Analysis of financial information whereby some item is expressed as a proportion of some other item.

ream   A standard measure for paper; 500 sheets.

red herring   The preliminary prospectus given by brokers to potential investors. Also the major venture capital magazine.

red tape   The excessive use of bureaucracy and paperwork.

REG   Regional Enterprise Grants.

registered office   The address to which all official correspondence goes, which may be different from the business address.

research department   The department within a brokerage firm that analyses securities and markets using both fundamental and technical analysis.

reserves   The name given to all the undistributed profits accumulated by the business.

response rate   The percentage of people responding to a direct mail advertising campaign.

restricted stock   Stock that cannot be sold except under certain circumstances, such as first offering the stock back to the company.

retail investor   An investor who buys and sells securities on their own behalf.

return   The percentage profits realized from an investment over a given period.

revenue   The amount of sales of a business covering both cash received and money owed on invoices sent.

risk   The measurement of the potential of losing money on an investment, because the security's value declines sharply.

risk averse   An investor who chooses securities so as to minimize risk.

risk/return ratio   Various measures, such as price volatility, for calculating the relationship of the increased risk versus the greater return.

ROCE   Return on capital employed. An accounting ration expressing the profit of a business for a financial year, as a percentage of the capital employed.

ROP   Run of paper. This is a cheap form of display advertising, whereby the publication has freedom to place the ad where they wish.

router   A device for connecting your company Internet server or local network server to the Internet via a leased line.

royalty   The money paid to an owner of intellectual property such as a trademark, copyright or patent.

S&P 500 Index Standard & Poor's 500 Index. A daily measure of stock market movement based on the average of 500 popular stocks on the NYSE.

sales promotion A short-term sales campaign where the customers are offered additional incentives, such as a price reduction, to purchase a product or service.

science park A collection of new buildings on a landscaped site designed to be attractive for high-tech companies and their employees.

search engine A program for locating information on the Web on a specified topic. The search engine actually searches a massive database, accumulated by so-called 'Web crawlers' which continuously search the web for new information.

seasonality A regular event, such as summer, that causes sales to rise or fall in response.

secured creditor Someone lending money to a business whose debt is secured by linking it to an asset, such as a building.

seed capital Initial venture capital funding for a business to develop an idea into a product.

SERPS State Earnings-Related Pension Scheme. The UK state pension entitlement that an employee builds up through the payment of national insurance contributions.

server An important computer in a network that provides database access or message routing for other computers.

share capital The capital of a business pledged by the owners or shareholders.

share option Incentives scheme whereby staff in a company have the option to buy a given amount of shares, at a given price, at a given date in the future.

SITPRO Simplified Trade Procedures Board.

size of market In retail, the number of potential customers in a specific market segment. In securities, the number of shares in an order a market maker will handle at a given price.

sleeping partner A person who has put up capital for a business but does not intend to take an active part in running the business.

small-cap company A company with a market value of between $100 million and $1 billion. *See market capitalization.*

SMART Small Firms Merit Award for Research & Technology.

SME Small to medium sized enterprise. Euro-speak for a company below a specific size, such as 50 or 250 employees.

SMP Statutory maternity pay.

SMTP Simplified Mail Transfer Protocol. A system allowing computers to exchange electronic mail messages in transit from the sender to the receiver.

soft loans Money loaned at a low rate of interest, or which only needs to be repaid if the business makes a profit.

SOHO Small Office, Home Office.

sole trader A one-person business.

specialized fund A mutual fund focusing on investing in a specific industry or business sector.

speculator An investor who is willing to take large risks by purchasing high-risk securities, which have the potential of returning very high gains.

split Increasing the number of shares without affecting their overall value. For instance, a two-for-one split doubles the number of shares and halves each share's value.

SSP Statutory Sick Pay.

stand-by advertising An advertising scheme whereby potentially unused advertising space is sold at a markedly reduced rate (eg stand-by airline seats).

stock A stock or share conferring ownership in a company.

stop-loss order An order to a broker to sell at a specified price, so as to limit possible losses.

suits A term used by 'techies' for professional management brought in to run a start-up company.

surfing A popularist term for people who browse the Internet looking for information.

sweat equity A person who works for free for a company in return for equity. Some lawyers and accountants help start-ups to launch in this way.

SWOT analysis Strengths, weaknesses, opportunities, threats. A technique for analyzing the strengths etc of your business.

tax avoidance Legal actions taken to reduce the amount of tax paid.

tax evasion Illegal actions taken to avoid paying tax and making a false tax declaration.

tax loss A loss that has been legally created to reduce or eliminate taxable profits.

TCP/IP Transmission Control Protocol/Internet Protocol. The standard set of Internet communication protocols that manages packet transmission and error checks across networks.

tech stocks The share of companies in high-technology fields such as computers, communications, consumer electronics, media and biotechnology.

techie A person with significant technical expertise. *See suit.*

technical analysis Analysis of securities and the market based on charts and computer models used to identify price trends.

TECS Training and Enterprise Councils.

telnet A system that allows you to connect to computers and type commands remotely, as if you were in front of the computer.

term loan A loan for a fixed amount with a fixed repayment schedule, normally from a bank.

test mailing A small-scale mail shot in direct mail to assess the probable level of response to a mail shot.

ticker symbol   The stock market symbol designating a particular company.

trade cycle   The observed behaviour of the economy which cycles from an 'upturn' encouraging investment and expansion, to a 'downturn' of cost-cutting and job losses.

trademark   Something that identifies a product or service in the eyes of the customer.

trade sale   Sale of a business to another company.

trader   An investor who buys and sells securities to take advantage of price movements in short time periods.

trial balance   The totalling each month of every page in the nominal ledger of a company.

triple witching   The last 'hectic' trading hour in which stock options and futures all expire. The third Friday of March, June, September and December.

true and fair   In accounting, the concept that financial reports have been prepared according to standard accounting principles.

UDR   Unregistered design rights.

undervalued   When the price of a security is below what is justified by its current price-earnings-ratio or asset value. *See overvalued.*

underwriter   An investment banker who handles the offering of a new issue of securities, buying them from the issuer and selling them for whatever they can make to investors.

uptick   The sale of a security at a higher price than the preceding sale.

URL   Uniform Resource Locator. The address of a page on the World Wide Web. Each page has a unique URL.

USM   Unlisted Securities Market.

USP   Unique selling proposition. A feature that is unique to a particular business, product or service.

value added   The difference in value between the cost of producing a product or service and the sales revenue generated.

vapourware   Software promoted by a company before the product is finished – in some case before it has even been started – to disrupt the market of a competitor.

variable cost   Expenses, such as labour and materials, that are 'directly' tied to the amount of work undertaken. Also called direct costs.

VAT   Value added tax. The tax paid by a business when it buys goods from someone, and charges tax when it sells them on, handing over the difference to the taxman.

VDU   Visual display unit. The display or monitor of a computer system.

venture capital   A source of finance for start-up companies and new business ventures involving investment risk.

videoconference   A discussion using audio and video, over a network, between two or more at different remote locations.

volatility   A measurement of the size and frequency of fluctuations in the price of a security, sector or the market.

volatility index   A measurement of the fluctuation of a stock over its 52-week high/low price range.

voting rights   The rights assigned to certain shareholders in a company, to influence the running of the business, such as the appointment of directors.

vulture capital   An investment fund that invests in ailing businesses, or a derisory small-business term for the venture capital industry.

WAN   Wide area network. The networking together of a number of local area networks, computers linked together using the telephone network, leased lines etc.

warrant   A right to buy stock at a specified price for a given period of time, called the term.

web casting   Web casting uses 'push' technology to send selected information to Internet users who have previously requested the information. *See push technology.*

Web page   A single file stored on a Web-connected computer containing (HTML) formatted text, graphics and hypertext links to other pages.

Web server   A computer that stores a collection of Web pages comprising a website.

website   A home page and its hypertext-linked, subsidiary Web pages associated with a single organization or individual.

work in progress   Products and services in the process of being produced.

working capital   Capital used in the day-to-day running of the business, comprising current assets less liabilities.

working life   The economically useful life of a fixed asset, such as equipment and buildings.

WWW   World Wide Web. The on-line library part of the Internet.

Index